Patricia C. Annable

Easter 1967

THE ✛ BIBLICAL SPIRITUALITY OF ST. JOHN

ALBA HOUSE
a division of
St. Paul Publications
Staten Island, N.Y.

THE ✝ BIBLICAL SPIRITUALITY OF ST. JOHN

Paul - Marie de la Croix, O.C.D.

Translated by JOHN CLARKE, O.C.D.
This book was first published by Desclée de Brouwer, S.A., Bruges.
L'Evangile de Saint Jean et son Temoignage Spirituel

Nihil Obstat:
John A. Goodwine, J.C.D. — Censor Librorum

Imprimatur:
✠ Terence J. Cooke, D.D., V.G.

New York, N.Y. — May 17, 1966

Library of Congress Catalog Number: 66-13033

The nihil obstat and imprimatur are official declarations that a book or pamphlet is free of doctrinal or moral error. No implication is contained therein that those who have granted the nihil obstat and imprimatur agree with the contents, opinions or statements expressed.

✠

Preface

It is characteristic of great works, especially of inspired writings, to offer an inexhaustible source of material for study and meditation. That is why the fourth Gospel has never ceased through the centuries to hold the attention of its readers and to give rise to many commentaries. The knowledge we have of this Gospel is deepening each day, and its "spiritual testimony" is becoming ever more evident.

This word testimony, so misused today, has a fulness of meaning in the writings of St. John. The apostle has laid a definite claim to his status as witness; he has reported exactly what he has seen. We know that he speaks the truth and that his testimony is authentic (19, 35; 21, 24).

This testimony expresses a plenitude of faith which he desires to see grow and develop in his readers. "But these things are written that you may believe that Jesus is the Christ, the Son of God, and that believing you may have life in his name" (20, 31).

The content of his Gospel is essentially spiritual. In fact, the Revelation coming to us through John is not just made up of rough facts. Each of these facts is a "sign" that contains a message and proposes a spiritual reality. Those who receive this teaching are empowered to become adorers in spirit and in truth (4, 23).

From faith in the "Word made flesh" (1, 14) there is born a "life in the Spirit" which the apostle himself experienced in the depths of his soul. This life is not simply an aspect among others in his Gospel, but it is the vital principle from which the soul of the true "child of God" is vivified.

For such a work to be profitable to all, John has carefully chosen and presented his material. He has "built up" nothing and has added nothing to the data revealed. What he gives us is the fruit of the Spirit's work in his soul.

The value of the teachings and principles of the spiritual life which have already been elaborated and will be elaborated in the course of time will always remain dependent upon the Gospels, and especially upon what may be termed John's "Spiritual Gospel." We shall always find ourselves returning to that well of Jacob (4, 6) where the gift of God is offered to us in its fullness, and we shall always have to meditate upon this Gospel which presents us with the Way, the Truth, the Light, and the Life.

N.B. The Johannine Gospel constitutes the real object of this study, but we have not hesitated to have recourse to the Apocalypse and frequently to John's first Epistle which appears to contain the apostolic and pastoral application of what is in the Gospel.

Because of their frequency, references to the fourth Gospel contain only the number of the chapter and verse. For Scriptural quotations we have used the Douay Version and the Confraternity Edition.

CONTENTS

20. THE HOLY SPIRIT AND THE SOUL   405

21. THE HOLY SPIRIT AND THE CHURCH   415

✠

CHAPTER 1

THE SPIRITUAL FORMATION OF
THE EVANGELIST

The fourth Gospel, which casts such a living and interior light upon Christ and His mystery, reveals likewise the soul of its author. John is careful to remain in the background and identifies himself only indirectly, and yet he is exposed in his work. This enables us to catch a glimpse of the manner in which God prepared him for his mission.

The apostle, who had the unique privilege of living in intimate and constant contact with Jesus, benefited also from other influences which were decisive, viz., those of the Baptist and the Virgin Mary. Finally, an exceptional longevity afforded Christ's disciple the opportunity of faithfully "pondering in his heart" the Master's words and works under the guidance of the Holy Spirit (Lk. 2, 19). The secret of the "spiritual" Gospel lies to a great extent in this formation.

We know St. John's parents through the Gospel. His father, Zebedee, owned a fishing boat on Lake Genesareth and "hired men" aided him in his work (Mk. 1, 20). So he must have had some wealth. As for Salome, his mother, she will soon join those women who were following Christ and ministering to the needs of the apostles. According to all probability she was closely related to the Blessed Virgin.[1] This excuses her boldness to a certain extent when she asks that her two sons, James and John, "sit one on his right hand and one on his left in his kingdom" (Mt. 20, 20-23).

This relationship likewise accounts for the privileged position of the two brothers in the apostolic group (Cf. Lk. 9, 54; & Ac. 1, 13, where John is placed immediately after Peter). The fact of John's being the beloved disciple of Jesus would have undoubtedly sufficed to assure him this position, but family ties probably had something to do with it. They help

1. Cf. note to John 19, 25: Bible de Jérusalem.

in grasping family traits and they permitted the Master to make Himself better understood by John than by any other.

These affinities, this relationship, the work of grace in his soul, all these explain in part why, when about to expire, Jesus gave John to His Mother and confided her to him.

However, a very deep formation was necessary to prepare the apostle for a spiritual understanding of the Master's teachings. According to all likelihood, John had begun to draw this formation from his family surroundings. The study of the Scriptures was one obligation from which no pious Jew would exempt himself. It was accompanied by prayer and the participation in the liturgical feasts. Like Mary his relative, young John must have been reared in the knowledge and love of God's word.

The evangelists have acquainted us with the fiery temperament of the one whom Christ was going to nickname "son of thunder" (Mk. 2, 17). John was to bring this same ardor to the examination of the Scriptures, to the penetration of their substance and spirit. And it was going to make him careful in gathering together everything that could help him in his research.

The Disciple of John the Baptist

Now the report spread abroad, not only in the "hill country of Judea" but all through Palestine, of the appearance of a prophet on the banks of the Jordan, announcing the coming of the Messias and administering "a baptism of repentance for the forgiveness of sins" (Lk. 3, 3).

This John the Baptist, whose fiery preaching drew the crowds, was also a relative of John the apostle. The Gospel shows us the latter desirous of knowing the prophet. Leaving "his father Zebedee, his boat, and his hired men," John went to the Jordan's banks to listen to the Baptist.

What he heard and saw was such a revelation to him that he decided to remain and become his "disciple" (1, 35). Three-quarters of a century later, when Christ had already taken complete possession of the mind and soul of John, the fourth Gospel bears witness to the decisive character of this encounter.

It is clearly stated in the gospel text that John did not come simply to listen but to become a disciple of the Baptist. "Again the next day John was standing there, and two of his disciples . . ." (1, 36).

This title helps us understand that John really placed himself in the Precursor's school and submitted to his teacher's influence.

We find it somewhat difficult today to realize the prestige of one who effaced himself so completely before Christ as the dawn gives way to day. "He must increase, but I must decrease" (3, 30).

When this man with the violent and sharp word, this ascetic who ate "locusts and wild honey" (Mt. 3, 4), announced the proximate approach of the Messias, all Israel was shaken. When hearing the echoes of the voice of the greatest of the prophets reverberating across the desolate solitudes of the Judean desert, John was seized by the ardor and the note of finality that were manifest. Never had he heard the like. Never had the messianic prophecies and announcements been set forth with so much vigor and above all with such a certitude of immediate and imminent fulfillment. "But one mightier than I is coming. He will baptize you with the Holy Spirit and with fire" (Lk. 3, 16).

Never had the distinction between good and bad been made with such violence. "Brood of vipers! who has shown you how to flee from the wrath to come? Bring forth therefore fruits befitting repentance. For even now the axe is laid to the root of the trees" (Lk. 3, 7).

All that John had learned concerning the prophets of old was being enacted before his very eyes. Crowds were approaching the Baptist from all sides and among them Pharisees and Sadducees mingled with soldiers and publicans which was very unusual (Mt. 3, 7; Lk. 3, 12; Mk. 1, 5). All spoke to him as a teacher whose authority was not to be questioned, and they asked: "What must we do"? As for the people: "They were in expectation and all were wondering in their hearts about John, whether perhaps he might be the Christ" (Lk. 3, 14).

We get here an inkling of the Baptist's prestige from these words of St. Luke. And it helps us understand why, even after his death, many continued to take him for the Messias (Lk. 1, 66). Had not his preaching drawn to the Jordan's banks even greater crowds than those which followed Christ?

As for John the apostle, he kept before him the sight of those crowds descending into the muddy waters of the Jordan river to be baptized, as well as the spectacle of this extraordinary man, a new Elias, preaching penance and announcing the good news (Lk. 3, 18).

The Synoptics, especially St. Luke, have preserved the essential part of this preaching. However, the fourth Gospel contains revealing data.

And first of all, there is that scene dear to the heart of the apostle since it recalled his first encounter with Christ. When Jesus passed by and John the Baptist pointed out the Messias with the words, "Behold, the lamb of God" (1, 29,36), John was actually at the Precursor's side. In order for these words alone to have led John to leave his master and to follow Christ, they must have been both the summing-up and the completing of a teaching that John the Baptist had given to his disciples.

It is noteworthy that this teaching has been summed up in a formula which remains central in the apostle John's writing. It opens his Gospel and remains present to the apostle's mind until fixing his gaze upon the Crucified, from whose side "came forth blood and water" (19, 34), he cites on this occasion the words of Exodus concerning the paschal lamb: "Not a bone of him shall you break" (19, 36).

John keeps this figure of the lamb always in his memory.[2] We find it again in the Gospel as well as in the Apocalypse where Christ is honored under the traits of a lamb immolated and living (Ap. 5, 6). That it pervades John's entire work is proof of the lasting and profound influence of the Baptist over his disciple.

Another proof of this influence comes from the Prologue. In this unique page, John wished to transport his reader to the very bosom of the mystery of God. "In the beginning was the Word, and the Word was with God: and the Word was God" (1, 1).

In these lines in which "time is assumed by the Eternal",[3] one single human being finds favor,[4] one single human name is pronounced and this on two occasions. "There was a man, one sent by God, whose name was John" (1, 6). "John bore witness concerning him" (1, 15).

This shows us the singular esteem with which the apostle regarded his first teacher. He could have been encouraged in this by Christ Himself, for had not Christ praised John very highly? "You have sent to John, and he has borne witness to the truth. He was a lamp, burning and shining" (5, 33,35).

John the Baptist, a prophet? "Yes, I tell you, and more than a prophet. This is he of whom it is written, 'Behold, I send my messenger before thy face, who shall make ready thy way before thee.' Amen, I say to you, among those born of woman there has not risen a greater than John the Baptist; yet the least in the kingdom of heaven is greater than he. But from the day of John the Baptist until now the kingdom of heaven has been enduring violent assault, and the violent have been seizing it by force. For all the Prophets and the Law have prophesied until John. And if you are willing to receive it, he is Elias who is to come. He who has ears to hear, let him hear" (Mt. 11, 9-15).

John approached this man of whom divine Wisdom spoke. We too easily see in him only the rough ascetic with the avenging word. John knew him and was not slow to perceive the richness hidden beneath a

2. The "paschal" lamb or, more probably, the lamb of the prophecy concerning the suffering Servant (Is. 53) who is pure enough to efface the sins of the people through his innocence. The question will be examined later.
3. L. Bouyer, The Fourth Gospel, Intro.
4. With the exception of Moses who symbolizes the Law.

rough exterior. Jesus had said of him he was the new Elias. Was this in order to point out the Precursor's role? Was it not also to indicate his fiery temperament and indomitable fortitude in the service of the living God? Was it not because, like Elias, John the Baptist combines strength with meekness and tenderness which the Gospel has revealed, and which John perceived better than anyone else when he drew near to him?

John the Baptist will salute Christ with words of unusual delicacy. He will permit us to glimpse his ardent soul's love for the Messias when he answers, with such sovereign detachment, the question of those who come to him. "No one can receive anything unless it is given to him from heaven. You yourselves bear me witness that I said, 'I am not the Christ but have been sent before him.' He who has the bride is the bridegroom, but the friend of the bridegroom, who stands and hears him, rejoices exceedingly at the voice of the bridegroom. This my joy, therefore, is made full" (3, 27-29).

Elias, on Horeb, had perceived Yahweh's presence in the gentle breeze (3 Kgs. 19, 12). At the Jordan, John the Baptist "will see the Spirit, as a dove, descending from heaven and resting upon Jesus" (1, 32).

If we complete the account given by John concerning Jesus' baptism with the accounts in Matthew (3, 13-17) and Luke (3, 21,22), we can see there the first manifestation of the mystery of the Trinity: The Son receives baptism from the hands of the Precursor; the Father's voice is heard in the heavens; the Spirit, finally, in the form of a dove, descends and remains on Jesus.

Now, who has been favored with this vision and who was the first to grasp its meaning, if not John the Baptist, the apostle John's master?

Keeping these facts in mind, we can glimpse the influence the last and greatest of the prophets exercised over the young disciple who came to place himself under his guidance.

Inflexible when it was question of defending, even at the price of his head, the demands of outraged morality—"It is not lawful for thee to have her" (Mt. 14, 4), he will tell Herod, guilty of having married Herodias, the wife of his brother Philip—the Baptist also has a humble soul: "The strap of whose sandal I am not worthy to loose" (1, 27); a tender and unselfish soul, "He who has the bride is the bridegroom; but the friend of the bridegroom, who stands and hears him, rejoices exceedingly at the voice of the bridegroom. This my joy, therefore, is made full. He must increase, but I must decrease" (3, 29).

John knew these were not only words. He had seen the Precursor in action. He remembered the day when he and Andrew had left him to follow Jesus (1, 37), the Precursor had shown this "perfect joy."

When with the Baptist, the apostle had learned what faith was. If, when yet in his mother's womb, the Precursor had recognized the Savior and leapt for joy at His approach (Lk. 1, 44), it seems he never saw Him afterwards. Will he not say, when pointing him out as the "Lamb of God," "And I did not know him" (1, 31)? Afterwards, Jesus and the Baptist had only few occasions, if any at all, of meeting one another. Conscious of his mission which was to withdraw after Christ's coming, John the Baptist kept his distance, even physically, in order not to hamper Christ's action. It appears as though the Jordan was symbolically placed between them (1, 28).

He was so well separated that he was acquainted with the Messias' works only through hearsay. Hence the reason for the messengers sent to Christ. "But when John had heard in prison of the works of Christ, he sent to him two of his disciples to say to him, 'Art thou he who is to come, or shall we look for another'" (Mt. 11, 3)? John the Baptist lived, then, by faith. This faith, profound and admirable as it was, knew times of trial; but it came forth victorious. The Master's words reported to him through his disciples suffice to confirm him in it forever: "Go and report to John what you have heard and seen: the blind see, the lame walk, the lepers are cleansed, the deaf hear, the dead rise, the poor have the gospel preached to them. And blessed is he who is not scandalized in me", (Mt. 11, 5).

Is it surprising that the disciple of such a man becomes later the evangelist of the faith?

Man of faith, the Baptist appears also in the Gospel as the man of the Spirit.

It is the Spirit, in fact, descending and remaining on Christ "as a dove" who enables him to recognize Christ and to testify that "this is the Son of God" (1, 32,34). Elsewhere, John terminates the interview with Nicodemus, in which the necessity of a birth from water and the Spirit is pointed out, with the Baptist's last testimony which ends with the words: "For he whom God has sent speaks the words of God, for not by measure does God give the Spirit" (3, 34). They make Jesus the one upon whom the Spirit remains. Even if they are not pronounced textually by the Baptist, these words show that John has made his own a thought he received from his master.

Besides, if John is anxious to report in full (8, 31-58) the impassioned discussion between Jesus and the Jews, during which the latter cry out with anger: "We are the children of Abraham. Abraham is our father" (8, 33,39), it is doubtless because it brings out the importance of a birth from the Spirit as opposed to a birth according to the flesh and from the bosom of the chosen people. But would it not also be because these words recalled to John very similar ones which he, as the Precursor's disciple, heard recently on the banks of the Jordan? "Bring forth therefore fruit befitting repentance, and do not think to say within yourselves, 'We have Abraham for our father,' for I say to you that God is able out of these stones to raise children to Abraham. . . . I indeed baptize you with water, for repentance. But he who is coming after me . . . he will baptize you with the Holy Spirit and with fire" (3, 8-12).

The relationship between John and his teacher is very close on the plane of "testimony." For if John the Baptist is the witness "par excellence," the apostle John has no greater desire himself than to be a true witness (1, 7,8,15,19,23,34; 3, 28; 5, 33,34,36), upon whose testimony we can and must believe that "Jesus is the Son of God, the one sent by the Father" (19, 35; 20, 31; 21, 24).

The study of such themes as: faith, birth, life in the spirit, testimony, which form the important themes of John's Gospel, uncovers a meeting of minds between the teacher and the disciple which cannot be merely accidental.

John undoubtedly was acquainted with the Scriptures, but it was the Baptist who revealed their inner meaning to him. "For all the Prophets and the Law have prophesied until John. And if you are willing to receive it, he is Elias who was to come. He who has ears to hear, let him hear" (Mt. 11, 13). Was this not a declaration that the Precursor gathered the entire Old Testament into his person and that he carried it within himself, bringing it to its completion? With him a new age was about to commence.

This presence of the Law and the Prophets in John the Baptist, this messianic sense, this ardent longing for the Redeemer, John assimilated them all through the teaching of the Baptist. Never did a son of Israel benefit from a formation as deep, extensive, and truly enlightened with the light of God. The Jews still dreamed of an earthly, powerful, and victorious Messias, but John the Baptist awaited the "Servant of Yahweh," the Lamb of God who takes away the sin of the world. And it was such a Messias that he taught his disciples to expect.

How can we forget that for John the memory of his first teacher blended with the picture of a true apostle: ardent, detached, intensely taken up with God's glory, who knows no greater testimony than that one shed his own blood! John the Baptist was first of apostles and first of martyrs.

Instructed by Herodias, Salome said to Herod: " 'Give me here on a dish the head of John the Baptist.'. . And grieved as he was, the king, because of his oath and his guests, commanded it to be given. He sent and had John beheaded in the prison. And his head was brought on a dish and given to the girl, who carried it to her mother" (Mt. 14, 8-11). This scene reminded him of the price to be paid for the glory of following Christ and bearing witness to the end.

If "testimony" holds such an important place in John's thought and word, may we not say it is because he was the Precursor's disciple at an impressionable age? Never will John forget that he had come in close contact and knew intimately one of the greatest, the purest, and most faithful souls that ever had been.

The Disciple of Christ

The Precursor had performed his office of bearing witness to Christ more perfectly in John's case than in the case of anyone else. He had turned him towards Christ. He had pointed out to him the "Lamb of God" and had even rejoiced when his disciple left him to follow Christ (1, 37).

That encounter with Christ must have been the event that really transformed John's life. Peter, Andrew, James, and Philip were drawn to Him of whom "Moses in the Law and the Prophets wrote" (1, 45). They too cried out: "We have found the Messias." But John had the conviction that his search for God had come to an end upon meeting with Christ. Everything came to Him with Christ: life, light, truth, and grace. In Jesus his life saw its fulfillment. "And of his fullness we have all received, grace for grace. For the Law was given through Moses; grace and truth came through Jesus Christ" (1, 16).

The object of our present study is what Jesus meant to John. We will try to envision the fourth Gospel as the apostle's testimony concerning Christ. With the aid of the Synoptics we would like to determine how Christ entered John's life and how He set about reforming his character and refining his spiritual sense. How did He succeed in preparing him to become the witness and spiritual teacher which his Gospel reveals?

We usually picture John with the best dispositions for receiving Christ's action in his soul. The reality is much different. The Gospel gives us a glimpse, along with the difficulties He encountered, of the method He employed in John's case and the foundation stones He laid in his soul for the edifice He wished to construct.

Whatever had been the shock sustained by John by his first encounter with Christ, it does not seem to have modified his character at least in the beginning of his life with the Master. Scenes reported by Mark and Luke show a man who is not only impetuous and fiery, but even violent and harsh. Tendencies in him which gave rise to generous decisions such as leaving his family to follow Christ can also draw him into the impassioned deed marked with bigotry (Mk. 1, 16-20). Is it not John who is referred to in that episode where "the disciples saw a man casting out devils although he was not of their number, and one of them came to warn the Master"? Jesus, perceiving a partisan spirit in this devotion to His cause, replied, "Do not forbid him; for he who is not against you is for you" (Lk. 9, 50).

Another incident shows John lacking that spirit of meekness which should animate the true disciple of Christ and accompany his zeal. Sent on ahead to prepare things in a village where Jesus and His apostles were soon to arrive, James and John were not well received by the inhabitants. Seeing this, they quickly retraced their steps and said to the Master, "Lord, wilt thou that we bid fire come down from heaven and consume them?" But Jesus reprimanded them, "You do not know of what manner of spirit you are; for the Son of Man did not come to destroy men's lives, but to save them" (Lk. 9, 54-55). Without a doubt, it was at this time that James and John must have been nicknamed by Christ "sons of thunder."

If we add to these two scenes that in which Salome, their mother, claimed for her sons (surely consenting, if not actually accomplices) a special place in the kingdom (Mt. 20, 20), we cannot doubt that ardor and generosity, but also violence, anger, and even harshness characterized the one who, through some strange aberration, is so often represented as a soft and almost effeminate individual. Indeed, with St. John, the notion of the kingdom of God was still conformed to the ideas of his times. His love for Christ is deep, and he is ready to serve Him generously, but his desire to occupy the first place shows the progress that still had to be made. No, he did not know "of what spirit he was."

Christ, however, needed this ardor and zeal. They were going to form the still imperfect, but necessary, foundations of the spiritual work to be realized in the apostle's soul. Were they not the counterpart of a jealous attachment to the Master's glory?

There is not a scene in which John is involved in which this attachment does not fail to appear with all the strength and finality of passion. John is not numbered among those whose head is independent of their heart. When he surrenders himself, it is entirely and without reservation. He cannot conceive of the half-measures or the prudence of a Nicodemus. His engagement attaches him to Christ with an extremely personal bond, and this attitude casts a decisive light over the entire Johannine Gospel. It explains why and how, in spite of his natural faults, John was able to advance so quickly in the ways of love and union.

There is, in fact, a spiritual life only in proportion to the existence of a bond between one person and another. There is nothing sentimental about this bond. John loved Christ because Christ had first loved him. He is "the disciple whom Jesus loved" (19, 26; 20, 2: 21, 7). His love for the Master is, first of all, the return of this love of divine charity with which Jesus has filled him. But, to be supernatural, this love does not have less need of a favorable terrain to spring up towards God and be rooted in Him. How would the lukewarm, those of whom John will say, "God vomits them out of his mouth," be capable of attachment, of dedication, of surrender to life and death (Ap. 3, 16)?

The fourth Gospel will never cease to bring us the conviction that the principle of unity of the Johannine thought and "spirituality"[5] resides in this capacity of personal attachment and surrender to Christ. The Johannine themes of "life," "light," and "truth," these great perspectives through which God reveals Himself to man, do not designate abstract entities, in any way. Each one of these expresses something of the infinite richness contained in Christ's Person.

Thus, John will always be careful to propose them to us in an extremely personal form, and never must they be separated from the Person to whom they refer. The "I" with which they are preceded makes this understood. "I am the way, the life, and the truth," "I am the light of the world" (14, 4; 8, 12). And it is under this eminently personal form that Christ's principal claims will be transmitted to us by the apostle: "I am the resurrection"; "I am the good shepherd"; "I who speak with thee am he (Messias)" (11, 25; 10, 11; 4, 26). In short, all goes back to that central and last reality, viz., Jesus, because He is God, is the fullness and the perfection of Being.

We are here at the opposite extreme of an abstract or intellectual vision, a vision absolutely repellent to the Semitic mind. It is clear that we have the most favorable terrain for the development of an intense spiritual life. And no less favorable for a spiritual development is that tendency in St. John to consider things, that desire to "see" things. The word is used constantly by him and belongs particularly to his role as witness. What is a witness if not one, to use John's own expression, "who sees with his eyes and touches with his hands" (1 Jn. 1, 1)?

Many are undoubtedly of the opinion that the spiritual life demands a disinterested attitude towards the world; that it suffers when a person becomes engaged in the realities of this world. Does not one render himself unfit for union with invisible and interior things when he permits himself to become occupied with the world? John shows how a deep

5. If we may use this expression unknown in John's era.

interior life can be accompanied by a very acute awareness of what is going on around us.

There is nothing better seen and better described than those scenes reported in the fourth Gospel, and especially those of the man born blind and the woman of Samaria (cf. cc. 4, 9, passim).

John attaches such an importance to the sense of sight that he continues to employ the expression "see" even when he is speaking of matters pertaining to faith. Thus, in Christ's words we have: "He who sees me, sees the Father" (14, 9). John's thought concerning faith could even be summed up in three sentences in which the word "see" recurs: "Come and see" (1, 39); "He saw and believed" (20, 8); "blessed are those who have not seen, and yet have believed" (20, 29).

The apostle's desire to see is proof of his realistic and objective temperament. The fourth Gospel gives many proofs of this temperament. Thus, in the scene of the Master's arrest, John does not lose his composure and having noted that Peter did not succeed in entering the courtyard, he intervenes and obtains permission for him to come in (18, 16). And again, when after running to the tomb, in spite of his highly emotional state, he keeps a sufficiently clear head and observant eye for noting down the minutest details (20, 5).

John has frequently been represented as an emaciated, ethereal youth, lost in some interior vision. Those who thus represent him seem to forget that Jesus went looking for this young Galilean fisherman on the shores of Lake Genesareth. Through his hard trade, he was forced to battle against the elements, to observe in the skies the signs announcing changes in the weather (Mt. 16, 2). Thus did he have to provide for his daily sustenance as well as that of his family. There is nothing poetic in all this! And this John, who dragged heavy fishing nets, coated his fishing boat with bitumen and its rigging with pitch, must have had, like Christ, the rough calloused hands of the workman.

Far from being an obstacle to an authentic spiritual life, this realism of a man accustomed to considering the things around him went to make up an excellent point of departure. Realism is the necessary atmosphere of the spiritual life and nothing is more contrary to it than day-dreaming. Saints are the most authentic realists, and God is Reality par excellence. If He Himself is invisible, the reality of this visible world created by Him is proof of His own Reality. In fact, we are united to this Absolute Reality only after we have learned to go to Him through the visible things He has made. Hence, the spiritual man has neither to turn away from the world nor leave it (17, 15). Rather he should strive to unravel the mystery of God through the world he sees around him.

In St. John's case, his intense desire to see prepared him to consider the spiritual life not only under the form of a union of love, but under that of the contemplative look. Having encountered Christ, his natural desire to see, just as his thirst to love, was concentrated henceforth upon Him alone. Had not the Master when calling him and his companion said to them, "Come and see" (1, 39)? These words, corresponding so profoundly with his own tendencies, were going to make him choose Christ as the unique object of his life. The desire to see would develop into the longing for vision, the ardor of his love, into the thirst for union with God.

The true spiritual life is to be found at the confluence of these two essential currents, seeing and loving. It even demands their fusion and it is identified with this fusion. The marvelous richness of the life of faith which will expand into eternal life and into beatitude is to be found here in germ. One word under John's pen expresses it better than any other, the word "knowledge." He uses it in fact to specify the activity of eternal life and the life of faith, and also to describe beatitude itself: "Now this is eternal life, that they may know thee, the only true God, and him whom thou hast sent, Jesus Christ" (17, 3).

Such was the one whom Christ chose to follow Him and He was going to prepare him for his role as apostle and evangelist. Using the positive traits of his temperament, He will direct these into very definite channels.

Like the other apostles John followed Christ on his apostolic journeys. He assisted at His miracles, listened to His teachings, shared in all His interviews. The affectionate confidence of the Master allowed him even to be one of the little group present on Thabor and in Gethsemani.

And even more, John will be the only one of the apostles present on Calvary right up to the death of Christ. Having assisted at Christ's trial from beginning to end, he will remain with Mary at the foot of the Cross. Who would think that his presence in these various circumstances was only chance? We may see in it not only a proof of his fidelity and love, but also a manifestation of God's designs upon him.

At Thabor John sees Christ transfigured before him. "And his face shone as the sun, and his garments became white as snow" (Mt. 17, 1-8; Mk. 9, 2-8; Lk. 9, 28-36). He sees His glory (1, 14), and like Moses on a former occasion, he enters into the cloud (Ex. 19, 9). In Gethsemani John beholds Jesus overwhelmed by depression and sadness. He hears Him murmuring those words, "My soul is sad even unto death. Wait here and watch with me. . . ." (Mt. 26, 38). He sees Him fall to the ground and hears His prayer, "Father, if it be possible, let this cup pass from me; yet not as I will, but as thou willest" (Mt. 26, 39).

John relates neither scene in his Gospel. Only an ignorance of his habits would make one believe he was indifferent to them. The study of the fourth Gospel shows the degree to which both scenes affected him. They appear as the two extremities of the mystery of the Incarnation that John had the mission to reveal.

On Thabor the Son of God is glimpsed in Christ and John states in the Prologue, re-echoing that manifestation on Sinai: "We have seen his glory" (1, 14). In Gethsemani there seemed to be no longer anything but a man crushed by suffering and agony, hardly human in appearance, "so marred in his look beyond that of man" (Is. 52, 14).

Setting the data of these two scenes side by side, John succeeded in giving us a formula of extraordinary compactness concerning the two natures in Christ. "And the Word was made flesh . . . and we saw his glory . . ." (1, 14). We see why it was necessary that he be present on Thabor and in the garden of Gethsemani and how Christ prepared him for his mission as author of the fourth Gospel.

The contemplative in John required that vision receive certain guarantees, and the one who was to make faith men's response to the gift of God really had to know the object of this faith with great certitude.

This friend of Christ, in whom the annihilation of the Word-made-flesh still met with resistance, needed this spectacle in the garden of Gethsemani in order to see the lengths to which Love intended to go for the sake of the Redemption.

As for his presence at the Cross, this was permitted so that he could see the mystery of divine love in its last dimension. For there on the Cross he saw the Lamb of God immolated and the Word made flesh, and he took both in at once and hence understood the mystery of a God-Man and His love for us.

The fruitfulness of John's spiritual message stems from the intensity of his personal union with Christ. The fourth Gospel is the expression of this love. It is a love John has received from Jesus and which he has returned in the ardor of his generosity and fidelity. He was able to penetrate deeper than anyone else into this love and Christ willed that he discover its living source, contemplate with his eyes its reality and symbol, at one and the same time. He desired that John penetrate this mystery and remain there. That is why He allowed him to look, along with Mary, at His transpierced Heart. He wanted him to see that blood and water flowing from it which are the physical and spiritual sources operating in the sacraments and in the Church.

In this glance upon the Lamb of God hanging on the Cross, on the water and blood escaping from His side, we have in germ not only the Johannine Gospel, but also all the elements which will nourish the apostle's spiritual life as well as our own.

Child of the Virgin

Formed by the Precursor, in whom the Old Testament calls upon the Messias for the last time, and having received from Christ a direct preparation for his mission, John seemed to be in possession of the necessary graces. Jesus' tenderness for this disciple whom He loved reserved for him other sources of enrichment and development. We wish to speak of the influence Mary was to have upon the one whom Jesus confided to her. And likewise, of the role which the Holy Spirit was going to play in the apostle's soul, particularly during the last part of his life, the one which would see the Epistles and Gospel come to light.

After Christ's departure, the apostle's life was no longer separated from that of Mary who, through the express will of the Savior, had become his Mother (19, 26).

In the ardent young man come to him upon the Jordan's banks, John the Baptist had a presentiment of the future disciple of the Messias and, with all his prophetic soul, he had prepared him for this role.

Mary herself received from her Son on the Cross the one whom, after her, Jesus had loved the most on the earth. Mary was going to continue the work undertaken in John's soul, with means and a love surpassing even those of the Precursor. For her as for the Baptist the end would remain the same: to turn John towards Christ, to have him discover His visage, to reveal to him His Heart, and have him enter more deeply into His intimacy and love.

How many years did she have for this work? We do not know, just as we do not know the place of their retreat. Jerusalem? Ephesus? Jerusalem and later Ephesus? This will be a disputed question for a long time. However, it is of little importance, the essential thing being to discover what John owes the Blessed Virgin in his spiritual formation.

What is lacking to the great majority of people is not so much an object upon which they can center the powers of their mind and the aspirations of their heart, as the opportunity of having known how to choose this object, then to remain turned towards it in patience and love. Patience is the sole revealer of hidden riches, and love is the sole creator. In this way they would have succeeded in perfecting themselves.

The grandeur of the contemplative life is to be found in the fact that, having proposed God as this object, this life effects a gradual transformation and divinization of one's being through that ceaseless look of love cast upon Him. And not the least of the paradoxes of this life is that it is animated with an extraordinary dynamism precisely at a time when it seems to be at a standstill.

Never did this statement receive such striking confirmation as in the case of St. John. After having turned towards God from his youth, John saw the object of his contemplation reveal itself to him in Christ. "No one has at any time seen God. The only-begotten Son who is in the bosom of the Father has revealed him" (1, 18). John is given the mission of rendering testimony. "I write of what we have seen with our eyes, what we have looked upon and our hands have handled of the Word of life" (1 Jn. 1, 1). And right to the end John remains turned towards this unique object, aided in his work by her in whom "the Word took his delight," who had lived the mystery of God in its fullness and kept in her heart the divine memories placed there by Jesus.

After Calvary the constant company of Mary was going to make of John the contemplative he had still not become. When living the mystery of the Incarnation and meditating upon that of the Redemption, Mary entered into the secrets of the contemplative life. She was no longer to cease advancing into the depths of these secrets through the silence and recollection afforded by this home to which she retired with John.

We do not know the exchanges they had one with the other and here suppositions are not permitted. But it is certain that living in Mary's company John was able to see much that was still superficial, incomplete, imperfect in his own love and knowledge of Christ. He believed he had loved his Master, but in Mary he saw the true contemplative; he saw too what an infinitely pure and dedicated soul, one fully united with Christ, could bring into the domain of knowledge and love of Christ.

He discovered that Mary, much more than the Baptist, carried within herself the entire tradition and all the hopes of Israel. She was the bridge and the mysterious bond joining the Old Testament to the New. She was the living Scripture, written not with words but with flesh and blood. She was invincible faith, indefectible hope, and perfect love. She was the spouse of the Spirit, His prayer and His living breath in the world. Leaning upon the Master's breast at the Supper John approached the furnace of infinite love, but in Mary he felt this flame ever burning. In her the divine Presence continued to pour forth peace, light, and love.

Though Mary and John communed in the same love, how much more did Mary's experience of things divine outweigh that of John. John had everything to learn from her in purity of outlook, faith, and fidelity. Not that their lives were to be identified. They could not, neither was it necessary. John had the obligation, after receiving Christ's message, to transmit it in theological and spiritual form. He had to make known life "in spirit and in truth" (4, 23). Mary, on the other hand, was to remain the soul and the heart of the Church.

Again, it was not so much upon the content of that message that John was to be enlightened by Mary. Rather it was upon the manner of entering into that message more deeply. He had to learn from her the lesson of "remaining" in spirit upon the Heart on which he had gazed with Mary on Calvary.

The Virgin's reserve, to which John's seems to correspond, signified the "silence" she was supposed to teach this soul so little inclined to be silent at the beginning and so filled with uncontrolled eagerness.

Mary had "known" how to listen to the word of God. And in her company John too learned how to listen and to hear. Music never finds a better echo than silence, and Christ's words will never resound better than in the heart that has learned to be silent. Mary's was the most silent of all hearts and she had gathered up all these words and meditated upon them in her heart. She had only to live in John's company for the disciple's soul to open up gradually to the possibility of receiving and "hearing" all that the divine words concealed.

Through Mary John had grown in his knowledge of Christ. Mary had forgotten nothing of the latter's infancy, His attitudes, and ordinary actions. She had kept these all in her heart. These memories shed light upon a personality specifically human, at least from all outward appearances, for "a man is always a child in his mother's eyes." Jesus, perfect God that He was, did not wish to escape this law. He desired to receive His weakness and human frailty from a woman and a mother. Who better than Mary could testify to them?

And yet such was her testimony and such was she herself that the traits of humanity which should have been a trial to John's faith in the divinity enriched and strengthened it instead. The information, so utterly human, which he received from Mary, established him firmly in his faith in Christ, Son of God. The Incarnation becomes for him a totally positive reality.

What he no longer beholds with his eyes he hears with his heart; he joins Him with his faith as a mystery into which he penetrates and in which he communes. He does this with Mary who, far from removing the mystery that was Christ, has enabled him to perceive its depths.

If it were our purpose here to meditate upon the Virgin Mary's life, we would first understand that each of the events composing it served to plunge her deeper into the darkness of faith. In the privileges and sufferings of her maternity, Mary found herself constantly confronted by the "interiority" of things. She tried always to unite herself with the message which the facts themselves conveyed to her and that profound sense of God they communicated to her. She lived them to such a degree that she was found worthy at the foot of the Cross to become the depositary and dispensatrix of these mysteries.

We cannot doubt that John was the first to draw from this treasury, and this in a privileged manner. When, in the evening of his life, he was drawing up his Gospel, he recalls the past and gives himself the title of the "disciple whom Jesus loved" (19, 26). An astonishment seems to pierce through from these words. They were written with great humility and a recognition that love alone made the choice. Here we see that baffling simplicity of those who have seen with their eyes things so great as never again to be really surprised at anything; and yet they seem to remain amazed and puzzled at what they have the mission to honor. If he is able to call himself the "disciple whom Jesus loved" without any feeling of complacency, it is because he has seen in Mary, much more than in himself, what it was to be loved by Christ.

Man of the Holy Spirit

If John learned how to listen to the divine Word by observing Mary, this interior voice was not simply the memory of words already heard and the recalling of facts already known. The entire Johannine Gospel reveals the existence in us of a "testimony" and a presence of Christ, as active and effective as the Word of God upon whom they shed light, viz., the testimony and presence of the Spirit.

Each of the apostles received the sacred testimony rendered to Christ in the form of a gift. The Gospel is its text and evangelization is born of it. But can we attribute to John a greater fullness of this gift? Could we say God was more liberal in his regard? We are not asking the question properly. By nature, God's gifts are indivisible. God is given entirely to each and He is all in all. The measure is full in each inspired author. But each one has his own grace and transmits the truth according to a mode decided upon by God alone.

John's insistence in bringing to light the Person and the role of the Holy Spirit is something proper to him. The stress he places upon interior testimony proceeds from an experience actually lived. And in his case its power was such that it realized what no human intellect could have conceived: that wonderful synthesis of Revelation known as the fourth Gospel.

True, there is in John's writings what we find in the others: what his eyes have seen, his ears have heard, and his hands have touched. But over and above all this, there is that unique arrangement of material, that clarity which makes of each word of Christ an overture to the world beyond the grave and of each of His actions a divine manifestation. It seems as though the Person of Christ were lighted up not from the outside but from within and that John sees all things in this light, without in the least going out from the limits set by faith.

The fourth Gospel is not only the work of a spectator, an historian, or a theologian; it is the work of a "witness" in the full acceptation of the word. And a witness of the same caliber as the Baptist who alone had understood that the theophany revealed "the Lamb of God" (1, 29,36). What the Father had taught the Precursor, John received from the Spirit sent by the Father and the Son. What he gives us in his Gospel is the object of his faith, and in that object, he gives us the one whom he loves: not Jesus of Nazareth, but the Son of God made man who has been revealed to him interiorly.

That sovereign mastery of the text is nothing but fervent docility to the breath of the Spirit who leads John into the things of God, unveiled as they are one after another to his loving gaze. His Gospel is written under the guidance of the Spirit of God, under the form of an interior colloquy with the Spirit who animates him.

Contemplative and Apostle

And all this does not allow us to place John in any other order than that of the normal development of the Christian life. "All things that are mine are thine" (17, 10). John is in possession of what procures the perfection of the Christian life. But if he is actually living the life of a child of God who draws freely from the divine treasury, he is still living in faith and hope, and in that indefatigable love which he teaches.

Totally Christian, John is also the contemplative formed by the Virgin and whom the Spirit keeps under His tutelage. What ordinarily hinders us from approaching things divine and is an obstacle to the knowledge of God is not so much the abundance or the absence of natural knowledge as it is the sense of the relativity of this knowledge, its subordination to Truth. Again, it is not so much the response we make to the seduction of so many attachments as the lack of that will which should be centered only on Him who saves.

John was seized by the Truth and everything fell into line in relationship to Truth. His human experiences were fully integrated with his experience of God. His glance, centered upon God, cleansed everything around him. Faith and hope were able to grow freely and give forth their fruit. His will remained united to the Master's and this attachment gradually detached him from everything else.

At the beginning of the spiritual life, the soul is restless and entangled in many things. She discovers only later that "very little is necessary" and finally that "only one thing is necessary" (Lk. 10, 42). A single look of knowledge and love upon Christ seems to have been the secret of John's introduction to the "life in the spirit." He reverts to that one essential thing and that unity in which his soul acquired perfect simplicity. His entire Gospel is filled with this taste for God. He lives it and he calls upon us to remain in it. Even those who are not contemplatives find in this Gospel the desire for and the foretaste of contemplation.

But John did not retire into solitude to enjoy the divine mysteries. His Gospel, his Epistles, the Acts of the Apostles and Tradition show him engrossed in the duties of his office. He too had "the care of all the churches" (2 Cor. 11, 28) of Asia. And God knows the state they were in.

The care of these churches is intimately associated with the apocalyptic visions of the seer of Patmos. Were we acquainted with this work only, what has been said above concerning the norms of the Christian life would seem to be contradicted. However, vision as well as prophecy, no matter how exceptional they may be, do not exclude faith. What they really do is show a special intervention of the Spirit.

In St. John they are exercised in relation to his apostolic work and its universality. But is it worthy of note that his Gospel is in no way transformed? It still remains the testimony of a believer and not a seer. It is always the apostle who is speaking both in the Gospel and in the Apocalypse, the apostle who has received a mission, who speaks what he has heard from God, and guides those who have been confided to his care.

If there is a time for contemplating and recollecting oneself in silence and prayer and if, in a certain way, this time must never cease, there is also a time when contemplation and prayer have nothing to fear from cares, trials, and solicitudes inherent in the apostolate. St. Paul gives us proof of this.

But in a much different way, St. John allows us to glimpse in his Gospel and especially in his first Epistle how much the care of the churches and of souls only served to intensify his prayer, bringing about in him a union between contemplation and the apostolate. A fact related by St. Clement of Alexandria illustrates how this union was realized between two loves, that of God and neighbor. When almost a hundred years old, John repeatedly told the youth of Ephesus, "My little children, love one another." And when they grew sad at this repetition, he said: "For this is the commandment of the Lord and it alone is enough."

The Beloved Disciple

"The disciple whom Jesus loved" (13, 23; 19, 26; 21, 20). This title through which John identifies himself and which distinguishes him from the other apostles is indicative of a privileged friendship with the Master. A secret and a mystery are certainly unveiled when someone is made known to us, not by describing him, but by presenting him in his relationship to another Person whom we know and by characterizing him by the love that Person has for him. That is why, no matter how perceptible this love may be, only those can understand it who actually experience it.

It is characteristic of love to isolate two beings in those respects in which they would otherwise be accessible to others; and how evident this law is with regard to Jesus and John! The latter's restraint, his silence on so many facts about which we would have liked him to comment, these are due undoubtedly to the fact that he shared these with the Master as a confidant and friend. The most ordinary event which may be easily expressed when one speaks with strangers reveals to those who love each other different and very secret angles perceptible to them alone. And in some strange way their love gives rise to a modest reserve that conceals the event entirely. There is no reserve like the reserve of two intimate friends, and the silence and reticence characterizing this reserve is evidence of this intimacy.

This very human and very lofty manifestation of mutual love is admitted implicitly by John when he called himself the "disciple whom Jesus loved." There are personal confidences of Christ that he does not betray, and his own can be guessed at only on rare intervals. Thus, while his title of "beloved" adds an inestimable value to his testimony, we can likewise be assured that this testimony draws out from the facts their most universal application, so that we may enter more deeply into their mystery. This comes to us as a right and enables us to be, along with John, the beloved of God.

CHAPTER 2

THE SPIRITUAL GOSPEL

A miraculous simplicity seems to conceal the real depths of the fourth Gospel. When approaching it after having read the Synoptics, we seem to be entering another world where everything is bathed in a new light. True, the Johannine Christ is the one with whom we are already acquainted and we come once again upon the broad outlines of His life. However, the day which sheds light upon these events and the atmosphere which surrounds them are different. Spiritual teachings of a very lofty nature take the place of those familiar scenes. We no longer come upon the parables.

The more we study this Gospel, the more we are convinced of its originality. Everything gives evidence of this: language, composition, extensive use of symbols. Would we meet this same originality in its end?

If the author's explicit intention is to bear witness to Christ's actions and words, "so that you may believe that Jesus is the Christ, the Son of God, and believing you may have life in his name," beyond this obvious teaching there are others which aim at extracting the meaning and import of the scenes recounted and of underscoring their spiritual lesson in the light of certain great themes.

When seeing things this way we are not complicating what is simple and building up theories where we are only asked to open the eyes of our heart. Rather we are trying to unite the author's thought and intentions insofar as this can be done. God, infinitely simple, is also infinitely profound. The fourth Gospel is undoubtedly the most pure expression of this divine simplicity and profundity. It retains and reflects the power and the light of this Word of Life whom the apostle "has seen with his eyes and touched with his hands" (1 Jn. 1, 1).

Style and Composition

St. John's style and language are not erudite. There is a simplicity about them that some would even term "poverty." His vocabulary, repeating as it does the same words, appears monotonous. Short sentences develop his thought in a very gradual way. "John attempts to study an object from its various angles and close in upon it as the waters of the rising tide instead of analysing and defining it."[1] Though he never tries to produce an effect, his innate simplicity obtains it for him.

His desire to transmit a teaching or to describe a spectacle leads him to use at times a grave and quasi-liturgical rhythm similar to a chant or the successive sentences of a prayer spoken to God. It is then the contemplative speaking, seized by the mystery of God. At other times, he is led to paint a scene he has long since witnessed with an exactitude, a vividness of detail, and a freshness of vision that are really astonishing. No sooner has the description come to life than he shows that not a detail, not a character-trait has escaped his watchful eye. It is then the witness carrying out his mission.

"Go, call thy husband and come here," Jesus will say to the Samaritan woman. And further on, having described the scene of the ointment poured out and having noted down Judas' words, "Why was this ointment not sold for three hundred denarii and given to the poor?", with a stroke of the pen which he drives in like the thrust of a dagger, John remarks, "Now he said this, not that he cared for the poor, but because he was a thief and, holding the purse, used to take what was put into it" (12, 6). Such care for objective detail is worth more to us than precious descriptions of the Savior's character and actions. Whether he is acting as a contemplative or a witness, the important thing for John is to see things as they actually are. His language and style mold themselves around the object to be described, but they reveal its depths. Thus, Christ appears in John's writings such as He really is: human and divine.

The serenity of the fourth Gospel does not render it impersonal. On the contrary, nothing is more living and more vibrant than this text through which a certain Presence never ceases to manifest itself. Abstract symbols and terms come to life. Under the most calm appearances we feel an interior flame burning throughout. Everywhere we devine "the fiery and stormy soul of the son of thunder" writes K. Barth. While ordinarily speaking the style is the man and nothing but the man,[2] here the style is still the man, but one totally seized by his mission of witnessing and presenting facts in such a way as to enlighten, enter into, and

1. L. Bouyer, The Fourth Gospel, Intro.
2. Buffon has written: "Le style est de l'homme...."

nourish those who will read these facts. "This is written that you may believe . . ." (20, 31).

Already perceptible through its language and style, the originality of the fourth Gospel is evident even more so in its composition. This latter follows a preconceived plan, maturely reflected upon, which introduces an arrangement much different from that of the Synoptics. Not only does John say nothing concerning the birth and hidden life of Christ, and in general about anything he has not personally assisted at, but he also makes a definite choice among Christ's teachings. He retains only seven of the miracles, and he does this in view of a very definite teaching to be imparted. With him, the miracle sheds light upon a teaching, which in its turn extracts the spiritual meaning of the miracle.

An analysis of the major themes around which his Gospel is organized enables us to discover the author's preoccupations. More deeply than the style, the composition of the fourth Gospel brings out into the light the spiritual tendencies of St. John.

If this Gospel follows a certain chronological order in its broad outline, it pursues at the same time another plan of the spiritual order in which themes and symbols play a major role. In their turn, these themes and symbols used by John have reference to a central Reality, the Person of Christ.

The simplicity of the fourth Gospel conceals then a very subtle arrangement. John does not recount any parables and he does not mention any teachings of Christ which lay down or recall the moral foundations of the Christian life. He passes over in silence discourses as important as that of the Beatitudes, and events as essential as that of the institution of the Eucharist, though he had even been its privileged witness. He keeps to himself the secret of the confidences received from Mary about the birth and infancy of the Savior. The other evangelists make frequent mention of the celestial world (angels, the intervention of spirits, etc), but John rarely makes allusion to these. His concentration evidently is elsewhere. He aims at having us discover in Christ what he himself found in Him: Life, Light, Truth, Grace, and Love.

Everything takes place in the fourth Gospel as though the apostle had wished to strengthen his readers against the temptation of attaching themselves to the accidental, even though this is linked to the divine, and he does so in direct proportion to the "marvelous" and the "supernatural" contained in this accidental element. Thus, in the Johannine Gospel there is nothing that lends itself to a "legendary" or "mythical" interpretation.

John retains the entire objectivity of the events he recounts, but he scrutinizes them in order to hear the Word speak through them. He goes right to the essence of their message in order to unite with the Word there. What John pursues in this Person whom he has seen with his eyes and touched with his hands is the hidden God whom the Spirit reveals.

The fourth Gospel shows that its author had a keen sense of composition, and the latter contributes much to intensifying the spiritual atmosphere of the Gospel. Thus, through the religious majesty of the Prologue, John succeeds at the very outset in snatching the soul from time and establishing it in the eternal. Thus also, he arranges his account in such a manner that, to a set of circumstances at its beginning, there corresponds another set of similar facts at its conclusion. There results from this a rhythm and a balance to which the soul is sensible even though it is not explicitly conscious of it.[3]

The spiritual character of the fourth Gospel is intensified likewise by the dynamism that runs through it from beginning to end. How can the soul possibly escape that intense drive which passes from the apostle into his readers? John is never content simply to treat a theme as an end in itself, but he must apply himself to showing its progress and development and influence in souls.

And so a simple study of the Gospel and its composition shows us how its author obeyed certain spiritual driving powers. However, we shall understand this much better still if we analyse the use he constantly made of symbols and signs.

Symbols and Signs

In fact, this is one of the characteristics of the Johannine Gospel. And it would be sufficient in itself to manifest the preoccupations of its author. Symbolism already appears on the most material plane, that of numbers. "Though we must guard ourselves against too much hair-splitting in the matter, yet it is difficult to deny that there is a symbolism in St. John that is not deliberate and consciously elaborated."[4] Examples of such a symbolism are so numerous in the fourth Gospel that they cannot be

---

3. At the conclusion of the Gospel, the testimonies of Peter and John (20, 6-9), that of the disciples (20, 19-35), that of Magdalene (20, 11-18), and finally that of Thomas (20, 25-29), all correspond to those initial testimonies of the Baptist, the apostles, the disciples (1, 19-34; 1, 35-51; 2, 11). It is clear that testimony and faith are the door through which John opens and closes his Gospel. To the Baptist's statement when saluting Christ as the Lamb of God (1, 29) there correspond the words of St. John applied to the Crucified, "Not a bone of him shall they break" (19, 36).

4. L. Bouyer, op. cit.

ascribed to chance.[5] In itself alone the fact would not be enough to characterize a spiritual tendency. But the use of symbols and signs is manifest under other forms as well.

Symbolism obliges the thought to move and develop on two planes: that of the symbol itself and that of the superior reality designated by the symbol and of which it is a reflection and an image. Of these two planes, one at least is non-temporal or spiritual.

Though Christ Himself is at the origin of the symbols with which the fourth Gospel is filled (and John would undoubtedly not have had recourse to them if He had not first used them in His interviews), it nevertheless appears that John was more attentive than the other evangelists in reporting them and more careful in underscoring their meaning and import.

In fact, it is in the fourth Gospel that we find the symbols of living water, bread of life, the Door, the Good Shepherd, the vine, etc. These symbols all have direct reference to Christ Himself. Their spiritual value acquires a transcendent import for, through each one, something of the divine Reality tends to be revealed to us. And the apostle points out this transcendence by declaring that Christ is the "true" vine, the "true" light.

The Johannine symbol has a transparency about it that allows a glimpse of the highest spiritual realities, those for which the soul hungers. That is why in St. John only the major religious symbols are to be found, those that are filled with the same essential signification in all religions, viz., water, bread, wine, light. In John's mind, bread, the vine, water, etc., are not only illustrations or comparisons which permit us to become conscious of certain characteristics of the "divinity." It is to Christ, to His Person, that they refer, and it is in Him that they find their plenitude of meaning. He alone fulfills them: "The Word was the true light that enlightens every man" (1, 9).

While Christ's parables are stories or pictures borrowed from daily

5. The first words of John's Gospel recall those of Genesis, for he intends to make the account of the "new spiritual creation" the work of the Word. Hence it opens upon a series of seven days like the creation account: 1st, 1, 19; 2nd, 1, 29; 3rd, 1, 35; 4th, 1, 43; then 3 days, 2, 1; and the 7th day the manifestation of Christ takes place.
The numbers "three" and "seven" are frequent.
— He makes 3 references to the feast of the Passover and each time in the same words: "The passover feast of the Jews was at hand...."
— There are 3 sojourns in Galilee (1, 43; 4, 46; 6, 1).
— There are 3 words from the Cross: "Behold thy mother"; "I thirst"; "It is finished."
— 7 miracles are reported: changing water into wine (2, 1-11); healing the official's son (4, 47-54); healing the paralytic (5, 1-15); multiplication of the loaves (6, 1-15); walking on the waters (6, 16-21); healing of man born blind (9, 1-41); raising of Lazarus (11, 1-46). The miraculous draught of fishes is considered an addition by a disciple.
— There are 7 testimonies: Baptist's (1, passim); the disciples (cc. 1, 2, passim); the Father's (5, 37); the Son's (8, 14); the works (5, 36; 10, 38); the Scriptures (5, 39); the Spirit's (1, 35; 15, 26).
— There are 7 declarations of Christ's nature: "I am the bread of life" (6, 35); "I am the light of

life, the Johannine symbols are totally absorbed into the reality that is signified, i.e., Christ.

Furthermore, the Johannine symbols do not simply present a spiritual reality, but it frequently happens that these symbols actually realize this spiritual reality. Thus, the cure of the man born blind does not only symbolize the ascent of his soul to the light; it really brings this about. John takes care to have note that the water with which the blind man washes is taken from the pool of Siloe. Now Siloe signifies "sent", and the one sent is Christ. Coming to Him, the blind man, at the same time as he receives sight, receives the true light, that of faith. Through the symbol of water we penetrate into the very mystery of Christ, the light and source of light.

In St. John's writings the symbol is closely attached to another reality: the sign. The term sign, "semeion," did not have the same meaning in his mind as it has in our own day, viz., that of a symbol buried in the unconscious and considered at the moment that it crops up into the consciousness; or again, what remains after drawing from the symbol, a devitalized symbol.

"In a world where everything draws its reality from the eternal Idea which it contains or represents, there are certain things, as there are certain events, which incarnate or represent this Idea with more perfection than others."[6] And it is here that the word "sign" is going to take its meaning.

This meaning can be affected by a bad character, as when the sign sets itself up in opposition to faith which has no need to see "wonders" in order to believe. This is the case when Christ says to the crowd eager for "miraculous signs," "Unless you see signs and wonders you do not believe" (4, 48).

But the word can also have, and it does have in St. John as well as in the prophets of the Old Testament, the meaning of "the symbolic act." In this case it does not appear essential that the sign be also a miracle. If it happens that it is a miracle in the episode of Cana of which John says: "This first of his signs Jesus worked at Cana of Galilee" (2, 11), the sign possesses nothing of this character in the washing of the feet and in the cleansing of the Temple, which are nevertheless both "signs." Every miracle is a sign, but not every sign is necessarily a miracle.

Miraculous or not, the sign is then essentially the means through which God gives man the power to discover Him at work in history, in events. The sign is a manifestation of God.

the world" (9, 5); "I am the door" (10, 7); "I am the good shepherd" (10, 11); "I am the resurrection and the life" (11, 25); "I am the way, the truth, and the life" (14, 6); "I am the true vine" (15, 1). L. Bouyer, op. cit. Introduction.
6. C. H. Dodd, The Interpretation of the Fourth Gospel, pp. 141-143.

It seems from this way of looking at it that all Christ's works and all His actions are signs, and all these signs are true since the one who performs them is the divine Truth and the Word made flesh. In this sense we may then say that each of the acts and words of Christ—and we know in the Johannine Gospel, Christ's words are actions and vice versa— contains in a certain way the whole truth of the Bible since each is performed or spoken by the living Truth itself.

The symbol evokes another reality; it raises up this reality in our mind which is turned towards it. The evangelical sign bears in itself the very Reality which it signifies.

Undoubtedly divine omnipotence is necessary in order that the sign be not only true, but effect what it signifies. But what is important to consider here is that Hebraic thought was in accord with such a conception of things.

In fact, contrary to Platonic-hellenism for which no encounter whatever was possible between the image and reality, for they are on two parallel planes, Hebraic thought placed no separation between the material world and the world of the spirit; each has come forth from the thought and will of God. God can, then, when He so wills, establish a communication between them . He can even bring it about that the signifying reality contain and realize what it signifies. Such will be the case with the sacraments.

God is Creator of all things. Because of this fact these things are not only linked up with Him, they are also linked up one with the other. More precisely, they are linked up in His Word, the all-powerful Logos, in whom He has created all: "In the beginning was the Word.... Everything was made through him, and without him was made nothing that was made" (1, 1,3).

Such as the Bible presents it, the notion of creation permits then a communication between the two orders of reality. There results from this, in this universe come forth entire from the hands of God, a veritable unity. The word "universe" underscores this unity.

However, this communication which was always virtually possible does not pass into act until the coming of the Word made flesh into the world. The notions of symbol and sign are going to acquire a new significance and import, far surpassing everything that has preceded them, because now the divine and eternal Word is incarnate, because God, through the Incarnation, "has effected an unforeseeable entry into the world which he assumes,"[7] because in the same Person, the finite and the infinite are henceforth united.

7. L. Bouyer, op. cit.

Through the path of symbols and signs we are led to the truth which dominates the entire fourth Gospel: that fact which is simultaneously historic and transcendent, viz., the advent of the Eternal into time.

But it is much more to a Person than to fact that we are led. The mystery of the Incarnation terminates in nothing else, in fact, but this Person. It is this Person in whom God and man are united.

Signs and symbols are referred to Christ who works miracles and wonders. The function of each is to reveal Him to us and, through faith, to make us believe in Him, to make us say when pointing to Him: "God is there!" In a word, the fourth Gospel leads us to two realities so intimately united that they are inseparable: the Word Incarnate, and our faith in Him.

Faith

Faith is the terrain upon which the entire fourth Gospel is constructed and it is faith that confers upon it its spiritual character. The ultimate reason for miracles and wonders is to arouse faith in man (20, 29). Signs and symbols have no value in themselves if, in the final analysis, the spiritual reality which they designate is not really existent or really attainable. And Christ is really attained solely through faith. It is the road that enables us to unite ourselves to Him. While entirely relying upon visible realities, faith receives from on high the power to show in what and how these visible realities are authentic signs of the Invisible.

Then, and then only, is that spiritual, coherent ensemble, that homogeneous entity which constitutes the fourth Gospel, realized. From the object to be attained, viz., God, who is Spirit; to the road which permits us to attain Him, viz., faith; passing through the visible realities themselves which deliver up to us the secret God has enclosed in them: everything is spiritual.

By its very nature, faith is not only spiritual, but it is also spiritualizing. It transforms us little by little into God, while it offers Him to us and makes it possible for us to unite with Him. St. John's Gospel, being the Gospel of faith, is also the road to this spiritualization for men.

"God is spirit" (4, 24). And God can unite only with him who will be born of the Spirit (3, 5), who will adore Him in spirit (4, 23) and who will love Him in spirit who comes to dwell in him (1 Jn. 4, 13), and who is Love itself.

Never until now was such a road opened to man. Will he know how to follow Him through faith, and through faith how to enter into possession here on earth of this heritage (3, 36) which is proposed to him? The fourth Gospel was written to permit him to do so, and that is why we can say with regard to it that it is the "spiritual Gospel."

Incarnation

"The Word was made flesh." If we wish to grasp the central fact of the fourth Gospel it is to this statement that we must return. Like every other son of Israel, John looked upon God as the author of all realities, spiritual as well as material. He realized that God was able to establish communication between them. But he had never envisioned the possibility that this union would one day be established in God Himself. The idea of an incarnate God, if only expressed in words, would have appeared to him as scandalous, blasphemous, and unacceptable.

In order to succeed in believing that the man who one day passed along the banks of the Jordan (1, 36) was God and that His flesh veiled the glory of the Word (1, 14) light and grace from on high were needed.

But, on the day when "grace and truth" (1, 17) came to him through Jesus Christ, John discovered in the Incarnation the furnace of light which was going to cast light upon the entire Revelation.

No one can doubt that the Incarnation and the Person of the Word made flesh constitute the center of the fourth Gospel. The teaching which is extracted from this Gospel is nothing else but a more vivid perception of this mystery, a communion with Christ incarnate, a faith and a transformation into Him.

Thus, the apostle whom Jesus loved was not content to contemplate his Master, or to live because of Him; he judged it necessary to consider, in relation to the Incarnation, the ensemble of realities in the midst of which this mystery had incorporated itself.

It was not possible that an event as prodigious and as transcendent as the coming of the Eternal into time, as the taking possession of the world by the Son of God, and the fact that henceforth He would "dwell among us"; in a word, an event such as the coming of Christ here on earth and the assumption by Him of a human nature, would not modify all perspectives and oblige us to reconsider all things in the light of this event.

The fourth Gospel has this remarkable thing about it, after having placed us face to face with the Word-made-flesh and after giving us a glimpse of this mystery's depths, it invites us to rediscover with it all things in the light of this mystery.

The years which flowed by until the drawing up of his Gospel were not used by St. John only for reliving in an interior way the mystery of God's love for man. They were employed in drawing out the consequences of the Incarnation, in the manner of conceiving our relationship with a world entirely renewed by this coming, as well as the way of regulating our conduct towards God and man. The fourth Gospel is not spiritual only because it draws souls along the path of faith and love, but because it gives them a complete view of the world in the light of the Spirit.

And John's merit consists in raising himself from the bosom of Israel's long traditions to this vision, and of giving himself up to the work of this renovation, of having understood that his message was to be entirely thought out in the light of the Incarnation.

History

St. John understood that the Incarnation demanded first of all a new vision of history. Undoubtedly for the Israelites, "human history was an instrument in the hands of God; it revealed the action of the divine hand."[8] God governs the world as its all-powerful Creator. It is easy for Him with the aid of material events to allow a glimpse of His designs to be had as well as the direction which He intends to set for humanity.

Although this direction and these designs remained enveloped in a certain obscurity, the announcement and the promise of the Messias conferred upon the events of history a complete orientation. Thus, contrary to many of the ancient concepts dominated by the notion of cycle and perpetual recurrence, the Jews considered time as an orientated reality, irreversible, dynamic. One was going towards something definite, history had a "sens."

However, in order that they might be able to be integrated into this new spiritual vision which the Incarnation brought, Jewish notions themselves were to undergo a change, they had to be refocussed. It was necessary that, without losing their reality and their historical import, the events and personages of Israel's history be brought around to the rank of preparation for the Event which transcended them all, at the same time as it fulfilled them, and polarised them. Without anything being denied their historic and religious role, Moses, David, and other personages of the Ancient Law were henceforth to be considered as figures of Christ, rough drafts fashioned in view of a model. In a certain sense, the Jews were to

8. L. Bouyer, op. cit.

have the courage to say of these men held in such veneration: "Christ must increase and they must decrease" (Cf. Jn. 3, 30).

But were they really decreasing? By reason of the transcendence of the Messias, Son of God, whom they prefigured and for whom they prepared, these personages and events were on the contrary promoted to an unforeseeable dignity. Their relationship to Christ conferred upon them a mysterious and quasi-sacred character.

The transcendence of Christ with regard to what preceded Him and the difficulty the Jews experienced in accepting such an upheaval in their way of considering their history are evident in several places in the Gospel. Thus, we have the occasion when Jesus complained to His listeners in the following words:

"This generation is an evil generation; it demands a sign, and no sign will be given it but the sign of Jonas. For even as Jonas was a sign to the Ninevites, so will also the Son of Man be to this generation. The queen of the South will rise in judgment with the men of this generation and will condemn them; for she came from the ends of the earth to hear the wisdom of Solomon, and behold a greater than Solomon is here" (Lk. 11, 29-31).

And more clearly still in that discussion with the Jews, Jesus will declare: " 'Amen, amen, I say to you, if anyone keep my word, he will never see death.' The Jews therefore said, 'Now we know that thou hast a devil. Abraham is dead. . . . Art thou greater than our father Abraham . . . Whom dost thou make thyself?' Jesus answered, 'Abraham your father rejoiced that he was to see my day. He saw it and was glad . . . Amen, amen, I say to you, before Abraham came to be, I am' " (8, 51-59).

In taking human nature, God had linked time with His own eternity. But, by becoming incarnate, God had likewise come to "fulfill" time which has flowed by since the origin of the world till the coming of the Messias. And this was done so well that from the time of Christ there is something that is radically new in the value and dimension of time. Before Him, it was a time of waiting, of preparation, of signs and figures. With Him there begins a time of reality, fulfillment, of communion with the divine Absolute.

This is the reason why, far from considering what preceded Christ as having henceforth lost its value and as disappearing before Him as the night gives way to day, John, entirely nourished on the Old Testament, discovers the real dimensions and meaning of the Old Covenant in the light of Christ.

The Johannine Gospel is built upon Jewish material and is in no way a product of Neo-platonism. Israel's history enters into it constantly and biblical reminiscences, particularly from Exodus, frequently appear. While drawing up his Gospel John had in mind the development of the history of the people of God, and it was in the light of Christ that he discovered its real meaning. Having perceived a real relationship between the Old Testament and Christ's life, John never ceased reading in the latter the history of Israel. One corresponds with the other, shedding light upon it and bringing it to completion. As Augustine expressed it: "Novum in vetere latet, vetus in novo patet."

We shall not read the fourth Gospel then with much advantage if we are ignorant of Israel's history, if we are not nourished upon the Old Testament as was John. And this, not only to make comparisons between the texts, but also to see how all things must finally be referred to Christ, not yielding their true meaning except in His light.

However, if all that precedes Christ terminates in Him, we must not think that with His coming history ceases to advance. When God enters His world, He does not interrupt its course of progress. On the contrary, He introduces into it a principle which is infinitely fruitful and communicates life from within. The Incarnation is an historical fact, and it is even the primordial fact of history. "No one has seen God at any time. The only-begotten Son, who is in the bosom of the Father, he has revealed him" (1, 18). It is then in both an historical and a spiritual way that the work inaugurated by the Incarnation continues; thus, it appears that there is nothing which stands out more in the Johannine writings and in the spiritual Gospel than the mystery of the Church.

Church

Present throughout the fourth Gospel, though in a hidden way for the most part, the Church is one of those realities which contribute greatly in conferring a spiritual dimension upon it. This statement will seem to be paradoxical since we have spoken with apparent reason of John's individualistic spirit; no other evangelist, in fact, insists as strongly as he does upon faith, insofar as it is a personal relationship between man and God in Christ.

Nevertheless, it is true to say that the fourth Gospel is "ecclesial," and this in direct proportion to its being spiritual. What does this mean? For St. John the Church is not separable from Christ. It is not only something that proceeds from Him on the historical plane, but it is His spouse. It is finally His sacrament.

On the historical plane the Church is attached to Christ. When he was writing his Gospel, the Church was already established. John, like Paul, had a personal experience of the sacrificial and sacramental life of the Church. "The communities to which the apostle writes are communities of believers."[9] They know the life of Christ, and they are united to Him through faith. They realize that He is the founder and the center of the Church, and that the latter has as its mission the communicating of His life to its members. Those whom John addresses are the "people of God," or to use Peter's own expression: "You, however, are a chosen race, a royal priesthood, a holy nation, a purchased people" (1 Pt. 2, 9).

And John has no difficulty in seeing in this people the continuer and the spiritual heir of that people in whose midst the divine Presence had resided and whom God had accompanied in its marches and guided all through its long history. Between the people and its God, a "Covenant" had been sealed which ensured its unity: "Thou art my peeple . . . I am your God." And better still, it was already under the figure of a spouse that God had willed to consider Israel.

Such a vision of things will be taken up and given depth by John. Everyone knows that the Covenant inaugurated with Abraham and renewed at the time of the Exodus (Ex. 23, 12) will be definitively established as well as spiritualized through the Incarnation (1, 14). Prefigured at Cana (2, 1), the messianic nuptials will be sealed on the Cross (11, 52; 12, 32).

Now the Church which was born from the opened side of Christ (19, 34) can do nothing else than perpetuate among us the mystery of the Incarnation and the Redemption, i.e., the mystery of the Word made flesh. Its mission is to lead us to Christ. "It has as its sole purpose the revealing of Christ to us, leading us to Him and communicating to us His grace. She alone can do this and she never finishes doing so. Never does the moment come either in the lives of individuals or of nations when her role must come, or even can come, to an end. If the world lost the Church, she would lose the Redemption."[10]

But to give us Christ "in spirit and in truth" (4, 24) she must give Him to us under the form in which "he has dwelt among us" (1, 14). And with astonishing depth John has understood that such was the economy of the sacraments of which the Church, as spouse of Christ, is both guardian and dispenser. She is herself the great sacrament containing all the rest.

Sacraments

Just as it is through Christ's "flesh," i.e., through the mystery of the Incarnation, that John united himself to the Word through faith, so he

9. Ed. Hoskyns, The Fourth Gospel, p. 51.
10. P. De LuBac, Méditations sur l'Eglise, pp. 175, 176.

understands that the sacraments have the mission, in uniting us to Christ's "body," of uniting us to God through faith.

St. John realized the priceless value of his encounter with the Word-made-flesh and of his human contact with Christ. But he knows also that this contact would have been fruitless without faith. "It is the spirit that gives life; the flesh profits nothing" (6, 63). John discovers in the sacraments the admirable means of having Christians encounter Christ and of permitting them, through the centuries, to establish this contact with the God-Man. But he does not forget that faith is necessary if we wish to recognize Christ through the veil of the sacraments. As the mystery of the Incarnation which they continue among us the sacraments are matter and spirit. It is substantially the same Christ and it is also the same essential mystery which they convey to us. They are simultaneously: figure, symbol, and reality.

We can understand how the sacramental economy, joined to the fact of the Incarnation, transmits the mystery of Christ to us in its veritable dimensions: historical, symbolic, and sacramental.

When reading the fourth Gospel we gradually become conscious of the fact that the whole history of the world is found there gathered together and fulfilled in Christ's Person; that there is not a single word or action of His which, besides having an obvious, historical, and material meaning, does not have also a spiritual meaning which transcends space and time.

Gospel of the Spirit

However, if the fourth Gospel merits the name "spiritual Gospel" it is because the Holy Spirit was not content with simply inspiring the apostle. He gave him an intimate experience of the things of God. Invading and penetrating St. John's soul, He marked it with His influence. And we must make an attempt to show the traits and the profound nature of this influence of the Spirit.

The Bible makes it clear to us that certain inspired men were only momentarily placed under the Spirit's influence. Without looking for extreme cases, we can verify this fact by looking into that of Saul as an example. (1 Kgs. 10, 6). But ordinarily the Spirit's action is neither extrinsic nor passing.

The inspired authors were men of God in whom the Spirit dwelt habitually and who were gradually transformed by Him. More or less perceptible, this action appears as sovereign in certain ones among them. This was especially the case in St. John, and it is because of this interior and continued action that his Gospel is the Gospel of the Spirit.

The form under which it appears allows us to state that the Spirit did not propose to John in an exterior way a truth which he was to enter into little by little. He did not invite him to transmit his message to us under the form of a set of ideas or a body of doctrine. Acting in the intimate depths of John's soul the Spirit revealed the living Person of Christ to him. God is not some kind of question concerning which we should make a general survey. Rather, He is a reality in the midst of which man may be placed, if God Himself takes the initiative. And the Spirit has this precisely as His mission.

What John had to know about the historic Christ, about His words, actions, attitudes, etc., was already a "fait accompli," and the Spirit did not have to give him the revelation of new words, or even to place in his memory words he had heard and forgotten. The Spirit had to give birth in John's soul to a more living light, a warmer furnace; and John had to "know" Christ "in the Spirit" and because of the Spirit in this renewed light and in this flame of burning love. And it is of this interior, experimental, intimate, and contemplative knowledge concerning Christ that John gives an account in his Gospel.

Contemplative knowledge and the contemplative life are not so much specified by their object as by the manner in which the soul enjoying this contemplative knowledge apprehends this object, and the depth at which the soul is united to this object.

In order to grasp this action of the Spirit, it is good to remember the manner in which the Jews of John's time conceived this action. It came from that "divine breath," that "ruah Jahweh" emanating from God Himself, and which, invading man's soul, communicated life to him. The important thing was to open oneself to this invasion, to be permeable in one's spirit to the Spirit of God, for man also is in possession of a "ruah" which renders him capable of this participation. In contact with the "ruah Yahweh," the ruah of man comes to life. A new life is born in him, life in the Spirit, the "spiritual" life.

Taking up this manner of looking at things, Jesus will say to Nicodemus: "What is born of the Spirit is spirit . . . You must be born again. . . . The wind (ruah) blows where it will and thou hearest its sounds but dost not know whence it comes or where it goes. So is everyone who is born of the Spirit" (3, 6).

It was thus that John conceived the influence and action of the Spirit. The living breath of God, He gives man the power to go to God and to receive Him as a Person, a life, a light, and a love. And no matter under what aspects we envisage Him, it will always be a question of a living totality as far as the Spirit is concerned.

The bent of John's soul recalls that of the souls of the sages starting out in quest of Wisdom. Their whole ambition was to enter into intimacy with this divine Wisdom, to know her, and to take her as their spouse (Wis. 8, 2).

But, while the wise men were always refused the opportunity of seeing this Wisdom whom they had chosen in their heart, it was given to John to know and to love incarnate Wisdom, eternal Wisdom that had come in the Person of Christ to pitch his tent in Israel. Better than anyone else, John, through his biblical formation and much more through the action of the Spirit, was to recognize in Christ the one who was prefigured under the traits of divine Wisdom. The action of the Spirit in John's soul was going to lead the apostle to a gradual interiorisation and to conduct him along the paths of interior unity.

A simple reading of the fourth Gospel brings out that "detachment" which characterizes the thought and style of its author. The images are few in number, and there are no parables or picturesque comparisons. "The Johannine similitudes are different from those of the Synoptics. They represent something higher. It is not a question of attracting the attention through picturesque comparisons to something that has escaped it. This attention is already captivated. Neither is there question of presenting new viewpoints in order to understand an object, but rather it is question of entering more intimately into an object now known, and of remaining there and trying to penetrate its depths.

"Like John the Baptist, the Johannine similitude must 'decrease' so that what it presents, though still veiled, may 'increase.' It must give up that glittering detail of the parable and be content to be the simple focal-point in which the only Light of invisible realities will shine forth.

"John's similitude aims at the heart of the Eternal and in order not to blur the infinite riches of the Eternal's simplicity the image must despoil itself and accept this privation of detail. Hence, the rarity of John's symbols. He is trying to lead us beyond the diversity and multiplicity of details. Finally, all is unified in those few exalted notions in which Life and Light dominate."[11]

One might say that face to face with the divine, John experiences that impotency which took hold of the authors of the Old Testament. They admitted their inability to break God down into His attributes, and preferred to say: God is One, God is Unique, God is Truth, the Living One, the Holy One. John is not unaware that the expressions: Life, Light, Truth, Love designate a Reality whose light pales when it is refracted in

11. L. Bouyer, op. cit.

the poor language of men; but that contemplation restores this light to its original splendor by bringing it back to its Source.

The reader of the fourth Gospel must tend towards this contemplative knowledge with which John was inundated. Human efforts in themselves alone are powerless to attain this, but the purifying, illuminating, and unifying action of the Spirit can bring it about. To read the fourth Gospel by simply stopping at the words and ideas, and even meditating upon them, is to remain on this side of what is essential and living in it. We must try to unite ourselves with the mystery concealed in its lines and which the Spirit reveals to us. For the one who lives in the Spirit and because of the Spirit, the Johannine text bears witness to the mystery it seems to veil and which in reality it never ceases to reveal.

The fourth Gospel bears witness to a God who is "one," but also to a God who is supremely personal. No other evangelist has brought out in such vivid light the relations which, while uniting the three Persons, reveal their transcendent Personality. The fourth Gospel is "spiritual" in the measure in which the Unity of nature and Trinity of Persons are stated and manifested in God.

When we see the simple and unadorned words which Christ made use of in order to make us enter into the mystery, and how John knew how to set up this same atmosphere in his Gospel, we can understand the depth to which he must have lived this mystery. Does not the alliance of the Unity and Trinity in God consititute the nourishment par excellence of the contemplative life? There is no knowledge except of "persons" and there is no communion except in "unity."

And John has arrived at this profound spiritual unity which engenders "simplicity," a reflection of the divine simplicity. His Gospel, fruit of this unity, like his life summed up in love of neighbor, bears witness to it.

We have been led to consider the fourth Gospel under some very varied angles. We have supposed it built upon very definite systems in which we have attempted to enclose the Johannine thought: chronological, liturgical, geographic, symbolic, and historic planes. Each one of them has some foundation, and not one of them is totally satisfying or can account for a reality of another order which, containing all these, surpasses them all.

Like all contemplatives and mystics, John has been profoundly attracted by those two complementary aspects of the unique Reality: God's transcendence and immanence. This transcendence and immanence, present and operative in the Word made flesh, enveloped, impregnated, and penetrated him through and through. He never ceased to be drawn and fascinated by them. Living because of Christ's Spirit, John entered into a knowledge of God's mystery. He did not look upon this mystery as from a distance, but as a reality into which we must penetrate and live at every instant and whose action in us is transforming even here on earth.

"Whoever believes has eternal life" (3, 16). "Everyone who loves is born of God" (1 Jn. 4, 7). "He who follows me has the light of life" (8, 12). "If we walk in the light as he also is in the light, we have fellowship with one another" (1 Jn. 1, 7). "We are called the children of God, and such we are" (1, 3).

These words extracted from the Gospel and the first Epistle of St. John are identical in meaning. They testify to the possession of the same object, simultaneously transcendent and very near. All of these words help us understand that God can be known and loved and possessed in his Son Jesus, tasted and experienced in His Spirit. If their peremptory, even sharp, character strikes us, their real power resides more in their simplicity and poverty. Nothing greater has ever been expressed in language more simple. Some would have the "seer" of Patmos express his experiences in fulminating sentences. There is none of this. Just as such humble and lowly material as bread and water give us Christ and the Trinity, the most unassuming words in John's mind appear as the least unworthy vehicle for expressing such things as Life, Eternity, Divine Sonship.

In John's Gospel all tends towards unity. The commandments become the commandment. "And whatever we ask, we shall receive from him, because we keep his commandment, that we should believe in the name of his Son Jesus Christ, and love one another" (1 Jn. 3, 22). "If you keep my commandments, you abide in my love" (15, 10).

We must love one another and keep the commandments. Is this the real message of the fourth Gospel? Is this all that John wishes to give us? Let us carefully read his words: "And he who keeps the commandments abides in God, and God in him. And this we know that he abides in us, by the Spirit whom he has given us" (1 Jn. 3, 24).

Thus, John declares that not only does God abide in us, but that we can have assurance of this life in Him and of His infinite love: "We know that he abides in us by the Spirit whom he has given us." And his Gospel bears witness to this reality; it testifies that the Spirit brings us overwhelming certitude of the divine indwelling in the depths of our being and the immanence of our own being in God. It gives evidence of the gift of God to His creature, and the presence in us of Him who makes us children of God. If the fourth Gospel reveals a transcendent and immanent God in us, if it is spiritual, it is because it testifies in favor of a mystery in the very midst of our own life; of a life that surpasses life, and which is the very Life of God.

CHAPTER 3

THE PROLOGUE

The Prologue, that majestic portal preceding the fourth Gospel, is not an introduction creating an atmosphere or setting the reader in a favorable environment. Neither does it have as its purpose the presenting of a plan or the great guiding themes of the Gospel, though these may be detected in it. It is something else altogether.

At the beginning of his Epistles St. Paul addresses an act of thanksgiving to God. The Prologue itself is John's act of thanksgiving before the mystery which is revealed to him.

He speaks in it not of personal memories, but of what has appeared to him: God and His mystery.

It is a hymn that springs up from his heart and which he allows to rise to his lips. Hence, that rhythmic and poetic incantation. It develops on the fringes of the divinity for it is a human voice that speaks; but it addresses itself to us as coming from the other world, because all takes place in God.

This is what makes it possible for John to bypass the heaviness and opacity of our mental universe, to reach one of total transparency, of liberty of spirit, where the poorest words are so charged with the infinite that they disappear before it.

At the outset, John places us in the heart of God, in the center of that eternity which proceeds from itself, perpetuating and fulfilling itself. "From everlasting to everlasting thou art, O God" (Ps. 88, 2). God is, and, in spite of appearances, the Incarnation will not be the coming of the Eternal into time, an instant when the Eternal comes to visit, for time is not something which, having come out from God, would have to return to Him. Time is, in the bosom of eternity, something identified with it. There is no other reality but God. Thus, John succeeds without any effort in placing us in God, in setting history in the very reality of God.

From the time that God dwells in it, history is without mystery. It is one and true, in God who is One and Truth. For God nothing "passes," the past does not exist. Everything is done eternally because God is.

It is something unique that the Prologue makes us sense this absence of alternation in God, or rather this perfection of reality and unity in Him through the alternation of the times used, relieved of all heaviness of "reflection," and through that thrust given to John's gaze which buries itself in the fathomless depths of the mystery.

No other mystic has gone so far into the "Presence" which gives to the intellect the power both to drink deeply at the divine fountains and to pour forth their riches to others, and which gives to love, the power of loving in loving Him.

John has "looked upon God." In His turn, God has in some way looked upon Himself in St. John and it is this image from eternity that the apostle sends back to us, in which life overflows into infinity and finds its pleasure and glory in itself.

There is nothing surprising about the fact that the Gospel takes up again the greater part of the themes of the Prologue. "The disciple is not above his Master" (Mt. 10, 24). And the one sent has no other mission but to repeat the words he has heard (8, 28). But John is alone in knowing what God has said to him without language, and the Prologue, though it offers many perspectives for analysis, remains a garden enclosed, without any other key but that of a look fully in accord with the Master's.

In the Gospel John will not "show," but he "will bear witness" only, not so much to exterior facts as to the divine Presence that gives them life and meaning.

In the Prologue, he withdraws totally before this Presence. And he gives us an inspired text with a purity attained by no other, and with an authority which has no equal but that of the very words of the Lord Himself.

"I write of what was from the beginning . . ."

When we compare the Prologue with the introduction to the first Epistle we are struck by the difference. The beginning is practically identical: "I write of what was in the beginning . . ." (1 Jn. 1, 1). And we come upon the same central idea. But in the Epistle it is the witness who is speaking, gathering together with great effort poor human data, powerless to express through them the unbelievable manifestation of the "Word of Life" (1 Jn. 1, 2).

In the Prologue, entirely in praise of the Word, no exertion is put forth. The text rolls along with a majesty and a serenity of expression.

Formerly, Wisdom had come to declare its divine origin and its joy to dwell "among the children of men" (Prv. 8, 31). There is an evident relationship with these texts which the Prologue enjoys; this relationship is not only literal, but essential. "Then the Creator of all things gave me his command, and he who formed me chose the spot of my tent, saying, 'In Jacob make thy dwelling, in Israel thy inheritance.' Before all ages in the beginning, he created me, and through all ages I shall not cease to be" (Sir. 24, 8,9).

In the fourth Gospel there are many other pages that can be set side by side with biblical texts, but the Prologue outweighs them all in the clarity and precision of its expression. Though the pronoun "I" is not used, the affirmation of the divine Person thrusts itself upon us and the coming of the Word is an accomplished fact. This coming is presented in the Prologue, accompanied by the circumstances surrounding it and its witness and herald, John the Baptist.

It is a fact as concrete as possible and no doubt can be associated with it: He who "was born not of blood, nor of the will of the flesh, nor of the will of man, but of God. And the Word was made flesh and dwelt among us" (1, 14).

Those acquainted with Scripture are not surprised that God made use of the reminiscences of ancient texts long studied and which John "kept in his heart" (Lk. 2, 51). God does no violence to those whom He inspires; and He despises nothing in which they are already steeped. But here, He goes even further; He sets His steps, if we may so express ourselves, in the steps of the apostle. Thus the strength enclosed in the Prologue bursts the old bottles and the new wine served there makes us forget the old, that of the Old Law. What the Prologue offers our thirst is nothing else but the very life of God, the living water of the Trinity.

The "Prologue" does not appear as such only because it is set before the Gospel; but the type of writings to which it is attached, as well as the unity of its movement as a whole, and above all the depth of mystery in which it is rooted, all these make of it a piece which has a purpose all its own.

Undoubtedly it is not accidental that the Gospel develops certain themes of the Prologue; but this seems to stem from the fact that these themes are imprinted in John's soul because of the effect of an experimental knowledge of God. John has the language of the mystics who are obliged to have recourse to images, even when they are speaking of what is most intangible and ineffable in God. He makes no appeal to analysis or abstraction, and much less does he use any form of philosophic thought.

Just as "his eyes have seen and his hands have touched," so his interior sense has been impressed by certain symbols and certain words of the

Lord. This "impression," not in the emotional sense, but in a very objective sense, guides him in the choice of what he will report in his Gospel; but the Prologue surrenders to us in some way the object of his contemplation in its native state and at its very source.

That this contemplation does not urge him to nourish himself upon personal memories, but rather draws him to consider before all else in Jesus the Word, the only-begotten of the Father, is proof of how faith outweighs every human sentiment in John and the place it holds in his life.

In John the divine life has taken precedence over everything else. If those whom he loved still had human names, the Word alone henceforth gives them a meaning by restoring them to their divine vocation. Not for a moment will John be able to go away from this vision of things since in Jesus Christ Himself he will see everything, in the light of the Word. When Jesus is silent, it is still the Word who speaks to the apostle's heart "as no man has ever spoken" (7, 46). Undoubtedly the "Word was made flesh and dwelt among us" full of grace and truth" (1, 14). But it is "the only-begotten Son" who has "revealed God whom no one has ever seen" (1, 18), and it is this Word who fills the apostle's soul to overflowing.

The Epic of the Word

Casting a studied glance over the Prologue, we can easily detect its progress from verse to verse, and its swift passing from one to the other of the themes to be dealt with later in the Gospel; Christ's miracles and teachings will both emphasize and elucidate these themes. The movement retains a distinct unity right up to verse 14. Its narrative character is evident from this verse to the conclusion. It treats of the Word's great epic in the adventure of that twofold creation: the ancient and the new, the latter being full of redemptive grace, eternal birth and alliance.

John reports Christ's words to Nathanael in the introductory pages of his Gospel. "Because I said to thee that I saw thee under the fig tree, thou dost believe. Greater things than these shalt thou see. Amen, amen, I say to thee, thou shalt see heaven opened, and the angels of God ascending and descending upon the Son of man" (1, 50).

The ladder was still empty when Jacob beheld it in his dream, rising from earth to heaven, used by angels awaiting the offspring to be born of the Patriarch (Gn. 28, 10-19). The ancient dream becomes a reality with the advent of the Son of God. In His heart the angels were tracing out that path towards heaven of which Jesus was speaking, and upon that path the Word advances filling the entire distance between heaven and earth. The perspective, however, no longer shows the human progeny born of Jacob and tending towards the Messias; it springs now from that divine line whence Jesus derives both His origin and the power to bring forth children to God for His glory. It is truly a question of the things of God, of God's word, and of an accomplishment to which nothing can be added and from which nothing can be withdrawn.

We understand better, consequently, why John will be silent about the birth and childhood of Christ. The Book open before him is not one with roots in the flesh, but one with foundations in eternity. This is what gives meaning to what takes place.

John has seen these "greater things" promised to Nathanael and his companions. It is these that he repeats and his canticle springs forth; it is divine music, simple and unadorned. No human passion troubles it. Its pure note re-echoes continually, enriched with many inflections which reach out farther and farther until they attain an endless eternity where duration has no meaning.

"In the beginning was the Word, and the Word was with God, and the Word was God"

As at the beginning of time, evoking the beating of the Spirit's wings "hovering over the waters" (Gn. 1, 2), the first words of the Prologue slowly unfold.

But John ascends beyond time. The extraordinary economy, the fewness of the words employed bear witness in their own way to the fact that they did not exist yet, that nothing existed, outside the Word in the beginning.

The Word, God, Being. Here we have a threefold identity of a unique Reality, subsisting alone in its magnificent strength.

At Horeb, time was opened and through this opening the infinity of God, the divine immensity had made its appearence. "I am who am. . . . This is my name forever; this is my title for all generations" (Ex. 3, 15). But the Being had revealed Himself in such crushing plenitude that from then on men will fear to appear before Yahweh: "to see his Face" or "to die" are one and the same thing.

In the Prologue the same verb "to be" claimed by the Word of God is found to be so charged with the absolute that all usage of it to specify human realities seems henceforth improper.

Its power is no longer used by man, nor in relation to him, but God gathers it into Himself, and it is in Himself that Being has its "rebondisse-ment." There is society in God.

Everything possible is contained in Him, carried by Him. There is nothing outside this dialogue He holds with Himself. God withdraws into His own absolute being.

This is a mystery whose revelation causes us nothing but amazement. It is not the amazement, however, of a transcendent spectacle that would overwhelm us by that sudden encounter between nature and the divinity as on Horeb; neither is it like that other encounter, totally interior, which reveals to Peter the sanctity of God present before him in Christ's Person. (Lk. 5, 8). It is rather the amazement we experience from the mystery itself, the knowledge of which is so soul-filling and satisfying. At one stroke we attain the Ultimate and everything is expressed of the Ineffable. The fact that we are able to contemplate this mystery, which seemingly remained an eternal secret, testifies already to the fact that we are in contact with it.

"All things were made through him, and without him was made nothing that was made"

Being takes its participated sense now from creation. Through the balancing of words, in the springing up of the Word in the bosom of God, His Work appears; there is no other work but His, and it has no meaning and no end except in Him.

"All". . ."nothing." Because this is the realism of Truth, mystics will take up these two extremities of the absolute, viz., todo and nada, which refuse existence to what is not God. The work of the Word is not a mirage, an illusion, an appearance; this is the world that is not, vanity, Nothingness. The work of the Word places us before and in a true world, just as He Himself is True. It is a substantial world, because He has made it such. God does not make nothing, He makes His work. He considers it, He creates it, He fashions it. It is not a game of chance, for there is no break of continuity between Him and His work. The work of the Word is a fruit which tastes of God.

All Scripture, and in particular Genesis, the Psalms, the Sapiential Books vie with one another in honoring creation as a hymn of praise to God, as a positive reality. However, this work, though distinct from God, is not exterior to Him. He carries it in Himself. "Nothing" is without Him, and "all" is through Him. If the terms "transcendence" and "immanence" can be applied conjointly to God, it is because God is not an "object." He is the unity of the multiplicity He creates. From Him and from Him alone, each thing draws its own individuality, for nothing exists that can know a dependence on anything outside of Him; but in Him too, each thing knows a communion with all other things, for nothing exists which does not have in Him a sharing with everything that is.

"He was the life of every being"[1]

And this is understood of that primordial push which we call existence and which sustains existence in everything that lives. But how can we not be struck by this insistence in employing the verb "to be"? "He was the life of every being" (1, 4).

The life of creation is frequently taken as synonymous with physical life. Besides, the existence of creation, that magnificent and admirable testimony of the divine omnipotence, appears to us as a gift, an excessive liberality. Thus we commonly say: "God gives us life," detaching it in some way from its Author for our profit.

But John did not write: "He gave life to every being." He wrote: "He was the life of every being."

Thus, in a more or less remote fashion, all life is a sharing of the divine life, a participation in the Word of God.

It is not only a "gift" but a "participation," and this is not only something more, but something of a different order. Participation means that God never ceases to be present to beings, to inform them interiorly, to be their very life. This is not to be taken in the sense of a subordination of God to what He would have communicated of Himself to His work, but just the contrary, viz., God anterior to His work, distinct from it and freely pouring Himself into it by a continual creation, whom nothing limits, nothing contains.

As the Word was with God from the beginning, so He never ceases to be with His work. He does not only give life to this work, He "is" this life; thus created life itself is a hymn of praise to the Father. Its form is multiple, but whatever that form may be, it conceals within itself a sacred mystery. "And God saw all the things that he made and they were good" (Gn. 1, 31).

An artist can take pleasure in his work. When it is a question of the Word's work, it is in God that God takes pleasure. Thus we sense already that this work is visited, permeated, and worked through an immense sign of love.

1. The "Bible of Jesuralem" translates Jn. 1, 4 in this way.

"And the life was the light of men"

With the last-born of creation God does not seem to have acted as He did with His other creatures. ". . . and breathed into his nostrils the breath of life . . ." (Gn. 2, 7). His Word did this. "Let us make man to our image and likeness . . ." (1, 26). God's breath completes the work of the Word and man becomes this work in which the Word expresses Himself with the breath of God.

John does not take up the text of Genesis literally, and yet from the moment in the Prologue when man appears, he is raised above the entire creation through a singular capacity and vocation. To be, to live are not enough in this new world which rises with him. He must "see." Light is his end, his nourishment. He receives it with life. It is the same thing for him. It animates and informs him.

The compactness alone of the words in this declaration which breaks forth from John as a cry of joy helps us understand the plenitude with which man has been filled. "And the life was the light of men" (1, 4). Life is the source of this light with which man is invested and invaded, and this light is the very light that visits creation, that of the Word.

But if it still remains possible, on the cosmic level, to see in light a physical reality distinct from its Author, it is not the same with the light that invades man.

Capable of communicating itself to other created beings, the life of the Word conceals infinite riches and the humblest of creatures is made to hear a note of these riches. Man is made to hear another which is perceptible to his spirit. When revealing him to himself, this note fills him beyond his own limits.

The simple fact of existing does not bring to reason any light on God. We know from experience that humanity, separated from its Creator, no longer recognizes Him as such. However, the breath which has created man has endowed him with a sense that makes him capable of being an image and a likeness. He arrives at this in the light of the Word who made him, and he never really becomes himself except in this light. Without it he remains mutilated, incomplete; the work of God in him is unrecognizable. Only the Saints, because this light dwells and shines in them, can give us some idea of what a man is.

These scales of participation in being which come to us from infinite Life are only an infinitesmal part of what life is in itself. There are infinitely more creations in creation than we can know. But among them there is also a certain continuity.

Pascal has brought out into the light the radical distinction and infinite distance between the different levels of creation. His three "orders" know among themselves immeasurable distances, and what makes them incomparable one with the other is forcefully brought out. And indeed, from organic life to that of the spirit, and from the spirit to that of charity the difference in nature is such that it seems there can be no possible passage from one to the other. The sacred text restores this unity. When stating of the Word that He was the life of every being, and that the life was the light of men, it reveals the origin and the sacred character of every life, its expansion by degrees of existence in the light, its ascensions without end until it reaches the plenitude of God. Man is the being who has his sources in the humblest origins and the highest splendors.

"And the light shines in the darkness, and the darkness grasped it not"

The mystery of this verse is difficult to decipher. It seems to introduce into the story of creation a world about which we know nothing except the name of its prince, Satan. Until now, the Prologue invited us to consider only the infinite ocean of God's being; it underscored a plenitude so perfect and a continuity so intimate that it would seem impossible for created beings to be outside the sphere of divine influence. But here we see darkness rising up. This darkness is not the absence of being, an emptiness of light. It actually exists since it opposes God. God does not allow it to be at rest. He visits this darkness with the same light which we know to be so overwhelming, and yet this visitation is met with opposition.

If we hold to this translation: "The light shines in the darkness, and the darkness grasped it not," this aggressiveness of the darkness appears to cover Satan's action, and that of all those who, having accepted him as chief, form this "world" which will refuse to "know" or to recognize the true Light.

If we translate: ". . . the darkness did not comprehend the light," we can think that John designates only men who since the Incarnation have not welcomed Christ. In one case or the other, there is no question of a dualism, for there is no equality between light and darkness. On the one hand, the sovereign God is supremely good; on the other, we have darkness which the Light still visits and which rebels, although its chief has been conquered forever.

It hardly seems possible, however, to restrict this opposition between light and darkness to the epoch where the Light came into the world, since John just a few lines further on does not separate the illumination brought by Christ to humanity from that which enlightens all men from the beginning.

"The Word was the true light that enlightens every man who comes into the world. He was in the world and the world knew him not"

We must then envisage this darkness in its widest sense: all men who turn away from the Light through the centuries, and Satan who has never ceased to be the prince of darkness ever since the original fall.

When the true Light came into the world, the darkness, in the person of Satan, sought to grasp Him and inflict a mortal wound upon Him. But the very bruise which the Prince of darkness plans signs his own defeat.

God tempts him, in fact, through this light spread among men and in this world which is his realm. And it is also among them that Satan fails to grasp Him and falls. How can we fail to recall here the Protoevangelium? "She shall crush thy head, and thou shalt lie in wait for her heel" (Gn. 3, 15). The victory is God's.

The Gospel will show, especially in Chapter 12, that Christ's hour is that of the judgment of darkness by the light and of the definitive condemnation of Satan. "Now is the judgment of this world; now will the prince of this world be cast out" (12, 31). He will drag along with him in his fall all those whose "father" he is.

Nothing appears in the Prologue of these results about which the Gospel speaks. The serene statement of the glory of the Word of God is found in the the former.

It is because the existence and the malevolent activity of the darkness take nothing away from God. He is the Author of all that exists. The darkness subsists only through Him, and it is unable to escape from the world of God or to destroy itself.

It cannot hinder the work of God from continuing. As mysterious as this is, we must say that the darkness too is the work of the Word. Our faith demands our adherence to this most disturbing and frightening mystery which has cost God and humanity so much. It contains the whole problem of evil and eternal punishment: of evil, that worm in the fruit given us to eat, and of eternal punishment, the existence of which we can understand only as existing in the very bosom of God. But this mystery contains that of the Redemption and salvation.

St. John has seen those "greater things" (1, 50) which we shall one day gaze upon. He has seen the work of the Word returning entire to His glory and that of His Father. This is the mystery of life, the mystery of the incomprehensible effusion of the Word into a work which, betraying Him, remains nevertheless entirely subject to its Conqueror. Just as the Word is with God, His work remains linked to God. Eternally it shares in the Life that has brought it into existence.

The Johannine Gospel will speak to us of the Son's love for the

Father and the first Epistle: "God is love" (1 Jn. 4, 8). The Prologue itself shows us the supreme peace, the blessed fulfillment of all things in the bosom of divine life. And if, after having read the Gospel, we return to the Prologue, we shall have to say, even after reading this terrible and mysterious verse: all is love.

"There was a man, one sent by God, whose name was John"

After that grand flight into eternity, the Prologue re-enters time and even the apostle's contemporary world. "There was a man, one sent by God, whose name was John."

Nothing is retained of all those centuries of a history so dear to the Chosen People. Everything recedes into the background before this man "sent by God," and this event about which he is to testify. What is the meaning of this silence? Everything takes place as though John had been visited by a light which has no concern for anything but the divine world: the divine life, the work of the Word orientated towards its completion. Now, in spite of the great signs with which God has marked the stages of history, we know that history has identified itself more and more with darkness from which God is seemingly absent. The world will not take up its true direction except with the visitation of Him who brings it salvation, regenerates it, and sanctifies it again. And so the herald who opens up the way is saluted and honored in the Prologue.

In our mind it would have seemed more "a propos" to bring to light the dignity of the Mother of God. The choice made by the evangelist is directed by another necessity: the role of witness assigned to John the Baptist is essential, not to the coming of the Messias but to the mission Christ comes to accomplish. The importance given to the witness underscores the singularity of the event: the unique event which is going to judge the world and decide its history.

"This man came as a witness, to bear witness concerning the light"

It would seem that such a statement is useless. Does not a lamp lighted in a dark place spread its light? There must have been more than merely external darkness involved in order that a testimony in favor of the light was still necessary.

The light that John the Baptist announces does not come to dispel material darkness, but to strike the blind, to open their eyes through the voice of one among them who himself has seen and borne witness: "in order that all may believe through him" (1, 7).

And if this is not enough, then the miracle of the man born blind will manifest once and for all the power of Christ, the Light.

Faith is still possible for those who do not see; but it is still necessary in order to come to the light.

What inaugurates these new times is the testimony concerning the light, and it is done without subterfuge, even roughly. The refusal which he opposes to this light encloses the blind one forever in his own night.

This will be the same for all times, but in order that no one will be mistaken by the voice heard, the apostle adds:

"He was not the light, but was to bear witness to the light"

Such humility is the guarantee of the authenticity of testimony: the witness withdraws, but what he has seen remains. Christ, the true Light, will one day give the reason why the soul will never be misled by the voice to which it listens. "And when he has let out his own sheep, he goes before them; and the sheep follow him because they know his voice. But the stranger they will not follow, but will flee from him, because they do not know the voice of strangers . . ." (10, 4,5). "He who is of God hears the words of God" (8, 47).

What has remained hidden from men, but what the Baptist glimpsed: the mystery of the sufferings and the Passion of Christ, as well as the manner of designating Christ, "Behold the lamb of God," is not taken up here by the apostle. In a much more vast movement he contemplates what would be the possession of the entire world if, suddenly cured of its blindness, it was to raise itself from its darkness and open its eyes upon the "true Light."

"It was the true light that enlighteneth every man"

With this statement it seems all is said. But John is about to undertake the retracing, not from the outside, but from within as one speaks of a reality known with ineffable certitude, the "journey" of this Light with which he is filled. Almost word for word, John restates the beginning of the Prologue: "It (the Word) was the true light that enlightens every man."

But he emphasizes "true" which marks the abyss between the work of the Word and the choice made by man. Man is spoken of here in the singular; it is the man envisaged under the light of faith, man the work of the Word, and it is of his silent dialogue with the Word that John is going to speak.

"He was in the world, and the world was made through him, and the world knew him not"

Visited by the Word, this world which belongs to Him, which is His work, persists in ignoring Him. Better than any other expression of sadness or revulsion, the painful astonishment of the apostle underscores the scandal of this ignorance, but also the marvelous benignity of Him who "comes."

The "coming" of anyone whosoever is never a matter of indifference to another person; he who comes brings with him a world of intentions which will be expressed by what man calls happiness or misfortune. But when the one who comes is this God whose presence in the world already testifies to his solicitide and benevolence, how explain why the whole world did not go to meet Him?

St. John does not say that the world was mistaken about Him and did not recognize Him: the testimony was there, convincing enough. Neither does he speak of indifference, but of "knowledge," that word as ancient as the Bible, expressing a relationship founded upon love. St. John unveils the Word's intentions when coming into the world. He came to be "known" by it, i.e., to love it and to be loved by it, "and the world knew him not."

In his astonishment, the apostle insists on the part of love which should have guaranteed to his coming a welcome without any reservations. "He came among his own and his own received him not" (1, 11).

Among His own ... into His own possession undoubtedly, since the world is His; but among His own, since in this world, He has chosen His house, the country and people of His predilection.

This verse condenses the entire history of the Hebrew people: its separation from other strange nations, its espousals in the desert, its long time of trial where the whole people received promises of fidelity from Yahweh: "I have loved thee with an everlasting love, and therefore have I drawn thee, taking pity on thee" (Jer. 31, 3). Finally, the announcement of His coming. It is truly among His own that He has descended, and to designate them Scripture has employed such terms as "child" and "spouse." Israel is sometimes His first-born, His child of predilection, and sometimes His well-beloved to whom He will restore all her beauty, soiled through infidelity. (Ez. c. 16).

None of the reproaches of the prophets attains the depth of suffering contained in those simple words: "He came among his own and his own received him not."

However, John does not dwell upon it, but passes on. The decisive mark of divine inspiration which animates the text is there, in that extraordinary faculty of suggesting a fact concerning life, love, suffering or joy; of condensing into a few brief verses things which, if all were written, "not even the world itself, I think, could hold the books that would have to be written. Amen" (21, 25). The refusal, the rejection of Him who comes, the Passion, the Cross: everything is said with those words: "His own received him not." It is the most sober statement possible made of that check put on Christ's coming.

"But to as many as received him he gave the power of becoming sons of God"

However, it is a question of the Word who comes, of His work which continues and knows no check. It is this that John contemplates, and with that eagle-like flight which characterizes him he climbs back into the light; and he will not stop till he reaches the divine Sun which fascinates him so. "But to as many as received him he gave the power of becoming the sons of God...."

Dwelt in by the Word, John is freed from the darkness. He sees into the Kingdom. He has found a Father when finding Christ, since in receiving Him he has received the power of becoming "a child of God." But he is not alone in this world, in this true childhood, that of the children of God, which is neither that of the senses, nor of appearances, nor of reason, but of the divine benevolence alone. All those "who believe in his name" are with him. All those who have heard this voice, testifying concerning the Light, have ceased to be blind. They see, they know their Father. The Word communicates His own life to them. He who was with God, who is God, gives them the power to go right to the source, to mount up to the mystery of His own plenitude. "Who were born not of blood, nor of the will of the flesh, nor of the will of man, but of God" (1, 13).

John has attained his end. Nothing earthly encumbers him any longer. It is the entire work of the Word that he embraces with one single glance in His victorious journey. It is completed and it continues, it takes its delight in this world now uniquely God's, where the children of the Father are forever reunited; where the children contemplate without end Him who has come from on high, from the bosom of God.

The glory of the only-begotten Son

The end of the Prologue falls back into a meditation, stirred no longer by that breath which dictated to the apostle words whose meaning and depth will never be exhausted. It seems that the first part has sprung up from a mind so invaded by the light that no human genius, no matter how great, would be able to be compared with it. We must go to the very words of Christ to find again not only the authority, but that extreme compactness of teaching and power which characterize these verses.

Henceforth, though always in the same great rhythm, will appear simply the apostle's own reflection upon the great mystery proposed to him.

In this verse: "And the Word was made flesh, and dwelt among us, and we have seen his glory" we are right in seeing the key-word of the whole Johannine Gospel. The "Word made flesh" will remain for Christians, for all those who through the centuries keep their eyes fixed upon Christ, the pole of contemplation, the source of their faith, hope, and love.

"And the Word was made flesh." John makes accessible to us in human language what he has seen, whose testimony he has received, and the reason he will testify himself until the end of time.

Such is the sense and center of our life. Such is henceforth the bond of a world which draws meaning and direction from it.

All flesh has access to the Word, is heard in Him who has made Himself one of us, passible flesh like our own.

"And he dwelt among us," as He had promised; as a father with his children, as a bridegroom with his bride. Other translations use a verb which emphasizes His repose, His complacency to be among us.

Joy thrills in the apostle's heart. It is no longer the sadness of refusal which now returns to his mind, but this thought alone: The one who has come to us, hidden, veiled by the flesh, is also Uncreated Splendor whose glory he was able to contemplate. "And we have seen his glory—the glory as of the only-begotten Son of the Father—full of grace and truth."

He has seen resplendent the whole interior beauty of Christ, the beauty that belongs to the only-begotten Son, in whom are all grace and truth in their plenitude. The mission of the apostle will not be to unveil this glory, which God alone can do in the secret of hearts, but to render testimony to the Word.

The Word has come, but His word will not continue to be heard except through those who, having heard and received it with faith, transmit it. He continues to be delivered up to the mercy of His own, among us still and always, at once flesh and Word, hidden and glorious, such as He appeared to His contemporaries. For us, as on the first day, the choice is given and the Baptist's voice opens the way: "This is he of whom I said, 'After me there comes one who has been set above me, because he was before me.'"

"Who is and who was and who is coming" (Ap. 1, 8). These words John has placed in the beginning of the Apocalypse as an echo of the words of his Master, as a sign for all generations to recognize Him, the divine Being always like Himself, who never ceases establishing His kingdom of grace and truth.

"And of his fullness we have all received"

The apostle's meditation is complete. With emphasis he renews his statement: "Yes, and of his fullness we have all received."

What he considers here is not the Word only, but His gifts inseparable from His manifestation and the infinite riches with which He is filled. He does not say that He has poured out a few crumbs of these riches, though these would be priceless, as a rich man chooses from his treasures some precious pearls and makes presents of them. No, God is Himself the indivisible treasure with which the one who receives Him is filled: "And it shall be given to you, good measure, pressed down, shaken together, running over, shall they pour into your lap" (Lk. 6, 38).

All that can be received by a human heart expanded by grace is given. "Grace for grace," the apostle stresses, in order to express the superabundance which is ceaselessly being reborn: "For the Law was given by Moses; grace and truth came through Jesus Christ." The state he has so recently known and which so many around him still know constrains John to cast a look into the past. "The Law was given to us. . . ."

When evoking Moses, when speaking of grace and truth, the apostle recalls that theophany of Sinai, where Yahweh revealed Himself as "rich in kindness and fidelity" (Ex. 34, 6). In Christ this kindness has developed into "grace," the supreme manifestation of the divine benevolence; and fidelity, into "truth," for in Him it becomes the reality without end or change of Love, His very "truth." Where God has delivered up His own Son, there can henceforth be no question of a renewal of His "fidelity." With Christ we have the truth, and we are in love forever.

What a distance between these times of figures, signs, preparation, and expectation, and that into which humanity has just entered since God has given His only Son. He has come, and behold the Law withdraws before grace, the letter before the Spirit, shadow gives place to the Light, signs to the Truth.

It is then that, before this revelation of divine Love, in a burst of fervor and thanksgiving, John gives us for the first time the Name of peace and salvation, of grace and truth, the Name which henceforth becomes common property between God and man: "Grace and truth have come to us through Jesus Christ."

And as though it were necessary once more to urge men to recognize the Invisible in the flesh, John terminates in these words: "No one has at any time seen God. The only-begotten Son, who is in the bosom of the Father, he has revealed him."

It is impossible for us to see God here on earth, for in us there is nothing that measures up to God. Our eyes, our body of flesh veil His splendor from us and hold us off from what our wounded nature is unable to contemplate. But the only-begotten Son, Jesus Christ, has been made flesh to make known God to us and so that we may be born to this eternal life which is His own Life.

CHAPTER 4

THE WORD OF TRUTH

I. THE WORD

"In the beginning was the Word ..." (1, 1). The term "Word" as applied to the Son of God may surprise us since Christ Himself does not seem to have used it. Neither is it employed elsewhere in the Johannine Gospel, or in the Synoptics. It appears again in the "prologue" of the first Epistle (1 Jn. 1, 1) and in the Apocalypse (19, 11-13).

The term is used five times in the Prologue. The author's purpose of bringing it to our attention from the outset is evident. What was John's reason for conferring this title upon Him whom we "have seen with our eyes and touched with our hands" (1 Jn. 1, 1). What is the meaning of the term? Is its function the casting of a light upon the Gospel as a whole in the place he has assigned to it?

Logos

Though we do not have to eliminate entirely the possibility of some kind of relationship between Philo's "logos" and that of John, yet studies on the latter's tend to set its origin in the Bible. We find the notion and even the term itself in the Scriptures, and especially in the Sapiential Books, where its meaning approximates that in John's Prologue. As a matter of fact, the same meaning was applied to "Word" (an expression used for God's creative and directing power) and to such terms as "Wisdom," "Spirit," and even the "Law." It tends to become a divine hypostasis. God speaks, manifests Himself, acts in and through His Word.

When using the term "Logos," in Latin "Verbum," John is drawing from an authentically biblical source. If he had a preference for this term over others, it is apparently because he judged it alone to be capable of expressing the only-begotten Son's function. He became incarnate precisely to "express" ("dire") God to us, to manifest Him, to reveal Him. "No one has at any time seen God. The only-begotten Son, who is in the bosom of the Father, he has revealed him" (1, 18).

God, who expresses Himself in His Word, expresses Himself to us by sending His Word.

John meditates upon this revelation, whose witness and confidant he has been. He attempts to point out its transcendent value and infinite power. True, he retains the Master's words, and especially those in which Jesus has said He is the Light and the Life. However, John experiences the need of mounting up to the ultimate Reality and Truth of this Life and this Light, to their very source.

In this way, he is led to penetrate into the mystery of the triune God, such as Jesus revealed it to His apostles on the evening of the Last Supper. His contemplative gaze discovers the perfect image of the Father in Jesus; better still, he discovers the fullness of the divinity eternally in act: true God of true God, Christ is not only the One who has come "to declare His Father to us" ("nous dire son Père"). He is also in Himself the One who expresses Him essentially, eternally, and totally. By nature He "is" His Word. It will be sufficient for Him to be among us what He "is" in Himself, to utter this Word which He is, in order to express God to us, to reveal Him to us.

The title "Word" appears to be intimately and inseparably linked to the Father's Person, as is the title "Son," though under a different aspect. There is no Word unless Someone bears it within Himself as the very expression of His being. It is the "Logos endiathetos," i.e., the internal mental Word, infinite intelligence contemplating Self. There is no "logos prophorikos," Word externally expressed, unless Someone utters it. This Someone is the Father. The Word is the fruit of the activity whereby the Father contemplates Himself. And the Word is also the One who reveals Him. The Word is eternal, and eternally in act.

Nothing was capable of "expressing" this Thought eternally in act except this Word which is perfect, continued, eternal, and absolute Act. The "Word" is precisely the One who is not satisfied with "revealing" God to us through words, but who manifests His life to us simultaneously with His absolute truth. The Word is the Act expressing God perfectly since He is God Himself.

However, the revelation of the Trinity enables John to place in this term "Word" the infinite riches which the word "Son" contains.

The "Word" is spoken by the Father through the process of "generation." This act of understanding is also an act of love. That is why John joins the two terms, Word and Son, in the Prologue. The Son, equal to the Father, reveals Him because He is His Word; and this Word expresses God perfectly and fully because He is His Son.

The revelation the Word brings us of His Father: "He who sees me sees also the Father" (14, 9), is not confined to words. In the human sense of the term, words are only one of the forms revelation uses to express God to us, and they are not necessarily the most expressive. Along with words, Christ makes use of actions and mysteries. The very life of the Word "made flesh" and even more so His "Person," will be supremely revealing. For St. John, the expression "Word" is co-extensive with God. And the revelation the Word brings us is in itself co-extensive with His very being. Under penalty of mutilating itself, hence of denying itself, truth can be nothing else but entire. In the same sense, St. Paul will say of Christ: "In him dwells corporeally the fullness of the divinity" (Cor. 2, 9).

We should not, then, seek in this expression "Word" a kind of new contribution capable of changing the atmosphere of the Gospel by its presence, or of substituting or superimposing some kind of abstract concept on Christ's historical and incarnate Person. In John's thought, "Word" expresses the entire and divine reality of Him who came to reveal the Father.

The expression "life" which John joins to the term "Word" in the prologue of his first epistle changes nothing in what we have said, any more than the word "flesh" in the expression "Word made flesh": "I write of what was from the beginning, what we have heard, what we have seen with our eyes, what we have looked upon and our hands have handled of the *Word of life*" (1 Jn. 1, 1).

In each case, John refers to the same reality. Neither life nor flesh can effect change in the Word. God does not take on life, He is its very source; He is the living God giving life to others. He is our life only because He is life in Himself, or rather, He is being, i.e., the only life, the source of life.

Perhaps John is simply varying the account in Exodus where God reveals Himself to Moses as "I am who am" (Ex. 3, 14). Life and being are here identified. At the most, we can say that the expression "Word of Life" means not only the life of God insofar as He is being, but also insofar as He shares it with others through His creation. This is exactly what the Prologue will say: "All things were made through him . . . He was the life of every being" (1, 3,4). In the expression "he was" there is a difference of the transcendental order with the life such as man receives and possesses it. On the one hand, we have the Word who is eternally in Himself and through Himself; on the other, we have beings that receive life as the river proceeds from its source.

And with even greater reason, neither can the flesh modify anything whatsoever in the Word. The flesh is "for us." If we may so express ourselves, in the hands of the Word the flesh is a means of manifesting what He is. It is somewhat similar to the voice which manifests thought, i.e., the sound strikes the ears and resounds in the mind. Or again, matter, arresting light, renders it visible, without adding anything to it. In the Prologue the term "Word" expresses simply and fully the divine reality insofar as it is communicable and communicated.

It is not only possible but even probable that John, acquainted with Greek thought, was not unaware of the advantages afforded by using the word "logos" when writing in his day. However, John is not only a follower of Philo or of any particular philosophy, but also he gives to the word "Logos" a plenitude of meaning which it had never yet had. It is not around the word "logos" that he builds a Christ upon whom this word confers new meaning; rather it is from the reality of Christ such as it was revealed to John that the expression "Logos" or "Word" draws its whole significance.

John chose this expression not to enrich revelation with a contribution borrowed from some philosophical system (the thought alone of such a mixture would strike him with horror), or because it already made up part of the patrimony of the Old Testament; he chose it because it appeared to contain and to express the data of revelation. He had no intention of adding anything whatsoever to revelation; but at the termination of the reflections which matured slowly in his mind, the expression "Word" came to him as the most suitable for expressing in great simplicity Christ's infinite richness.

The Word is the replica of the "Word" spoken by Yahweh at Horeb. It reveals to us the triune God, while the word at Horeb revealed the one God.

God expresses Himself (se dit) in His Word, and this simple Word expresses the entire content of revelation. Furthermore, it reveals the very being of the Son of God and what He actually is in the Father's bosom, for to declare of Christ that He is the Word is equivalent to introducing us into the eternal generation of the Son by the Father.

John's Prologue and Gospel have no other object except this revelation. The former offers the "Word" for our meditation, while the latter shows us the Word made "flesh."

The biblical notion of word

Christ is the uncreated Word that never ceases to be spoken by the Father and He speaks it in its entirety. We are assured that the Father, having given us His Son, will also express Himself fully and perfectly to the world.

St. Paul points this out when, using expressions borrowed from Alexandrine theology about Wisdom and the Logos, he writes: "God, who at sundry times and in divers manners spoke in times past to the fathers by the prophets, last of all in these days has spoken to us by his Son, whom he appointed heir of all things, by whom the world was made; who, being the brightness of his glory and the image of his substance, and upholding all things by the "word" of his power, has effected man's purgation from sin" (Heb. 1, 2,3). This "word" resembles no other.

Undoubtedly the prophets transmitted not only human words but the word of God to the people. Because of this St. Paul describes their words as "living and efficient and keener than any two-edged sword" (Heb. 4, 12). But they are still words. Such is not the case when the living Word, the Logos, comes.

God expresses Himself in this Logos, and He reveals Himself. This revelation has within itself a teaching which we shall discover through the pages of the New Testament, but it does not limit itself to words even though these are pronounced by Christ: it consists before everything else in the manifestation of the living Word, Christ. To say that God has spoken to us through His Son does not mean only that He has placed words in His mouth, as He did in the case of the prophets, but that He has expressed Himself, pronounced His ineffable Name in the Person of His Son.

The Word is the Logos perpetually in act. That is why He can pronounce the Name of God, or manifest it. Christ will be glorified on the evening before His death for having accomplished His mission. "And now, Father, do thou glorify me with thyself, with the glory I had with thee before the world existed. I have manifested thy name to the men whom thou hast given me out of the world" (17, 5,6). This manifestation of God's Name is realized in those who listen to and keep the living Word that is Christ. "They are thine and thou hast given them to me, and they have kept thy word" (17, 6).

This Word's transcendence in relationship to all others does not hinder its being placed at the end of a long tradition: "God, who at sundry times and in divers manners spoke in times past to the fathers by the prophets, last of all in these days has spoken to us by his Son" (Heb. 1, 1). This continuity of the "divine word" asks that we examine the living Word which is Christ in the light of the biblical notion of word.

As in the greater part of the ancient religions, the biblical "word" is a reality which is both active and revealing. It bears testimony in a special manner to God's creative power: "And God said: Be light made. And light was made" (Gn. 1, 3). It is evident that John has the account of creation in mind when he writes in the Prologue: "All was made by him and without him was made nothing that was made" (1, 3).

The Word appears, then, as the Creator of all things, and this creation springs into being at the command of His omnipotent Word, as in Genesis.

There is no abatement in the creative power of God's Word throughout biblical times. The Word commands and guides the Chosen People through Moses and the prophets; and it is this Word also that, in the Ten Commandments, "the ten words," (for, even when written, the divine Word keeps its name and power) furnishes this people with a code through which it will abide in the ways of life and salvation.

The divine "word" expressed through the prophets and in the Torah soon becomes so normal and necessary to Israel that it cannot conceive of its ever being absent. And the greatest possible chastisements are God's silences. "Yes, days are coming, says the Lord God, when I shall send famine upon the land: Not a famine of bread, or thirst for water, but for the hearing of the word of God. Then shall they wander from sea to sea and rove from the north to the east in search of the word of the Lord, but they shall not find it" (Am. 8, 11).

The divine Word is omnipotent and effects all it proclaims. It is "like a projectile which, proceeding from Yahweh's mouth, attains its goal." "For just as from the heavens the rain and snow come down and do not return till they have watered the earth, making it fertile and fruitful, so shall my word be that goes forth from my mouth; it shall not return to me void, but shall do my will, achieving the end for which I sent it" (Is. 55, 10,11).

Besides being the Lord's creative and omnipotent command, the Word also reveals. God makes known His will to men when He speaks, but He also makes Himself known by revealing Himself. He incorporates Himself in history, dominating and regulating its development and giving it a definite direction. God stands at the beginning and end of all events. "Who has performed these deeds? He who has called forth generations from the beginning" (Is. 41, 4).

God has confided this "word" to His Servant. As a "two-edged sword" He has placed it in His mouth in order that He may make righteousness and truth triumph upon the earth (Is. 51, 4), instruct and sustain men (Ibi. 49, 10-13), save and judge them (Ibi. 49, 6). He invites all to listen to His Word: "Whoever among you fears the Lord heeds the voice of His servant" (Ibi. 50, 10).

When personifying Wisdom, Sirach frequently identifies it with the Word. Both proceed from God's mouth. Their activity and their origin intermingle. "The source of Wisdom is the word of God in the heavens" (Sir. 1, 5).

Finally, the Psalmist sees the principle of light, strength, and joy in this Word; it is the path and the lamp guiding the believer's steps (Pss. 119, 105).

This Word, intervening in history to regulate its course, marks one of the aspects of the mission of the Servant of Yahweh, the Messias, who will come to enlighten and to save the world through His Word.

True, we are still far from the Prologue and the Johannine Gospel. Nevertheless, it will suffice for Christ to lay claim to all that has been said of the Word in order for the expression to reveal its true meaning.

Words and the Word

It is noteworthy that the expression "the word of Yahweh" or the "word of God" disappears from the New Testament. It is never said that the word of God was spoken to Jesus. Why is this? It is because the evangelists are convinced that the Word of God is Jesus Himself in Person.

If the divine words transmitted through the prophets were treated with such veneration and respect by the Chosen People, what is to be said of the words spoken by the divine Word incarnate? This "word" is totally His: "If anyone love me, he will keep my word, and my Father will love him and we will come to him and make our abode with him" (14, 23). It is also His Father's: "My teaching is not my own, but his who sent me" (7, 16). And, finally, the Holy Spirit alone can give us a proper understanding of it: "Many things yet I have to say to you, but you cannot bear them now. But when he, the Spirit of Truth, has come, he will teach you all the truth. For he will not speak on his own authority, but whatever he will hear he will speak, and the things that are to come he will declare to you. He will glorify me, because he will receive of what is mine and declare it to you" (16, 13-15).

But in spite of the respect in which they were held, the evangelists do not necessarily repeat Christ's words literally or under the same form. This statement would be surprising if we did not find in it a new proof that these words did not have in themselves a reality separable from the total reality of Christ.

True, no evangelist and not even St. Paul expressly states that the "Word" is Jesus. This statement, reserved for St. John, was nonetheless prepared over a long period of time. Thus, in the fourth Gospel the "Word" assumes everything that it represented in the biblical tradition.

"If you keep *my* commandments, you will abide in my love" (15, 10).

Just as words had become *the* word when passing from the Old Testament to the New, as the author of the epistle to the Hebrews has us understand, so also we can say that *the* commandments become *the* commandment into which they are all combined and fulfilled. "This is my commandment, that you love one another as I have loved you. All the things I heard from my Father, I have made known to you" (15, 12,15).

What is impossible when it is a question of words—to make known all that Christ has taught—becomes possible if Christ is identified with the Word, if he is Himself this Word, for He makes Himself totally "known."

Christ, the living Word

But the true meaning of Christ's mission, a mission which sheds light upon the veritable significance of the "Word" in St. John, is given to us in the "sacerdotal prayer." "Father, I have manifested thy name to the men whom thou hast given me out of the world. They were thine, and thou hast given them to me, and they have kept thy word. Now they have learnt that whatever thou hast given me is from thee; because the words that thou hast given me I have given to them" (17, 6-8).

If Jesus manifests this "Name," it is because He is the Father's living "Word." Seeing Him, "we see the Father" (14, 9). When manifesting Himself, when expressing Himself, He expresses the Father (en se "disant," il "dit" le Père).

This "Name" likewise emphasizes the unity between Him and His Father (17, 11,12), and that is why when listening to Jesus we listen to the Word: and this Word does nothing else but "utter" the Father, revealing Him in the Person of the Son.

"I have given them thy word" (17, 14) means: In order to reveal Thee, to manifest Thee, I have given Myself to them; I have surrendered Myself in the fullness of a gift which corresponds with what the Father has done with His Son for the world (3, 16). When giving Myself, I have revealed to men the infinite reality of God, His absolute Truth, in this living, subsisting, and eternal Word. And that is why Jesus can add: "Father, sanctify them in truth. Thy word is truth" (17, 17). "Just Father, the world has not known thee, but I have known thee, and these have known that thou hast sent me. And I have made known to them thy name, and will make it known, in order that the love with which thou hast loved me may be in them, and I in them" (17, 25).

The entire mission of the "one sent" from the Father will have been: "I have made known to them," and it will be until the end of time and throughout eternity: "And I will make known to them," revealing and manifesting His Father's "Name."

But in order that this "Word" be living and truly revealing, it is necessary that the mystery of God which is fully in Christ, "in him dwells corporeally the fullness of the divinity" (Col. 2, 9), pass over into us.

Simple words, such as those spoken by the prophets, did not suffice here. The living Word of God had to speak Himself, and He had to do so from the fullness of His being and from the plenitude of the Spirit. "For he whom God has sent speaks the words of God, for not by measure does God give the Spirit" (3, 34). And He does not simply pronounce these words by mouth, but through His entire humanity which is at the service of the divinity.

If two beings, intimately united here on earth, already have so many ways of understanding one another and of communicating with each other, if everything between them conveys a message, viz., gestures, attitudes, reticences, looks, decisions, hesitations, etc., then how much more will He who is the "Word" and the "Revelation" arrange things in an infinite variety of ways so that He can reach us and speak to us of the Father? "No one has at any time seen the Father. The only-begotten Son, who is in the bosom of the Father, he has revealed him" (1, 18).

We are invited to become attentive and to listen to this living Word in order to learn: "This is my beloved Son in whom I am well pleased: hear him" (Mt. 17, 5). The Word of God is His Son and the word of the Son is His entire Self. "God has spoken only one Word and this is His Son. Consider Him well and you will find everything in Him" (Ascent of Mount Carmel, Bk. 11, c. 22).

"For in her is the spirit of understanding: holy, one, manifold, subtle, active, undefiled. . . . For wisdom is more active than all active things and reacheth everywhere . . ." (Wis. 7, 22,23). This praise of Wisdom is applicable to the "Word" also that has come "to dwell among us," entering into intimate contact with us, penetrating into the very depths of our soul. And He does this not only through words, i.e., discursive knowledge, but through the diverse and infinitely rich ways of intuitive and affective knowledge, of the knowledge of love which communicates the divinity through the way of interior experience and makes the soul adhere to this Word and become one spirit with Him.

The living Word bears witness to the truth

However, the incarnate Word's mission, meaning, and essential function is Testimony: testimony concerning the living truth which is Christ, about the eternal truth which is the Father. Testimony and Truth are inseparably united, the one leading to the other. "I have given them thy word. . . . Thy word is truth" (17, 14,17).

As long as we do not see the Father's "Witness" and "Envoy" in the Word, His mission of making us "children of God" goes unaccomplished. For the child of God is one who "receives the word," makes it his own, and in whom the word bears fruit. Then only does he have "eternal life": "He gave the power of becoming sons of God to those who believe in his name" (1, 12). "Amen, amen, I say to you, he who hears my word and believes him who sent me, has life everlasting" (5, 24).

Here, then, is the mission of the Word made flesh: The Word through his "Testimony" leads us to the "Truth"; and it was this mission He proclaimed to the world the last day of His life and it made Him the Word of Truth (18, 37).

II. TRUTH

Few notions have been changed so much from their primitive meaning as the notion of truth. We call truth today: the correct apprehension of an objective reality. If modern man continues to tie these two notions of reality and truth together in his mind, he nevertheless realizes how much his apprehension of reality is burdened with many imperfections; he knows, too, that he cannot attain objective reality without unconsciously mingling elements of subjectivity with his observations. Finally, and perhaps above all, he is aware that the truth he arrives at is marked with the sign of relativity. Hence, he joins the real skepticism of Pilate who allowed the words: "What is truth?" to fall from his lips.

It is not, however, a Roman functionary's reply that interests us here, but rather the words which preceded it and were the occasion for it: " 'Thou art then a king?' Jesus answered, 'Thou sayest it; I am a king. This is why I was born and why I have come into the world, to bear witness to the truth.' Pilate said to him, 'What is truth?' And when he said this, he went outside . . ." (18, 37,38).

"What is truth?"

It is noteworthy that John is the only evangelist to report this scene, as though he alone had understood the place truth was to hold in the Word's message to men.

What should hold our attention is Pilate's skepticism as contrasted with Christ's confidence, the latter claiming that His mission here on earth is to bear witness to the truth. One could not have presented the problem better.

What is this truth for which Christ has come into the world and to which both his life and death bear witness? What is this truth with which He does not hesitate to identify Himself? "I am the way, and the truth, and the life" (14, 6).

The truth with which we are dealing in the fourth Gospel is not something simply opposed to error. True, it may happen occasionally that the evangelist uses the word in its ordinary sense, and in this way it is opposed to what is objectively false or subjectively appears as such, and to whatever is lacking in sincerity. According to its customary meaning, the idea of truth is opposed to error, and more frequently to falsehood (for with the Hebrews truth is a moral category). This signification is found in that opposition between Christ and Satan. While the latter is a "liar" and the "father of lies" because "he has not stood in the truth" (8, 44), Christ is true, and sincere, and always speaks the truth: "If I speak the truth to you, why do you not believe me?" (8, 46).

We have here one of the accepted meanings of the word truth, but not the one to which John would lead us and which, derived from the first, retains before all else a moral significance. "But he who does the truth comes to the light" (3, 21). The expression "to act in the truth" or "to do the truth" comes from the Old Testament and has the meaning of: being faithful to the manifest will of God. It is certain that a conscience, faithful in fulfilling what it judges to be its highest duty, is conformed with God and is gradually transformed into Him, connaturalized. To do the truth means "not to sin against the light" (Newman). If the light shines in a soul, it is because the soul has triumphed over evil, falsehood, and darkness. It is in the statement on the "light" that the expression "to do the truth" is found: "For everyone who does evil hates the light and does not come to the light, that his deeds may not be exposed. But he who does the truth comes to the light" (3, 19-21).

Christ, eternal Truth

However, the special meaning of the word "truth" in the fourth Gospel is on another plane. This word designates the unchangeable, last, and absolute Reality because it is divine. Truth, thus envisaged, is nothing else but God Himself.

When Christ turns to His Father and directs this prayer to Him:

"Father, sanctify them in the truth. Thy word is truth" (17, 17), the term "word" refers to the Son as the Father's Word. And this Word is true because it is the divine Reality revealed and identified with God. In John's writings, truth used in this way is capitalized. There is no truth except the Truth, i.e., God. Thus, in John's Gospel, the word "truth" means eternal Reality insofar as it is revealed to men, or this reality in itself.

When Christ says: "You are seeking to kill me, one who has spoken the truth to you which I have heard from God" (8, 40), this means that Christ has revealed eternal Reality; in other words, that He has revealed His Father to men. Now such a revelation is not possible except for one who, knowing God intimately, can express Him perfectly because He is God of God. "No one has at any time seen God. The only-begotten Son, who is in the bosom of the Father, he has revealed him" (1, 18).

God alone can reveal the divine and eternal Reality, the divine and eternal Truth. That is why, with reference to Christ, to affirm that He is the Truth Himself (14, 6) and that He speaks the truth to us, or that He has come "into the world to bear witness to the truth" (18, 37), i.e., to reveal the Father, all this is one and the same thing.

Christ, the living Truth

In order to read the fourth Gospel correctly, it is not sufficient to know that all we find in it is true and worthy of our faith; neither is it enough to believe that this truth brought to us by Christ is not relative truth, subject to change. We must believe that this truth is unchangeable, absolute, definitive, and eternal. We must understand that in Christ, and not only in His words, man arrives at the apprehension of absolute Reality. This reality is manifested in Him, and it is identified with Him. He is this reality. In other words, Truth is not a "thing" but a divine Person. That is why we cannot know the Truth in the same manner as we attain other human knowledge, viz., by being content to study and assimilate its elements, and enter into them intellectually. The truth, since it is a Person, must be "known" in the biblical sense of the term, i.e., man must be united to it through love, and adhere to it vitally. He must live with it and in it. He must be "established in the truth" (8, 44), becoming one with it. Using Christ's own expression, he must be "of the truth."[1]

1. "In the Bible, the usage of the word "truth" proceeds from the sense of "reality," what is real, ultimate, to "knowledge of the real." The knowledge of God (which) is eternal life (17, 3) is the apprehension of ultimate reality. This reality is above and beyond phenomena and appearances. This eternal reality has been manifested in Christ who, as the Logos, is not only the bearer of divine

From the moment the word "truth" ceases to cover simply an abstract notion and becomes a living and personal Reality, it undergoes a complete change in character, it begins to take on its true image, viz., the image of Christ.

It appears, as a consequence, that Truth demands of those who wish to come to it and be united with it a personal attitude; and it is here that we come upon, this time on the level of divine realities, that "moral" sense that truth had in the tradition of Israel, viz., that demand of loyalty, sincerity, fidelity of mind and heart. Christ will make the attempt to have the Jews understand this: "If you abide in my word, you shall be my disciples indeed, and you shall know the truth and the truth shall make you free" (8, 31,32).

To extract the real meaning of Christ's words, it is sufficient to substitute the abstract terms for "the one" whom they designate: If you abide in Me (for Christ is the Word), you will be my disciples indeed. Then, you shall know Me, and I will make you free, with the freedom of the children of God which I have come to bring to humanity. In other words: If you are faithful to me in spirit and in act, if you become interior souls through a spiritual indwelling of you in Me and I in you, you shall be permeated by my Spirit; you will be vitally united to the living Truth, and this Truth will infuse its life into you; it will make you enter into absolute Reality, into unveiled light. All falsehood, pretence, illusion, error will be dissipated through this association with Truth and eternal Reality. There is no slavery for the one who abides in the Truth. In you the Truth will be victorious over the devil; he not only "tells lies" (8, 44), but also "has never stood in the truth" (8, 44), i.e., his very being is expressed in a refusal of the truth, in an opposition to God.

The Truth is victorious over darkness since it has conquered Satan, "the prince of darkness." It is victorious over the world because it has reduced its falsehood, illusion, and seductions to nothing. It unties all chains and removes all veils. If the Word is the epiphany of the Logos, Truth is the full affirmation and manifestation of whatever exists.

We can see why John, nourished on the Old Testament and conscious of the transcendence of Christ's revelation, has set down the two revelations of Horeb and Christ in his Prologue to distinguish them one from the other. Each revelation has placed man face to face with God's Reality,

grace, but also divine Truth, and the one through whom this Truth is revealed to men. He is not only the revealer of Truth; He is Truth itself (14, 6). The identification of this ultimate reality with a Person who is set in history transforms the meaning of the term. The expression means in every case that the relation of men to Christ, through whom they "know the truth" is infinitely closer than that of the disciples with regard to the Master. To know the truth, it does not suffice that they listen to His words; they must be united to Him who is the Truth" (Dodd, Interpretation of Fourth Gospel, p. 177).

but while "the Law was given to us through Moses," through Jesus Christ "grace and truth came" (1, 17).

We can see why Christ was able to place His entire mission under the sign of truth when He came to the end of His earthly sojourn: "This is why I was born and why I have come into the world, to bear witness to the truth" (18, 37).

Love of the Truth

If God alone is supreme Truth and Reality, then all things have their being and truth only in Him. This notion is linked up with the idea of creation which John attributes to the Person of the Word: "All things were made through him and without him was made nothing that was made" (1, 3).

All things were directed towards Truth by the very fact of their existence. In this sense, we may say that creation and Truth coincide in God. He made them and they are true only in the way He made them. The truth of things is their very existence.

Coming into the world, the Word, author of all that exists, enables man to join this creation through Him, to join it "in truth," to discover it in the infinite purity of its Source.

But if we are to discover what is, in the light of Truth, i.e., in Christ, how can He speak of truth as a reality distinct from Himself? If He has said: "I am . . . the truth" (14, 6), elsewhere He states: "Whoever is of the truth hears my voice" (18, 37); and again: "This is why I was born and why I have come into the world, to bear witness to the truth" (18, 37). What are we to think of this apparent contradiction?

Even among men, love of the truth is the most detached sentiment there is. They love it for itself and not for their own profit; we could say that they are constrained to express it by an irresistible force and, if necessary, to sacrifice themselves for it without any other advantage than that of having remained faithful to it. We may ask ourselves, whence comes this unselfish and strong love for truth in men? Revelation furnishes an answer. Truth appears in revelation as the deepest and most indestructible root which fixes man in God, even when man is unaware of His Name. Man's nobility resides in his detached love of Truth, even though he senses this only indistinctly.

God does not will that this love for truth remain without an object. It must be fully satisfied. But this presupposes that man accept no compromise, that he pursue truth without allowing himself to stop at anything, and that he do this with pure motives. It is noteworthy that in the fourth

Gospel Christ asks nothing else of His interlocutors but a submission to the real, to the truth, as though this disposition, faithfully adhered to, sufficed to lead them to the recognition of what He is. "If I speak the truth to you, why do you not believe? He who is of God, hears the words of God" (8, 46).

Is not the frequently repeated expression with which Christ opens up the greater number of His discourses striking: "Amen, amen, I say to you" (En vérité, en vérité, . . .)? It is as though he said: Behold your thirst for truth is about to be satisfied. Follow the path traced out by my words and you will arrive at a knowledge of the Truth which I myself am (Cf. 1, 51; 3, 3,5,11; 5, 19,24,25). From this respect Christ professes for the Truth, we may draw an important conclusion regarding the very essence of faith.

Undoubtedly the faith He requires of us must be directed towards Him, His Person. However, could we not say that it is directed through Him to Truth? Are not all things, including faith in Him, to be directed towards it (truth)? Certainly, the day men realize who sent Him and who He is, viz., Creator of all, outside of whom nothing exists, the identity between Truth and Him will be fulfilled.

But in the meantime, He leaves Truth to its own resources, i.e., to its power of attracting the hearts of men and making its demands upon them. And does not the Church herself leave to truth this privileged place, when she has the Christian say in the act of faith: "I firmly believe because Thou art Truth itself"? And this, as though Truth had an existence in itself. In fact, we know that Truth does not exist more than Goodness, Mercy, Justice, and that we are dealing here with the divine perfections. It is very noteworthy, however, that in the fourth Gospel, the Holy Spirit is called three times by Jesus: the Spirit of Truth. He is the one who will teach the apostles "all the truth" (16, 13). Christ does not hesitate, then, to reserve for Truth the capacity and appearance of an hypostasis, and to make it appear both the first stimulus of our faith and its last point of reference. In fact, "to believe" does not mean giving our assent to a fixed program or to a certain number of truths; it means surrendering ourselves entirely to "Truth," consenting to follow "Truth" without any limits or conditions wherever it leads us and in whatever it demands. This attitude is necessary and decisive.

This pursuit and love of truth are the very soul and life of faith. In their absence, faith quickly becomes a tree deprived of vitality, no longer bearing fruit. That is why Christ prefers to use, not the word "faith," an abstract expression which is static more or less, but the verb "believe" which is really dynamic.

To believe means to have been seized by the Truth and to have surrendered oneself to it; it means to have decided never, at any price, to allow oneself to be separated from it.

This absolute and unconditional submission to Truth as such is primary and indispensable in faith. The account of the cure of the man born blind shows a love and respect for truth in him which, along with his good will, seem to constitute a sufficient foundation for faith to "take hold" in his soul (9, 7,9,11,15,25,31-33). In a second encounter, Christ will say to him: " 'Dost thou believe in the Son of God?' 'Who is he, Lord, that I may believe in him?' And Jesus said to him, 'Thou hast both seen him, and he it is who speaks with thee.' And he said, 'I believe, Lord.' And falling down, he worshipped him" (9, 35-38).

"Whoever is of the truth hears my voice"

Do not Christ's words to Pilate mean the same thing? "Everyone who is of the truth hears my voice" (18, 37).

"To be of the truth" means to be so deeply marked with its seal that we cannot cease tending towards it, for we have been created by it and for it. It means that we have retained the divine imprint in us, the Creator's luminous image, and we recognize Him in every "truth," just as the smallest drop of dew reflects the sun shining upon it.

It seems also that only the one who is "of the truth" has a soul sufficiently receptive to perceive the truth under any form it presents itself.

It is not with the intelligence only, or with such and such a faculty that we perceive the truth. Being coextensive with God, the truth forms us gradually according to its infinite dimension. When we believe, we are brought to that transcendent and immanent Reality that confers upon us, simultaneously, its object, Truth, the light in which we attain this object, and the strength to abide in it. Truth's presence and activity in us make it possible for us to be born to it, at the same time we discover it.

The role of the Spirit of Truth, Christ's Spirit, at work in us appears to be to have us pass from a purely human concept of truth to a divine notion of it.

Humanly speaking, truth appears to us first as a "body" of truth; then, when we penetrate it more, as a birth to something; finally, as a communion with this something which is never totally fulfilled. But in God, the Truth is much more than that. It has no other object in Him than itself, and this object is perfectly known, since it is God contemplating Himself. Furthermore, the Truth in God is not a thought antecedent to the act by which it is apprehended. It is this act itself through which God is and expresses Himself eternally to Himself in His Word; and this so perfectly that the Truth in Him is simultaneously Life and Light. It is Light in proportion to His splendor, brilliance, and clarity, when in us this Light is only an incandescent point in the darkness, which is continually irradiating and which rises in us little by little as a dawn filled with purity and splendor.

The simplicity of this divine Truth can be termed light, for the word "light" calls up in our mind a simple, unique, immaterial and total reality, as light has no division, it fills everything, coincides with everything, makes all things appear and be at the same moment.

This light of Truth cannot be expressed with words, and contemplation attains only its luminous fringe. It remains an intimate perception, the results of the Spirit's touch, shedding light interiorly upon the truths of faith.

"It (the Word) was the true light" (1, 9), i.e., the light of truth which sets free (8, 32), for, while flooding the soul with its brightness, it casts out darkness.

The surest guarantee of the purity of our faith is a detached love of the truth; Christ is content with it when He encounters it in a soul, and in itself it is sufficient to bring the soul to Him. To be authentic, this faith must become a purely spiritual testimony; if it is supported by signs and wonders, it has to leave these behind finally so that it advances solely upon the strength of Truth, a strength which takes possession of the soul.

Such was the Baptist's faith, for it was deprived of what established the disciples' faith, and placed simply under the breath of the Spirit whom he saw resting upon Jesus.

John the Baptist confessed Christ and was His perfectly detached witness; Truth had invaded his soul, filling it with a boundless joy: "But the friend of the bridegroom, who stands and hears him, rejoices exceedingly at the voice of the bridegroom. This my joy, therefore, is made full" (3, 29).

John the Baptist, more than any other, was filled with the light of Truth. And Christ was to bear this testimony concerning him: "He was the lamp, burning and shining; and you desired to rejoice for a while in his light" (5, 35).

He was the lover of the Truth. In its brightness, he recognized Christ.

Pilgrims of the Truth

In God, Truth is light, perfect, transparent, and without any shadow; in man, however, it is otherwise. Even though Truth reveals itself to him, even though he can possess it in its fullness in the Word, nevertheless it must trace out a path in him, and this path is painful, often even tragic. Truth is conformed to God's image and not man's; thus, when it enters into him, it appears as a crushing and obscure reality, and his being cannot sustain its weight and its demands upon him. Truth cannot be grasped by his mind because it is infinitely above it, and it cannot even be expressed; it asks to be lived, suffered in its whole being, and it is then that it reveals itself, slowly and painfully: "But he who does the truth comes to the light" (3, 21).

But man cannot "do the truth" except by acting against himself. Though there is something in him that waits upon Truth, longs for it, desires it, and is filled with it, yet there are areas of darkness and a power of darkness fiercely opposing Truth's entrance. And it is not a question here only of the obstacles opposing Truth. "Yet men have loved the darkness rather than the light, for their works are evil" (3, 19). We are dealing here with that "submission" which Truth demands of those who would place themselves under its instruction.

To engage oneself upon the road of truth is equivalent to placing oneself in the hands of God, feeling the pitiless rigor of that hand weighing down upon us, beholding our faculties, one after another, captivated by Him; for in us, Truth is not necessarily accompanied by light. Light comes only afterwards, and submission to the Truth must often be effected in the darkness. And before the light dawns, we must "do the truth" in the sweat of our brow; worse still, we must walk under the shadow of contradiction, defeat, and in an absence of realism. In order to submit themselves to Truth, the prophets already experienced these bitter things, and John the Baptist more than any other (Mt. 11, 3).

"He who does the truth comes to the light" (3, 20). In these words we seem to glimpse Truth's painful progress, fulfilling itself in man's heart. We seem to feel the different types of opposition tumbling down under its blows and the various defenses melting away, until truth finally expands in its own light. However, its light seemingly shines upon nothing but a ruin.

All spiritual men and women have explained the soul's strange adventure when engaged upon these obscure paths of Truth, and how Truth breaks asunder, little by little, the human limits and modes of thinking, feeling, and loving. If Truth were not divine, if it were not Reality perfectly simple, unique, filled to overflowing, it would not be this destroyer with which the Saints are seized. Truth is the remedy which, while wounding our eyes, cures them.

This Truth Christ came to bring to the world, but the world, almost totally, did not wish to receive it. Certain ones, however, were receptive, in spite of the difficulty of understanding it and standing up under its burden. Jesus was aware of the harsh struggles for which His disciples had to prepare themselves, yet He leaves them; He leaves them alone in the world, witnesses of this Truth, its prisoners, its apostles, and this Truth was to embrace the world after having burned itself into their hearts. "But I speak the truth to you; it is expedient that I depart. For if I do not go, the Advocate will not come to you" (16, 7).

The Spirit of Truth

The Advocate, the Spirit of Truth—it is in a totally spiritual and interior visitation, unknown to the flesh and the world, that the Truth will come to them: "The Spirit of Truth whom the world cannot receive, because it neither sees nor knows him. But you shall know him, because he will dwell with you, and be in you" (14, 17).

With the Spirit of Truth it will still and always be the Word of Truth who will come to them, for the Father will send this Spirit to them in His Name: "But the Advocate, the Holy Spirit, whom the Father will send in my name, he will teach you all things, and bring to your mind whatever I have said to you" (14, 26); ". . . the Spirit of truth who proceeds from the Father, will bear witness concerning me" (15, 26). "But when he, the Spirit of Truth, has come, he will teach you all the truth . . . he will receive of what is mine and declare it to you" (16, 13,14).

The Truth revealed through Love

Conjointly with the Spirit of Truth, who will sustain and enlighten them, Christ sanctifies them in this Truth which He Himself is, and fortifies them with its all-powerful strength. "Holy Father, keep in thy name those whom thou hast given me. . . . Sanctify them in truth. . . . And for them I sanctify myself, that they also may be sanctified in truth . . ." (17, 11,17,19).

Christ's disciples will experience, then, not only the weight of this truth, but also its intimate visitations and infinite dimensions in the midst of worldly struggles and in the very depths of the darkness into which they will be plunged. Truth will be at stake in a difficult and humanly desperate undertaking, but the grace of the Son and the Spirit will be there. Inhabited by the fullness of Truth to which the Spirit will lead them, men will finally enjoy a full revelation of it insofar as it is possible on earth. It is not without reason that John, having had experience of this, associates "grace" with this Truth.

If "grace and truth have come to us through Jesus Christ" (1, 17), it is because love is Truth's last secret, and it is this love that the Word made flesh has rendered accessible through His Person. He is the Truth, and He has revealed to men that Love was the torch for the light from which this Truth had appeared to them, a light veiled and hidden from human eyes but shining for those in whom the Spirit dwells.

Few men have known how to recognize the Truth in what manifested it with the greatest purity, viz., charity. "There was in him no stately bearing, nor appearance that would attract" (Is. 53, 2). Becoming incarnate, the Truth renounced the power to fascinate men by its light. It desires rather to show itself under the appearances of one who gives his life for those whom he loves. And nonetheless, each of the words of this Man attest that: "grace and truth came through Jesus Christ."

In a word, it is to the very bosom of God, about whom the Word has come to testify and whom He has made known to men, that this Reality, viz., the Truth, transports us. Hence we understand why, having arrived at the end of His mission here below and being called upon to give before God and men the real significance of His mission, Christ pronounced those words: "Thou sayest it; I am a king. This is why I was born and why I have come into the world, to bear witness to the truth. Everyone who is of the truth hears my voice" (18, 37).

CHAPTER 5

THE WORD WAS MADE FLESH

"In the beginning was the Word, and the Word was with God, and the Word was God" (1, 1). These words could furnish material for an eternal hymn of praise. But to this praise should be added, in view of God's infinite and merciful love, a thanksgiving and an admiration that know no limits. For the "Word was made flesh" and He has come "to pitch his tent among us."[1]

The revelation of the Word made flesh lies at the very heart of the Prologue. Everything in it converges towards the mystery of the Incarnation and everything springs forth from this mystery. "And of his fullness we have all received, grace for grace" (1, 16). It is the most precious cornerstone upon which rest the salvation of the world and the power given to men whereby they may know and love God and be united with Him forever.

"The Word was made flesh." Under John's pen these simple words are enough in order to add to the Word's transcendence the certitude of His humility and goodness and closeness to us, and in order that the step taken by God reveal the inexpressible dimensions of love to us.

And yet this term remains confined to the Prologue and is not to be found in the Gospel. It is because, having clothed Himself in our humanity and having entered time, the Word is henceforth in John's mind the one who has assumed a body similar to our own, the one who now carries the name: Jesus Christ.

But thanks to the Prologue we shall never be able to forget that the one whose actions and words are reported in the Gospel is in possession of the plenitude of the divinity.

The Synoptic Gospels reveal the mystery of Christ little by little. Here it is revealed from the very first line. John has simply a greater facility for presenting the wonderful simplicity and marvelous transparency of a humanity through which the Son of God comes to us.

1. 1, 14. dwelt: the Greek term has the meaning: "he pitched his tent."

Dimensions of the Mystery

"The Word was made flesh" (1, 1). John desires that the mystery of the Incarnation manifest itself through the declaration of these words alone, and that it thrust itself upon our mind in all its true dimensions.

While the term "Word" brings to our mind the transcendence of Him who is Life, Light, and Truth, the term "flesh" manifests His appearance in our human condition and His permanent dwelling in the midst of sinful humanity.

When these words are set side by side, they emphasize the distance that separates the two natures in Christ, and also the intimate union God has effected between them through an act of His omnipotence. Of all the expressions that could have been used to designate Christ, that of "Word," placing us as it does in the presence of a God who contemplates and "expresses" Himself eternally, is the most opposed to "flesh" that can possibly be imagined. Between the two, the contrast is absolute, and that is why the expression "Word" is the most proper for setting us before the mystery and revealing its depths.

Not only is the contrast between the two words absolute, but their juxtaposition surpasses the understanding. The Latin and Greek sentences expressing the fact, viz., "Et Verbum caro factum est" and "Logos sarx egeneto," in which the two terms are joined by no intervening word, stress even more the abysmal depths separating them.

Two thousand years of Christianity has dulled the sentiment of scandal which the Jews experienced so deeply when they were placed face to face with the truth of a God incarnated and crucified in His flesh. Paul had experienced it himself before his own conversion and he was able to understand it better than anyone else. And yet, far from minimizing the difficulty or removing the "scandal" he brings them into full light. With the ardor of a convert, he openly declares to his former co-religionists: "But we, for our part, preach a crucified Christ, to the Jews indeed a stumbling block and to the Gentiles foolishness" (1 Cor. 1, 23). In another declaration which shows the deep sincerity of his conversion, he cries out: "For I determined to know nothing among you but Jesus Christ and him crucified" (1 Cor. 2, 2).

In his own way, so different from Paul's, John says nothing else in his Prologue when he sets up the image of an Incarnate God in all its stark reality: "And the Word was made flesh."

The farther apart two poles are, the stronger must be the current if it is to draw them together. John, who was not unaware of the omnipotence of divine love, does not have any fear of stressing the infinite distance that separates the Word from the flesh. He knows, in fact, the source whence springs the spark that unites divinity to humanity.

Just as strongly as it reveals the distance between them, the expression "The Word was made flesh" points out the union of the two terms that compose it. It is a union so close, so decisive, that henceforth John considers only the living and mysterious reality which is born of it: Jesus Christ.

As the prophet had announced, the Messias does more than establish a mediation or set up a Covenant between God and humanity. He Himself is this Covenant. "I have preserved thee and given thee to be a covenant of thy people..." (Is. 49, 8). And that is why Christ will say at the Last Supper: "This cup is the new covenant in my blood, which shall be shed for you . . ." (Lk. 22, 20).

The mystery of love shines forth in the Word made flesh, for love alone is able to reduce distances even to the poinnt of abolishing them entirely. The expression "Word made flesh" brings out the perfection of this love which lies at the basis of the mystery of the Incarnation. To express this love the apostle relies upon this expression which brings out the liberty and spontaneity with which the mystery is accomplished. The Word, he says, "was made flesh" without any obligation, without any intervention, without any constraint, in a freedom as sovereign as that with which the Father "has given his Son" (3, 16). The unity is perfect between the Father's decision and that leap of loving obedience on the part of the Son. "Behold, I come to do thy will, O God" (Ps. 39, 8; Heb. 10, 7). We are in the presence here of that free display of love in the bosom of God's omnipotent will.

John's glance is centered upon this sovereign liberty which nourishes his own adoration and love. He discovers in it what unites the inaccessible and inscrutable nature of a God whom no one has ever seen (1, 18), to that reality which no one would have ever dared to place in contact with the divinity, and much less unite to the divinity, viz., humanity. And John designates this humanity by what manifests it most: the flesh.

If the idea of sin is not directly aimed at here, as in St. Paul who gives to the word flesh the sense of "the body of sin," it is implicitly contained in it. The Word was made flesh in view of the Redemption; and the Word rendered itself capable of thus becoming "the lamb of God who takes away the sins of the world" (1, 29,36), expiating for them and shedding His Blood on the Cross through love.

The expression "Word made flesh" stresses two major orientations of the Johannine thought in a positive way. It enables us to consider alternately and simultaneously the infinite distance and the close union between these two terms. But whether the soul contemplates this infinite distance or sees in Christ's Person that union realized, it is always confronted with mystery.

Under John's pen, these words are something else besides a solemn declaration or marvelous revelation which changes the face of the world. We sense here the fruit of an adoring contemplation and vibrant love in the apostle's soul.

St. Paul's soul may be expressed in these words: "And the life that I now live in the flesh, I live in the faith of the Son of God, who loved me and gave himself for me" (Gal. 2, 20). St. John's soul is manifest in the expression: "Verbum caro."

True, he was not the first to surrender himself to the consideration of this mystery with the fervor of an intimate friend and the astonishment of a mystic. St. Paul has also made this same attempt when he wrote to the Philippians: "He emptied himself, taking the nature of a slave and being made like unto men" (Ph. 2, 7). In these words, he attempted to throw light upon the love which lies at the basis of such an unheard of step.

It is also love which is for St. John the real motive for the Incarnation, but the incidence here is not the same. In St. Paul, the movement suggests that of the eagle hovering in the heights and suddenly allowing itself to fall to the earth: "Who though by nature God, did not consider being equal to God a thing to be clung to, but emptied himself, taking the nature of a slave ..." (Phil. 2, 6,7). It is also the divine eagle that John considers. But what he beholds especially is that supremely positive movement by which He decides to swoop down upon the earth in order to take up our humanity and in doing so to become totally ours and to make us totally His.

The "Verbum caro factum est" of this Gospel reveals an infinite "elan" and an infinite condescension.

The positive role of the flesh in salvation

When making the choice of the term "flesh" to designate Christ's human nature, John wished to point out the extremity to which love brought the Redeemer, and no term could make this better understood than this one. However, in John's thought the role of flesh is positive because it constitutes one of the privileged instruments of salvation.

If he had written his Gospel shortly after Christ's death, perhaps John would have been tempted to speak of "man" rather than of "flesh" and to write: "The Son was made man," instead of: "And the Word was made flesh." Many of the witnesses of this humanity would still be living and would have remembered the one who was going about the towns of Judea and Galilee preaching the Gospel, and who died outside the gates of the city. But when John was actually drawing up his Gospel, the Church was already established and the last witnesses of Christ's humanity had disappeared.

Now in his desire to bear witness to past events upon which humanity's future rests, John takes into consideration the countless generations that will come until time is no more. These future generations, given birth through the Church and reared in her bosom, will be called upon to enter into contact with Christ. But they will never meet the "man" and they will not see Him. The eyes of faith alone will aid them in discovering and recognizing Him. Where will those eyes behold Him if not in this Victim the Church immolates upon the altar and offers them as their daily food?

Such is the form under which Christ continues to make His Passover truly present and active among His children, without any prejudice to His presence through grace in the depths of their souls. Keeping his eyes fixed upon Christ as He knew Him on earth, John associated the sacrament of His Body and Blood with His coming here on earth in the flesh. "And he dwelt among us. And we have seen his glory" (1, 14).

The Eucharist is not the only reference the fourth Gospel makes to Christ's humanity and more particularly to His flesh and Blood. There are others as well. In fact, we would be very much mistaken about this Gospel if, along with its very pronounced spiritual character, we were not to discover in its author a very strong desire to place us always and very concretely in the presence of Christ's humanity.

First, there is that declaration of the Baptist which John retains and which colors, we might say, his entire Gospel. "Behold the lamb of God." Then there is the discourse after the Supper, and the Passion. There, indeed, the power of Christ's humanity and His sacred flesh is sanctified.

Could we not say that the discourse after the Supper is a divine act of thanksgiving which Christ has the apostles make on the night of their First Communion? And the Cross is not absent, upon which tomorrow will be suspended the body which the Master gives them now as food.

None of the Synoptic accounts gives to Christ's Body the attention given it by John in his account of the Passion. He seems to have eyes only for this Sacred Body. And the closer the end approaches the more he fixes his gaze upon it. He notes all that takes place regarding that Body right up until the moment when his loving contemplation is rewarded by the sight of the Blood and water flowing from the transpierced side (19, 34).

"Blood and Water"

This is a sight of such lofty significance that John solemnly declares: "And he who saw it has borne witness, and his witness is true; and he knows that he tells the truth, that you also may believe" (19, 35).

It is because he had contemplated the Body with such faith and love that John saw what no one else noticed, and yet it had within itself a very deep meaning and spiritual power. This Blood, flowing out with the water, signified the birth of the Church and the sacraments; it is Christ's Mystical Body being born from His own Body and Blood; it is the door opened upon the fathomless depths of divine love, and that Heart is the furnace of that love.

The quotations from the Old Testament which John joins to his own account show him entirely absorbed by the contemplation of Christ's Body. "Not a bone of him shall you break" (19, 36); "They shall look upon him whom they have pierced" (19, 37).

From that glance of faith upon Him, John receives life, and it is the very life he sees flowing, so to speak, from that pierced side and immolated flesh. He now understands why the Savior's flesh must be placed at the service of love and how it has become the omnipotent instrument of salvation. And the Resurrection which rendered this flesh glorious increases John's concentration upon it, if this is possible.

When transmitting to us Christ's words to the Magdalene who had "undoubtedly cast herself at his feet to embrace them,"[2] John gives us to understand that this flesh will have a role to play when, once glorified, it will be vivifying and sanctifying.

Decisive too is this role of Christ's flesh in the apparition to the apostles on the day that Thomas is among them. "And after eight days, the disciples were again inside, and Thomas was with them. Jesus came, the doors being closed, and stood in their midst, and said, 'Peace be to you.' Then he said to Thomas, 'Bring here thy finger and see my hands, and bring here thy hand, and put it into my side; and be not unbelieving, but believing.' Thomas answered, 'My Lord and my God!' Jesus said to him, 'Because thou hast seen me, thou hast believed. Blessed are they who have not seen, yet have believed' "(20, 26-29).

In this scene we see underscored both the role of the risen Christ's flesh as pledge of redemption and salvation, and the need of a by-passing of this same flesh in an act of faith. In other words, this flesh must be present to us and yet we must be detached from it: "Unless you eat the flesh . . . the flesh profits nothing" (6, 53,63). John's entire message is contained here: the Incarnation, the sacraments, and faith.

Rehabilitation of human nature

The meaning of the mystery of the Incarnation would not be fully grasped by simply contemplating the Word or even by realizing the merciful love which prompted the Word to "make himself flesh." It is necessary also to consider the effects resulting from the Incarnation in favor of humanity.

It appears that when becoming incarnate, Christ has not only effected the world's salvation; He has likewise rehabilitated human nature, associating it in a most intimate way with salvation, and promising the whole man glorification.

Would Christ have assumed flesh if it were capable only of sinning or if it were radically evil? Would He have come to liberate us from sin by making a pact with it? We cannot admit such a thing, and St. Paul seems to confirm this. "We have not a high priest who cannot have compassion on our infirmities, but one tried as we are in all things except sin . . ." (Heb. 4, 15). "By sending his Son in the likeness of the flesh, he has condemned sin in the flesh" (Rom. 8, 3).

In Christ, the flesh is not only an element of this human composite which is inseparably body and soul; in Him, the entire human nature is united to the divine nature which sanctifies and divinizes it. The Word did not have to "purify" it since it was created good. "God saw all that he made and it was good" (Gn. 1, 31). This flesh was in Christ such as it had come from God's hands. In assuming human nature, Christ renders all condemnation of matter and flesh impossible.

It is true that the flesh was the great victim of Adam's fall, and it carried the fall's painful stigmata. It seems that it was rendered definitely incapable of rehabilitation because of the numberless disorders, sins, and shameful deeds performed through it. But this would be to misunderstand the omnipotence of divine love. Christ comes to "save that which was lost," all that was lost, and the more profound and irremediable appeared the fall, the greater the salvation (Mt. 18, 11).

God had placed in this flesh, when He created, certain powers and riches which man did not know how to cultivate or even preserve. On the contrary, he had wasted them and turned them from their true purpose. In man, the flesh was so corrupted that it became incapable of obeying the spirit. By becoming flesh, God restores all these riches and reveals them to man. To enter into possession of these riches, it is enough for man to seek them at their source, in the humanity of Christ.

The Savior does not take flesh simply to offer it in reparation for sin

2. P. Mollat, Evangile selon S. Jean, Bible de Jérusalem, p. 193.

to His Father; He also reveals divine love to men which is willing to restore humanity to its integrity. It is not enough for Christ to carry in His flesh the weight of men's sins in order to purify it in them; He wills to assume in this flesh the entire sinful man, so that the entire man can become divinized.

To be saved in his flesh and to make of his flesh an instrument of salvation, man must not forget that this flesh suffers in Gethsemani or on the Cross, that it becomes food for bodies and souls, that it is the unifying power gathering together all into a unity in the Mystical Body; he must not forget that this flesh, through Christ's eyes, voice, actions, steps, and understanding, is a means of singing of creation, of praising God, of manifesting tenderness, friendship, mercy and love to his brothers.

God has resolved to rehabilitate and restore to its true mission this flesh which peoples of antiquity frequently divinized, considering it the source of delights or adoring within it the reflection of invisible beauty; or inversely, upon which they set no value at all, corrupting it with illicit pleasures, crushing it under inhuman burdens, torturing it and casting it as food to the beasts.

The Word was made flesh, and behold this flesh was suddenly restored to the role assigned to it by God from the beginning and which had been so quickly lost. In the Word made flesh the material world becomes once again conscious and capable of a sacrifice of praise. In Christ, God is henceforth an integral part of His creation and gives this creation, even in the flesh, the possibility of reflecting light, life, and grace. In Christ, the permanent indwelling of the spirit in matter makes an endless act of thanksgiving, a eucharist, possible.

The soul no longer exercises an uncertain, questionable control over the body, for there is a lasting, absolute, and definite consecration of the former over the latter. The anointing received by Christ (3, 34) is poured forth upon the flesh which the hypostatic union places under the Holy Spirit's tutelage in a most constant and intimate manner. John sees in Christ's baptism the principle of an assumption of our nature, and the possibility of a communication to men, through the Word made flesh, of this Spirit who rested upon Him. "I beheld the Spirit descending as a dove from heaven and it abode upon him" (1, 32). "And no one has ascended into heaven except him who has descended from heaven" (3, 13). The flesh of the Risen Christ becomes for our flesh a pledge of resurrection; through its glorification and return to the Father, He confers upon it the possibility of being associated with the soul in eternal glory. The mystery of the Ascension enables us to understand this and furnishes us an assurance of it.

Because God has become incarnate, henceforth no rupture is envisaged in the divine plan of our salvation. The great redeeming wave takes hold in our nature of both its material and spiritual parts with one single stroke, one single flow of grace. It penetrates one and the other, illuminating and transforming them. It is the entire man that it takes and divinizes. "Now this is the will of him who sent me, the Father, that I should lose nothing of what he has given me, but that I should raise it up on the last day" (6, 39). And that other passage in which the entire divine plan is summed up: "No one can come to me unless the Father who sent me draw him, and I will raise him up on the last day" (6, 44).

The flesh is united in Christ's victory

Christ's coming in the flesh is not only a sensible sign of His love for us, revealing God's infinite condescension. It is the point of departure of a re-ascension which leaves behind it only what refuses to be assumed.

On the wood of the Cross, although sin was effaced and the Redemption accomplished, the role of the flesh did not terminate there, but was just beginning. Chained until then to sin and death, the flesh is henceforth united to redeeming love and its victory. It becomes forever, in the Risen Christ, the source of life, light, and grace. Through the centuries it will serve to build up one by one the cells of the Mystical Body of Christ. Through the power of this immolated and risen and life-giving flesh, man is made a sharer in the divine nature. In this flesh, man possesses even here on earth the pledge of future glory and the vision of God.

There are those who say that man is united to God only through the highest faculties of his spiritual being. Such a viewpoint does not take into consideration the way God came to us. It is a way He would have us follow in our going back to Him. Christ's plan does not consist in effecting any kind of divorce or separation in man's nature, but rather of having him realize his nature by respecting and fulfilling its unity.

Man's higher faculties have not been assigned the role of a relay station between matter and God. Though these powers do share in a privileged way in the assumption of our nature by Christ, yet we must not forget that the entire nature of man is promised divinization whatever be its various infirmities and limitations. Each man is destitute of intellectual abilities, no matter how humble and miserable he may be.

Human nature is undoubtedly endowed with many perfections in Christ, but it was not in virtue of a perfection of intellect or will or sense nature that He can be called "perfectus homo," or that Pilate presents Him to the people saying "Ecce homo." It is because in Christ an integral human nature is united to the divine nature.

In Christ this unity is so perfect that His human nature becomes a source of divinization for all men. Through it, as through a marvelous filter, the purified cosmos passes. It takes up its original function and becomes again that instrument from which God awaits perfect praise.

The grain buried in the ground springs up and ripens in God's sun; it becomes material for the Eucharistic sacrifice and for Christ's flesh through man's efforts and offering. And man also is this grain that gathers up, breathes in, and assimilates into his entire being all the matter and all the powers of the cosmos. And henceforth he is able to make these ascend towards God in Christ to whom he is united.

This work which is perfected in each man and each cell of Christ's Mystical Body is also realized in the Church herself. It is to her that Christ has confided the power of communicating to humanity the fruits of His redemptive Incarnation. This it does in the sacrament of His Body and Blood. The Church is Christ poured forth and communicated to men. But since it is born from Him on the Cross and since it is His visible Body, the Church may be considered in some way as the "flesh" of Christ. Imperfect as are her members, she is nevertheless the community of those in whom Christ lives, the visible branches of the Invisible Vine. We continue to touch, see, and hear the Word made flesh through our contact with the Church, and we recognize Him with the eyes of faith.

We can establish undeniably that, in her, Christ's mission of saving souls is continued and accomplished. True, it is done in a manner that bears the mark of our human condition; but in eternal life this "assumption" of the body will make it possible for the total Christ to be constituted in glory.

However, at the right hand of His Father Christ remains still the Word made flesh, and the seer of Patmos perceives in the flesh of the Lamb standing before the throne of God the marks of His suffering (Ap. 5, 6). In a parallel manner the glorious Church will also remain the one which, having fought on earth, keeps the traces of their combats, sufferings, and victories in the flesh of her children.

The redemptive value of suffering

There is still another aspect of the mystery of the Word made flesh; the one which makes it possible for Christ to assume the life of abjection and suffering. And we should bear in mind that the apostle of Thabor is also the apostle of Gethsemani, the Passion, and the Cross.

These images of Christ's sufferings are more deeply imprinted on

John's heart than on the heart of anyone else. It was given to him to see the Face of Jesus drenched in bloody sweat, and to hear His voice appealing to His Father to let the chalice pass (Lk. 22, 42) ; later, on the Cross, he heard him speak the words of dereliction (Mk. 15, 34). John beheld Christ's flesh humiliated, scourged, crowned with thorns, covered with dirt and spittle, and finally mockingly clothed in a purple cloak. Not for a moment did his eyes leave that flesh when, on the Cross, it experienced the pangs of death.

John has seen the Blood falling to the ground from those pierced hands and feet, and that body, exhausted by thirst and shaken with agony, gather up the last vestiges of its strength to offer itself in one supreme holocaust. Finally he has witnessed Christ's dead body surrender that secret of an eternal love in that blood and water flowing from the pierced heart.

His intimacy with Mary, who had entered into all her Son's sufferings and suffered the passion in her own soul, allows John to enter more deeply in the sufferings of the Lamb of God. In his writings the revelation of love is intimately linked to that of Christ's sufferings. "In this we have come to know his love, that he laid down his life for us" (1 Jn. 3, 16).

"For thou wast slain and hast redeemed us for God with thy blood"

If the Word was made flesh it is for the purpose of assuming all the suffering of the world, the flesh bearing a very large portion, and also to reveal to men the fruitfulness of this suffering when it is imbued with love.

Till then humanity had tried to cast out suffering, and when it did not succeed it saw in suffering a punishment for sin. The best tried to bear it patiently or even to make of it a means of purification.[3] But no one had ever imagined that the flesh could become an instrument of salvation and healing for humanity.

Isaias had pointed out in his hymn of the Suffering Servant that a man would come who was "despised and the most abject of men, a man of sorrows and acquainted with infirmity; his look was as it were hidden and despised. Whereupon we esteemed him not. Surely he hath borne our infirmities and carried our sorrows . . ." (Is. 53, 3,4).

Men would see in him only a being "punished and struck by God," but it would be revealed that these sufferings endured by Him would be wonderfully fruitful. "But he was wounded for our offenses, he was

---

3. In particular in the "Book of Job."

bruised for our sins. The chastisement of our peace was upon him, and by his bruises we are healed" (Is. 53, 5).

Thus had the prophet spoken. Comparing the Servant to a "lamb led to the slaughter," he stated, "Because his soul has labored, he shall see and be filled. By his knowledge shall this my just servant justify many, and he shall bear their iniquities" (Is. 53, 11).

Also, He will be glorified, for "he hath delivered his soul unto death and was reputed with the wicked. And he hath borne the sins of many and hath prayed for transgressors" (Is. 53, 12).

For the first time undoubtedly, suffering, sickness, and sorrow under their varied forms were set forth not only as an expiation inflicted by God, but also as a positive means of salvation. If this prophecy still retained anything obscure for John, the Cross was going to dispel this. Looking upon him "whom they pierced" (19, 37), John understands why the Word was made flesh. This flesh is for Him the means, not only of becoming "the man of sorrows and acquainted with suffering," and the "lamb who takes away the sin of the world" (1, 29,36), but it is also the means of delivering Himself up to death and to make this death the highest testimony of love ever given. "Greater love than this no man has that a man lay down his life for his friends" (15, 13).

John points out this power of Christ's flesh in his epistle. "And the blood of Jesus Christ, his Son, cleanses us from all sin" (1 Jn. 1, 7). And again, "Jesus Christ the just is a propitiation for our sins, not for ours only but also for those of the whole world" (1 Jn. 2, 2). And we read in the Apocalypse that the twenty-four ancients, prostrating before the Lamb "as though slain," sang a new canticle, "Worthy art thou to take the scroll and to open the seals. For thou wast slain and hast redeemed us for God with thy blood, out of every tribe and tongue and people and nation" (Ap. 5, 9).

The flesh is visited by grace and promised glory

"Lamb of God" and "Word made flesh" (1, 14,29). It seems these two visions of Christ remain ever present in John's mind. In his work, from beginning to end, he "confesses that Jesus Christ has come in the flesh" (1 Jn. 4, 2), when he salutes the Lamb of God who takes away the sins of the world. This same Lamb is shown immolated on the night of the Passover (19, 36), and in the Apocalypse it is shown victorious forever in the heavenly Jerusalem (Ap. 19, 22).

Throughout the Johannine message, we come upon the thought which influenced its author to confer upon Christ the title of "Word made flesh."

This thought never ceases to develop in two apparently opposed, but actually complementary, directions. On the one hand, John exalts and glorifies this flesh whose power penetrates our own flesh with a ferment of immortality, communicating to the soul grace and salvation; on the other, in this same sacrificed flesh, he discovers the mystery of suffering and the redemptive fecundity of self-immolating love. John knows that henceforth there will never be in this world a physical suffering, a moral agony, an abasement or a humiliation which cannot be referred to the humanity of the Incarnate Word. There it will find its justification, its meaning, and even its transfiguration through a union with Him who has assumed them all in His love.

John realizes also that, for this lowly flesh of ours, there no longer is any real obstacle on the road of its rehabilitation and glorification except the one man places there himself.

The Word was made flesh in order to work out our salvation, and He brings this about by the fullness of His presence. The amplitude or scope of that presence in the world extends from the lowest depths of physical and moral misery to the highest summits of the mystical life and union with God.

There is not a prisoner tortured in some gaol and abandoned to the worst end, not a patient afflicted with some malady, whose sufferings go on increasing until death, who cannot say that this abjection, misery, and despair into which they are plunged were not visited, assumed, and even surpassed by the suffering and dereliction experienced by Christ Himself. And in Him they can find an omnipotent support.

And no less must be said of those mystical heights which some souls touch for an instant with the impression of experiencing a foretaste of heavenly joys; there is no comparison whatever between these and the joys Christ experienced in His soul which already enjoyed the beatific vision (2 Cor. 12, 2-4).

Christ welcomes and embraces humanity with His arms extended on the Cross. His sufferings are deeper than our stains and His flesh shares a happiness to which none of our ravishments will ever attain. Having sustained the one and experienced the other, the Word made flesh will make us share in His brightness and glory after conferring life upon us through His grace.

"The Word was made flesh, and of his fullness we have all received, grace for grace" (1, 14). "Father, the hour is come, glorify thy Son, that thy Son may glorify thee, even as thou hast given him power over all flesh, in order that to all thou hast given him he may give everlasting life" (17, 1,2). "Father, the glory thou hast given me, I have given to them" (17, 22).

CHAPTER 6

THE PORTRAIT OF CHRIST

John tried not to merit that reproach addressed to his companion Philip: "Have I been so long a time with you, and you have not known me" (14, 9)? His Gospel shows how well he applied himself to the task of getting to know Christ. He was not content to remain simply at Christ's side during a period of three years. Neither was it enough for him to listen to His discourses. Realizing that Christ was the one sent from the Father, he looked upon Him with an adoring fervor filled with love. And later on under the Spirit's guidance he succeeded in mounting to the very source of His activity. His knowledge of Christ had become contemplative knowledge.

This contemplation, so evident in the Gospel, is linked to a perfect objectivity. It unites the perspicacity of one adept at observing and noting down revealing data to the fervor of the disciple and the tenderness of the friend. Each one of these data retains a special and personal meaning and is possessed of numberless implications. John does not resurrect the past; he offers for our meditation a present which never ceased to be living for him and in which he would have us commune.

His testimony is never second hand, for what he speaks about he has either witnessed or heard directly. The fourth Gospel opens on the day when John encountered Christ on the Jordan's banks, and it closes with the last apparition with which he was favored on the shores of Lake Genesareth. However, this Gospel does not touch only upon external realities; it reaches to the very heart of the personality it depicts, viz., the mystery of Christ. It leads us beyond visible realities into invisible ones which give meaning to the least of Christ's words and actions. If the portrait which it sketches is so strikingly life-like, it is because this Gospel has not only a spiritual dimension, but a supernatural one as well. Thus, it is not at the first reading that Christ's portrait comes forth from this work; it rises little by little and impresses itself progressively upon us in its divine and human Truth, and this "revelation" illumines the entire Gospel.

The Hidden God

A man like other men, One who remained until now unknown among His own: such is the Jesus of the first pages of the Johannine Gospel. Unknown, in spite of the Baptist and his powerful voice which attracted crowds to announce His advent. "Make straight the way of the Lord. He who is coming after me is mightier than I. In the midst of you there has stood one whom you do not know. He is the one that is to come after me" (1, 15,23,26; Mt. 3, 11).

And what is even more strange: He is unknown even to the Baptist: "And I did not know him" (1, 31. Cf. Lk. 17, 21).

What an admission this is! But still more, what a revelation it is about Christ who does not only will to remain in the background, unknown, but whose voluntary effacement has the depth of a mystery about it. Jesus remains the Hidden God, the "Deus absconditus" of Scripture, until that very moment when the Spirit Himself, resting on Him, points Him out to the Precursor. "And I did not know him. But he who sent me to baptize with water said to me, 'He upon whom thou shalt see the Spirit descending, and abiding upon him, he it is who baptizes with the Holy Spirit.' And I have seen and have borne witness that this is the Son of God" (1, 33,34).

An instant before, Jesus was still only one of the Israelites come to the banks of the Jordan to listen to the Baptist, a Jew among others, whom no one had taken notice of in the midst of the crowd of penitents.

This is the way He appears in this scene and it is the way He will remain. With great reserve, yet very clearly, the Johannine account enables us to see that Jesus does nothing to push Himself forward, just as He had done nothing to stand forth from the generality of men. He passes by in silence and it is the Baptist who points Him out to his disciples: "Behold the Lamb of God" (1, 29), he says.

Jesus, nevertheless, continues walking and does not stop until He hears the Baptist's two disciples coming to Him: "But Jesus turned round, and seeing them following him, said to them, 'What is it you seek?' They said to him, 'Rabbi, where dwellest thou?' He said to them, 'Come and see' " (1, 38).

Christ does not steal away: "He takes care of those who seek him"

(Sir. 4, 11), but in such a way as not to impose Himself. He does not bring forth His titles or an origin which would have won for him some consideration. When Philip announces to Nathanael: "We have found him of whom Moses in the Law and the Prophets wrote," he adds: "Jesus son of Joseph of Nazareth" (1, 45). And that reply of Nathanael: "Can anything good come out of Nazareth?"

We do not know which is to be admired the more: the humility of Christ which reveals Him to little ones and hides Him from the wise and prudent; or the faith of those who, in the son of the carpenter, do not hesitate to recognize the Messias. We are reminded here of the prophet's words: "Who hath believed our report? And to whom is the arm of the Lord revealed" (Is. 53, 1)?

Humility and Simplicity

Even during His public life, Christ will depart from this reserve only when the demands of His mission determine Him to do so. This reserve and complete absence of affectation seem so natural to the disciples who surround Him that John does not even think of calling our attention to them. "Come and see.... And they went and saw where he lived" (1, 39).

The home of Jesus! No one, not even John who actually saw it, judged it necessary to describe it. Undoubtedly because it was according to the Master's image! A house among many others, hidden, humble, ordinary; nothing singled it out as the "home" of God among men. Better than the cloud, humility withdrew it from human gaze.

There is the same simplicity, the same freedom from affectation at the wedding of Cana. Jesus was invited to it like many other guests, along with His Mother and His disciples. That the Mother and the Son were invited together shows that Jesus was there as a close neighbor or as a distant relative. This all goes to show the degree to which He identified Himself with the human group to which He belongs, and intends in no way to act contrary to the customs, usages, and habits of His milieu. "They invited him and his disciples" (2, 2). To invite to a village wedding One who had already acquired the reputation of a "rabbi," perhaps even of a prophet, and to feel he would not decline the invitation, is this not a revealing sign of that simplicity which struck the humblest and encouraged them to come to Him without fear (Mt. 19, 14)?

If we have trouble imagining Him in this noisy atmosphere, exchanging remarks with the guests and entering into the general mirth, He Himself had no trouble suiting Himself to His surroundings. Also, His presence spread no gloom over these rejoicings, however prosaic. Better still: far from tempering the festivity with a note of gravity, Jesus and Mary will busy themselves with undoing an accident which, while placing their hosts in an embarrassing situation, threatens to compromise the joy of the guests.

Free from all affectation and egoism herself, Mary is attentive to the needs of others. "They have no wine," she whispers to her Son (2, 3); and the simplicity with which she warns Him casts a vivid light, not only upon the charity of them both, but also upon the loving and confiding intimacy which united them. In spite of appearances, the objection which Jesus seems to oppose to the very reserved suggestion of His Mother, and the words of the latter to the servants, "Do whatever he tells you" (2, 5), enable us to measure that simplicity even better.

Doubtless one would have to be the Blessed Virgin to understand that her Son had not refused her, and that these words: "What wouldst thou have me to do, woman? My hour has not yet come" (2, 4), contained a mysterious power which confidence would succeed in expanding.

Jesus heard Mary's prayer: the water was changed into wine. "This first of his signs Jesus worked at Cana of Galilee and he manifested his glory, and his disciples believed in him," (2, 11).

But, John, although very attentive to the consequences of the miracle, underscores the quietness with which the miracle was performed. He did not fail to note down that only the attendants had any knowledge of the prodigy (2, 9). "Every man at first sets forth the good wine, and when they have freely drunk, then that which is poorer. But thou hast kept the good wine until now" (2, 10). The humor of the scene did not escape him and he hints that Jesus experiences it too, He who allows the steward of the feast to be astonished when He could have so easily spared him this surprise. But the nuance is so light that it does not distract from the principal idea: this miracle is a sign and it sufficed that this sign revealed Christ's glory only to His disciples and stirred up their faith in Him.

Between the lines we discover that human slant, filled with the simplicity, goodness, and even the mischievous *bonhomie* of Jesus. Only a witness could have reported this scene with such finesse, and John's respect for His Master does not prevent him in any way from bringing to light the rich aspects of that highly endowed personality. Far from presenting Him as aloof and distant, He brings Him to life before our eyes, showing Him to us full of delicacy towards His Mother even at the moment when it seems, dare we say it, that he was failing in consideration for her; he shows Him capable of enjoying the unforeseen in a situation, all the more when He is in a position to direct the events towards a happy conclusion.

The Divine Wisdom incarnate

The Cana episode has a much more important meaning than that of helping us realize the simplicity and charity of both Jesus and Mary. Cana is the point of departure of Christ's mission of salvation. Humanity to which He has been given is there awaiting Him; it is a question of going to it with all the resources of His divinity and humanity; with all those qualities of fortitude and meekness, of delicacy and authority which seem to us men hardly reconcilable and even opposed one to the other, but which the Master will prove through His mission of redeeming love to be complementary.

And that is why, from the apostle's testimony, an overall impression is drawn, and it is best expressed in the term "wisdom," that supreme wisdom present in all the proceedings and activities of Christ.

The manifestation of this wisdom is accompanied in Christ by a profound knowledge of the human heart: ". . . many believed in his name, seeing the signs that he was working. But Jesus did not trust himself to them, in that he knew all men, and because he had no need that anyone should bear witness concerning men, for he himself knew what was in man" (2, 23-25).

This wisdom, while fulfilling it, unites with that divine Wisdom proposed to the men of the Old Testament. We can set side by side with Christ, uncreated Wisdom, who "from the beginning is with God" (1, 2), who is "come out from God" (17, 8) and comes "to dwell among us" (1, 14), that passage where Ben Sirach pronounces the eulogy of Divine Wisdom: "Then the creator of all gave me his command, and he who formed me chose the spot of my tent, saying, 'In Jacob make your dwelling, in Israel your inheritance.' Before all ages, in the beginning, he created me, and through all ages I shall not cease to be. In the holy tent I ministered before him" (Sir. 24, 8-10).

In this Wisdom, we can truly see the "prototype of the Logos."

In John's Gospel, this divine Wisdom manifests itself in Christ as a faculty of assembling, utilizing, and regulating all the other faculties, with the possibility of making use of them at a time and in a way that is most suitable for His purpose, viz., the salvation of the world.

Jesus knows what is in man; He knows too what the will of His Father is. Between these two realities Wisdom throws up a bridge. Thus at each moment, through the best adapted ways which are both naturally and supernaturally effective, the end will be attained and the mission accomplished.

Characteristic traits

When we want to paint the portrait of a man we try to discover his "strong point," the unifying principle which bears within itself, and around which are gathered, all his interior qualities. Applied to Christ, such a method is doomed to failure because in Him we cannot find a definite "strong point" which would polarize all His other qualities. Wisdom alone, that supremely well-ordered unity, that living cohesion, accounts for the diversified aspects under which His character is proposed for our meditation.

An infinite gentleness and boundless meekness are united in Him to a strength, a demand, a sharpness which can be disconcerting. However, all this is "Himself," and we feel that in Him apparently opposite qualities not only do not neutralize one another or dissolve into some kind of synthesis or compromise, but rather each quality blends in perfectly with the other.

Besides, the fact that Christ is Incarnate Wisdom enables Him to utilize each of His powers and faculties in a most effective way. Thus, the revelation of God is brought about and light is given to men with an admirable certainty and constant efficacy.

Christ's character emerges from the shadows on the occasion of a task to be done, a truth to be taught, an error to be corrected, and a soul to be enlightened and saved. These are just so many circumstances in the course of which His character-traits are revealed and underscored; they are so many opportunities for us to enter more deeply into the mystery and knowledge of His Person.

While some men are unable to release their rich personalities and their learning unless confronted by a large crowd, there are others and perhaps they are in the majority who need the friendly atmosphere of a private conversation to make this same release. Christ appears at ease in either case. John has been careful to report His words addressed to large audiences, friendly or hostile, to the small group of the apostles, as well as His private interviews with such people as Nicodemus and the Samaritan woman. Undoubtedly these latter scenes give us an inkling of the divine teaching method, that delicately shaded psychology of Christ; but the chapters of John's Gospel dealing with the work of the Son, His testimony concerning Himself, on the light, in which we see him coming to grips with unfriendly listeners, all these are very revealing.[1] Here another facet of His personality is brought out: His strength of character, His love of truth, the demands of His charity.

1. Confer chapters 5, 8, 12.

The discourse on the bread of life, the parable of the Good Shepherd, the discourse after the Supper, all these offer still another aspect: the infinite riches of His Heart, unburdening itself to a circle of souls hungering for life and intimacy and union.[2] We cannot possibly consider all these various traits, but we shall consider some which delineate Christ's portrait from several aspects. These have come to us from John.

The interview with Nicodemus

The interview with Nicodemus brings out that singular aptitude in Christ of placing Himself on a level with His listener without for a single instant losing sight of the goal to which He wants to lead him. But at the same time as Christ seemingly goes out to His listeners, it is the latter who are being drawn to Christ.

"Master, we know that thou hast come a teacher from God..." (3, 2). This is the persuasive and typically oriental introduction used by Nicodemus, and Jesus immediately discovers in it his motive for seeking Him out. He knows He has before Him an undecisive and timid man, whose good will has limits that are easily reached and who would willingly accommodate himself to any compromise. That is the reason He sets before him a demand and a choice which throw this good and prudent man off guard.

Without hedging, Jesus tells this "teacher in Israel," who finds in Christ his real Teacher, this "confrere," whose limited knowledge Jesus easily sees through, that the one means of attaining the kingdom of God is to be "reborn of the Spirit." Nicodemus is dumbfounded and baffled. "How can this be done"? Of all the evangelists John is the most conscious of the irony of which Christ makes frequent use. It is because he discovers in it a weapon which divine Wisdom knows how to make very effective, that stroke which wounds and pierces the hidden abcess while removing it. "Thou art a teacher in Israel and dost not know these things?" In other words: Of us two, you are the one who carries the titles of teacher and doctor, and still you don't know that?

However, after removing that false "glory" men bestow upon one another or "draw from each other," and the high esteem Nicodemus had of himself, Jesus, aware of his good will, far from confounding him, tries to enlighten him. Thus, He reminds him of that teaching on the Spirit which he should know, for it has already been taught especially in the prophetic writings (Ez. 11, 19; 36, 37; Is. 44, 3; 59, 21; Jl. 3, 1-8). He

2. Confer chapters 6, 10, 14, 15, 16, 17.

certainly is soon conscious of his inexcusable ignorance. But did he really appreciate the charity accompanied by divine prudence with which Christ sets before him the redeeming mystery of the Cross? That mystery inseparable from the new birth?

Jesus will present it to him in a veiled way, under cover of an Exodus scene, familiar to this doctor versed in the Law. "And as Moses lifted up the serpent in the desert, even so must the Son of Man be lifted up, that those who believe in him may not perish, but may have everlasting life" (3, 14).

The Samaritan woman

In the interview with the Samaritan woman, the wisdom, kindness, and self-control of Christ shine out all the more as Jesus, to attain His ends the better, allows Himself to follow this woman through the meandering paths of her curiosity, her self-love, and even her banter. Father Lagrange has written of this episode that it was the "marvel of marvels," and it is true. Nowhere, perhaps, do we see the sovereign authority and the infinite meekness of the Savior so harmoniously and subtly united as He bends over His creature and succeeds in bringing her back to Himself after seeking her in the "distant country" of her indifference and sin.

The search will not be without difficulty. The divine Fisherman will finally make His catch, but it will struggle long before giving in. The Samaritan woman is extremely clever in eluding embarrassing questions and escaping Him who, with divine skill, will nevertheless end by breaking down all her defenses.

The exquisitely delicate nuances of the text scarcely bear commentary. They merit at least our pointing them out since certain traits of Christ's character and soul will stand out.

When narrating the episode, John has in his mind the great plain, arid and desolate, above which towered Gerizim and Ebal to the west, while Sichar was sheltered in the hollow separating them. John recalled that at the end of a journey Christ was tired, and the apostles, less exhausted, had left Him at the end of Jacob's well and went on into the neighboring town for provisions.

"Jesus, therefore, wearied as he was from the journey, was sitting at the well. It was about the sixth hour. There came a Samaritan woman to draw water" (4, 6,7). Breaking with the custom that Jews were not to associate[3] with Samaritans (4, 9) and that a Jew was not to talk with a

---

3. The Jews contracted a legal impurity when using the same instruments as the Samaritans. Such was the real meaning of "co-utuntur." D. Daube, the New Testament and Rabbinic Judaism.

woman, much less a woman of Samaria, Jesus starts the conversation. "Give me to drink" (4, 10). These introductory words are very natural at this place and hour, but they also remind us of several like scenes reported in the Old Testament (Gn. 24, 17; 29, 10). But above all, they give Christ the occasion for arousing in this woman a thirst for God which she was far from experiencing until then.

The Samaritan was not one of those who forget they are women even when asked for a favor. Instead of complying simply and kindly with the request of a pilgrim exhausted by fatigue and tortured by thirst, she takes advantage of the situation and expresses surprise: "How is it that thou, being a Jew,[4] dost ask a drink of me, who am a Samaritan woman?" (4, 9). "She does not let slip the opportunity of pointing out this departure from the usual behavior of the Jews,"[5] and of showing Him that necessity lowers all barriers. Jesus is far from these vain thoughts. He wastes no time, for His main desire is to rouse in her a real thirst for things divine. And how succeed, if not by stirring up curiosity in the Person to whom she is speaking? "If thou didst know the gift of God and who it is that says to thee: 'Give me to drink'. . ." (4 ,10).

The object of the conversation is promptly changed, and both the woman and Jesus, in spite of His real thirst, no longer think of drawing the water which continues to supply the topic of conversation. The interview will retain a slightly ironic tone owing to the woman and in spite of Christ's efforts. What does this stranger take himself for? After lowering himself to ask for a drink, now he claims he can give me living water and yet has nothing with which to draw? "Art thou greater than our father Jacob who gave us the well . . ."(4, 12)?

Jesus allows nothing to turn Him from His quest; gently, forcefully, and lovingly He insists: "Everyone who drinks of this water will thirst again. He, however, who drinks of the water that I will give him shall never thirst; but the water that I will give him shall become in him a fountain of water, springing up unto life everlasting" (4, 13).

Who is this man, this poor beggar, who just a moment ago craved a drink and now speaks of nothing but a gift? "If thou didst know the *gift* of God. The water that I will *give* him shall become for him a fountain of water . . ."(4, 10,14).

So strong and captivating is the magic of that word, so great the nobility of this stranger with majestic promises that the woman submits to His power even to the point of saying, "Sir, give me this water that I may not thirst, or come here to draw."

4. The woman recognized Him either by His accent or His clothing.
5. Lagrange, Gospel of St. John.

There is no question in her mind of anything else but material water. Perhaps even in her practical conclusion, "give me this water that I may . . . not come here and draw," we can see a somewhat impertinent summons, tinged with incredulity, for Jesus to manifest His power.

Christ feels that the irony, fickleness, and banter which continue to manifest themselves in the Samaritan run the risk of rendering the interview useless. He decides to turn her thoughts in another direction: "Go, call your husband and return here" (4, 16).

She parries this unexpected blow cleverly. "I have no husband." There is a little irony in Christ's concession that she was right in saying she had no husband, for she had five and the one she has now is not her husband; Jesus shows her He can read hearts and nothing is hidden from Him. It seems that the blow struck home! "Sir, I see that thou art a prophet" (4, 19). But with the same unconcern as before, she again changes the subject. Since the man is a prophet, she sets them both on the religious plane. She cleverly introduces a venerable tradition with a claim of little weight, and pointing to Gerizim towering over the plain, she says: "Our fathers worshipped on this mountain, but you say that it is at Jerusalem that one should worship" (4, 20).

Mildly, Jesus takes advantage of the diversion and draws from it the opportunity of making one of His most exalted revelations. The sinner before Him will be its first beneficiary, but through her this declaration will enlighten and nourish a multitude of souls in search of life and truth. Raising the discussion above the petty bickering over hills, He says: "Woman, believe me, the hour is coming when neither on this mountain nor in Jerusalem will you worship the Father. You worship what you do not know; we worship what we know, for salvation is from the Jews. But the hour is coming, and is now here, when the true worshippers will worship the Father in spirit and in truth. For the Father also seeks such to worship him. God is spirit, and they who worship him must worship in spirit and in truth" (4, 21).

These words of simple majesty and this profound teaching unsettle the Samaritan and give rise in her to better sentiments: that thirst, that expectation of a Messias as Savior. "I know the Messias is coming and that when he comes he will tell us everything" (4, 25).

Her real feelings and this initial humility which these words conceal permit Jesus to reveal what He wanted to teach her and what He had asked His disciples not to reveal: "I who speak with thee am her" (4, 26).

The question which had opened the interview: "If thou didst know the gift of God and who it is that says to thee, 'Give me to drink'. . ." has received its response. Obliging Himself to follow the meanderings of a purely natural mode of thinking and acting, Jesus has attained His ends.

Better still: when favoring this apparently ill-prepared and sinful woman with such a revelation, He has made it clear that His mercy is absolutely gratuitous.

"I came to save what was lost"

We willingly place side by side with the episode of the Samaritan woman, that of the one taken in adultery.[6] Here, it is pure mercy that is apparent and the Good Shepherd does not have to go out in search of His lost sheep. Bad shepherds have taken it upon themselves to bring her to Him.

St. Augustine sums up this story with this striking statement: "And then there remained only the two: misery and Mercy." Whether it belongs in John's Gospel or not, this marvelous account brings to light another facet of Christ's psychology, viz., His infinite respect for souls.

Jesus was teaching in the Temple, when a noisy crowd of men arrived: Scribes, Pharisees, Doctors of the Law, and some curiosity seekers. Pushing a woman before them whom they had surprised in adultery, they set her in full view of Christ. The Gospel text shows clearly that, when questioning Christ on her case, the intentions of these moralists were not pure. "Master, this woman has just now been caught in adultery. And in the Law Moses commanded us to stone such persons. What, therefore, dost thou say" (8, 5)?

Undoubtedly, to this hatred of Christ there were added certain bad dispositions, for the witnesses of this scandal were not on the scene by chance.

Jesus meets the noisy demonstrations of His questioners with absolute silence, and He even turns away from them. "But Jesus, stooping down, began to write with his finger on the ground" (8, 6).

Whatever the significance of this gesture is, it does impose silence upon them, while an uneasiness takes hold of the bystanders. The Pharisees and Scribes, however, have no intention of letting slip this opportunity of involving Christ in difficulty. They will not allow Him to escape through some subterfuge. Insistently they come back to the attack. Then, just as a bow held taut for a long time sends forth its arrow with great speed, Jesus, rising suddenly, hurls this challenge at them; "Let him

6. This episode can be attributed to John with only feeble probability. Many manuscripts place it after Luke 21, 38, or at the end of John's Gospel. However, since it remains practically in the body of the fourth Gospel and is very revealing as far as Christ's psychology is concerned, we will meditate upon it here.

who is without sin among you be the first to cast a stone at her" (8, 6). Then, "again stooping down, he began to write on the ground."

He needed no assurance of the effect produced. His words hit home and He knew it. Not one of these men but felt he was struck. "But hearing this, they went away, one by one, beginning with the eldest. And Jesus remained alone, with the woman standing in the midst."

Silence follows upon the tumult and the shouting. The apostles and a few curious onlookers, silent and stunned, await the outcome of this strange scene.

Christ, who had remained stooped, rises, and this time the arrow He has prepared is one of mercy. With infinite delicacy and compassionate love, He is going to direct it towards this sinner so that it will reach her heart.

Indeed, until now He had avoided her gaze in order not to trouble her any further. Were not the things she suffered already enough? Her shock at having been taken by surprise, her fright, her shame at being thus exposed to the eyes of all? But what do the silence and judgment of this Man, whom she can avoid no longer, reserve for her?

While Jesus was writing on the ground, she was unconscious of the work accomplished in her soul. He was aware of it, for He knows He has purified her heart in his love and transformed it. He looks at her and asks, "Woman, where are they? Has no one condemned thee" (8, 10)? As her gaze meets His she does not see the look of condemnation she feared, but a look of gentleness, reassuring her and giving her strength to murmur, "No one, Lord."

And it is to a soul totally renewed by forgiving Love that these saving words are addressed, "Neither do I condemn thee. Go thy way and from now on sin no more" (8, 11).

Renunciation and Detachment

Christ poured forth this mercy repeatedly, as is evident in the miracles John reports: the healing of the royal official's son (4, 43-54), the healing of the paralytic who was thirty-eight years lying under the porticoes of the pool at Bethsaida (5, 1-18), the miracle where He fed the crowd on the hillside (6, 1-15), and where He restores sight to the man born blind (9, 1-41).

Whatever be the symbolic meaning John attributed to these miracles, he always presents them enveloped in an atmosphere of quiet, humility, and detachment. If the thirty years of preparation were characterized by the mark of Christ's hidden life, this same sign is not absent from His public life. Indeed, it is with a kind of quiet reserve that Christ performs His miracles and immediately afterwards withdraws. With a word and at a distance, He cures the child of Capharnaum (4, 50); He disappears into the crowd immediately upon giving the infirm man the order to take up his pallet and walk. So perfectly is this done, that when the man is asked, "Who is the man who said to thee, 'Take up thy pallet...'" (5, 12), he cannot say. After the multiplication of the loaves which brought the enthusiasm of the crowd to such a pitch that they would make Him king, "he fled again into the mountain himself alone" (6, 15).

A similar attitude is evident in His actions on the eve of the feast of Tabernacles. "Leave here and go into Judea that thy disciples also may see thy works that thou dost, for no one does a thing in secret if he wants to be publicly known. If thou dost these things, manifest thyself to the world." To this advice of His relatives, Jesus replies, " 'My time is not yet come... I do not go up to the feast....' When he said these things he stayed on in Galilee. But as soon as his brethren went up to the feast, then he also went up, not publicly, but as it were privately" (7, 6-10).

Faithful to this attitude of reserve, Jesus disappears immediately after opening the eyes of the man born blind. And when questioned as to where Jesus was, he answered, "I do not know" (9, 12). The entire discussion between this man and the Jews, a discussion in which the crowd remained divided, takes place without Jesus putting in an appearance, and it is only by chance that He meets the man later and the latter makes his act of faith in the Son of man (9, 38).

Even the resurrection of Lazarus is enveloped in silence and reserve, since before performing the miracle Jesus had retired into the Jordan area (10, 40), and immediately after the miracle He goes into the desert of the Ephrem region (11, 5). Although the miracle itself cannot remain unknown, it nevertheless unfolds in an atmosphere of simplicity. It was suddenly that Jesus arrived on the scene since no one was expecting Him. Even Martha was unaware of His arrival. Jesus avoided all showiness, but contented Himself with speaking the words which restore life (11, 43).

The triumph following upon the miracle is very much subdued. Palms thrown before Jesus seated on the colt of an ass in fulfillment of the Scriptures, and the joyful cries of His countrymen, present to celebrate the Feast, who come out to meet Him, this is all He will consent to. He will not even agree to showing Himself to certain Greeks who ask to see Him (12, 12,21).

All this reserve and self-effacement, even in the thick of His ministry and mission, have struck John, and justly so.

The Synoptics frequently state that Jesus told His disciples not to dicuss what they had seen (Mt. 17, 9) and to be silent about his identity

(Mt. 16, 20). This prohibition, which appears in the Synoptics to be dictated by prudence and to be following a plan of progressive revelation of Christ's divinity, has a different significance in St. John's Gospel. Here it takes on the aspect of a character-trait, a mark of great detachment. What we see more is Christ's desire that all things be referred to His Father.

"I do always the things that please him"

Indeed, though the miracles and interviews reported in the Johannine Gospel show us the sentiments of Christ's soul and enable us to approach His Person, there is still an even deeper reality that remains to be discovered and John deserves the credit for having understood it.

The apostle grasped the fact that Christ's character could be explained only in the light of its eternal dimensions, and on condition that He never be separated from His Father. We have to discover in each of His actions and words the Father's witness and envoy; the One who expresses Him in a perfect and filial fidelity.

This essential dimension is never absent from the fourth Gospel, but is one of its characteristic marks. Just as when we apply the laws of perspective to a sketch, we give it depth and confer a new dimension upon it, so also, this relation to the Father brings to the fourth Gospel its true dimension, viz., the one that enables us to see in Christ "the one sent by the Father."

This title claimed by Christ is constantly on His lips. (It appears thirty times or more in John's Gospel). But the thought of this Father who sent Him does not only occupy His mind, it also controls all His dispositions. If He has come to save the world it is at the Father's command, and His mission as Savior cannot be separated from that of Revealer of the Father. The only-begotten Son has come to make "known" His Father (1, 18). "I came forth from the Father . . . I go to the Father" (16, 28). Christ refers nothing to Himself, but everything to the Father. And that is why He will instruct men to turn towards the Father and tend always toward Him.

He Himself is "ad Patrem" and this expresses His whole life. He desires nothing else but to be the living Word of the Father. He fulfills the will "of him who sent him" (5, 30; 6, 38); "I always do the things that please him" (8, 29). This renunciation confers a deep interior freedom and a sovereign strength to His words and actions.

We know ourselves how free and how strong we are when we act for others and for their profit. Our personal interest not being at stake, we are ready to bear anything, accept anything and demand anything.

What a father claims for his family, a mother for her children, and a servant for his master, all this is only a pale reflection of what Christ demands for the honor and glory of His Father. He seeks not His own glory, but the glory of him "who sent him" (8, 50). He does not seek Himself in anything He has done; He takes no complacency in Himself (Rom. 15, 3).

However, to say that there is no reference to self in Christ is not sufficient. What we come upon in Him is the very mystery of love itself, considered as a "belonging" to another, the inhabitation in this other. Christ does not only work for His Father, He is "in him" and it is "in him" that He accomplished all things. Now, the fact of Christ's being, not in Himself, but in His Father, explains His entire conduct, and makes us enter into the mystery of His Person.

Whatever be the demands of His role as the Father's "envoy," it does not superadd some kind of borrowed personality to Christ which would oblige Him to modify, go counter to, or reduce to silence His own personal reactions. Christ's intimate sentiments as Savior or Good Shepherd are in no way opposed to those which are consonant with His mission as "envoy," which obliges Him to defend at all costs the honor of Him who sent Him: all goes to make up His personality.

Christ, whose Heart has pity on our misery, who weeps over the City of Jerusalem, who has compassion on the multitude, who invites those heavily burdened to come to Him, this Christ has no other sentiments than those of the Word; and the Word bears within Himself and manifests to us with perfect fidelity all the Father's sentiments.

The Meekness and Violence of Love

We would be falsifying Christ's character if we were to reduce His message to scenes of gentleness and meekness. We must consider with just as much care those scenes in which there appear His strength, His sharpness, and even what we may call His violence, e.g., the cleansing of the Temple and His discussions with the Pharisees (Cf. c. 8, passim).

Conscious of the fact that such scenes are extremely revealing, St. John, far from tempering them, retains all their vigor and even emphasizes their power. Thus, he is the only one of the evangelists to point out that Christ's action of expelling the vendors from the Temple is not a simple movement of just anger, but a real indignation. It is not, in fact, with a cord taken up haphazardly, but with several from which He makes a whip, that He drives out those who "make the house of my Father a house of business" (2, 16).

John's memories are very exact. He points out that not only did Jesus expel all (2, 15) the merchants with their "sheep and oxen," but that He "poured out the money of the changers and overturned their tables. And to them who were selling doves he said, 'Take these away....'" The irresistible power of this anger, stopping only when the Temple has been restored to its purity of purpose, shocks only soft souls. The "son of thunder" sees here only the real mark of the "zeal which devours" Christ for the honor of His Father's house.

Jealous for God's glory

The description of the cleansing of the Temple is one example only of Christ's ardor and the jealousy of His love for His Father. If it is surprising to us, it is because this zeal is manifested in actions which seemingly are out of place in One who says, "I am meek and humble of heart" (Mt. 11, 29).

But there are other occasions even more symptomatic where this strength, instead of being released, remains contained and perfectly disciplined. And it is nonetheless more vengeful and terrible in its effects.

And it will no longer be a question of expelling the traffickers from a Temple of stone, but of forbidding those who live in their egoism, falsehood, pride, and injustice from entering the kingdom of heaven.

"He knows what is in man" (2, 25). When He accuses His adversaries of falseness, malice, hypocrisy, sectarianism, when He unveils their murderous desires, He is laying bare the absolute truth; His listeners feel this and are reduced to silence or forced to bury themselves deeper in their darkness, their falsehood, and their refusal to accept Him.

In many of the fourth Gospel scenes, it appears that Christ, far from extending the hand of friendship to His adversaries or of coming to an understanding with them, cuts the bridges between them and Himself and has no fear of harassing and confounding them.

Thus, in the following abrupt, absolute statements we see no room for any kind of reconciliation: "He who does not believe in him (the Son) is already judged, because he does not believe in the name of the only-begotten Son of God" (3, 18). "He who is unbelieving towards the Son shall not see life, but the wrath of God rests upon him" (3, 36). "But I know that you have not the love of God in you" (5, 42). "I have come in the name of my Father and you do not receive me. If another come in his own name, him you will receive" (5, 43). "If you were blind you would have no sin. But now that you say, 'We see,' your sin remains" (9, 41).

Pointing out the incredulity of the Jews at the end of Christ's ministry, John will write: "Now though he worked so many signs in their presence, they did not believe in him; that the word which the prophet Isaias spoke might be fulfilled, 'Lord, who has believed our report, and to whom has the arm of the Lord been revealed?' This is why they could not believe, because Isaias said again, 'He has blinded their eyes and hardened their hearts; lest they see with their eyes, and understand with their mind, and be converted and I heal them' " (12, 37-40).

We cannot read the eighth chapter without being deeply stirred. Jesus, attacking his enemies and unmasking their hypocrisy, animosity, and guilty desires, says: "You are from below, I am from above. You are of this world, I am not of this world. Therefore I said to you, you will die in your sins . . . I speak what I have seen with my Father; and you do what you have seen with your father. . . . You are seeking to kill me, one who has spoken the truth to you, which I have heard from God. . . . The father from whom you are is the devil, and the desires of your father, it is your will to do. . . . But because I speak the truth to you, you do not believe me. . . . The reason why you do not hear is that you are not of God" (8, passim).

This violence will not be refuted and this opposition will not surrender; even in the last moments of Christ's life, at the Supper, in His prayer to His father He will say, "I pray not for the world" (17, 9).

The Revelation of Divine Love

The same lips that pronounced the above words, also said: "As the Father has loved me, I also love you" (15, 9), and "Greater love than this no man has that he lay down his life for his friends" (15, 13). Christ, who condemned the Pharisees, called the apostles "my little children" (18, 33), and to the end He is ready to pardon His betrayer.

The same one expels the vendors from the Temple and pardons the adulterous woman; the one who hurls those avenging words at the Pharisees, "You will die in your sin" (9, 40), says of the Magdalene, "Her sins, many as they are, shall be forgiven her because she has loved much" (Lk. 7, 47). Christ, who said to the Jews, "You have the devil for your father" is also the Good Shepherd who "gives his life for his sheep" (10, 11); and who has greater care of the weakest of his flock than the one of whom Isaias spoke? (Is. 40, 11).

His tenderness for His disciples is evident on many occasions. It pains

Him that he must leave them, but He makes up His mind to do it, promising to prepare a place for them, to send His Spirit, and finally that He will some day take them to Himself. He pours out upon them tokens of His love by offering Himself in sacrifice and giving Himself as food. The desire of being united to them is within Him and He finds no rest till He finds a way of realizing it and making it permanent, definitive, by taking up His abode in them.

Finally, the discourse at the Supper terminates with that intense desire for unity, the ultimate fruit of love: "And the glory that thou hast given to me, I have given to them, that they may be one, even as we are one: I in them and thou in me; that they may be perfected in unity, and that the world may know that thou hast sent me, and that thou hast loved them as thou hast loved me. . . . And I have made known thy name to them, and will make it known, in order that the love with which thou hast loved me may be in them, and I in them" (17, 23-26).

If John, who set these two aspects of Christ, viz., gentleness and strength, in such vivid light, has understood how to blend them into a living unity, it is because he has grasped something of what divine love itself is.

The great majority of men frequently has only a partial and very imperfect vision of what divine love means. They see only one side of it, viz., the one that corresponds with their desires and feelings. Their idea of this love is associated with gentleness, tenderness, mildness, and merciful pardon.

However, divine love has another side to it which is essential and has been stressed in the Old Testament. It declares that this love is strong, jealous, inflexible, that "its flames are a burning fire" (Cant. 8, 6).

The "Deus aemulator," a God who is jealous because He loves, the strength of a love that "deep waters cannot quench, nor floods sweep away," all these are themes presented in the Sacred Scriptures. How would the Son of God, who had this love and "is" this love, allow any of this divine heritage to fall into disuse when revealing love to men? How could He sacrifice one aspect of it for another, even were this for the sake of rendering it more acceptable to men?

Love, like truth, is an indivisible entity, and Christ's love for men consists precisely in revealing divine love to them in its truth, no matter how hard this may be. Such was His mission on earth and it remains the same in each soul throughout time. It is because He is absolutely alone in "knowing" Love that He is able to present it in all its truthfulness, for He is this living Love.

St. John has understood the secret of this love because he lived in intimate contact with the Master and saw His Heart opened. Thus, he gives us a picture of love much different from what we imagined it to be. Our poor human psychology oscillates between poles that are not too far apart and our wisdom is most frequently only the golden mean. The Johannine Christ is of another dimension. If it is true that He possesses wisdom, it is not our wisdom, but uncreated Wisdom. The exigencies, the jealousies of divine love frighten us, shock us; but we are not capable of fathoming the depths of the tenderness and delicacy of this same love. We are equally powerless to attain either extremity of this divine love. The Saints alone would be able to say how these extremities meet. Having entered more deeply than anyone else into the depths of this mystery, St. John understood that its power of expansion was limitless. He understood that those final condemnations, those fearful judgments were expressions of Christ's love as real and authentic as His words of tenderness and His actions of devotedness.

Where we behold only unpitying harshness, John sees love. Because he "knew" Christ, because he had examined His interior character to a depth we do not attain, John had understood that a portrait of Christ would not resemble Him if it were only similar to a man, even though this man was the purest, the greatest, and the best. This portrait resembles Him only if it resembles God.

What is marvelous about the fourth Gospel is that it gives us a portrait of Christ in which, besides His human traits, we perceive a higher and very mysterious dimension, viz., that of His divinity.

John's Christ is simple, but this simplicity is not only human; it is divine, for it both hides and reveals to beings and to things that perfect presence which absolute simplicity alone is capable of doing.

John's Christ is wise, but this wisdom is not simply the fruit of a profound and perfectly balanced psychology, allowing its possessor to plan well, to judge, and make decisions with a superior lucidity. Christ's wisdom is divine, it is carried on in another world which escapes men and that is why they call "folly" the things this wisdom leads Him to do.

John's Christ is humble, but this humility is not only human in the sense of urging Him to make Himself smaller, more hidden. Christ is certainly hidden and this to the highest degree, but His humility transcends ours, for it urges Him to be glorified in Himself as well as to glorify His Father. It invites Him to give testimony and to draw attention to Himself, in order that in knowing Him we may know His Father. He is not only associated with His Father, united to Him: He and the Father are "one"; and that is why everything that procures His own glory procures glory for the Father also.

Such is His utter detachment that He can and must be "lifted up from the earth to draw all men to himself" (12, 32). His humility is so transcendent that it is identified with His glory, just as this glory manifests itself best in the abasements into which love draws Him.

John's Christ is expressed totally in love, but this love resembles what we term love only vaguely, for it is as vast as the divinity, it contains everything, embraces everything, transforms everything into itself. Thus, we cannot doubt that Christ's words and actions, which seem to us totally different from what we call love, are really its authentic manifestations.

If we would have such a love come into our souls, we must enlarge our concepts of love. And it is only when we shall have succeeded in discovering love in all Christ's actions, words, and attitudes that His portrait will become clear to us and we shall finally know Love.

CHAPTER 7

CHRIST THE LIFE

I. THE MYSTERY OF THE DIVINE LIFE

From the first reading of the fourth Gospel, the terms *life* and *light* appear as the major themes around which the Johannine thought revolves. But these themes are dependent upon a Reality that is above them and assumes them into itself. Indeed, the life to which John refers is not some obscure and impersonal force, but the reality communicated to us by the Savior, viz., His own life.

This life is a light for man. "And the life was the light of men" (1, 4); this light, qualified at times as the light of life (8, 12), and at other times as the light of truth (3, 21), emanates from Christ Himself: "He was the true light that enlightens every man" (1, 9). Chosen by Christ Himself and transmitted to us by John, these great themes stress the essential aspects of His plan of Redemption.

Nevertheless, the revelation they give us bears especially upon Christ to whom they refer and who fulfills them. The essential thing is to realize that He is this Life and this Light, being the living Truth.

The following questions could arise: Is Christ life and light in Himself and in an absolute manner, or is He these only for our sakes? Do the terms have a transcendent signification coming from an eternal reality in God? Is the Word life and light by nature? Or are we simply dealing with functional characteristics having no significance except in relationship to us? Is it through the gift He makes of Himself that Christ becomes life and light for us?

If human words, in some way, are deprived of their usual meaning when they are applied to God, and if from this aspect we can say that God is in Himself nothing of what we term life and light, it must still be affirmed that Christ is in the most perfect manner and in the highest degree whatever He communicates to us. He could not be our life, if He were not life in a supereminent degree; He could not be light of the world and the light of men, if He were not the light in Himself. To carry out His office as Mediator it is necessary that He be first in Himself what He is for us. While an ordinary intermediary is content to transmit to others what he does not possess essentially as his own, a Mediator by definition must be what he communicates and this to a perfect degree.

There is no opposition then, but rather a link between the Person of Christ and His mission. We cannot fully understand the real value of the gifts Christ confers upon us unless we first consider in Him the Word who possesses these gifts as His own, and this is the role of the Prologue; secondly, we must consider Christ who communicates them to us, and this is the role of the Gospel, which instructs us particularly in the nature of this light and life and in their communication to men.

Life is present throughout the fourth Gospel. Intimately linked to the Person and presence of Christ, it shines out in each of His words and actions and miracles. It is identified with Him. To approach Christ is equivalent to approaching life's very source and to be united to life. To possess Him is to possess life for "He who has the Son has the life" (I Jn. 5, 12).

Life is a mystery and it is the divine mystery par excellence; that is why it is the privileged manifestation of God. Before all other things, it is life that Christ has come to bring to men. The gift of life contains all other gifts.

Sermons, actions, miracles, all these introduce us in a gradual way to life and teach us the ways through which it is born, develops, is nourished, is restored if we lose it, and finally affirms its victory over death in a very definite way.

Nevertheless, all these things would still not suffice to reveal its secret to us. What does Christ mean when He states that He has come to give us life? (10, 10) His passion and death alone will aid us in discovering the answer. The mystery of life is not elucidated except in the light of the sacrifice of love of the Good Shepherd who "gives his life for his sheep" (10, 15).

We must make our point of departure from that fundamental affirmation of the Prologue: "In the beginning was the Word, and the Word was with God, and the Word was God" in order to arrive at the other affirmation which flows from it: "He was the life of every being...."[1]

Life, that essential first reality upon which all others rest, has its source in the Word who possesses it as His own in an absolute way. He does not have life, but He is life and all beings draw their life from His.

1. Bible de Jérusalem, (1, 4.)

The mystery lies in this that between the divine life and that which God communicates to His creatures, there exists simultaneously an infinite distance and true relationship authorizing us to speak of a participation; and it is a participation which does not hinder the divine life from remaining without any proportion or similarity to everything we can know or imagine. That is the reason we shall not be able to become conscious of the revelation contained in the Johannine Gospel, unless we break asunder the narrow confines in which our concept of life is enclosed; unless we cast ourselves into the infinite ocean of being and of the divine life; unless we try to see that God has placed in us the desire and thirst for His own life.

The first thing necessary is to cast aside all fixed ideas and place ourselves face to face with the mystery proposed in the Prologue: "In the beginning was the Word." There is perfect identity between this Word and the God of Genesis who revealed His name to Moses; but this time the divine reality is there actually living before us. This reality comes to us "in Person." This life which Christ brings to us is the very life that made the men of the Old Testament tremble with fear. Before it, Abraham, Moses, Isaias, Daniel, all hid their faces and fell prostrate upon the ground in mortal terror. "Woe is me, I am doomed; I have seen the King, the Lord of hosts" (Is. 6, 4).

Before this mystery we must "remove the sandals of our daily existence" as did Moses, and consider the communication it is making to us; we should try to visualize the abyss between ourselves and God, between our life and His. Then only will there begin to appear before us in its true dimension the mystery of a life which *is* in itself and for itself; it is immense, infinite, unique, and yet interiorly rich with an infinite communion of divine and eternal exchanges among the Persons. We get the true dimension of a life which remains inaccessible to us, as a mountain whose ascent no one can undertake nor even see its summit. We get the true dimension of a life which remains inaccessible to us as a mountain is related to nothing, and leans on nothing for support. It is immutable and supremely active and is without beginning or end. For God is through Himself, in Himself, and with Himself. He creates and contains all things in Himself, and beings have life only in the measure they have received it from Him.

Every human life is a life received, shared, and communicated; it is always dependent upon another, upon which it leans, seeking in it what it lacks and which it will never possess as its own. It is limited, fragile, passing, always in danger, forever compromised, menaced by adverse forces which may at any moment overwhelm or extinguish it. In spite of all these things, a human life still remains something great, exalted and unique; even its very brevity confers upon it a tragic and heart-rending beauty. But what is all this when compared with the formidable mystery of the divine life, of that "infinite ocean of being"?

We are always coming in contact with this mystery of the divine life, but this contact with this inscrutable reality is salutary. In fact, we must learn how to live in the presence of the life of God, until that moment when its infinitude impregnates and penetrates us and casts us down in adoration before it. We must allow ourselves to be borne along on the immense wave of this limitless ocean until we cry out with the apostle: "Oh, the depth of the riches of the wisdom and the knowledge of God!" (Rom. 11, 33).

If the thought of death frightens us at times, our fright should be even greater before this "life" without end and without limits which is none other than the very life of the living God.

Life transmitted by Christ

The mystery of life in God is a purely spiritual reality in the bosom of which reality "life" and "word" are identified. By the very fact that God utters or expresses His Word, the divine life is in infinite and eternal act. But when it is a question of beings like ourselves, God can no longer be content with expressing Himself, in order that life be communicated to these beings. It is further necessary that the Word come to us, this creative, illuminating, and all-powerful Word. When giving us His Word He gives us life in Him.

Furthermore, it is necessary that this life be manifested to us under a form that we can understand. That is why God makes our own nature the channel that the divine life borrows to communicate itself to us. It is a nature, totally like our own, that the Word assumes to come to us and give life. And this life is not however a life of the same nature as our own, but His own, viz., the divine life.

However, Christ's human nature has as its function the revealing of this divine life to us before communicating it. It is in seeing Christ actually living a life similar to ours under our very eyes that the mystery of the divine life will be revealed to us, drawn from that fountain eternally springing up.

Christ's Person is then the whole revelation of God and the communication of life. The epiphany of the Word made flesh is a theophany incomparably more revealing than all those of the Old Testament, for it is supremely personal, without any intermediary, total, immediate, and both interior and exterior. But the revelation of life demands that Christ be living in us personally in order to be realized. And His teaching will progress in us to the same degree as our union with Him. The mystery of the divine life cannot be received except from Christ and it cannot be perceived except through Him. We shall know God is life in direct proportion to Christ's having become our life.

"Life" and "kingdom"

John always speaks in the present when he refers to this life which Christ possesses and brings to us. "He who has the Son has the life" (1 Jn. 5, 12). Whether he is dealing with its birth in us (3, 3), its development (4, 14), its increase in us through our submission to the word (5, 21), through eating the Eucharist (6, 54), or through faith (3, 16), John always refers to it as a reality given right now. And this life is eternal life. (6, passim; 1 Jn. 1, 1). These two latter expressions which are characteristic of the Johannine Gospel and practically synonymous are closely related to that other reality which has the name "kingdom of God" or "kingdom of heaven."[2]

The opening of the interview with Nicodemus shows us that John is not only acquainted with it, (how could he forget a reality so frequently spoken of by Christ?) but also that there is a link between the notions of *kingdom* and *life*. But is there in St. John a passage from one to the other? Would the two terms kingdom and life be practically interchangeable for him, and this to such an extent that where the Synoptics say: "enter the kingdom of heaven, possess the kingdom," John would say: "enter into life, possess life"? Such a statement would be rash. We are in fact in the presence of two notions which, for all their close dependence one upon the other, are nevertheless really and clearly distinct.

In the Synoptics, especially in St. Matthew, the kingdom refers to a reality the notion of which is inherited from the Old Testament and is rich in meaning. God is the unique King of this community which His Son has come to found. He has come to instruct Israel concerning this kingdom and the necessary conditions for entering into it. It is established in a very hidden way, but its modest beginnings conceal a limitless power of development which will never cease till the end of time. This kingdom is conquered by fidelity, and it demands that one follow the straight path of obedience and renunciation. Open to the little and the humble of heart, it is closed against the proud who boast of their justice. Sinners will enter it before them. Its charter is the Beatitudes. These announce it and present

---

2. St. Matthew uses the expression "kingdom of heaven" 51 times.

it as a reality which, though destined to expand fully in the next life, begins to be set up here on earth. Those who are "poor in spirit," who "hunger and thirst after justice" (Mt. 5, 3, 10) enter into possession already of this kingdom which is "among us" (Lk. 17, 21). Often compared to a banquet to which, through the Son's voice, the Father convokes His children, this kingdom, of which so many parables give us an idea, finds a rough draft in the Church.

St. John is acquainted with all the above ideas. And he is not unaware how much the words "kingdom of God," "kingdom of heaven" underscore the family aspect of eternal life: the sharing in common of all God's children in an identical life, in the same banquet at the Father's table; and he stresses these things by making eternal life the privilege of "the children of God," viz., all those gathered together in their Father's house and sharing the same meal prepared for them.

However, even though leaving somewhat in the background this really important aspect of the development and growth of the kingdom, John applies himself to revealing what constitutes the essence of this spiritual kingdom, viz., the communication of the divine life itself, the sharing in the very life of God; in short, he shows what flows directly from the fact of our divine filiation or adoptive sonship. And is this not what stands out in the parables as a whole, especially the parable of the Prodigal Son?

Consequently, anxious to point out what makes us children of God, John usually uses the word "life" or eternal life in preference to kingdom. Not that he does not appreciate the richness of the latter expression. He prefers to go directly to the reality, instead of using images of a feast in which the description runs the risk of appealing to our earthly imaginations.[3]

Life possessed here on earth

However the ideas of development and growth are not absent from this eternal life, this free and indivisible gift of God. In fact, in each child of God *life* is a dynamic reality both perpetually becoming and growing. Furthermore, the notion of unity that dominates the entire Johannine Gospel is itself included in the idea of life (cf. 17, passim), for the pres-

3. Such a passage could be misunderstood if poorly interpreted: "And I appoint to you a kingdom, even as my Father has appointed to me, that you may eat and drink at my table in my kingdom; and you shall sit upon thrones, judging the twelve tribes of Israel" (Lk. 22, 29-30). Cf. the request of the mother of the sons of Zebedee, "Command that these my two sons may sit, one at thy right hand and one at thy left hand in thy kingdom" (Mt. 20, 21).

ence in each of the same divine life works ceaselessly "in gathering into one the children of God scattered abroad" (11, 52).

What John intends to point out in these words of life and eternal life is the continuity which joins this world to the other through the apparent rupture of death; the spiritual realities which are the lot of the children of God here below and those which will make their beatitude in heaven. Is not the divine life *even now* infused into their souls, and do they not live from it now?

Before Lazarus' tomb Christ strongly affirms the permanence of this life in the believer's soul. "He who lives and believes in me, shall not die" (11, 26), and "He who believes in me, even if he die, shall live." Death has no power over this divine life.

To some the *kingdom* is a reality whose definite establishment must be postponed until the Parousia. Nothing like this is to be feared when we conform our idea of life with that presented in John's Gospel. Life is identified with the possession of God in Christ and with our status as "child of God" (11, 25).

The many statements of this nature found in his Gospel allow no doubt of the orientation of John's thought. Whether it is question of faith (1, 12), of love (1 Jn. 5, 1), of fidelity to Christ's word, he returns always to that basic certitude enunciated in his first Epistle: "And this is the testimony, that God has given us eternal life; and this life is in his Son. He who has the Son has life" (1 Jn. 5, 12). John's gaze and thought are fixed upon a total presence that exists now in the immediate present, viz., Christ, and not some distant reality.

According to him, what forms the major preoccupation of the Christian is not so much the entrance into the kingdom promised as a reward for his fidelity at the end of his life, but rather the participation offered here and now in a "life" (1 Jn. 5, 11) in the Son (1 Jn. 4, 7). His concentration will be on an approach to Christ, a belonging to Him, a receiving of Him, and union in Him. To be in Jesus Christ is to have eternal life, for "he is the true God and eternal life" (1 Jn. 5, 20). Was this not what his Prologue would have us understand under another form: "But as many as received him he gave the power of becoming the sons of God, to those who believe in his name" (1, 12)? The interview with Nicodemus is very specific about the nature of this birth announced in the Prologue. Having started out by speaking of the kingdom of God, the interview proceeds to speak of nothing else but birth and life (3, 3-8,15,16). The Epistle states that this life is not only a hope for the future, but a reality of the here and now. "Behold what manner of love the Father has bestowed upon us, that we should be called the children of God; and such we are" (1 Jn. 3, 1).

The more we reflect upon the Johannine concept of things, the more we discover the degree to which it points to a renewed concept of the life of the child of God, i.e., the Christian. Life here on earth takes its true supernatural dimension from this fact, since it is no longer only an expectation, a trial and an experience; but it is also and already, though in a hidden fashion and in faith, a *possession* and even at times an *experience* of the divine life in the soul.

Our ideas concerning the next world become more elevated and spiritualized. To those striving to live in divine intimacy, eternal life appears as the full development of a reality of which they are already actually in possession of assurances and guarantees. Also, life here on earth becomes authentically spiritual since the life of the Spirit is already in act in it. In fact, there is no spiritual life except the life which permits us to know God "in spirit and in truth" and, at least in a certain measure, of experiencing Him. For such a knowledge is likewise one of the characteristics under which John presents eternal life to us (17, 3), and hence it is formed and commenced here on earth. It comes to us and it develops through the knowledge of God "in his envoy, Jesus Christ" (17, 3).

Intimately connected with our very existence of which it is both the soul and the hidden fount, this life is also closely united with this existence. It utilizes it to realize and develop itself. Indeed, it is not sheltered from dangers which threaten this existence; it undergoes the blows of these dangers and it can be always lost (1 Jn. 1, 9). In a word, this divine life is, in the child of God who is faithful in preserving it at the price of a generous struggle, the source of a plenitude which generates a real joy (15, 11; 16, 22).

Thanks to this change of perspective, the entire aspect of the Christian life is transformed. Instead of introducing into the kingdom a "human" concept of happiness as often happens, and at the same time of paradoxically lowering a barrier of separation between this life and the other, the Christian penetrated with the Johannine thought suddenly discovers that he actually carries in himself what will go to make up his eternal beatitude: this divine life, actually hidden, but which will appear tomorrow in glory (1 Jn. 3, 2).

The child of God is permeated through and through here on earth with the divine life and this in direct proportion to the way he applies himself in allowing Christ, His Father, and the Spirit to take up their abode in him (14, 22). The kingdom of God is not only among us, but in the midst and in the intimate depths of the soul of each of us.

The Christian is careful then to know the one who dwells in him, filling him and communicating eternal life to him. He discovers this great hidden treasure: the indwelling of Christ in the soul, through the Spirit.

It is an indwelling in which he has no difficulty in recognizing this "fountain of water springing up into eternal life" (4, 14) about which Christ spoke with the Samaritan woman. Hence, in the midst of difficulties, trials, and sufferings, the Christian is fully conscious of himself as being intimately and constantly united to God and sharing in His life. Kept by the Father and the Son (17, 11), and handed over by them to the Holy Spirit (14, 16; 16, 7), he realizes that within him he possesses the seed of eternal life; he knows that even now he is the child of God (1 Jn. 3, 2) since the Spirit lives within him. Thus, he tries to cooperate with the planting of this grace within him and bringing it to fructification. He lives the life which Christ came to give him. He realizes it has on earth limitless possibilities of development and depth. For this the necessary condition must be realized in him, viz., close union with Christ, the principle and source of life. "He who has the Son has the life" (1 Jn. 5, 12).

Life and the sign of the Cross

This divine life brought by Christ knows in itself neither shadow nor limit. It is eternal life, perpetually springing up and infinitely superabundant (10, 10). It is affected, however, in the fourth Gospel, by a very particular characteristic which John never ceases stressing. It carries the sign and the stigmata of the Passion. The life communicated through Christ to us comes through His death.

Life, Truth, and Light. It would be dangerous for us sinful and weak creatures to consider these notions of Life, Truth and Light, on a purely abstract and philosophical plane; to imagine they can be joined and attained by us without first having undergone the necessary trials and purifications. John never considers them in the abstract. To him they are always: Life of Christ, Light of Christ. Better still, Christ is there in Person. How could John possibly separate himself from the concrete way in which they had been presented to him, viz., in Christ. Undoubtedly God could have communicated Life and Light to us in a direct way and without any other condition necessary for receiving them than the presence of our own good will. John, however, as we see, is a "witness" of a Reality, Christ, who is woven into the texture of life. John bears witness to the fact that God has spared men any conditions necessary for entering into the possession of Life, Truth, and Light; and that He has asked His Son, at the cost of His sufferings and death, to create from these very sufferings and death new conditions through which men will have access to this Life, Truth, and Light.

Through this, the veritable dimension of divine things will be revealed to men: the dimension which love confers upon these things. And at the same time, this Life which will come to them will be able truly to appear to them as the very Life of Christ. And it will not be a present that one offers without any pain or sacrifice, but it will be a gift that is at once onerous and loving; and this love will be in direct proportion to what it has actually cost.

If then in the Johannine Gospel Christ appears as the Life, this Life is always marked with the sign not only of gift but of sacrifice. The Life received from Him is a life that has been "offered up." He does not give us "Life" except in giving "His" Life.

Allusions to the sacrifice and death of Christ are always combined with the statement that Christ is the Life and the source of Life. These allusions are mostly always hidden and veiled, and yet there is a transparency about them, e.g., the name, Lamb of God, with which the Baptist salutes Christ (1, 29,36); the allusion is more concealed in the episode at Cana, but very clear in the episode of the Cleansing of the Temple (2, 19-22). Both introduce the dimension of the Cross in the work Christ has come to accomplish here on earth at the command of His Father.

In the interview with Nicodemus, that bond between Life and Sacrifice is underscored in a very positive way. Jesus has just pointed out to this "teacher in Israel" that it is necessary to be born again, i.e., to take on an entirely new spiritual life; his listener is far from suspecting that this birth must issue forth from a death. Jesus is not unaware of this. But He knows too that a too clearly expressed declaration of the mystery of the Cross would produce nothing but scandal and revulsion in the mind of Nicodemus. However, He judges that at the time when this new birth is revealed to the world, it is impossible to pass over in silence the price this life has cost, as well as the way through which it will actually come to men. He speaks of it then in veiled words, the sense of which, though hidden to Nicodemus, is clear now to us.

"And as Moses lifted up the serpent in the desert, even so must the Son of Man be lifted up, that those who believe in him may not perish, but may have life everlasting. For God has so loved the world that he gave his only-begotten Son, that those who believe in him may not perish, but may have everlasting life" (3, 14-16). Through a death and a death on the Cross life will be communicated to the world.

Other allusions are evident in the Johannine text. "I have sent you to reap that on which you have not labored." These words Christ will speak to His disciples at the time of their return from the Samaritan village where they bought supplies. It was the occasion on which Jesus had revealed "the gift of God" to the Samaritan woman. And He adds: "Others have labored." Who else if not the Master Himself. He sowed in tears and lets us reap in joy (4, 38).

We cannot read Chapter 5 without the image of Christ's death and resurrection coming before our eyes as the principle of life for the world. (Cf. 5, 19-47) The idea underlies everything and it is this that confers upon Christ's declarations their real meaning (5, 21,24,25). Of the bread which comes down from heaven and gives life to the world Christ will say: "This is my flesh for the life of the world" (6, 51); and again, "Unless you eat the flesh of the Son of man and drink his blood, you shall not have life in you" (6, 53). He could not state more clearly that life comes to us through his death.

Later, John, reporting the Master's words, "When you have lifted up the Son of man, then you will know that I am he . . ."(8, 28) teaches us that the Revelation of the Living God whose Name is Life will come to us only through the Cross. And this same truth is taught by Christ when, as the Good Shepherd, He does not give life except by giving His own life. "I came that you may have life and have it more abundantly. I am the good shepherd. The good shepherd lays down his life for his sheep" (10, 10). "And I give them eternal life" (10, 28).

With the episode of Lazarus, a figure of Christ's victory over death, the idea is enriched and made even more precise since life comes forth literally from the tomb (11, 25,43). A new allusion to life which comes from death is met with in the words of Jesus to Andrew and Philip. "Amen, amen, I say to you, unless the grain of wheat fall into the ground and die, it remains alone. But if it die, it brings forth much fruit. He who loves his life, loses it; and he who loses his life in this world, keeps it unto life everlasting" (12, 24). And again, "And I, if I be lifted up from the earth, will draw all men to myself" (12, 32).

The Passover will set a seal upon this mysterious truth of a Life which comes to us marked with the sign of death, as Caiphas had unknowingly prophesied. "You know nothing at all; nor do you reflect that it is expedient for us that one man die for the people, instead of the whole nation perishing" (11, 50). The hour had arrived when all that had been pointed out or even only suggested is going to be fulfilled. Henceforth, it will be impossible for Christians when considering Christ as the source of life and eternal life not to recall that this life came to them through death on the Cross.

This conviction, firmly anchored in the apostle's heart, will be further enriched during the final hours preceding the Master's sacrifice. In fact, in the entire discourse after the Supper there is no longer question of life coming forth from death, but of love carried to the length of total sacrifice and rendering this life communicated to the world fruitful. Christ had only recently said that He came "in order that they may have life and have it more abundantly" (10, 10). He revealed the price of purchase: "Unless the grain of wheat fall into the ground and die . . ." (12, 24). And now returning to what He had said, "If it die, it brings forth much fruit" (12, 24), Jesus insists upon the limitless fruitfulness of this divine life granted at such a high price and offered up in a love so great that there cannot be a greater (15, 13), and He will be able to say, "He who abides in me, as I in him, bears much fruit" (15, 5,8).

Such is the atmosphere in which Christ intends to reveal the Christ-Life. It is as deeply life-giving as it is admirably balanced. And is it not even now that this divine life is offered for us in plenitude and totality? But is it not also always marked with the sign of the Cross, and does it not come to us in this way? The Johannine realism is to be found here.

II. CHRIST, OUR LIFE

It seems that Christ, to help us better understand the nature and role of this life he brought, did not hesitate to make certain analogies between it and human life, and to set their respective needs in parallel lines.

Life on earth requires a *birth*; afterwards there is a development from an internal dynamism ensuring its continuity and advancement. Life is also acquainted with the necessity of a *victorious struggle* against interior and exterior dangers that menace it; life must be *nourished* and *sustained* constantly; life, finally, tends towards a *full expansion* which, in creatures endowed with a spiritual life, aspires after a stable and definite fulfillment.

The miracles and discourses reported in chapters 3, 4, 5, 6, and 11 of John's Gospel and in this order seem to contain teachings based on the above data, transposing them to the supernatural plane.

Birth from on high

"As the Father has life in himself, even so he has given to the Son also to have life in himself."[4] The Son dispenses this life first by giving us the power to be born into it. This is the object of His interview with Nicodemus.

"Unless a man be born from on high . . ." (3, 3). The word which qualifies this birth means both *again* and *from on high*.[5] However, we

4. "Comme le Pere dispose de la vie, ainsi a-t-il donne au Fils d'en disposer, lui aussi" (Bible de Jérusalem, 5, 26).
5. Greek word "anothen" means both "de sursum" and "iterum."

want to retain the latter sense here. How would not a birth from on high be basically *new* since, in contrast to all carnal births which borrow elements from the surrounding realities of the cosmos to form new life, birth in the Spirit comes totally from on high! It is not a question, as Nicodemus imagined, of being "born a second time," nor of being born in the sense of a renewal or an imperfectly realized purification, as this does not eliminate what radically existed beforehand. Rather it is a question of being born "from on high," and from this supernatural origin proceeds this absolute newness of life.

Nicodemus judges it impossible and unthinkable and so casts aside the true meaning of the term *born from on high*; he favors one of the conceptions current in ancient times, viz., regeneration, without of course judging this concept acceptable. "Can a man enter a second time into his mother's womb and be born again?" Jesus brings him back to the real birth, the birth from on high, by revealing its spiritual nature: "Amen, amen, I say to you, unless a man be born again of water and the Spirit, he cannot enter into the kingdom of God. That which is born of the flesh is flesh; and that which is born of the Spirit is spirit. Do not wonder that I said to thee, 'You must be born from on high' " (3, 5-7).

Jesus brings out the most tangible element and the external condition for this birth, viz., baptism. The water constitutes the matter and expresses its purifying aspect. But Christ adds another element conferring upon it a supernatural value, viz., the Spirit. Since it is question of a birth or an entrance into a life, Jesus specifies that this life is that of the Spirit. Even though it is invisible and escapes our influence, it is nevertheless real. And He makes a comparison with the wind: though we are certain of its effects, we neither see it and we do not know whence it comes or where it goes.

Although this "birth of the Spirit" far surpassed what was said in the Old Testament about the effects of the Spirit (some of which were: making the prophets speak, being a principle of interior renewal) it should not have remained inconceivable to a teacher in Israel but should have fallen in line with a fulfillment of the Scriptures.

When making a contrast between birth according to the flesh and that according to the spirit, was Jesus pointing out likewise the activity required of a man to be born to the spiritual life, since his passivity is complete when he is born according to the flesh? This is not certain. We are not prohibited from thinking so and the expression, "You must be born from on high" seems to imply it. In fact, if God alone can effect birth from on high, and if baptism of water for the greater number of us who are baptized is conferred without our own initiative, on the other hand, birth according to the Spirit demands our effective participation during our whole life. The point of departure for our "spiritual life" is due to the action and grace of God; but this same life is not maintained and not developed unless our activity corresponds with the gift of God.

Christ finally gives us a glimpse of the condition necessary for this birth "from water and the Spirit," viz., His Passion and Death on the Cross. He presents this truth to Nicodemus under a figure taken from Exodus as he would not be able to make any clear allusion to an execution and death. The necessity of so concealing this teaching because of the state of his listener must not veil its great importance in our eyes. We are at the very heart of the mystery of salvation here.

Baptism is necessary in order to unite us to Christ's death which effaces our sins. Just as the brazen serpent was raised on the standard and cured those who looked upon it, so the Son of Man will realize our salvation when He is raised up on the Cross (Nb. 21, 6-9). This is His role as Redeemer.

In a few extraordinarily compact statements Christ points out to Nicodemus and to all men the conditions of this new birth without which no one can enter the kingdom. John insists on the last of these conditions in reflections that are closely intermingled with the Master's words. Christ had said: "Yes, God has so loved the world that he has given his only-begotten Son . . ." and John added: "so that all who believe in him will not perish, but have eternal life" (3, 5,16). The Father's love is expressed in the gift of His Son and the Son's love is expressed in the gift of Himself on the Cross. And our response to this love is faith; the result of this encounter of our faith with divine Love is salvation and eternal life. All this is summed up in a few lines containing John's thought.

Even when reduced to its point of departure, viz., birth, our Christian life places us before the mystery of death and love. As joyous as are this birth and our accession to life, it is impossible to forget the price that was paid for them. Just as a mother who buys with her own life the coming of her child into the world, so Christ must give His life in sacrifice to give us this spiritual birth.

A fountain springing up unto life everlasting

Jesus revealed that man must be reborn of water and the Holy Spirit. Using this same symbol of water, He explains certain traits of this life to the Samaritan woman. Here He no longer envisions it as purifying but as life-giving. The water becomes *living* water; it is the principle of a constant, spiritual renewal. The important word in this interview is *fountain*. The woman quickly grasps this although a slave to earthly realities.

Christ says: "He, however, who drinks of this water that I will give him shall never thirst; but the water that I will give him shall become in him a fountain of water, springing up unto life everlasting" (4, 14). She immediately requests: "Sir, give me this water that I may not thirst or come here to draw." We are being introduced here to the first of two main ideas in this interview: that of life envisaged as a fountain perpetually springing up and renewing itself. Jesus had said to Nicodemus: "God has so loved the world that he has given his only-begotten Son" (3, 16), and now to her He says: "If thou didst know the gift of God. . . ."

If to "be born from on high" is an unspeakable gift of God's love for man, to realize that this life remains a fountain perpetually springing up in us, the principle of a renewal drawing the soul towards eternal life, this is a revelation even more overwhelming.

Jesus had spoken of the need of being born of water. This water would remain immobile and dormant though filled with a supernatural power. But here we are shown its rich and hidden potentialities. The marvel of this interview is that this water gives life and is actually living; it stirs up in souls the most profound and revealing insights that could be given of divine life. And this simply because Christ speaks of *living* water.

The place—that great arid plain, bathed in the sun and set over against the rough slopes of Ebal and Gerizim; the hour—noon; the nature of this water hidden in Palestine's deepest well—it is not the still, motionless water of a cistern, but water incessantly renewed from a spring; all these facts, even the effort a man must make to draw out this water to quench his thirst, speak silently to the soul and teach a lesson.

Between water stagnating in a cistern and this living and life-giving water, there is a distance as measureless as that between the baptized soul that allows the gift of God to lie dormant within it, and those for whom this gift is a fountain of life, forever springing up and bubbling over and productive of good works.

Bouyer writes: "The mysterious power of this water given by Christ is such that the one who has drawn at the fountain uncovers a fountain within himself. What he has drawn is divine life, love perpetually in act. He cannot have this love within himself, without loving; he cannot possess this gift, without giving himself and without discovering new possibilites of self-giving whose measure will be known only in eternity."[6]

This divine life comes from heaven and yet, as the Gospel account gives us to understand, it buries itself in the innermost depths of the hum-

6. L. Bouyer, The Fourth Gospel, p. 102.

blest being. It is a current as interior as it is divine, for this fountain of life is found only in these interior depths of the soul. A certain recollection is necessary if it is to be perceived. Man must recollect himself in order to gather this water and to experience its power and live with its life.

But while it invites us to a recollection upon a presence and a living love, the Gospel account encourages us on to ever higher ascents. The ascents, so well expressed in the image of a water springing up from the earth, are what the apostle would have us see since he himself experienced them and lived them. John would undoubtedly have agreed with Gregory of Nyssa's expression concering divine life: it was a going "from beginnings to beginnings through endless beginnings."

Rivers of living water

"Now on the last day of the feast, Jesus stood and cried out saying, 'If anyone thirst, let him come to me and drink. He who believes in me, as the Scripture says, from within him there shall flow rivers of living water.' He said this, however, of the Spirit whom they who believe in him were to receive" (7, 37-39).

Hence we have: birth to divine life, its springing up, renewal, and fecundity. Christ has set this life before the soul and He has pointed out its progress which is both mysterious and endless. And here these "rivers of living water" which flow from Christ are the Spirit. We are presented with those extensions this life is destined to know because of the Spirit who is given by Christ. If Christ is the source of this life and its eternally active principle, the Spirit is the "life of this Life." He is at work in us from the very beginning of this life (3, 5) and He is needed in order that its activity develop. Without the Spirit, the believer could not become "an adorer in spirit and in truth" (4, 23).

Thus this adoration which is the manifestation of the spiritual life demands the presence and action of the Spirit of Christ in the soul; to Him pertains its deepening and development.

How rich and new is the life of him in whom the Spirit of Christ dwells! This divine presence fashions him in the innermost depths of his being and flows into his conduct. The one in whom Christ and the Spirit dwell acts according to norms which do not come under the ordinary ways of seeing, feeling, and acting. Not that the human faculties are in any way impaired; on the contrary, they remain highly adapted to surrounding realities. But there is something about the conduct of such a one that is not easy to explain. He alone who lives under the Spirit's guidance can explain it, while others perceive its effects. The matter is somewhat comparable to a tree which, though remaining rooted in the earth, sways to the breeze which the spectator notices without feeling its effects upon him as he is sheltered from the breeze; or it is like the tree that remains verdant and alive in the midst of a drought simply because its roots have found an invisible spring.

We see then: if the Spirit did not come to follow up and perfect Christ's work, a certain depth and richness of development would be lacking to the life brought to us, to say nothing of the possibility of an experience of God.

There is another deepening of the divine life linked no longer directly to the Spirit's action in us, but to the revelation of divine love. The life such as Christ brought it to us is not limited to a birth, followed up by a development and a constant renewal. This life tends towards a definite goal which is union, and this union does not attain its purpose unless it produces fruitfulness in unity. . . . Then only does the divine life in us attain its ultimate dimension and meaning. . . . However, these high revelations concerning the divine life in us are too intimately connected with the last declarations of Christ to be separated from the context in which He placed them. Jesus will await the last evening of his life to reveal the mysteries of His intimate life, union, and unity with Him (Cf. cc. 16 & 17 below).

But He does not wait to prepare them to receive the "bread of life," that food through which He will renew their strength daily and teach them to live not only "from," but "because of" Him.

The living bread

The discourse on the bread of life which follows the multiplication of the loaves was destined in Christ's mind to prepare His listeners for the institution of the Eucharist. It formed the bond between the miracle that they had witnessed with their eyes and this other miracle which was to furnish them with spiritual food, viz., divine life. The transition from one to the other would be difficult (6, 26,27).

That God, in the Person of His Son, had willed to reveal to men that He was Life, a totally spiritual life, was easier to admit than the idea of this bread capable of appeasing the soul's hunger and sustaining its very life. Minds were able to arrive at the notion of a God as material provider for His people: yesterday, the manna in the desert; today, the multiplication of the loaves. They could understand how God led souls along the paths of life through the Law and through Wisdom. "He that shall find me (Wisdom) shall find life" (Dt. 8, 3). Israel realized when it approached God it was approaching Life. "For in thee is the fountain of life" (Ps. 36, 10).

But that one must eat "the bread which comes down from heaven and gives life to the world" (6, 33), and that this bread is Christ's flesh which has become nourishment: "I am the living bread that has come down from heaven . . . and the bread that I will give is my flesh for the life of the world," this was what was a stumbling block. "This is a hard saying. Who can listen to it?"

However, Christ's statements were clear and allowed of no debate. "Amen, amen, I say to you, unless you eat the flesh of the Son of man and drink his blood, you shall not have life in you. He who eats this bread shall live forever" (6, 54,59). There is no longer question of a birth to a life from on high, nor of a life springing up in us as a fountain. It is now life in its most incarnate form. The apostle places before us flesh, but flesh for our flesh. Our flesh is to receive and assimilate it. John will use the most material and concrete term, viz., "eat"; he will use this eight times so that no error is possible as to how this life is to be incorporated into ours. Christ makes Himself food, and our daily nourishment must be His flesh, and it is to be our bread. "And the bread that I will give is my flesh . . ." (6,51).

This bread is not an earthly bread, but one that "comes down from heaven" and that is why it is the "bread of life" (6, 35,48) not only for our body but more so for our soul. It is unlike the manna Moses obtained from Yahweh in the desert. Undoubtedly this too came from on high: "He rained manna upon them for food and gave them heavenly bread" (Ps. 77, 24). But the real heaven is not the one over our heads; rather it is God Himself. That is why Christ says: "Your fathers ate the manna in the desert and have died. This is the bread that comes down from heaven, so that if anyone eat of it he will not die. I am the living bread that has come down from heaven" (6, 49-51). Christ alone is the "true bread from heaven" and He alone truly "came down from heaven to give life to the world."

Thus the function of the eucharistic nourishment is brought to light and St. John uses the word bread to stress it. He calls this bread: the bread from heaven, the true bread, the bread of God (6, 33), the bread of life, the bread which gives life to the world, and finally the living bread. (Cf. 6, passim). A teaching is evidently hidden in these words and it will allow us to discover the nature of the life this bread brings us and also the fruit that should mature in the one partaking of it.

"He who eats me, he also shall live because of me"

"This is the bread that has come down from heaven; not as your fathers ate the manna and died. He who eats this bread shall live forever" (6, 58). Although it is truly a food, it is not like other material foods. Its power to nourish is essentially spiritual. If a body is needed to assimilate material food, what is necessary to receive and assimilate a spiritual food? The Gospel gives the answer: "It is the spirit that gives life; the flesh profits nothing" (6, 63). The bread of heaven surrenders its power only to those who eat it spiritually, i.e., those who receive it in faith, that spiritual organism of the children of God.

In faith, it reveals what it is in itself, viz., "a bread of life," a bread which gives life (not an earthly life but "eternal life") and gives it right now! "He who eats this bread has everlasting life" (6, 54). This bread nourishes the whole man when it is received in the flesh and in faith, if we may so express it. And that is why Christ will be able to say of the entire man: "And I will raise him up on the last day" (6, 54).

Again, to give forth all its power, this bread must be desired with a true, spiritual desire; we must hunger for this flesh and thirst for this blood. "Lord, give us always this bread!" (6, 34). To those seeking it with the right intention and with faith Christ says: "He who comes to me shall not hunger, and he who believes in me shall not thirst" (6, 35). Why is this so? Because this bread is not a food assimilated by the one who eats it; rather it is a living bread, so living that it assimilates the one receiving it and gives him a share of its own life. It is not only "a bread of life," but it is a "living bread" (6, 48,51).

When Christ desired to give this bread the power to nourish, He was simply acceding to the needs of our nature which demands daily sustenance. But as living food, the Eucharist communicates its own life and brings about a transformation in the soul. It fills the soul far beyond its desires so divinely does it nourish it. "He who comes to me shall not hunger . . ." (6, 35); and yet it constantly increases this desire while it creates the soul anew.

In fact, though the power of this bread is divine and does not lessen with time, as is the case in earthly foods, man must still make use of it as he does ordinary food, i.e., constantly. "Unless you eat the flesh of the Son of man and drink his blood, you shall not have life in you" (6, 53). Our life must have constant recourse to this food because it needs to be sustained at all times.

This need of a perpetually renewed and entertained dependence with regard to Christ introduces an indispensable complement to the teaching given by Him to both Nicodemus and the Samaritan woman. Indeed, the revelation of a birth from on high, a birth in the Spirit, as also the teaching concerning the fountain of water springing up unto eternal life, both these teachings could have given man the impression that the divine life was in his possession henceforth; and that life of the spirit, that subtle, flowing, invisible, and intangible life dispensed him from making any recourse to anything else and set him up in some kind of autonomy.

The discourse on the bread of life reminds him that this life "in the spirit" subsists only on condition of being constantly attached to its source. It asks that one come as a poor man, a beggar stripped of everything, in order to ask from God the alms of life. To cease coming to Him and to stop being nourished by Him is tantamount to ceasing to live spiritually. "Unless you eat the flesh of the Son of Man and drink his blood, you shall not have life in you" (6, 53). In other words, the one who comes to Christ saying: "Give us this day our daily bread" experiences a marvelous growth and enters gradually into the depths of the divine life.

It is noteworthy that in the announcement concerning the Eucharist the first stage of a teaching is introduced which will be later taken up again in the discourse after the Supper. In fact, we read here: "He who eats my flesh and drinks my blood abides in me and I in him" (6, 56). This expression "to abide" is one of the major themes of the discourse at the Supper. And we also have: "As the living Father sent me and as I live because of the Father, so he who eats me shall live because of me" (6, 57).

We come in contact here with a profound teaching. It throws light upon what must be understood when we say Christ is our life in the Eucharist. "To abide in him" and "to live because of him" are characteristics of this life which Christ reveals and communicates simultaneously. Although these are granted conjointly, they act ordinarily only successively. For the divine life to be operative in us, it is first necessary that we learn "to abide" in Christ, and that Christ be able to abide in us. The Eucharist furnishes the means for this each day. Every day, in fact, the Eucharist makes it possible for us to "live with" Christ, "convivere" as the words of the "O Sacrum Convivium" have it. This is the first step. And the second consists in "living from," and the last "in living because of." Through these repeated contacts and through that encounter realized with Christ at this depth and with this intimacy a knot is tied. It is no longer question of two beings associated in the pursuit of the same end and walking the same road, but of a union so close that they are veritably present to each other, living in each other. This mutual indwelling, making it possible for one to abide in Christ and Christ to abide in him, terminates in a mysterious symbiosis, through which one being lives from the other and "because of the other."

If this is possible in the realm of earthly love which unites two beings, what possibility will be offered man whom the Eucharist makes live not only in Christ but also because of Christ? This means that a soul is so totally invested with Christ's presence, thought, and will, that Christ becomes the principle of operation in him; the "I" of his being, so to speak, more truly than his own personality which is now absorbed, dissolved, and entirely united with Him.

We have not gone far enough. The words: "As the living Father has sent me and as I live because of the Father, so he who eats me shall live because of me" (6, 57) invite us to seek a model in that relationship between the Father and the Son; and even more than a model, a principle of union between us and Jesus. The Eucharist produces union and this union brings on a transformation into Christ. This transformation brings it about that His love becomes the principle of our life. We live because of Him, but this means to live "for" Him. From the union flows our consecration to His service, just as the Son who lives because of the Father lives also for Him who sent him. So through the Eucharist there is realized a "consecration" of our life to the very life of God. And this life of God is divine and eternal. Hence the discourse on the bread of life closes with the words: "This is the bread that has come down from heaven; not as your fathers ate the manna and died. He who eats this bread shall live forever" (6, 58).

Healing and restoration to life

Union with Christ is the goal to be attained, and that is the reason He returns to it and insists upon it at length in the final discourse (cf. c. 16, passim). However, Christ would have been very unrealistic if, at the same time as he proposed this ultimate development, He did not keep in mind the frail vessels into which this life is infused; and of how men can become both oblivious of God's gift and even lose it after having received it. Christ would not have been able to call Himself our life if, while giving, developing, and nourishing it, He did not also sustain, preserve and heal it; and finally, if He did not restore it to those who lost it and assure them its eternal possession without the possibility of any longer losing it.

These different aspects are present in the fourth Gospel. In chapter 4 there is the restoration to life of the royal official's son at Capharnaum. In itself this miracle of restoring to health a child at death's door is already meaningful. But John's insistence on Christ's words: "Go, your son lives" (4, 50) makes it even more meaningful. It shows clearly that in John's eyes Christ is "the living God who gives life" (2 Kgs. 2, 2-6).

The scene at the pool of Bethsaida sheds light upon another aspect, that of healing instead of restoring to life. The child at Capharnaum had been struck down suddenly by the ailment from which he was dying (4, 47). The paralytic, on the other hand, dragged out a languishing existence; he was permanently established in his malady, we might say. "Now a certain man was there who had been thirty-eight years under his infirmity" (5, 5). He needs a cure. (John uses the verb "cure" seven times in this account).

" 'Rise, take up thy pallet and walk.' And at once the man was cured. And he took up his pallet and began to walk" (5, 8,9). Later meeting him in the Temple Jesus says to him: "Behold, thou art cured. Sin no more, lest something worse befall thee." This helps us understand that the essential thing for him is the life of the soul, not physical life. Christ has come then to cure all ailments, those suddenly placing life in danger and those that are paralysing in their effects. "It is not the healthy who need a physician, but they who are sick. I have not come to call the just, but sinners to repentance" (Lk. 5, 31).

"He who believes in me shall never die"

Christ does not only heal and restore strength to a life shaken or endangered by illness. He is absolute Master of life. And the raising of Lazarus to life is striking proof of this. But here again, this life restored to a dead man, making a living being out of a corpse, should be considered from the spiritual aspect. Christ did not raise Lazarus to add "a single cubit" to his life (Lk. 12, 25), and He does not do it as proof of His omnipotence. He does it in order to place man face to face with another life, transcending mortal life and corporal death. His words to Martha are to be taken in this sense. "Thy brother shall rise again. . . . I am the resurrection and the life; he who believes in me, even if he die, shall live; and whoever lives and believes in me shall never die. Dost thou believe this?" (11, 25,26).

At the tomb and before this corpse which is about to come forth at the sound of Christ's voice, there is no question of life or death in the human sense of the term, but of eternal life. And we must view this scene in this light. "As the Father raises the dead and gives them life, even so the Son of God gives life to whom he will" (5, 22).

To this divine privilege the Son joins that of judgment which follows immediately after death. "All judgment has been given to the Son" (5, 22). And to hear His word and believe in the Father who sent Him is to have "life everlasting" and it is already to have "passed from death to life." Christ is Master of this eternal life. "For as the Father has life in himself, even so he has given the Son also to have life in himself" (5, 26).

It is of little importance that death has laid men in the tomb. At Christ's call, at the sound of His voice, "they will come forth from the tomb, and they who have done good shall come forth unto resurrection of life" (5, 28). Answering the call of His voice will be proof that death had empire only over the body and that the soul was always living, having remained united to Christ, i.e., to Life.

The risen body will rejoin this life of the soul, and this resurrection will be the work of the Word made flesh. Assuming our nature, He has clothed it in His own immortality and has made the entire man share in this life of which He is the fullness. The Jews were very blind who searched the Scriptures, hoping to find the source of life in them, when this life was there before them in Person. "You search the Scriptures, because in them you think that you have life everlasting, and it is they that bear witness of me, yet you are not willing to come to me that you may have life" (5, 39,40).

These perspectives upon the life beyond the grave, this contemplative glance upon the eternity of life or eternal Life promised to anyone who "lives and believes in him" (11, 26) are the seal placed upon the revelation of Christ the Life, the central theme of the fourth Gospel. From our birth into this new life right up to eternal life, Christ appears in John's Gospel as the source of Life and its principle of development. He is the one through whom we are promised eternal life in both body and soul.

The sacraments and the divine life

Have these aspects of the divine life, viz., its birth in us, development, nourishment, healing, and promise of eternity exhausted the mystery of the life Christ came to bring us? As necessary and enlightening as they are, it is necessary for us to recognize the fact that these are only elements and conditions and supports of this Life. In its ultimate reality this life has not yet been unveiled to us.

If we consider the different aspects thus far envisioned, we can see that they correspond with the sacraments which belong to the order of means. Whatever be their necessity and importance in the economy of salvation, nevertheless the life they are supposed to give birth to and develop and sustain in us both exists before them and will survive them. Undoubtedly until the end of the world, it will be necessary that there be a birth from water and the Holy Spirit, and the divine life will always have to spring up in us from the Spirit's action. We shall have to feed our soul on the bread of life, heal its languors and wounds and mortal falls in the Blood of Christ. But we must always remember these sacraments are only the channels of this Life. What is this Life and how are we united with it?

Love only can project a light upon the mystery of Life. Is it not love that we encounter at its very source? Even on the creature level, human life is transmitted as a gift of the whole being which, desirous of surviving itself, communicates its living forces or gathers up this life in the inmost depths of its being. This law is in the creature because it first exists in God. Having decided to communicate His own life, He takes on this task in Person, and the gift He makes to us is accomplished in an act of total love. "Greater love than this no man has than that a man lay down his life for his friends" (15, 13). And again, "The good shepherd lays down his life for his sheep" (10, 11).

Thus this life is to be found in Christ indissolubly linked up with love and sacrifice. It is from love that it is born in us. We have already remarked this but would like to repeat it: it is in His death that Christ communicates life to us, and the parable of the Good Shepherd brings this truth out into the light. Between life communicated and life sacrificed, there is more than a relationship. The life of which Christ makes the sacrifice and that which is communicated to us are identical. In Christ's death, Life is revealed to us under its true image, for it is only through love that life becomes fruitful.

This is the reason why the revelation of life is necessarily linked with the revelation of union and unity. And it is there that we shall have to go to seek the very Reality of this life, its secret, and its true dimension.

"Who has the Son has the life"

What John knew and experienced concerning divine life he found in an intimate contact with Christ. True, the sacraments introduce the soul to this union, but John knows by experience that this union is effected essentially from a realization in the depths of the soul; it stems from that "abide in me and I in you," "abide in my love," or again from, "we will come to him and make our abode with him" (15, 4,9; 14, 23).

However, John does not fail to set before us both the function and absolute necessity of the sacramental life. As witness of the Word incarnate, his intention is to transmit the Master's teaching faithfully. As the apostle of a Church which was to confront the centuries and to communicate Christ's life to men, he grasped the role of the sacraments. What would a life be, in fact, which would remain at the mercy and personal inspiration and good pleasure of each if it was not to be conveyed by any particular institution? Christ intends to have this life reach us through channels instituted by Him and these alone can communicate it to us in all fidelity and purity.

This does not mean we should take the means for the end, nor the channels for what they have a mission to convey. That is why what remains absolutely essential in the apostle's eyes is the reality of this life received and shared in. In a word, John really understood that this life was not separable from Christ and that it was identified with Him. He is the life and He alone possesses it and communicates it to us by giving Himself.

If life is a divine mystery, it is also a living and adorable presence; it is the living God come to dwell among us and giving us Himself. This revelation we come upon in those opening lines of the first Epistle, lines sparkling with the apostle's certitude of having met Life and of being united with it forever: "I write of what was from the beginning, what we have heard, what we have seen with our eyes, what we have looked upon and our hands have handled of the Word of Life. And the Life was made known and we have seen, and now testify and announce to you, the Life Eternal which was with the Father, and has appeared to us" (1 Jn. 1, 1). And we find it more distinctly once again in those words of the same Epistle, about to end: "Who has the Son has the Life" (1 Jn. 5, 12).

CHAPTER 8

CHRIST THE LIGHT

Is light something entirely different from life, or is it only the aspect this life takes on when it is communicated to beings of a spiritual nature? John's manner of introducing the idea of light: "He was the life of every being, and the life was the light of men" (1, 4) inclines us to admit the latter viewpoint. In fact, the sentence of the Prologue appears to mean that when communicated to men life, enlightening their minds, gives them birth in God. Light is the life and food of minds, the principle of their development and fulfillment.[1] Bodies stand in need of the vital force which perpetuates them in being and bears fruit. Minds need light (and truth) to live.

When it is communicated to men the divine life becomes light and this light permits them to know the truth. "The Word was the true light" (1, 9). Everything blends closely together in God for He is indivisibly Life, Light, and Truth. Does this mean that the notion of "light" and the word itself do not enrich the notion of life in an immeasurable way?

Several passages in the fourth Gospel and the first Epistle state that, though Christ is light for us, "I am the light of the world" (8, 12), He is also light in Himself. "I have come in light . . ." (12, 46). "God is light and in him there is no shadow of darkness" (1 Jn. 1, 5). Hence, just as we cannot reduce life to a merely functional reality, neither can we reduce light. "God is light." But the divine nature is simple. Light is not an element composing this nature, God's attributes and perfections not being subject to enumeration. As the prism refracts the sun's pure and blinding rays into various colors, so the varied richness we discover in God is simply the refraction of His absolute simplicity and dazzling purity. However, through the word light man perceives an authentic perfection in God which is not to be confused with the others even though

1. The two notions of light and truth are realities joined together in John's writings.

it is vitally linked to them. In God, light expresses a reality which had to be revealed to us in a special manner.

If the revelation of the "light" as such had not been made to us and had not been united to life, something essential would have remained unknown to us. It is infinitely precious to us to know that light is a manifestation of the divine life. The life that God communicates to us is not an obscure force, some uncontrolled attraction towards an object or an ideal more or less clearly perceived. It is not a longing for something about which we are in ignorance. If the divine life surpasses all our desires and aspirations, it does not do so by overwhelming us in some violent flood or by making us share in some cosmic communion with the Life of the All. The divine life surpasses all our aspirations by manifesting itself to our being and especially to our spirit as a peaceful visitation, an introduction to the kingdom of light and perfection.

Notion of light in Primitive Religions

When we study the apostle's words: "He was the life of every being and the life was the light of men" (1, 4), and when we place this statement in its historical context, we find that it marks the conclusion of a long search on the part of humanity for the role of light in the life of men and its full expansion.

The greater part of ancient religions have applied the notion of light to the divinity. This identification between light and the divinity is easily explained in the Orient in particular where light is so brilliant and all-pervading and where its action is so clearly linked to the appearance and development of life. Egypt, for instance, sang of light with great fervor. We see this in the lines addressed to Amon, the great solar god:

"Hail to thee peacefully residing in thy Temple,
Lord of joy and powerful apparitions!
The gods are pleased at thy sight
And men are happy at thy risings.

"Thy love appears in the southern heavens
And thy tenderness in northern skies.
Hearts are ravished by thy beauty
Arms made helpless by thy love.
Hands cannot reproduce thy perfect form
And hearts forget all having contemplated thee!"[2]

2. Hymn to Amon, Papyrus Boulaq.

Contrary to these primitive religions that divinized light, God Himself is light in the land of Israel.

In the realm of philosophic thought, light has frequently symbolized knowledge, that light of the mind. When looking at it this way, philosophers have often made of the divinity perfect knowledge and intelligibility, the highest possible light. They have placed the divinity on the highest rung of a ladder and human knowledge was set on the lowest rung. Whatever the distance was between man's intelligence and the divine, between human reason and the ultimate Reason for all things, between human wisdom and divine Wisdom, ancient thought[3] ordinarily established no break of continuity between them. When proceeding from men to God, one mounted towards a higher knowledge, a greater intelligibility, more light; but there was no change of "order."

Biblical thought, on the contrary, cast aside this concept of things because for it, between God and man, there is no common ground. He is an entirely different Being. Does this mean that the Bible repudiates the teaching that man carries in his intelligence a spark of the divine, placing him on a level higher than other creatures and making him lord of the universe? The Bible recognizes the fact that human wisdom, though limited, is not misleading and that it goes to meet divine Wisdom without being able to attain it. Hence, far from condemning the natural lights of human intelligence, the Bible assigns to these lights that heavenly origin which ancient thought also attributed to them. But this origin does not do away with that abyss between our intelligence and the divine.

This teaching, according to which there is no opposition but a difference of order between the two lights, that of revelation and reason, appears to be reflected in the Prologue. When the apostle writes, "He was in the world and the world was made by him" (1, 9), very likely he is speaking of the time of the Incarnation. But undoubtedly he is alluding to the fact of man's capability of becoming aware of the existence of Him "through whom everything was made" by means of the light of reason (Wis. c. 13, passim).

However, the biblical concept of light is referred directly to the supernatural reality of which God is the source and of which He will make humanity the beneficiary: first by tracing out for humanity roads of approach, viz., the Law, Wisdom, the Word, the Spirit, and then by sending into the world His Word, or uncreated Light. This light alone deserves the title of "true light" for it is the Word alone that enlightens man, in a hidden way first, and then in a personal revelation.

3. These philosophies considered in a general way.

The biblical notion of light

Biblical texts repeatedly state that God is light. He manifests Himself on Mount Sinai during the Exodus and He is surrounded by fire and flame and a dazzling light accompanies all these manifestations. A column of fire guides the Hebrews through the desert. When at the Parousia Yahweh returns to the Holy City, His presence will be as the light of a bright fire; the city will be entirely lit up with the Lord's glory (Is. 4, 5). "Arise, be enlightened, O Jerusalem, for thy light is come, and the glory of the Lord is risen upon thee . . . but the Lord shall be for thee an everlasting light . . ." (Is. 60, 1,19).

The Psalmists vie with one another in honoring Yahweh as the "luminous one, the magnificent one" (Ps. 75, 5). Being light, God cannot but enlighten and illumine those who contemplate and approach Him. The countenance of Moses reflects "rays of light" because he spoke with the Lord (Ex. 34, 29). Frequently the Psalmists implore Yahweh to show them "the light of his face," for this light is a source of salvation for man. "Yahweh is God, he enlightens us. Yahweh is my light and my salvation, whom should I fear" (Ps. 26, 1)? "Many say, 'Who will show us good things?' Raise the light of thy countenance above us, O Lord!" (Ps. 3, 7). "Make thy face shine upon us and we shall be saved" (79, 20). "Thou art my lamp, O God; my God enlightens my darkness" (Ps. 18, 29).

God's light is the source of salvation when enlightening minds and guiding them along His paths which are also paths of life. Thus, the pillar of cloud guides the Hebrews to the Promised Land: "in the night showing you the way by fire and in the day by a pillar of cloud" (Dt. 1, 33).

The Psalmists apply the role of light to knowledge which simultaneously reveals the word of God and His law and guides one to them. "The commandments of the Lord are clear, enlightening the eyes" (Ps. 17, 9). Psalm 118 sings of the Law throughout, the spiritual light of the believer: "Thy word is a lantern for my feet, and a light to my path. . . . The declaration of thy words gives light, it teaches the simple. . . . Show forth thy shining face to thy servant and teach me thy laws" (118, 105, 130, 135).

The authors of the Sapiential Books make light Wisdom's possession, and in Wisdom they see "the brightness of eternal light, the unspotted mirror of God's majesty, and the image of his goodness" (Wis. 7, 26). "She is more beautiful than the sun and above all order of the stars. Being compared with the light, she is found before it. For after this cometh the night, but no evil can overcome Wisdom" (Wis. 7, 29).

When it enlightens this light brings life. There is no question of a cold splendor falling indifferently on creatures. Those whom it enlightens are those who allowed the light to come to them by following the paths of goodness and justice. "Light rises for the just man and gladness for the upright of heart" (Ps. 96, 11). "To the righteous he arises as a light in darkness" (Ps. 111, 4).

Finally, it mercifully upholds those who experience suffering, difficulty, and trials. The divine light is a light of love. "Have mercy on us, O God of all, and behold us, and show us the light of thy mercies. And send forth thy fear upon the nations . . ." (Sir. 36, 1).

Gathering together so many statements which make of divine light the principle of life, truth, knowledge, and salvation, we can understand why it was sought for and awaited by humanity lying in the darkness and "in the shadow of death" and crushed under misery, sin, and error. "For with thee is the fountain of life and in thy light we shall see light" (Ps. 35, 10). From each of these oppressed hearts there ascended towards God, that light more desirable than the day after a long night, a cry full of hope. "My soul waits more expectantly for the Lord, more than the night watchman for the coming of the dawn" (Ps. 129, 6).

The Messias, Light of the Nations

This cry for light is directed chiefly towards Him in whom all place their hope, the Messias. They counted on Him to be the light of life and truth, the living way that leads to salvation and the brightness that triumphs over darkness and evil. They expected Him to bring light into the world or rather that He would be that light.

Such a conviction permeates the entire Bible, but it is especially apparent in the Prophetical Books. Isaias is the herald of the light identified with the Messias. He praises this "star" rising out of Jacob, spoken of already in the Book of Numbers (Nm. 24, 17), the Messias, "Light of the nations" (Is. 49, 6). His writings symbolize the hope of a people waiting for Him who is to come.

"For Sion's sake I will not hold my peace, and for the sake of Jerusalem I will not rest till her just one come forth as the brightness and her savior be lighted as a lamp" (Is. 62, 1). They await Him to whom Yahweh has said: "Behold, I have given thee to be the light of the Gentiles, that thou mayest be my salvation even to the farthest parts of the earth" (Is. 49, 6); ". . . that thou mayest say to them that are bound: Come forth. And to them that are in darkness: Show yourselves" (Is. 49, 9).

The prophet is so positive the Messias will bring light to the world that he cries out: "The people that walk in darkness have seen a great light. To them that dwelt in the region of the shadow of death, light is risen" (Is. 9, 1).

This prophetic hope visits hearts right until the time of Zachary who, filled with the Spirit, salutes the Precursor of the Light in John the Baptist: "And thou, child, shalt be called the prophet of the Most High, for thou shalt go before the face of the Lord to prepare his ways, to give to his people knowledge of salvation through forgiveness of their sins; because of the loving kindness of our God, wherewith the Orient from on high has visited us, to shine on those who sit in darkness and in the shadow of death, to guide our feet into the way of peace" (Lk. 1, 76-79).

"The Orient from on high. . . ." Through these words seemingly borrowed from primitive religions, as though he had wished to associate them also in the good news of salvation, the old prophet extolled the coming of the true light, the coming of Him who would say very soon: "I am the light of the world."

No wonder then that Christ, so long expected and who had come to answer those expectations far beyond what anyone hoped for, should lay claim to all that was attributed to the Messias! Why should He not present Himself as the face of God turned towards the world, as the Divine Son coming to enlighten humanity and to snatch it from darkness? He comes and "the light shines in the darkness" (1, 5). Why should He not have manifested Himself at once as the light of truth, for "He was the true light" (1, 9), the light of salvation and life, not for His own only but for the whole world: "I am the light of the world. He who follows me does not walk in darkness, but will have the light of life" (8, 42).

"I am the light of the world"

Deeply rooted in the Old Testament as was the notion of light when applied to God and especially to the Messias who was to come, as rich in meaning as it already is, it is going to appear infinitely more so in the fourth Gospel.

In St. John, the light ceases to be applied simply to the manifestations of the divine power and mercy, or to be only something hoped for; it has become a reality. It is identified with a Person that has come into the world, viz., the Word of life, Light of Light, "being the brightness of (God's) glory and the image of his substance" (Heb. 1, 3). This Person is at once the source and the furnace of this light. "God is light, in him there is no darkness" (1 Jn. 1, 5), writes St. John and Jesus Christ, the only-begotten Son of God, is God. After a long and anxious expectation, "the true light that enlightens every man" has come into the world.

The theme of light reinforces the theme of birth in the fourth Gospel. And light appears in it as the symbol of a spiritual birth. Furthermore: To those who are born spiritually, light does not simply bring the possibility of seeing what exists, but of discovering the order of beings, their meaning, their ultimate purpose of existence.

When Christ says, "I am the light of the world," He intends to tell us: I am the one through whom the world is revealed as it is and takes on a certain meaning. This meaning remains hidden from those who see only with the eyes of the flesh. Without me, the world is only what the senses apprehend. Through me and in me, it becomes the work, word, and language of God.

The divine light reveals the "inwardness" of the world. Just as the light of day reveals what the darkness concealed, so also Christ is the ray that illuminates the secret life of a world in which every creature is linked to its Creator.

The light likewise reveals men to one another. The "light of the world" permits them to know and recognize one another, to direct themselves in the world. The world and man become mutually permeable and intelligible. They are the data of one and the same problem the solution of which appears only in the divine light, manifested in Christ.

Regarding this light, there is no question of some kind of esoteric knowledge, but rather of a lived experience of the word of God in His Son. To approach the light, there is no question of having recourse to a cult or some kind of initiation. A giving of oneself to the spiritual order suffices. And the bond which ties the soul to this order is the Spirit. "That which is born of the flesh is flesh; and that which is born of the Spirit is spirit" (3, 6).

The Gospel, and especially John's Gospel, does not conduct us to a religion of mysteries. It proposes the religion of a hidden God, the object of faith. When He reveals Himself, He cannot do so in a fragmentary way, under such an aspect, but in a "comprehensive" way for it is always God who reveals Himself in "Person."

The Bible is not a book of initiations, but of Revelation. Thus, no one can claim to know God except the one to whom He makes Himself known. God remains the Master and He is the Light. It is not and cannot be separated from Him. If He communicates light to man it is because He gives Himself. Man does not learn God, but God teaches him that He is hidden; the Bible is nothing else but the book in which God makes Himself known by hiding Himself, i.e., by instructing man always more and more in His transcendence and immanence. The light does not "become greater" and God does not become "more" God because of anything man himself does. But God takes possession of man, and thanks to His light man sees and knows. He is born to the light as he is born to life. "Believe in the light and you will be sons of the light" (12, 36).

Thus, the religion of Israel is in no way a religion elaborated by men. We must not allow the Mosaic rites and cult to create any illusion. When Moses gathers the People of God together, the Light is both "behind" and "before" this people. It is "behind" it, in an "elsewhere" from which this people is excluded; a terrestrial paradise which remains a promise. The Bible is the revelation of this "elsewhere" and the light projected on man shows him he is of much more worth than he imagines, that he is made for something greater. So much so, that darkness for man consists in not being aware of his true image, his real fatherland. And as long as he is unaware of this, he is no better than the grass that withers, the body that is consigned to the worms.

But this Light is also "before" the people. All the appeals contained in the Old Testament have no reference to a moral conduct which through its own power sanctifies man before God, but to a "salvation" which conducts them to the true light. If the Old Testament was content with a rational conduct born of a natural morality it was because man was wandering. It is by groping that he must look for the road to the "promised land" which, lost in the "past" shines still before him as a promise, as a land whose prophets repeat to him that "Yahweh is the eternal light."

Is the Book of Wisdom anything else after all but the balance-sheet of an effort pursued according to human ways, attesting to the existence of another reality which God alone can reveal and provide? And the canticle of Zachary really expresses this fact: Behold He has finally appeared who will teach the nations their true destiny, behold the light of salvation has risen.

The Old Testament does not identify God with light as though He were a sun-god and light constituted part of His substance. Rather it sees light in Him because it is God's very nature to make light and to be the light which enlightens and saves, mercifully, while manifesting itself.

The struggle between light and darkness

John states: "God is light, in him there is no darkness." It is a fact, however, that in the whole Johannine Gospel, beginning with Christ's own declarations, the light never appears alone and completely independent. It is always linked with darkness and presented as opposed to darkness. Light does not exist in a state of peaceful repose, but rather as the result of a struggle, a victory. This does not mean that light does not pre-exist darkness and is not infinitely superior to it; but it does mean that light manifests itself only after tracing out a path in the midst of darkness. This darkness, of course, is considered as the opposing forces in the service of the evil spirit.

Whatever be our mode of translating the passage in the Prologue: "And the light shines in the darkness; and the darkness grasped it not" (to grasp it, to comprehend it, to welcome it), it is under the aspect of an opposition, a contradiction, and a conflict that John introduces the notions of light and darkness.

We are dealing here with something extremely important because these two notions are identified with real, living personalities, viz., Christ and Satan. It is not so much the aspect of a moral conflict that John presents and opposes light to darkness, but rather as two worlds irrevocably opposed one to the other. However, darkness is practically identified with illusion which is real evil. Satan, prince of darkness, is likewise prince of illusion, falsehood. The contradiction between Satan and Christ is absolute, Christ being "light" and "truth." "He was the true light. . . ." Different categories of moral faults have as their true foundation illusion, falsehood, and a refusal to accept the truth. Whoever turns away from truth and light is enveloped in darkness and is seduced by sin.

"The light has come into the world, yet men have loved the darkness rather than the light, for their works were evil. For everyone who does evil hates the light, and does not come to the light, that his deeds may not be exposed. But he who does the truth comes to the light, that his deeds may be made manifest, for they have been performed in God" (3, 19-21).

These reflections of the evangelist bear witness to the Master's teachings and the manner in which He intended the problem of light to be approached and solved. For it seems that Christ did not begin by giving his listeners any definition whatsoever of light or by recalling to their minds what the Old Testament has said of it. Indeed, He supposes the Scriptures are known which confer on light the meaning of life, truth, and salvation, and occasionally He refers to them. But it is not on this ground that Christ places Himself. He sets Himself upon a practical plane: men are awaiting the light announced to them. The herald of its advent, the Precursor has borne witness to Christ the Light "in order that all might believe through him" (1, 7). Now the light is actually present, and He is the "true light." Although we are dealing here with a spiritual reality, this light does not need proof or justification. Just as physical light strikes the eyes, so the spiritual light thrusts itself upon minds. Light does not prove itself, it declares itself simply by shedding light.

And nevertheless, though the Word —"the true light that enlightens every man that comes into the world"— has Himself "come into the world," yet "the world knew him not." Men do not see this Light or they turn away from it because the eyes of their soul are sick, and consequently: "their whole body is in darkness" (Lk. 11, 34).

Whence comes so strange a blindness? How can men prefer to the light this darkness which all tradition likens to death and from which they long so ardently to be delivered? Is this not the very reason for their calling upon the Messias? And behold He brings them the light and they turn from it! It is because the light, desirable in itself, brought out into the open what they wished to keep hidden, viz., the evil in their hearts holding them prisoners. Is this so powerful that the divine light itself, for which they were created, cannot deliver them?

Unlike Paul, John has not painted a dark and sad picture of the original fall and its consequences. In him, there are none of those cries which Paul addresses to the Liberator (Rm. 7, 24). Does this mean that John does not know, from experience and from what he sees around him, the inexorable law of sin? It is sufficient to read the fourth Gospel, the first Epistle, or the Apocalypse in order to convince ourselves that such is not the case. But for John, the despotic power of evil and its spread are summed up in one word, synonymous with darkness and likened to the kingdom of darkness, viz., the world.

The World under Satan's domination

In John's mind, the world is that totality of men who refuse to accept God as they are prisoners of sin. It is also the sum-total of the powers of darkness that fight against the light. It is the empire of Satan, the symbol and manifestation of evil. It is enough to consider the apostle's insistence on the the use of the word in order to grasp the degree to which he was haunted by the empire of sin and the depths of darkness to which it plunges humanity.[4]

This conviction does not lead the apostle into an analysis of the law of death dwelling in man and setting him at variance with himself in the innermost depths of his being. Rather the vision of sin which holds the world captive turns John towards the two principal protagonists in the fight: on the one hand, the Lamb of God who takes upon himself the "sins of the world" (1, 29) and delivers us from them through His Blood; on the other, the prince of darkness, the "prince of this world" (12, 31; 14, 30; 16, 11), Satan, whose formidable influence renders man practically powerless to extricate himself from sin and darkness.

True, sin in itself is sufficient to make man a slave. "Amen, amen, I

4. In chapters 14, 15, 16, 17, the word appears no less than thirty-eight times and it means not the universe or the totality of men in general, but those opposed to God.

say to you, everyone who commits sin is a slave of sin" (8, 34). But the devil makes this slavery worse still, more insupportable. "Why do you not understand my speech? Because you cannot listen to my word. The father from whom you are is the devil, and the desires of your father it is your will to do" (8, 43).

The devil is a "murderer from the beginning" (8, 44); in him there is no truth; he is a "liar and the father of lies" (8, 44). "The whole world is in the power of the evil one . . ."(1 Jn. 5, 19). It is he whom we must conquer if we wish that "the word of God abide in us" (1 Jn. 2, 14). It is he who makes this world an object of covetousness,—covetousness of the flesh and of the eyes,—and who turns us away from God by tempting us with the allurements of riches and possessions. Likewise, "he who commits sin is of the devil, because the devil sins from the beginning" (1 Jn. 3, 8).

It is "to this end the Son of God appeared, that he might destroy the works of the devil," for to commit sin is to be "of the evil one" (1 Jn. 3, 8,12), while he who is "born of God" is delivered from sin and from the evil one who "does not touch him" (1 Jn. 4, 7; 5, 18).

We would not understand the opposition between light and darkness if we did not see in it, before all else, a struggle to the death between Christ and Satan. Jesus salutes the hour of His Passion and Death, the hour which is likewise the time "when the Son of Man will be glorified" (12, 23): "Now is the judgment of this world; now will the prince of this world be cast out. And I, if I be lifted up from the earth, will draw all things to myself" (12, 31).

The Victory of the true Light

With the Passion, the struggle between light and darkness, entered into from the first hour, reaches its zenith. Having won the victory over the prince of darkness, Christ has saved the world over which shines the light of salvation. "I am the light of the world. He who follows me does not walk in the darkness, but will have the light of life" (8, 12).

This struggle occupies Christ's mind to such a degree that He never ceases making allusion to Satan until his last interview with His apostles. He does not mention his name[5] in order not to trouble the painful peace and tender intimacy of those last moments; instead He makes frequent mention of this "world" against which the apostles must be on their guard and defend themselves, for the world is the empire of the Evil one. The

5. Except three times: 14, 30; 16, 11; 17, 15.

world cannot receive the Spirit of Truth (14, 17); its peace is deceitful (14, 27). It will apparently seem to triumph (14, 30) and the powers of darkness will be unleashed against the children of the light. Because the latter are not "of this world," the world "will persecute them" and this to such a degree that "whoever kills them will think he is offering worship to God" (15, 19,20; 16, 2); but the disciples are to have no fear, for the "prince of this world is condemned." Christ's departure should not be the cause of sadness. Undoubtedly in "the world you will have affliction" (16, 33), but "take courage" for Christ has overcome the world (16, 33).

When leaving the world, Christ does not abandon those He leaves behind. He places them in His Father's care after having communicated His light to them. "The words that thou hast given to me, I have given to them. Holy Father, keep in thy name those whom thou hast given me" (17, 11).

His all-powerful prayer continues to keep them, not by withdrawing them materially from the world where they must live and work; "Father, I do not pray that thou take them out of the world, but that thou keep them from evil" (17, 15).

Then will be accomplished what Christ the Light had in view: having been brought to the light, they will arrive at the truth through Christ's grace. They have received the true light about which John spoke in his Prologue; they have received it and now they are "sanctified in the truth" (17, 19). Not being of the world, they can be sent into the world to bear witness to the Light and Truth.

Associated in His struggle and victory, the disciples will be given a share in His triumph, i.e., in His "glory," that eternal brightness of the divine light. "Father, I will that where I am, they also whom thou hast given me may be with me; in order that they may behold my glory, which thou hast given me . . ." (17, 24).

The struggle between light and darkness terminates in this: those who have followed Christ the Light and fought with Him will themselves be transformed into light (Cf. 2 Cor. 3, 18). If they have "walked in the light," they will be the light just as God Himself is the light for: "God is light, in him there is no darkness" (1 Jn. 1, 5).

"He who does the truth comes to the light"

The necessary conditions for liberation from darkness, sin, and the devil, as well as for advancing in the light are conversion of heart and life lived "in truth" (4, 23).

However, this divine light ordinarily remains hidden, though, in exceptional circumstances, it can become visible as at the Transfiguration. The Incarnation veils the light emanating from Christ. To discover it men must have pure eyes and a "good will." The divine light which has come to them is then unveiled. It springs forth at the confluence of a twofold advance: that of God towards man, and of man towards God. Man should remember that since God has taken the first step, he should walk with Him (1 Jn. 4, 10).

"The Word was the true light . . . he came into the world . . . he was in the world . . . and all was made through him" (1, 3). Christ did not judge it any more necessary to explain Himself concerning the light, than the life. He was content to present Himself as eternal life and teach men the paths leading thereto in order to come to Him. He does the same regarding light. Whether spiritual or physical, light thrusts itself upon us and manifests its beauty, power, perfection as soon as it is perceived. The important thing is to be in a state capable of "seeing" the light.

Thus, Christ took His stand on that declaration: "I am the light of the world" (8, 12) with all the consequences flowing from it: The necessity of acting in the truth, for "he who does the truth comes to the light" (3, 12); the necessity of following this light and of "walking while it is light" (12, 35), for "he who walks in the darkness does not know where he is going"; the necessity of "believing in the light" in order to become "children of the light" (12, 36). In these few statements is contained all Christ's teaching on the light. Nothing is more simple, more clear, but also there is nothing more demanding, more peremptory. Can we even speak of a teaching here? It is question more of a declaration, but one that has the weight and import of a revelation.

The Johannine Gospel is a real reflection of this absolute demand. For St. John, there are no half-measures between light and darkness, but rather a very definite opposition: one belongs in one category or the other! He will write in the Apocalypse: "God vomits out of his mouth" those who try to make compromises (Ap. 3, 15). John is without pity for the Pharisee and without indulgence towards Judas.

With him, the "moral" world is cast off; he does not stop at its standard, but abandons it to God to be judged by Him alone: "Because if our heart blame us, God is greater than our heart and knows all things" (1 Jn. 3, 20). The faithful must choose between one of two worlds, viz., that of light and that of darkness. He must choose without faint-heartedness and it seems even without any possibility of back-tracking. "Whoever is born of God does not commit sin, because his seed abides in him and he cannot sin . . ." (1 Jn. 3, 9).

John is not unaware, however, of the fact that man in reality does not cease to fall into sin. The weaknesses that do come will be judged by the Father and Christ; and the apostle makes it understood that a renewal can always be had by a simple glance upon Christ the light.

Moreover, John declares clearly that the light does not illumine the intelligence first, but the heart. Everything in the intelligence is accomplished when passing from the pole of faith to the pole of the will. It is faith that receives the communication of light and it is the heart that keeps it without fail. That is why the fourth Gospel appears under this aspect, much more as an ascesis than as a moral code. The light does not visit man unless he detach himself from all that is not God, unless he turn himself away from all false lights, illusions of the universal "maia," traitorously presented and proposed by the prince of darkness and falsehood. It is "detachment of heart" which keeps man in the light of God, and only an adherence without compromise to Him who is the light can keep man from the darkness which is in him as well as around him.

"Men have loved the darkness rather than the light, for their works were evil. For everyone who does evil hates the light and does not come to the light. . . . But he who does the truth comes to the light" (3, 21). To be in the light it is not enough to see, but one must love. There is only one equation in St. John: Light-Truth-Charity. It opposes its contrary: Darkness-falsehood-evil.

The sharp, absolute quality of these views introduces into the soul an extreme simplicity, a divine simplicity which relieves the soul of all complexity, disturbances, divisions, and sets it on the road to God.

John's approach is one of dedication and combat. The faithful one, the "child of light," does not fight for himself but for Christ's sake. He remains totally in ignorance of himself and his personal victories. "Progress" is not to be sought as an end in itself. By engaging himself in the struggle the faithful soul becomes a child of God. Whether saint or still imperfect, his condition remains the same as long as he fights against the darkness. And no matter what his spiritual stage may be, the struggle must never cease. It is up to God to judge the distance between perfection and his present state. In this way, there results for the soul a freedom from too much self-concentration. What the soul must do is enter more deeply into what it knows has to be done to attain eternal life.

John requires of the child of light "spiritual" dispositions rather than "moral." What he wants of him is that he recognize the truth, and having done so, that he conform his life to it through an inclination of the will, through a very definite choice.

The concluding sentence of his first Epistle stresses this "spiritual" plane, and not the "moral." "Little children, guard yourselves against the idols. Amen" (1 Jn. 5, 21). Everything becomes an idol, in fact, as soon as worship is offered it, consent is given. There are always God and false gods confronting us. The son of light, the child of God, is the one to whom God is always present and the one chosen in preference to everything else. All outside God is taken as a stepping-stone for advancing towards Him.

And nevertheless, this peremptoriness, this truly fierce demand, redolent of the Old Testament, is softened and tempered in John's Gospel through his teaching of friendship. This uncompromising demand does not issue forth from a hard Master's will, from an implacable and "jealous" God, but from a God of love who has revealed Himself as a Friend. "I will no longer call you servants but friends" (15 ,15). That dynamic quality in John's writings stems from this certitude. For him, to recognize the truth is to recognize God as Creator, Lord of all, the inaccessible and transcendent God; it is likewise to discover the Redeemer, the one who has come among His own and who has first loved us; the Good shepherd, the one who gives himself as food and shows us His Heart transpierced. Everything proceeds from love and calls upon love in return. Those absolute and intransigent choices imposed upon us by the Light still remain choices of love and preference.

Water quenches the thirst, bread nourishes, the heart is warmed, tears flow, humility overflows, and it is a humility of abandonment, of a recognition that admires another that is greater and better than self. Such are the fruits of the divine light that invades the soul. Each of the scenes described in the Johannine Gospel, each of the deeds through which light is given, a dialogue is begun, and contact is established between the soul and God, each of these confirms it for us.

But what is the condition? On condition that the soul enlightened by the truth surrender itself to it in an act of faith, penetrated, moved, vivified, and constantly renewed through love.

The man born blind and the miracle of the light

"He who does the truth comes to the light" (3, 20). "While you have the light, believe in the light, that you may becomes sons of the light" (12, 36). These two declarations sum up that admirable account of Chapter 9, in which the twofold miracle of conferring light is described with such astonishing sharpness of observation on John's part.

John has deliberately placed it immediately after one of Christ's discourses to the unbelieving Jews, beginning with the words: "I am the light of the world. He who follows me does not walk in darkness, but will have the light of life" (8, 12). It terminates in that declaration which stresses the symbolic meaning of the miracle, viz., opening the eyes of faith and of the heart upon Jesus the light of the world and "seeing" the true light.

"And when he found him, he said to him, 'Dost thou believe in the Son of God?' He answered and said, 'Who is he, Lord, that I may believe?' And Jesus said to him, 'Thou hast both seen him, and he it is who speaks with thee' " (9, 35-38).

There now follow the works of Jesus which bring out the close bond between the Light considered as manifesting the Truth, and the "judgment" which results from men depending on their attitude towards this Light of Truth.

" 'For a judgment have I come into the world, that they who do not see may see, and those who see may become blind.' And some of the Pharisees who were with him heard this, and they said to him, 'Are we also blind?' Jesus said to them, 'If you were blind you would not have sin. But now that you say, 'We see,' your sin remains" (9, 39-41).

Are not the following reflections with which the apostle ends the interview with Nicodemus a faithful echo of the Master's teaching: "Now this is the judgment: The light has come into the world, yet men have loved the darkness rather than the light, for their works were evil" (3, 19).

The blind man's physical cure has a significance and worth in itself, but its real meaning lies on the spiritual plane. It means that we open our eyes to the true light only when we open them to the grace of faith, through that good will and singleness of purpose of which the blind man is a perfect model.

"Dost thou believe in the Son of Man?". . ."Who is he, Lord, that I may believe in him?". . ."Thou has both seen him, and he it is who speaks to thee.". . ."I believe, Lord."

The full meaning of the account is to be found in the play on the two words: "to see" and "to believe," He only truly sees who believes. "Blessed are they who have not seen, but have believed" (20, 29). The miracle may very well be the point of departure as it is in this case; light is given only through faith. It is only in faith that the mystery of Christ, the Light of the world, is brought out in its full brightness.

Again, it is necessary that man walk continually with the aid of the light received in order to remain in the light: "Walk while you have the light."

We must use the light we already possess if we are to come closer to the light. If it is true that we must see in order to walk, it is even more true that we must walk in order to see. We have to put to work what has been given us of the light, and we do this by "doing the truth" (3, 21), for this is the condition for "coming to the light." A life lived in the truth and the light is the only means of becoming a "son of light" (12, 36), i.e., of having an intimate revelation of Christ interiorly.

But what is meant by "walking in the light"? Christ tells us: it is "believing in the light." And this helps us understand that this path of light is first of all a "path of faith," a path of darkness. We are right in asking whether we must enter into darkness, i.e., renounce our own lights in order to see those which come from God, just as we receive Christ's life by sharing in His Death.

Christ has taught us the law of life in these words: "Amen, amen, I say to you, unless the grain of wheat falls into the ground and dies, it remains alone. But if it dies, it brings forth much fruit. He who loves his life, loses it" (12, 24,25). Light itself will not come to us unless we renounce our own lights by entering upon the paths of humility of heart and spirit. God resists the proud and gives Himself to the humble (Prv. 11, 2). This is the lesson Christ draws from the proud Pharisees who have come into this world, that they who do not see may see, and they who see may become blind" (9, 39).

It is not only because Christ has become the true light that we must follow Him, as the similitude of the the Good Shepherd teaches us. It is also because this humble progress, accomplished through confidence and perseverance, is necessary so that the light in us "does not become darkness" (Mt. 6, 23).

We have received life from God, but we must always remain dependent upon Him in order to keep this life alive and to sustain it. So also must we, having become "sons of light," turn incessantly towards the source of light and remain under its rays, "walk" in this light of faith. In God, light is neither of the same order or nature as what we call light. Also, on the road by which we go to Him, faith, the light at times will appear obscure to us. And nevertheless, whoever has faith in Christ is enlightened through the "true light that enlightens every man" (1, 9), the divine light itself.

"He who follows me does not walk in darkness"

The collection of statements on the light is elucidated by the figure of the Good Shepherd. In this figure we see a revelation of God's merciful tenderness towards men, and a love so great as not to hesitate to "give his life for his sheep" (10, 11).

Are we supposed to see a relationship between these passages concerning the light and the similitude of the "Good Shepherd"? At least, must we consider the latter as furnishing us with an important complementary lesson on the light?

When presenting Himself as the Light of the world, Christ had added: "He who follows me does not walk in darkness, but shall have the light of life." Coming at dawn and calling his sheep enclosed in the sheepfold where they spent the night, He "makes them come out," and when He "has let them out, he goes before them; and the sheep follow him because they know his voice." He leads them to pasture, i.e., to eternal life of which He is "the door": "I am the door of the sheep. . . . If anyone enter by me he shall be safe, and shall go in and out, and shall find pastures." This door opens out upon life and salvation (10, 1-18).

Finally the Good Shepherd knows His sheep. "I know mine and mine know me." This "knowledge," which is so intimately linked to faith and is its delicious fruit, enlightens souls with the most penetrating and revealing light because it is the light of love.

All these declarations show us that faith, while retaining elements of darkness, proceeding from its nature and our limitations, remains nonetheless a light because it places us in contact with the Person of Christ. It makes it possible for us to live in close association with Him.

Fidelity to the Light

Whatever be the place assigned by John to the opposition and combat between light and darkness, and whatever be the importance of progress in faith and purity of intention without which there is no possibility of becoming "children of light," it is really as a contemplative that John considers this light which is Christ.

This contemplative manner of considering the light is in no way opposed to a realistic attitude. For it is only by being victorious over darkness, i.e., the devil, the world, and sin, and by taking the only road that leads to it, viz., faith, that God's children can come to the contemplation of divine light. Furthermore, he who desires to become a child of light must not only "do the truth" and walk in the light, but observe the commandments that are summed up in the precept of charity. The one who would claim to be in the light while hating his brother would in reality be in darkness: "He who loves his brother abides in the light. . . . But he who hates his brother is in the darkness, and walks in the darkness, and he does not know whither he goes; because the darkness has blinded his eyes" (1 Jn. 2, 9-11).

The light enlightens and abides in a soul only if it is constant combat against evil, faithful in following Christ and obeying His commandments, especially that of love of neighbor. The light, flower of the soul, expands in the soul tried by temptations and always tending heavenward. John realizes nothing is more dangerous and illusory and deceptive as a contemplation of the Light that does not have as its foundation fidelity of the soul in grace and truth. It remains true nonetheless that it is towards the Light, envisioned under its contemplative aspect, that the apostle has turned with the deepest and most vital tendencies of his being.

Identity between Light and Truth

A proof of this thirst for light coming by way of contemplation is given to us through the ever growing identification between Light and Truth in the Johannine Gospel. A like movement can be seen in his Epistle and in the interior of the Prologue itself.

In the very beginning of the fourth Gospel it is said that the Light has come into the world and to it man has opposed the darkness of his sin. It is under a moral angle that the notion of light is introduced, and that is why John writes, "He who does the truth (i.e., conforms his conduct to demands of God and his conscience) comes to the light" (3, 21).

But Christ insists later upon "testimony," and it is clear that this notion comes simultaneously from light and truth. To give testimony is the same as shedding light upon the truth, vouching for the truth. The Jews understand this very well when they answer Jesus' statement, "I am the light of the world" by saying, "Thou bearest witness to thyself. Thy witness is not true" (8, 12,13).

An identification between light and truth becomes more intensified when Jesus states, "If you abide in my word, you will know the truth," for He had told them not long before, "I am the light of the world" (8, 12,31).

The cure of the man born blind is performed especially to "open the eyes" of the spectators. Closing themselves off from the light, the Pharisees close themselves off at the same time from the truth. Their blindness hinders them from seeing in Christ the Light, Christ the Truth.

Finally the identification is virtually accomplished when Christ uses the expression "believe in the light" (12, 35), for it would have no meaning if light was not the same as truth. Thus, from moral rectitude which allows the soul to approach God (3, 20) we have passed into faith which develops into contemplation (12, 35). "Believe in the light" means: May this light that I am, become for you the living truth which gives life. Place yourselves under its rays, contemplate it, nourish yourself in it, allow yourself to be assimilated by it, become light in it, for this light is the light of truth. Better, it is its very ray.

It is in the sense of an identification fully realized between light and truth that we must understand these words: "I have come, a light, into the world that whoever believes in me may not remain in darkness" (12, 46). He who believes in me, he who believes I am the truth, will be in the light by that very fact. That is why in that all-important declaration, "I am the way, the truth, and the life" (14, 6), Christ has no longer any need to mention "light." Included in the Truth and intermingled with it as its radiance, light takes henceforth the name "glory"; and the Spirit whom Christ sends to us from the Father is called the "Spirit of truth" (14, 17; 15, 26). He is also light and fire, but the light and fire He brings to souls is the radiance, the splendor, the flash of truth.

And that is why the entire mission of Christ could be expressed in His words to Pilate: "For this was I born and for this came I into the world to bear witness to the truth" (18, 37).

John as a contemplative submits to the fascination of this Truth's splendor. The light is not so much what one contemplates as the means through which one contemplates. Light possesses its own beauty, but this beauty would remain invisible if it did not strike against objects which through it are clothed in beauty. On the contrary, Truth is in itself the supreme object of contemplation. If light is part of Truth, what one aspires to know and to see in the ray of divine light (which is called glory) is Truth. We have already remarked how often the word "see" is used in this Gospel and at times even in a surprising manner. It is applied to the mystery of faith in that passage, "He who sees me sees the Father" (14, 9), and in that other which is even more strange, "He who is unbelieving towards the Son will not see life" (3, 36).

John reports these expressions which he has heard from the Master's lips, but they are fully in accord with his contemplative temperament. Because what he longed to see more than anything else were the eternal realities which only the eyes of faith help us to distinguish here on earth, but which we shall "see" in the splendor of eternal light. John is no less the mystic of light than of love. Speaking of eternal life, he writes, "This is eternal life that they may know thee, the only true God, and Jesus Christ whom thou hast sent" (17, 3).

"We shall see him as he is"

"The only true God," i.e., the God of truth. As for "knowledge," this is what enables us to see in the light of love. Christ, the Light, is then essentially the one who reveals the Truth which He Himself is, the one who makes us share it, and promises the soul a blessedness which is expressed in terms of light and vision by John.

However, whether he is dealing with light, faith, or eternal life, John uses the word "see" as though it best expressed the nature of his own deep-seated desire. The blessedness of the children of God, "sons of light," is that they will be like God and they "will see him as he is" (1 Jn. 3, 2).

"To see God as He is." A better expression could not be found for expressing that intense desire to contemplate the divine Truth in the light of glory. If John attributes to faith a place of primary importance, it is because it is the only road which leads "in truth" to the vision of God as He is in Himself. In John, the veil covering the divine light here on earth is much less that of faith than that of the Incarnation, for John's faith seems to be so living that in him it is almost a means of "seeing." This idea comes to light in the Prologue. The Word's divine glory was obscured and veiled by His flesh. Yet so profound and ardent is the thirst he has for contemplating and seeing Truth in the divine light that John sees this glory through what seems to be made for hiding it. "And the Word was made flesh and dwelt among us. And we have seen his glory" (1, 17). The light of the Word shines through Christ's humanity and John is not hesitant in conferring upon it the name "glory." He goes as far as saying: "we have seen it."

There is, however, a great distance between this glory of the Word made flesh, even when shining through on Thabor, and the glory Christ has from the Father as the only-begotten Son. But for St. John whose contemplative soul pierces through the veils and joins those eternal realities in Christ's flesh, this glory is not substantially different from the glory of the Word. Made up here below of humility in love, constantly referred to the Father and setting itself radically in opposition to the glory men seek, this glory bears solemn testimony to the divine nature and is a prelude to the light of glory. John, who discovers it in Christ even on earth, is drawn towards it. It is the highest object of his contemplation as it was the all-important object of Christ's last interviews at the Last Supper. It is then, in fact, that the Master confers upon "glory" its real meaning.[6] We should note John's fervor and enthusiasm (etymologically speaking) when he reports Christ's revelation of this glory into which He is about to enter through His Death and of which He will make His

---

6. The word "glory," already so far removed in our modern language from its Gospel meaning, is uniformly mistakenly employed in the Gospel even when its content changes profoundly in meaning. The word "glory" is used for the glory man refers to himself and also for divine glory. And the Latin verb "clarificare" is translated simply to mean glory, whereas it really expresses the ideas of: "making clear," "rendering luminous," "clothing in light," and is applied exclusively to the glorification of the Son by the Father and vice versa.

disciples beneficiaries. Far from suffering humiliations and annihilations from this death which is so close, Christ's glory is viewed by John as exalted. "The hour has come for the Son of Man to be glorified" (12, 23). "And I, if I be lifted up from the earth, will draw all things to myself" (12, 32), i.e., to eternal life and then to glory. "Now he said this signifying the death he was to die" (12, 23).

After Judas leaves the Cenacle, thus setting the stage for the drama, Christ immediately turns His thoughts to the glory that will come to His Father. "When, therefore, he had gone out, Jesus said, 'Now is the Son of Man glorified, and God is glorified in him. If God is glorified in him, God will also glorify him in himself, and will glorify him at once'" (13, 31,32).

When He tells his apostles, "Where I go you cannot come" (13, 33); or, "Let not your heart be troubled. You believe in God, believe also in me. In my Father's house there are many mansions . . . I go to prepare a place for you. I am coming again and I will take you to myself" (14, 1-3), it is of this glory Christ is thinking.

The picture of the sufferings awaiting Him on the Cross do not discourage Him. The Cross is the vantage point to which He is led by love and from which He sees all the infinite horizons of heavenly glory due Him as Son of God. However, He does not dwell on it, but rather on the glory His Death will procure for His Father. He reflects upon all that He will do in favor of His own, once He has returned to His Father to share His glory. It is then that He will send them the Spirit. "He will teach you all the truth . . . He will glorify me, because he will receive of what is mine and declare it to you" (16, 13). This means: He will render fruitful the ministry of those who remain united to me, in such a way that they will bear fruit for the Father's glory.

Then comes the sacerdotal prayer in which John points out Christ's revelations: "These things Jesus spoke; and raising his eyes to heaven, he said, 'Father, the hour has come! Glorify thy Son, that thy Son may glorify thee . . . in order that to all thou hast given him he may give everlasting life . . . I have glorified thee on earth. And now do thou, Father, glorify me with thyself, with the glory that I had with thee before the world existed'" (17, 1-5).

Being the Light of the world and revealing Thee to men, "I have manifested thy name to men" (17, 6), I have made "your glory absolutely manifest to all the inhabitants of the universe."[7] "Now I come to thee" and "I pray that for those whom thou hast given me, I may be glorified in them." For them, it is "in being sanctified in truth" that they will be

7. S. Cyril of Alexandria.

glorified, i.e., made sharers in divine glory, "this glory, Father, which thou hast given me" (17, passim).

United to me in an inexpressible union, "I in them, and thou (Father) in me," they will be "there where I am" i.e., in the bosom of the Father, and with me, "they will behold the glory which thou hast given me" (17, passim), that glory which the Word made flesh enjoys in the splendor of His triumph.

Christ, Light and Love

Thus the revelation of the Light comes to an end. It appears as the radiance of the divine Truth Christ made known to us. The great contemplative aspiration which awakens in the apostle at sight of the Light Christ has brought to the world and which He is actually in His Person, comes from the fact that this light is the Light of divine Truth itself, the object of his ardent desires, and the substance of eternal life.

We may also consider this same contemplative aspiration as flowing from the apostle's attachment to Christ. Until the time his mortal life will be completed by that final encounter with Christ in glory, John will hear the Master's words resound in his ears: "I am the light of the world ... he who follows me will have the light of life" (9, 5; 8, 12). "I am the way, the truth, and the life" (14, 6). "I have come a light into the world, that whoever believes in me may not remain in the darkness" (12, 46). "Believe in the light, and you will become children of light" (12, 36).

For John, the light was the Person of Christ. Jesus is the living light of his mind, heart, and soul; and just as he was unable to imagine a road which this Light did not light up, a way upon which the Good Shepherd did not precede him, so John was unable to envision eternal life otherwise than as this reality which will give him light and will permit him to see it forever.

Faith carried within it the hope of seeing Christ again, of being able to contemplate His face forever. Those cries of the Psalmist found an echo in John's heart: "Who will show good things to us? Raise the light of thy countenance above us, O Lord!" (Ps. 4, 7).

Yahweh had answered the expectation and desire of humanity. "My eyes have seen thy salvation." For John, Christ is the central point of this Light of Life and of Truth; also in order to honor the Light, it is rather the language of love and of loving knowledge John desires to use. Here on earth, Jesus had been for him "the light of his eyes," and beatitude will be contemplating this Face in eternity. The "Holy Face" is not only the one he contemplated upon the Cross bloody and disfigured, it is also that of an immolated and victorious God, God of God, Light of Light.

"I am the Light."

Christ has been, then, for John the Light, the True Light, and the apostle's grace has been to discover in Jesus the very glory of the Son of God come in the flesh.

"The Word was the true light that enlightens every man. . . . And the Word was made flesh and dwelt among us. And we have seen his glory, the glory as of the only-begotten Son of the Father . . . full of grace and truth."

CHAPTER 9

THE GOSPEL OF FILIAL ADOPTION

St. John desires to point out from the beginning of his Gospel the close bond that exists between the coming of the Word into the world and the revelation He makes of His Father and our adoption as sons of God.

No sooner has the Prologue apprized us of the fact that to "receive" the Word is equivalent to "becoming children of God" (1, 12), than it gives the Word His title of only-begotten Son (1, 14,18). This Son has come to reveal His Father and to make us know and love Him (1, 18; 14, 7,21).

This is the ultimate purpose of the Incarnation, viz., the revelation of a Father to whose love His children have been restored (1 Jn. 3, 1). To limit the motive of Christ's coming to redemption from sin is to deprive His mission of one of its all-important characteristics; it is stopping at the means and not really seeing what constitutes the real purpose of this mission.

Christ the Redeemer is ever "turned towards" His eternal Father. And what He brings us is exactly what He is in Himself: He is Son of God and He intends to make us sons of God, to share in His own blessedness as Son.

True, Christ became incarnate "for us and for our salvation," but He nonetheless remains turned towards His Father even in carrying out His mission as Redeemer. He has come first to obey Him, pay Him homage and love and set Himself up as His real adorer and servant.

The Father's Envoy

"For God so loved the world that he gave his only-begotten Son" (3, 16). This gift and this Envoy to whom there will be made frequent allusion in the course of the Gospel have as their object man's salvation; however, though He comes among us with great love, Christ is really fulfilling His Father's will. He looks upon Himself primarily as His Envoy. He is the "missionary" par excellence. And coming into the world, He cries out: "Behold, I come to do thy will, O God' " (Ps. 39, 8).

Not to place this declaration at the beginning of the Johannine Gospel as a guiding light would be to falsify its perspectives and deprive oneself of the opportunity of understanding the true meaning of this Gospel.

The other evangelists present Christ in His humanity. They reveal the presence of the Word in Him only little by little. And this revelation is completed when He consummates His sacrifice. The Synoptics place before us the announcement of a kingdom into which men are invited to enter. Christ is the road to this kingdom and it belongs to His Father who is also our Father (20, 17).

In the fourth Gospel John presents Christ as the only-begotten Son in the bosom of the Father and this is his point of departure. Being made flesh, He reveals the Father's glory and His love for us. As a consequence, the stress is placed more upon our status as children of God than upon the kingdom. Men are turned towards this supernatural reality of which they are made sharers even here on earth.

At the same time, the Redemption is presented as the accomplishment of a mission confided to the Son by the Father (3, 16). When He becomes incarnate and makes Himself one of us, the Son is turned towards us; but more essentially still, He remains "ad Patrem." This is the reason that the mission "of the one whom the Father has sent" (3, 17, used forty-two times in this Gospel) consists not only in saving men, but also in leading them to the Father. After redeeming them He becomes their Way to the Father. He takes upon Himself the leadership of this humanity (14, 3) which He has acquired through His Blood (Ac. 20, 28; Ap. 1, 5; 5, 9).

This attitude of Christ, revealing so much of His Father whose living and perfect image He is: "He who sees me sees the Father" (14, 9), is the real norm of our own condition and attitude as children of God. In His own Person He offers us the model of a Son; in His conduct, the perfect attitude of a son. If we make this attitude our own, it will bring about our resemblance to Christ, uniting us to Him and making us the Father's beloved sons (14, 21).

True, God "expresses" Himself to us in His Word, but this revelation is not only in the intellectual order. It is likewise of a most intimate nature where the relationship between Father and Son alone can help us understand it. Thus, John does not say: "No one has ever seen God. The Word has revealed Him." He says rather: ". . . the only-begotten Son, who is in the bosom of the Father, he has revealed him."[1]

---

1. "Exegesato" is the Greek expression, i.e., explained, recounted in His own person and through His own life.

We are in the realm of love and generation. The Word reveals the Father to us by talking about Him, but the Son reveals the Father simply by manifesting His filial love for Him and the Father's love for us. If the "Word" can reveal "God," only a Word as Son of God can make known a "Father" in God.

This flow of love, intimacy, and union between the Father and the Son makes up the very substance of the fourth Gospel, and into this all the rest is woven. We must never lose sight of the special characteristic this "attitude" of Christ towards His Father confers upon the Johannine Gospel. Christ remains "ad Patrem" even in His surrender of Himself to humanity and in His life among men. Beyond what He reveals to "us" and His attitude in "our" regard, there is that divine Face turned from all eternity towards the Father, that immense field of His relationship with the Father, that ceaseless flow of love between them. And what concerns us, viz., our redemption—and we have a tendency to consider this the only reason for Christ's coming—draws all its value from this relationship between the Father and the Son.

We may now express the central truth of the fourth Gospel in three different ways which are complementary one to the other.

Christ is presented in this Gospel as the "Son." This term is a kind of common denominator extracted from the diversity of titles to which He lays claim, e.g., Son of David, son of Mary, son of Joseph, Son of Man, and only-begotten Son of God. Now there is no son without a father and to present oneself as a son is equivalent to admitting the existence of a father and attaching oneself to him.

One of the expressions always placed upon Christ's lips is: "He who sent me," and this designates the Father and makes of Christ both Son and "the one sent from the Father."

This "mission" enables Christ, through the totality of His actions, attitudes, and teaching, to make us know and love this "Father" (1, 18) who is simultaneously the Father of our Lord Jesus Christ and our Father (20, 17; 2 Cor. 1, 3). It gives that "filial sense" to those who are called to become "children of God" (1, 14).

The Revelation of the Father through the Son

John confers upon God the name of Father in the Prologue. Even the Old Testament bestows this title upon Him (Is. 64, 7; Wis. 11, 25; 12, 7). Here the divine paternity appears already as a reality and as such it far surpasses that sentiment of a Creator taking pleasure in the work which has proceeded from Him (Is. 63, 15). However, the revelation of a divine

Person generating another divine Person was going to enable men to discover in God a supereminent and transcendent fatherhood in God. It is one thing to be considered Father of the world and of a Chosen People; but it is something entirely different to be a Father, engendering a Son like unto Himself.

The Old Testament was unable to have a knowledge of a divine paternity thus understood, even when God the Father made His presence and love felt in the innermost depths of certain souls. The words of the prophets, which appear to us as containing in germ some information concerning the Trinity, remained a closed secret, e.g., "Thou art my Son, this day have I begotten thee" (Ps. 2, 7). The Old Testament data, however, did trace out a path to the revelation of the Trinity. It did so by stressing the divine fatherhood and extolling the fatherly love of Yahweh for His people; by familiarizing this people in a gradual way with realities that were seemingly personalized, e.g., the Law, Wisdom, Word, Spirit, by making this people understand that the divine unity was a unity of richness and of infinite plenitude and not one of solitude. They nevertheless remain without any comparison whatever with the revelations made by Christ.

John does not seem to have judged it necessary to aid minds in making this step gradually. From the very first page of his Gospel he sets the soul before the mystery of the Father and the Son. He speaks of the Word made flesh as the one "whose glory we saw, glory as of the only-begotten Son of the Father, full of grace and truth" (1, 14).

John is aware of the fact that such a revelation is the result of grace in the soul and that all human endeavors remain powerless to have the soul enter into the mystery. But he also realizes that Christ is in Himself the revelation of the Father: "He who sees me, sees the Father" (14, 9); ". . . the only-begotten Son, he has revealed him" (1, 18).

It is sufficient, then, that the revelation of the Son be made in order that revelation of the Father be made also (14, 8). And that is why the revelation of the Son is sovereignly necessary. He cannot reveal Himself without simultaneously revealing His Father. "I and the Father are one" (10, 30).

With the revelation of the Father by the Son we are in the presence of the mystery of a Person who experiences and lives this unity in fullness and who expresses in human words the meaning of this indwelling in the Father, this knowledge of the Father, this love of the Father for Him and through Him for humanity. Christ's unique and transcendent experience as man in His relationship with His Father has been transmitted to us by John, and he does so by trying to retain its whole revelatory power. And we have to try to become conscious of this before analysing its content.

Christ's filial experience

For us the knowledge of the Father is a very lofty and consoling reality, but we frequently perceive it in a remote and veiled manner. This knowledge, however, is immediate, total, and ceaselessly active in Christ. With Him it is not an object of revelation or teaching as it is for us; it is His very life and love. He is the only one who can speak of it as a lived experience, and that is why the things He said about it to His apostles, and which the Gospel has preserved for us are of priceless value.

Love keeps up a perpetual communion between those who love each other. When they speak of the object of their love, it seems to them that they alone understand what they are speaking about and it also seems to them that, in speaking about it, this love, which is their life, becomes more intensified within them.

Christ is alone in loving His Father perfectly and in understanding in what this love consists and in living it. But contrary to men, He both intends and is able to communicate the reality of this love to them by conferring upon them the status of children of God (1 Jn. 3, 1).

The apostle John's glory consists in having entered into this mystery of love and of having lived it himself in an intimate way; and he did this so well that some of it has passed over into his Gospel.

We are taught in theology that Christ enjoyed the beatific vision in His human nature, while we ourselves have to live by faith. Perhaps it would seem to us that we cannot place any hope upon a true filial experience of God. This would be forgetting that in Christ we really share in this divine filiation and we do so because we are intimately and vitally united to Him through sanctifying grace.

Christ is united to his Father through vision and glory and He is associated with Him. For us who are vitally united with Christ, something of this paternity is made perceptible to us, or at least comes to us "in Christ Jesus" through the Holy Spirit who proceeds from the Father and the Son. Is not this the meaning of the Master's words: "If anyone love me, he will keep my word, and my Father will love him and we will come to him and make our abode with him. . . . These things I have spoken to you while yet dwelling with you. But the Advocate, the Holy Spirit, whom the Father will send in my name, he will teach you all things, and bring to your mind whatever I have said to you" (14, 23,25,26).

The Christian, as child of God, is not confined to simply "imagining God as His Father; he has the interior experience of this through the Spirit of Christ who makes him say: "Abba, Father." "And because you are sons, God sent the Spirit of His Son into our hearts, crying, 'Abba, Father' " (Gal. 4, 6). "The Spirit himself gives testimony to our spirit that we are sons of God" (Rom. 8, 16). It is from this experience that we must start in order to understand the texts relative to the Father in the fourth Gospel.

Union of Father and Son

Christ is not as attracted by the exterior world as we are. Although this humanity which lives in illusion, in the shadow of death, in sin, is more present to Him than it is to us, for He beholds it in the divine light and without veils, what Christ contemplates first of all is His Father's bright and loving countenance. What He hears are those words which never fail to re-echo in His Heart: "Thou art my beloved Son . . ." (Mt. 17, 5).

The immediacy of this presence, that look which always encounters His, that bosom upon which He rests, that continual communion with His Father: "All that is mine is thine" (17, 10), that inexpressible oneness between them: "I and the Father are one" (10, 3), all this lies in the foreground of Christ's human life and experience. And we ourselves do not succeed in even imagining it.

John's merit consists in his having understood precisely these things thanks to his intimate contact with Jesus; so well did he understand them that the words uttered by Christ about His Father still retain for St. John their reality and significance. And they will retain these for us also if we make the effort at intimacy with Christ, and if we discover in him what made Him so much attracted to the Father, and not only what makes Him ours.

Before studying Christ's words concerning His Father, we must be fully penetrated with this intimate union, this constant communion between them. To be understood, Christ's teaching in this matter demands a knowledge of His nature as Son of God, consubstantial with the Father. It is only when we have been filled with what entirely constitutes Christ that we shall grasp the depth of a teaching which blends with the revelation of His very being.

Properly speaking, there is no such thing as a "teaching" of Christ concerning His Father; rather there is a living and total reality which identifies itself with Christ's being. It manifests itself in His love, obedience, confidence, His total self-abandonment into His Father's hands.

The Father is His very breath and His divine solicitude; He is the goal of all His strivings, forever present, forever sought, and forever attained; He is the object of His love, perpetually and perfectly possessed.

What being loved here on earth means for the one who loves: what he tends towards with his entire being and what he finds in the innermost depths of his being, sheds only a feeble light upon this perpetual and mutual presence of the Son to the Father and vice versa.

Undoubtedly when we set Christ's statements side by side, and join to these what we learn from His attitude and actions, we arrive at a theological and doctrinal ensemble which is priceless. However, what Christ wills to make known to us and what the fourth Gospel gives us is not only this teaching, but above all else an "atmosphere," a filial "sense," through which our conduct and our lives are transformed.

What we have to consider, therefore, in Christ is a God who is a "Son" and a Man who is "a son of God." There is not one single act of His, not a thought nor a sentiment which does not belong to a Son infinitely loving, obedient, confident.

We must also go beyond our concepts of human fatherhood, for this lies at the source of our physical life only, and is confined to a point of departure of an existence which later acquires a relative autonomy. It is not the same in God in whom paternity and filiation are perpetually in act. The Father generates the Son from all eternity, and at each instant of the same eternity the Son is generated. "Thou art my Son; this day have I begotten thee" (Ps. 2, 7). When applied to a God "who is spirit" (4, 24), the spiritual, subsistent relations of fatherhood and sonship bring about between the divine Persons a mutual, endless, and total embrace. There is nothing in the Father that is not turned towards the Son, nothing in the Son which is not "ad Patrem." As for the Spirit, He is eternally the Encounter of these two loves which blend into one.

"Sons" in the Son

There is nothing astonishing about the fact that Christ, "come that we may have life . . ." (10, 10) and who is Himself this life, has willed also to reveal to us in what this life consists, what is its nature, and what is the movement that animates it.

When we read: "I am the life . . ." (14, 6), we identify this life with the divine nature which Christ possesses as His own, and we are right in doing so. But this life is less a "possession" in Him than a "gift" ceaselessly received and perpetually returned.

The life Christ communicates to us is nothing else but that "élan" of love of the Son for the Father and of the Father for the Son. How would He transmit it to us without divine love which makes it live?

When He came among us, Christ never ceased laying claim to the status of one "sent from the Father." It is easy to deduce from this that this life He came to bring us is not a simple vital force placed at our disposition; it is the divine life itself, possessed in union with the Father and communicated in all its vitality.

How could this life in us not be an endlessly renewed élan or impetus at the same time as it is a gift constantly received? It contains in itself the entire love of the Son for the Father and the love of the Father for the Son. It likewise contains the Father's love for this world He intends to save by delivering His Son up for it, and the love of the Son offering the Father Himself for the salvation of men whom He loved even to total sacrifice of self.

The life communicated to us is one that is magnetic and orientated, and it is animated with the divine love that goes to make it up. It imprints in us that trinitarian character which it bears within itself.

True, it is "life" that Christ brings to us, but His "mission" as Son is completed by conferring upon this life a filial character. In fact, it is not only His own life as Son that He makes us share in, but His life communicated in the very act of His obedience to His Father, and in one great act of filial love. It is as the "one sent" by His Father that the Son communicates life to us.

Model of filial Love

"The Father has sent me. . . ." This expression so frequently repeated in the Gospel of St. John bears testimony to the Father's love for men, but also to the Son's love for the one whose will He carries out (8, 29).

The Son knows the reason for His coming into the world and He knows it with an infinite knowledge of love. He plunges into the Father's bosom and there He communes in His love for men. He contemplates this love for humanity and bears such a filial love in Himself that His love for us and for His Father flow together into that one great aspiration which forces Him to say: "Behold I come to do thy will, O God' " (Ps. 39, 8).

His coming here below is a manifestation of this filial love which has an infinite value, purity, depth and power. The movement which draws Him towards us is the revelation "in act" of this love. The one who, contemplating Christ with the eyes of faith and love, goes right to the source of these acts and to the first cause of His coming, encounters and discovers the Father; this Father who sent Him to us and who never stops sending Him.

When He reminds us the Father sent Him, Christ gives us the opportunity of discovering in the Father an infinitely merciful love and in

Himself a filial love which is the source and the model for our own. Look upon me, Christ could say to us, not only because in me "there dwells corporeally the fullness of the divinity" (Col. 2, 9), but in Me you can attain the Father's love and also the resource of filial love that must serve as model for you.

Christ's words, teaching these things, are essential; but the actions which accompany them bring us an even more important teaching. They show us that the life of Christ is a "mission," and like every mission, this one demands not only a constant bond of union between the one sending and the one sent, but also the return of the one sent to the one who sent Him.

"I came forth from the Father and have come into the world. Again I leave the world and go to the Father" (16, 28). "Father, I have glorified thee on earth; I have accomplished the work that thou hast given me to do. And now do thou, Father, glorify me with thyself, with the glory that I had with thee before the world existed" (17, 4,5). "But now I am coming to thee . . ." (17, 13).

Christ has given Himself with an absolute love and an act of perfect obedience, but it is question of an act accomplished in time, a transitory act. Christ cannot forget His origin and never stops longing for His return to His Father (14, 28). Eternity is the only "air" He breathes, the only one suitable for His eternal nature. As ardent as is His love for us, life with His Father still attracts Him and draws Him. Undoubtedly we are dealing here with the Word, but Christ's human nature shares in this irresistible attraction in virtue of the hypostatic union, and the Ascension is a visible manifestation of this.

Repeating so often: "The Father has sent me," Christ allows His thoughts, desires, citizenship to appear (Phil. 3, 20). He makes us understand that His city is in heaven with His Father: "Where your treasure is, there is your heart also" (Mt. 6, 21). Christ is "drawn" towards the Father, and His love for us is such that He desires nothing but what He desires for Himself. "And I go to prepare a place for you, and I am coming again, and I will take you to myself; that where I am, there you also may be" (14, 3).

Christ is so attracted towards His Father and His thirst for returning to Him so intense that He is astonished that the apostles are in such pain and anguish at seeing Him about to leave them and not rejoicing with His joy (14, 28; 16, 5).

Hence, how could an "envoy" not talk of the Father when this "envoy" is the Son, with a heart filled with love for that Father, and come to save men and lead them into the house of Him who is both His

Father and theirs? How could He stop revealing to them what attracts His gaze, occupies His mind, His will, and His love? "From the abundance of the heart the mouth speaks" (Lk. 6, 45).

How would His words and actions not reflect His constant contemplation and pre-occupation: to accomplish the Father's will and transmit His words (17, 8), to make Him known (17, 26), ensure His glory (17, 4), and at the same time to give Him in all His actions the signs of His submission (4, 34)? "I do always the things that please him" (8, 29).

We believe that Christ's mission consisted solely in revealing the truth to us, saving and giving us life. True, He did come to assume this role, but if He carried it out, it was chiefly because it was the Father's will and because this mission had been confided to Him by the Father. This constant pre-occupation to obey the Father's will is manifest in all His acts. Through each of these acts He intends to show His disciples that "he loves the Father and does as the Father commanded him" (14, 31).

Thus, once His mission is accomplished and His Father is glorified through His works (16, 15), Christ does not delay an instant. He asks His Father permission to return to Him (17, 4), and to be glorified "with the glory that I had before the world existed" (17, 5). "I have manifested thy name to the men thou hast given me out of the world," and henceforth: "they have learned that whatever thou hast given me is from thee; because the words that thou hast given me I have given them. And they have received them, and have known of a truth that I came forth from thee, and they have believed that thou didst send me" (17, 6-8).

"Now I leave the world and go to the Father" (16, 28). Now "I am coming to thee" (17, 13). The only thing He asks of the Father is to watch over these whom He has confided to Him and whom He has kept "while I was with them" (17, 12). These men have been so loved by Christ that He did not hesitate to "sanctify himself," i.e., to sacrifice Himself for them, "that they also may be sanctified in truth" (17, 19). And yet He never fails to see in these men before all else "those whom thou hast given me" (17, 9).

It seems He cherishes them in a special manner because of this and He has watched over them and kept them from all evil. "They were thine and thou hast given them to me" (17, 6). We are struck by Christ's extraordinary insistence in returning to this thought. He asks permission to "give eternal life to all those whom thou hast given me." This eternal life is "to know thee, the only true God and Jesus Christ whom thou hast sent." The work He has done on earth is what the Father gave him to do. He has manifested His Father's name to "those whom thou hast given me out of the world." "And now they have learned that whatever thou hast given me is from thee; because the words thou hast given me I have given them" (17, passim).

It is for "those whom the Father has given" Him that Christ prays, and it is these also "whom the Father has given Him" that He begs the Father "to keep." But now that He has given them the Word of the Father, i.e., Himself, and "the glory that thou hast given me," He returns "to the Father," but not without directing this last request to Him: "Father, I will that where I am, they also whom thou hast given me may be with me; in order that they may behold the glory which thou hast given me" (17, passim).

The mission confided to the "one sent" by the Father is to reveal Him. The many statements we find in the Gospel and especially in the discourse after the Supper confirm the words of the Prologue: "The only-begotten Son, who is in the bosom of the Father, he has revealed him" (1, 18). This means that the Revelation of the Father, holding as it does such a place of importance in this Gospel, makes of it a Gospel of "the children of God," to whom is announced the good news of their adoption, as St. John states in his Epistle:

"Behold what manner of love the Father has bestowed upon us, that we should be called the children of God, and such we are. This is why the world does not know us, because it did not know him. Beloved, now we are the children of God and it has not yet appeared what we shall be" (1 Jn. 3, 1,2).

Filial Love and fraternal Charity

Christ fulfilled His mission by being exactly what He was supposed to be, viz., the only-begotten Son, the perfect Son, the natural Son. And that mission was to save men, to reveal the Father to them and lead them to him; it was a mission which was doubly filial since it was as "Son" that He carried out the Father's will, and it was to those who were to become "sons of adoption" that He revealed His Father. Through His life, actions, and teaching He reveals in Person what it is to be a Son. In Him, the message and the Person form one entity. And in Him too, the revelation of the Father is linked to the revelation of the Son Himself. And that is why he can say: "He who sees me, sees the Father" (14, 9).

He reveals to us what we are and must be, contenting Himself with living in our presence His life "as Son." His words and actions reveal His sentiments concerning His Father. To become perfect children of God we must model our attitude upon His.

Consequently, the rule of the Christian's conduct must be summed up thus: Live as a true child of God. And Christ must be the sole model for us because He was the perfect Son and the Beloved of His Father. The fact is of extreme importance, for it makes the atmosphere in which the Christian must live very specific. It confers a definite orientation upon his actions, disposes his heart, and invites him to come to God with well defined feelings: those of a child coming to his Father.

Likewise, we find here the basis for social morality, since the attitude of each towards his Father influences his attitude towards the children of this Father, viz., his brothers. And to discover what our attitude towards them should be, we have only to consider what Christ's was. He has laid down the rule of conduct in the matter of fraternal charity by saying: "Love one another as I have loved you" (13, 34). Since He was God He could have made this rule of conduct flow from a law which He enacted for our observance. However, He did not will to give any other than one He put into practice and left as a model. Because He was Himself the Son of God and gave us the power of becoming "sons" too, He looked upon us as His own brothers. This filial attitude has certain aspects in it which St. John helps us discover in this Gospel.

Adoration, Obedience, and Confidence with regard to the Father

Two texts make adoration the first duty of the Child of God. Christ makes it understood when He declares, after expelling the money-changers from the Temple: " 'Do not make the house of my Father a house of business.' And his disciples remembered it is written, 'The zeal of thy house has eaten me up' " (2, 16).

More explicitly He will say to the Samaritan woman: "Woman, believe me, the hour is coming when neither on this mountain nor in Jerusalem will you worship the Father. But the hour is coming, and is now here, when the true worshippers will worship the Father in spirit and in truth. For the Father also seeks such to worship him" (4, 21-23). An echo of this teaching is to be found in the opening sentence of the prayer taught by Christ: "When you pray, say: Our Father, who art in heaven, hallowed be thy name . . ."(Mt. 6, 9; Lk. 11, 2).

If adoration is the first duty of the children of God, it is merciful love with regard to them that is brought to light as far as the Father is concerned: "God has so loved the world as to give his only-begotten Son. For God did not send his Son into the world in order to judge the world, but that the world may be saved through him" (3, 16, 17). This mercy is the superabundance of the Father's love for the Son, so to speak. This love overflows from Christ as "Head" of the Mystical Body and becomes "merciful love." The adoration of the children of God is permeated with this merciful love which gives it a note of humble but infinite confidence.

Speaking of this paternal Providence to which man must abandon himself, Jesus concludes His interview with His apostles in these words: "Fear not, little flock, for it has pleased the Father to give to you a kingdom" (Lk. 12, 32). This brings us to those words of the fourth Gospel: "I am the good shepherd, and I know mine and mine know me, even as the Father knows me and I know the Father" (10, 14,15). These are words inviting us to seek in the infinite love of the Father for the Son, the source of that admirably compassionate and merciful love of the Good Shepherd for His sheep.

Adoration of the Father, united to a humble and loving confidence, takes on the form of obedience in practice. Not a servile obedience, but a filial obedience so frequently exemplified by Christ in the fourth Gospel. John reports Christ's words carefully which re-echo the words of the Psalm: "Behold, I come to do thy will, O God" (Ps. 39, 8).

First, there are those words: "My food is to do the will of him who sent me, to accomplish his work" (4, 34). And those other words: "I seek not my own will, but the will of him who sent me" (5, 30). Jesus declares to His apostles: "I have not spoken to you on my own authority, but the Father who sent me, he has commanded me what I should say, and what I should declare. The things that I speak, I speak as the Father has bidden me" (12, 49,50).

In the accomplishment of His Father's will, He sees the real reason for His coming upon earth: "I came down from heaven to do the will of him who sent me" (6, 38). And to this same obedience belong those words pronounced by Christ at the moment He sets out irrevocably upon the road of oblation: "That the world may know that I love the Father, and that I do as the Father commanded me. Arise, let us go from here" (14, 30). Thus, from the first word, "Behold, I come to do thy will, O God" to the last, falling from the lips of the Crucified, "It is finished," i.e., everything is accomplished that you gave me to do, the Son's love for His Father takes the form of obedience.

To be surprised at the attitude of the child of God being summed up in obedience as exemplified by Christ would show that we have scarcely reflected upon what such obedience really means. And especially upon the love of which it is a sign. It is a love replete with humility and molded by the spirit of service.

The more we meditate upon Christ's obedience, the better we grasp that this obedience contains within it and sets to work all the virtues to be practiced by the child of God. Christ makes this understood when He says: "He who has my commandments and keeps them, he it is who loves me" (14, 21).

Christ's obedience manifests itself mostly in the form of service; and the "Servant of Yahweh" knows the mind of Him whom He serves because He is His beloved Son. Through service, the accomplishment of His Father's will, He keeps up an intimate communion with Him in love. "And he who sent me is with me, he has not left me alone, because I always do the things that are pleasing to him" (8, 29).

But above all, this obedience bears the characteristic of self-resignation, a dependence which repairs the independence and disobedience of the first Adam, introducing that filial atmosphere of love which is the great Christian revelation.

Not for a single moment, in spite of the power He possesses, does Christ aspire to anything else but the position of "Servant," one coming in the name of one greater and carrying out his orders. It is the words of His Father which He speaks (8, 38). "He speaks what he has heard and seen with his Father." "His doctrine is not his, but the Father's who sent him" (7, 15). He teaches men what the Father has taught Him (8, 28).

The same may be said of the works. They are the "works of him who sent him" (9, 4), for "he does nothing of himself" (8, 28). He acts in "the Father's name," by His power and in such union with Him that "the Father who abides in me, he does the works" (14, 10). They are the Father's works, and the glory of these works seen by men accomplished by Christ must go to the Father. In fact, the Father's work and that of the Son is one thing, viz., "the work of God," the important thing being the mission of the "one sent" by God and men's faith in Him. "This is the work of God, that you may believe in him whom He has sent" (6, 29).

True, He claims the whole responsibility and He speaks with authority; it is also on His own authority that He works His miracles (11, 4). However, nothing He says or does is to be referred to Him. He refers all these to one whom He calls His Father, and who must be sought, not here below, but in heaven whence Christ comes and to which He will return having accomplished His work (3, 13; 8, 23). Instead of presenting Himself as the final authority, as the term in which all ends, Christ presents Himself as the Door opening upon the Father, the Way to the Father, and as the Father's voice speaking to the world.

In the fourth Gospel we see a great absence of selfishness on Christ's part, and we see an unfathomable humility to which we may pay little attention and yet it is the very essence of the Incarnation. To St. Paul's

"He emptied Himself taking on the form of a slave . . ." there succeeds a series of acts which gives rise to that other great Christian principle: "For no one lives to himself . . ." (Rom. 14, 7).

Christ did not please Himself, and drawing others to Himself He does so only because He is the Way to the Father (12, 32). In a word, He wills to be for all what He is in Himself: "ad Patrem."

Christ has desired to give a foundation in His own life to that precept of St. Paul: "For if we live, we live to the Lord." And we end up with those other words of Paul to the Corinthians: "For all things are yours and you are Christ's and Christ is God's" (1 Cor. 3, 23).

"And Christ is God's." This is certainly what Christ would have men understand. His reference to the Father, His belonging to Him, His obedience, these are not those of a Servant only, or an envoy, but of a Son.

The Son is the Father's. He belongs to Him, but because He is a Son it is a relationship based on love. It is in this same spirit that He reveals Him and tries to turn us towards His Father. That is why, while making us understand our obligation of preserving a relationship of absolute dependence on God and fulfilling His will in all things, Christ does not fail to stress the fact that He is our Father. St. James will say: "Every good gift and every perfect gift is from above, coming down from the Father of lights" (Jas. 1, 17). "For this reason I bend my knees to the Father . . . from whom all fatherhood in heaven and earth receives its name" (Eph. 3, 15). And St. John: "He has so loved the world that he has given his only-begotten Son . . ." (3, 16).

That is why, a knowledge only of Christ's love for us helps us discover the Father's love. In fact: "If you had known me, you would have known my Father also. . . . He who sees me, sees the Father (14, 7,9).

The Father loves the Son

To reveal His Father as infinitely good, perfect, and loving procures for Christ an infinite joy. We feel this from the sound of His words when He speaks of the one He loves and by whom He is loved in return. The love of the Son for the Father and the Father for the Son is evident in a series of declarations which are complementary one to the other, blending into a unity.

Although the apostle John was a witness to the Transfiguration, and the Baptist acquainted him with the baptism scene at the Jordan, yet he does not report the twice-repeated words of the Father: "This is my beloved Son in whom I am well pleased" (Mk. 9, 7; Lk. 9, 35). But we come upon their equivalent in the Baptist's last testimony: "For he whom God has sent speaks the words of God, for not by measure does God give the Spirit. The Father loves the Son, and has given all things into his hands" (3, 34,35).

Christ wills to convince us of the Father's love for Him and through Him, of His love for us: "For the Father loves the Son and shows him all he does" (5, 20). He does not hesitate to unveil the secret of an intimacy which is the source of eternal and infinite joy: "And he who sent me is with me; he has not left me alone, because I do always the things that are pleasing to him" (8, 29).

This inter-communication is so perfect that: "All things the Father has are mine" (16, 15); "Father, all that is mine is thine, and all that is thine is mine" (17, 10). So total is this that each belongs to the other and is in the other: "Believe the works, that you may know and believe that the Father is in me and I in the Father" (10, 38). And this mutual indwelling tends to make them one: "I and the Father are one" (10, 30).

Christ, the Way to the Father

How can we be astonished that Christ has so much at heart the desire to communicate to the children of God this love of His Father which makes up His own life and joy and must be ours. This will be one of the themes of the "Sacerdotal prayer" at the Supper.

What He desires for them is eternal life: that life in which men are destined "to know thee, the only true God, and him whom thou hast sent, Jesus Christ" (17, 3). To lead them to it, He has "manifested the name of the Father" (17, 6). He has made them understand that all that has been given to Him comes from the Father" (17, 7). He has revealed the Father's love, a love of which He is the first beneficiary, but which is promised to men. For it is the same infinite and divine love the Father gives the Son and all His other children.

"I in them and thou in me; that they may be perfected in unity, and that the world may know that thou hast sent me, and that thou hast loved them even as thou hast loved me. . . . And I have made known thy name, and will make it known in order that the love with which thou hast loved me may be in them, and I in them" (17, 23-26). Christ wills to arouse such a filial love for His Father in souls that the certitude of going to Him and of living with Him forever may be the great hope of the children of God.

What, in the Synoptics, is proposed to us in parables where the Father is represented to us as a king or the father of a family offering a banquet to His children, is stated here with the aid of Christ's words alone. But how loving and urgent they are since they form His last will and testament.

"In my Father's house there are many mansions. Were it not so, I would have told you, because I go to prepare a place for you. And if I go and prepare a place for you, I am coming again, and I will take you to myself; that where I am, there you also may be" (14, 2,3).

Christ alone has the power to develop this filial sentiment in us. Being the only one who "knows" the Father, He is the only one able to make Him known: "And you do not know him, but I know him. And if I say I do not know him, I shall be like you, a liar. But I know him, and I keep his word" (8, 55). And His totally divine way of making Him known is by making us really and truly children of God, sons of God (1 Jn. 3, 1).

Christ is the Way to the Father, the road outside of which no one can come to Him (14, 6). It is true that He is the Way of knowledge and revelation, but through Him we actually realize union with God. It is through Christ and "in Him" that we become children of God. This status having been lost through sin is restored to us through Him who, both God and man and sent by God to represent humanity, restores it to us through His Incarnation and Redemption.

If He offers us the opportunity of becoming children of God it is because He wants us to become His brothers. This grace of adoption is the supreme grace that He merited for us: "To those who received him he gave the power of becoming the children of God" (1, 12).

This is the new and supernatural creation of which John sings in his Epistle and Gospel (1 Jn. 3, 1,2; 1, 12; 3, 7,8). And Christ's supreme joy is to increase the number of those who "adore the Father in spirit and truth" (4, 23).

"Enlarge the place of thy tent, and stretch out the skins of thy tabernacles. Spare not: lengthen thy cords and strengthen thy stakes. For thou shalt pass on to the right hand and to the left, and thy seed shall inherit the Gentiles, and shall inhabit the desolate cities" (Is. 54, 2,3).

What was formerly applied to Jerusalem by the prophet in these words takes on full meaning when we see in it the expansion and extension of the Mystical Body of Christ, of that immense multitude of the children of God, of those who have become sons "in the Son," and whose number daily increases.

From all these hearts inhabited by the Spirit there arises that cry of adoption into the divine family: "Abba, Father" (Rom. 54, 2). And that word "Father," which fell from Christ's lips as an aspiration of adoration and love, is now and always will be repeated by multitudes who find in it the source of eternal beatitude.

Children of God

It is Christ's mission to obtain this divine adoptive sonship for us. But this status of "child of God" is something so great that, to restore it to us, He willingly surrenders all His powers and even His life to obtain it. The mystery of the Cross is the efficient cause of our becoming sons of God. "For this reason the Father loves me, because I lay down my life that I may take it up again" (10, 17). These words of Christ set us in the right direction, because they apply directly to the sacrifice of Calvary and present it to us as an offering acceptable to the Father. The text clearly says that the Father accepts this sacrifice only insofar as it is an act and a proof of love: the greatest and purest that can be: "Greater love than this no man has, that one lay down his life for his friends" (14, 3).

If the Father consents to His Son's voluntary sacrifice, it is because it is an act of obedience towards Him who intends to reconcile His children to Himself through this sacrifice. Only an act of filial dependence and love could restore our status as children. It is not only because He is "God" that Christ can make us "children of God," but because He is "Son" of God. Our divine sonship is possible only in virtue of the Son's coming, of His redemptive action, as the expression of his filial love, and of our incorporation in Him and of His return to the Father, "that where I am, you also may be" (14, 3). It seems then that our adoptive sonship, resembling that of Christ's sonship, comes from the Father and returns to the Father.

If there is a sonship and an adoption it is because the Father has "sent" and "has given" His only-begotten Son. And if the children of God experience the full development of the new life Christ has acquired through His Blood, it is because, having returned to the Father, He will have them come to the place where He is (17, 24).

Thus the divine sonship which is at the very heart of the Johannine Gospel must follow the bent traced out in the entire Gospel and which the Prologue already pointed out: The coming of the Word from His Father, His incorporation into humanity, and His return to His Father.

Our divine filiation comes from the Father and goes back to the Father. Christ is the Father's Envoy and He is the one who reveals the Father. He is the Worker of this filiation and the Way through which the children of God regain their original home, or better, the bosom of the Father. But it is the Father who is the Alpha and Omega.

"Beloved, we are now the children of God"

When speaking to us about the Father, about His goodness, mercy, providence, etc., the Synoptic Gospels have used touching images and parables. The most beautiful of these, along with those of the lilies of the field and the birds of the air, is undoubtedly the Prodigal Son.

John's Gospel retains nothing of all this, even though it is the Gospel of divine fatherhood and our adoptive sonship. It is because the apostle John knows these in reality and has actually lived them "in spirit and in truth." He knows by experience that nothing can give an idea of this great reality. Undoubtedly the Master Himself did not hesitate to use these comparisons and parables in order to prepare minds to reach them better. But John has experienced the reality in the innermost depths of His own being; and he cannot stop singing of it in his Epistle as the only real happiness that exists, and that it is possessed and experienced here on earth.

"And the Life was made known and we have seen and now testify and announce to you, the Eternal life which was with the Father, and has appeared to us. What we have seen and heard we announce to you, in order that you also may have fellowship with us, and that our fellowship may be with the Father, and with His Son Jesus Christ" (1 Jn. 1-3). He has no doubt that his readers know the Father, as he does, in the intimacy of their souls. "I am writing to you, little ones, because you know the Father" (1 Jn. 2, 14).

He knows the possession of the Son cannot actually be without possession of the Father. "No one who disowns the Son has the Father. He who confesses the Son has the Father also" (1 Jn. 2, 23). The purpose of his teaching is to have his followers "abide" in the Father as well as in the Son. "If that abides in you which you have heard from the beginning, you will abide in the Son and in the Father" (1 Jn. 2, 24).

If "the great love" of Christ is having given His life for us, then the greatest love of the Father is to make us "His children," for such is our calling, incomprehensible as it may appear: "Behold what manner of love the Father has bestowed upon us, that we should be called children of God, and such we are.... Beloved, now we are the children of God" (1 Jn. 3, 1,2).

This status as children of God, enrapturing the apostle and containing that promise of a share in the divine life, does not simply lead to personal happiness. We cannot be "children of God" without at the same time being united to all His other children. Our happiness will not be perfect unless that of our brothers develops and completes it.

Eternity is not enough to characterize this happiness; what is also needed is the riches and depth of the relationship with others which eternity both permits and sustains. It is not only to the Trinity that we shall be united eternally, but also to all those who, in Christ, have become children of the Trinity and our own brothers.

The divine Fatherhood must then be inseparably linked, in our mind and heart, to this family whose Father He is and which has been gathered together at the price of Christ's Blood.

Hence, we are not surprised that eternal life is considered as a "house" in which "there are many mansions" (14, 2). The Father is "Father of the family," and the multiplicity of mansions lays stress upon the wonderful richness of this family's unity.

By insisting that this condition of "child of God" is something actually conferred upon us "right now" (1 Jn. 3, 2), John wants us to understand that it is not only the source of a filial life, but also of a fraternal life; and it is such a form of life that John desires to see develop in all those whom he calls "his little children." He hopes ardently that they know, as he does himself, the joy of knowing themselves "born of God" (1 Jn. 4, 7; 5, 1), and of "abiding in the Son and in the Father" (1 Jn. 2, 24). This "fellowship with the Father and with His Son Jesus Christ" is "this eternal life which has appeared to us" (1 Jn. 1, 1-3).

For St. John it is not necessary to await the next life in order to experience in the depths of the soul the Father's love for His children, and for us to try to return this love; or to realize among all the children of God a union of charity which is simultaneously the fruit and the manifestation of our divine adoptive sonship in Christ.

It is within the mystery of this spiritual rebirth, within the dynamic vitality of this adoption as sons, that John strives to "dwell" himself and to have us dwell too. This "new birth" (3, 3) announced to Nicodemus is seen here endowed with all its powers of life and grace. The experience of the aged apostle helps him contemplate it in the "children of God." In them he beholds the splendor of divine love, its perpetual and marvelous creation; and the words with which he had summed up the Savior's mission: "that he might gather into one the children of God who were scattered abroad" (11, 52) are being fulfilled and will know their final realization in eternal life.

✠

CHAPTER 10

THE HOLY SPIRIT

The Word holds first place in Revelation because of the Incarnation. Being made flesh and having dwelt among men (1, 14), what the Word is in Himself has been revealed to them, viz., Light, Life, Truth. The Father is the Object of this revelation which He brings us (1, 18) and Christ's purpose is to make us "children of God" (1, 12).

However, His work would have remained incomplete if He had not revealed the Holy Spirit to us, for without Him there is no true knowledge of the Father and the Son, as He is their bond (16, 13); neither would there be a true child of God (Rm. 8, 14,16). But how was He to reveal this Spirit to men?

We are able to form an idea of the Father because of His name. We are aided in this by human comparisons, fatherhood, sonship, etc. We come to the Son through all those ways which His life and word have traced out for us. The Word made flesh is the Bridge by which we are enabled to come to God. Each of us can still continue to see, understand, and touch the Mediator through the testimonies made of Him (1 Jn. 1, 1).

The Person of the Spirit

The Holy Spirit seems more mysterious. Not because He is more "spiritual" than the Father or the Son, for God is "spirit" (4, 24), but because we approach Him through a totally spiritual mode that is often dark. But the very thing that hides Him and renders Him remote for carnal minds, reveals Him to the true children of God, to those born of Him (3, 5,7), in whom He dwells and who are influenced by Him.

Far from being an abstract reality, the Holy Spirit is presented in the fourth Gospel as a Person. He is clearly pointed out in several passages where there is mention of the "Paraclete" (14, 16,26; 15, 26; 16, 7). The

Paraclete is the "defender," the "advocate"; He gives "testimony" of Christ (15, 26); "He will convict the world of sin" (17, 8); He will teach all truth (16, 13); "He will not speak on his own authority, but whatever he will hear he will speak, and the things that are to come he will declare to you" (16, 13); "He will glorify Christ" (16, 14); ". . . he will receive of what is mine and declare it to you" (16, 15).

It is evident all these statements refer to a Person. They lay stress upon His activity with men. When we consider the activity of the three Persons, it appears that, though the Father is first, since He sent the Son to save the world (3, 17), the Son Himself, having completed His work, sends us from the Father a third Person who, having prepared Christ's work from its very beginnings, is given the mission of following it through and bringing it to perfection in souls.

This succession in the Persons is pointed out repeatedly. Thus, when Christ cries out in the Temple on the feast of the Tabernacles: "If anyone thirst, let him come to me and drink. He who believes in me, as the Scripture says, 'From within him there shall flow rivers of living water.' He said this, however, of the Spirit whom they who believed in him were to receive; for the Spirit had not yet been given, since Jesus had not yet been glorified" (7, 37,38).

Jesus always speaks of the Spirit as the one whom He will send once He has returned to the Father (14, 12,16,17); or whom the Father will send in His name (14, 25,26); and finally whom He will send, though the Spirit proceeds from the Father also (15, 26).

This succession is even more clearly stated in the following texts: "It is expedient that I depart. For if I do not go the Advocate will not come to you; but if I go I will send him to you. But when he, the Spirit of Truth, has come, he will teach you all the truth" (16, 7,13).

These passages describe the Spirit as the one who continues Christ's work and who, though His action is a prolongation of that of Christ, nonetheless accomplishes a distinct personal work.

His action prolongs that of Christ, first in the baptism scene on the Jordan. The Baptist sees the Spirit descend upon the Messias "as a dove from heaven, and it abode upon him" (1, 32), according to the sign that had been given him in order to recognize Christ (1, 33,34). Then in that statement of John the Apostle which seems so closely connected with the scene of the Jordan: "For he whom God has sent speaks the words of God, for not by measure does God give the Spirit" (3, 34).

It is in virtue of this plenitude of possession of the Spirit that Christ will communicate the Spirit to His apostles, at the end of His mission and after His resurrection from the dead. " 'As the Father has sent me, I also send you. When he had said this, he breathed upon them and said to them, 'Receive you the Holy Spirit; whose sins you shall forgive they are forgiven them . . .' " (20, 21,22).

The Spirit's action is nonetheless distinct from that of Christ. The Spirit appears at the beginning of this new life without which "no one enters the kingdom of heaven" (3, 5). The life demands that one be "born of water and the Spirit" (3, 5). For only "that which is born of the Spirit" (3, 6) shares in "this birth from on high" (3, 3), which we owe to "the son of Man who is in heaven and who came down from heaven" (3, 6).

Furthermore, not only is the Spirit necessary for this birth from on high, but the permanence of His action in those who share in this spiritual regeneration is indispensable (1 Jn. 3, 24), though it remains invisible and mysterious to man. It is compared to the wind. "The wind blows where it will, and thou hearest its sound but dost not know where it comes from or where it goes. So is everyone who is born of the Spirit" (3, 8).

I. OLD TESTAMENT DATA ON THE SPIRIT

This collection of texts which place the Spirit on a high personal plane, pointing Him out as a Person co-equal with the Father and Son, takes on a fuller meaning when compared with texts from the Old Testament. St. John, who was acquainted with the images and symbols used in the Bible to signify the Spirit, found them frequently on the Master's lips; and Christ's teaching is made clear in the light of these Old Testament data.[1] It is helpful to recall these to our mind. The Holy Spirit assumes them into Himself while renewing and transcending them.

In the Old Testament the Spirit was considered as the breath emanating from Yahweh. This "ruah Yahweh" took complete possession of man. The prophets were the best examples of this action of the Spirit. The "ruah" manifested itself in two directions that are apparently very different but actually are complementary. On the one hand, it makes the "nabis" (those professionals of this religious exaltation), enter into an ecstacy or trance, and on the other, it places the words of Yahweh in the mouths of the "inspired." Although the two forms had not ceased manifesting themselves up to and including Messianic times, the importance

1. The interviews with Nicodemus and the Samaritan, the discourse on the bread of life, the promise of living water, all take on a fuller meaning when studied in the light of Biblical data, as will be shown later.

given to the word as the privileged manifestation of Yahweh's spirit did not stop growing, and it is in this sense that we find the "prophetic" evolution (Is. 1, 10; Jer. 1, 9; 2, 1; Bar. 1, 21; Ez. 2, 1).

We can see that the manifestations of the Spirit tend gradually to become a stable or permanent taking possession of the person rather than something transient and limited. Thus, the "judges" were clothed in this Spirit, but the "King of Israel" much more so, and he will appear more and more to become the permanent depository of the Spirit. Of David we could already say what will be said of Christ: "the spirit of God was upon him" (1 Kgs. 16, 13), consecrating him for the salvation of his people. When speaking of the Messias, Isaias declares that there will rest permanently upon Him "the spirit of wisdom, and of understanding, the spirit of counsel, and of fortitude, of knowledge and fear of the Lord" (Is. 11, 2). This permanence of the Spirit in those permeated with it enables them to be instructed in the "secrets" of the Lord (Am. 3, 7).

But it is above all in the mode of an "interiorization," and then in a more individualized sense, that we see the Spirit's action evolve. He works "in hearts"; He is at the service of divine Providence; He sanctifies the heart of someone chosen by God for some special mission: "Behold my servant, I will uphold him. My elect, my soul delights in him. I have given him my spirit" (Is. 42, 1).

Instead of manifesting Himself through the wind, the breeze, the tempest, the fury of natural forces (1 Kgs. 16, 15; cf. also Jgs. 9, 23), the Spirit tends not to act through a control over souls and minds (3 Kgs. 19, 11,12). In the full sense of the term, He brings about a complete possession of the individual, and we are able to follow its progress in Isaias, Jeremias, the Psalms, and the Book of Job.

In other words, the Spirit of God is shown here as the "generator" of what would be termed today a "spiritual life" (which is better termed: life in the spirit). He is at the source of those relations of man with God. He communicates to man God's thoughts, desires, and plans, and invites man to respond "in spirit." He makes of him, not only an instrument, but a "witness."[2]

---

2. In Chapter 61 the prophet declares: "The spirit of the Lord is upon me, because the Lord hath anointed me; he hath sent me to preach to the meek, to heal the contrite of heart, and to preach a release to captives, and deliverance to them that are shut up." (61, 1). And Christ, having read this passage in the Synagogue at Nazareth, will say: "Today this Scripture has been fulfilled in your hearing" (Lk. 4, 21), thus laying claim to these words of the prophecy. And these declarations make of the mission and action of the one upon whom God makes His spirit descend, the "Servant" of Yahweh, who bears witness to Him. And to this same role of "witness" the disciples will be invited by the Master: "But when the Advocate has come, whom I will send you from the Father, the Spirit of Truth, he will bear witness concerning me. And you also bear witness because from the beginning you are with me" (15, 26,27).

Isaias would never have been able to give us such a portrait of the Messias if this interiorization had not occurred;[3] and if he had not experienced the Spirit destined to open not only ears (Is. 50, 4), but also hearts and transform them.[4]

Finally, and undoubtedly this is essential: In the Old Testament there is a coincidence between a revelation which becomes more and more explicit and exterior and the fact of this Spirit concentrating upon certain chosen ones, e.g., Judges, Kings, Prophets (Jgs. 14, 6,19).

The New Testament will show us that the choice will finally rest upon a unique Person: the Anointed of Yahweh, who alone will receive the Spirit in His plenitude. "I beheld the Spirit descending as a dove from heaven, and it abode upon him. And I have seen and borne testimony that this is the Son of God. . . . For he whom God has sent speaks the words of God, for not by measure does God give the Spirit" (1, 32,34).

Hence we find the activity of the Spirit reach its highest point in that concentration upon the Anointed of the Lord. It was permanent, interior, and spiritual.

But what profit would it be for us to grasp this, if the nature and role of the Holy Spirit remained hidden from us? The Old Testament had recourse to images and symbols in order to reveal these to us. These will be taken up in the New Testament. And more than any other, the Johannine Gospel enables us to see that Christ Himself made ample use of these.

Symbols of the Spirit

Throughout the Old Testament the Holy Spirit is revealed under two types of symbols: first, under the symbols of power and violence, and second, under those of gentleness and slow and silent penetration.

The Spirit of Yahweh swoops down upon the prophets and the inspired ones with a sudden violence, similar to that of the eagle pouncing upon its prey or the lion upon the animal it makes its food. Coming upon them, He arouses in them an exaltation or even effects an unusual be-havior (1 Kgs. 10, 6; 10, 10). He confers unusual powers or extraordinary strength upon them (3 Kgs. 18, 46; Jgs. 14, 6). The wind, tempest, and fire are frequently associated with these interventions of the Spirit.

---

3. Cf. "The Servant of God" Is. 42, 1-9; 49, 1-6; 50, 4-11; 52, 13 to 53, 12. Filled with the Spirit of God the Servant is separated and chosen to be his witness before the nations; the prophet will insist on those sentiments of meekness, humility, and patience.

4. As Ezechiel will soon say: "And I will give you a new heart and a new spirit within you; and I will take away the stony heart out of your flesh, and will give you a heart of flesh. And I will put my spirit in the midst of you, and will cause you to walk in my commandments . . ."(36, 26,27). Confer also: Is. 7, 10.

Wind and Fire

In the New Testament these symbols will remain representative of the Spirit's omnipotence and His taking possession of souls and bodies; the "violent wind," sweeping through the Cenacle on Pentecost, and the tongues of Fire resting upon the apostles, are manifestations of this. Through these symbols an essential aspect of God's Spirit and His action upon souls can easily be grasped.[5] John the Baptist refers to it when saying of the one coming after him: "He will baptize you with the Holy Spirit and with fire" (Lk. 3, 16). The Canticle of Canticles helps us see this violence and strength as expressive of the ardors of love (Cant. 8, 6-7). At this epoch, assimilating love to the Holy Spirit was far from being accomplished.

In this same group of symbols can be placed those images which attribute to the Spirit creative and organizing powers. Thus, in Genesis the Spirit hovers over the primordial chaos as the eagle over the nests of its young. "The life-giving breath of God is about to give life to beings" (Cf. Bible de Jerusalem, p. 39).

Water as symbol of the Spirit

Contrary to this power and violence, the symbol of water is introduced under the most varied forms and represents the gentleness of the Spirit, His interior, transforming action. The Spirit descends upon man and penetrates his spirit just as the rain coming from on high penetrates the earth.

Isaias uses this symbol when he describes the Spirit's action: "For I will pour out waters upon the thirsty ground, and streams upon the dry land. I will pour out my spirit upon thy seed and my blessing upon thy stock" (Is. 44, 3). And Ezechiel associates the Lord's gift with the image of streams of waters which will bring renewed life to the dry lands: "And I will pour upon you clean water.... And I will give you a new heart.... And I will put my spirit in the midst of you" (Ez. 36, 25,27). The coming of the Spirit is compared to a "ritual cleansing," a benediction. "And I will hide my face no more from them, for I have poured out my spirit upon all the house of Israel, saith the Lord God" (Ez. 39, 29).

The Covenant itself in which the Spirit of God is contained and which expresses this Spirit with a special fullness will penetrate the people with

---

5. Cf. the Hymns for Pentecost: "Fons vivus, ignis . . .''; or again, the prayer to the Holy Spirit: "Reple tuorum corda fidelium, et in eis ignem. . . .''

its power, and will renew it: "This is my covenant with them, saith the Lord. My spirit that is in thee, and my words that I have put in thy mouth" (Is. 59, 21).

Evocative and rich as are these images and symbols, they can only succeed in orientating minds: "To transpose them such as they are to the interior life we run the risk of reducing the Holy Spirit to a natural element, very subtle and pure, but nevertheless of the material world."[6]

And yet through these symbols Israel gradually comes to understand not only the role played by the Spirit in the midst of the people (Is. 63, 9,10), but also the intimate nature of this Spirit who works to instill divine holiness (Ps. 51, passim).

From the earthy images of the divine breath of Psalm 104, "If thou sendest forth thy breath, they are created, and thou renewest the face of the earth," we pass on to that mysterious and spiritual reality that enters the New Testament with Christ.

Making Wisdom the object of their meditation, the authors of the Sapiential Books were in immediate proximity to the Holy Spirit. It is difficult to discern the depths of the mystery of God into which they are plunged. The life of the Trinity was not yet revealed and it was not possible for them to attribute the perfections which astonished them to one or other of the Persons. However, there seems to be an inkling of this relationship in the bosom of God. In particular what will be the grace of Christ and the gift of the Spirit springs from their writings still inseparably blended. They would not as yet have any idea of such high realities as the mutual complacence of the divine Persons and their particular and common beauty. And nevertheless in the light of what we "know" today, there is nothing that enables us to approach the revealed mystery as much as Chapters 1 and 24 of Ben Sirach. Now that we possess "the whole truth," thanks to the Holy Spirit, we should take up these inspired pages and complete them with the fully informed faith we have.

II. NEW TESTAMENT DATA ON THE SPIRIT

Passing over from the Old Testament to the Gospel, we go from figures and images to reality. Undoubtedly the ancient data still exist, preparations remain good and symbols keep their value and are directed towards their fulfillment. However, the appearance of the Person of Christ and the Revelation of the Trinity oblige us to consider the Spirit, His nature and role, under an entirely new light: the light the Trinity now casts over all things.

6. L. Guillet, Thèmes bibliques.

The Scene on the Jordan's banks

Priests and levites were sent from Jerusalem to ask of John the Baptist: " 'Who art thou?' And he acknowledged and did not deny; and he acknowledged, 'I am not the Christ.' And they asked him, " 'What then? Art thou Elias?' and he said, 'I am not.' 'Art thou the Prophet?' And he answered, 'No.'

" 'Why then dost thou baptize, if thou art not the Christ, nor Elias, nor the Prophet?' John said to them, 'I baptize with water; but in the midst of you there has stood one whom you do not know. He it is who is to come after me, who has been set above me, the strap of whose sandal I am not worthy to loose.' These things took place at Bethany, beyond the Jordan, where John was baptizing. The next day John saw Jesus coming to him, and he said, 'Behold the lamb of God, who takes away the sin of the world! This is he of whom I said, "After me there comes one who has been set above me, because he is before me." And I did not know him. But that he may be made known in Israel, for this reason have I come baptizing with water.'

"And John bore witness, saying, 'I beheld the Spirit descending as a dove from heaven, and it abode upon him. And I did not know him. But he who sent me to baptize with water said to me, "He upon whom thou wilt see the Spirit descending and abiding upon him, he it is who baptizes with the Holy Spirit" And I have seen and borne testimony that this is the Son of God' " (1, 19-34).

The scene of Christ's baptism at the Jordan ushers in His public life. It is comparable to a great portal opening upon the revelation of the three Persons and especially upon the Holy Spirit. Water appears as a sign and its symbolism will teach us a definite lesson.

Very frequently already water has characterized the different stages of history. First, at the time of a separation of the waters all things were created thanks to the Spirit who hovered over the waters (Gn. 1, 2). Secondly, after the Deluge a new humanity was born, and it was the waters that had carried this humanity on its surface (Gn. 6, 13 to 8, 22). Thirdly, under Moses' leadership, himself having been drawn from the waters (Ex. 2, 10), a people had to be gathered together and had to be saved from the waters of the Red Sea. Something new was born to God when that primordial chaos had withdrawn behind the waters, when the sin of Babel was buried in those waters, and when barbarous idols were renounced; and beyond those waters an ever-new and endless Covenant with God was offered to men.

Water had played a concrete and definite role in the history of salvation, not only as a symbol but as a creature. God had utilized it effectively to inaugurate the new order and had made choice of it for merciful ends. Inert in the beginning of the world, it obviously received a certain fecundity from God. Filled with His wrath at the time of the Deluge, it had destroyed evil which then reigned upon the earth. It had used this same destructive power with regard to the Egyptians, while it opened up a road to the Promised Land for the People of God. An effective mission is conferred upon water, according to God's will and the effusion of the Spirit; it does not yet have the power of the sacraments, but the power of an instrument with which God acts in the history of salvation. In this history the Jordan is called upon to be a line of demarcation between the times already passed and those just begun by the Messias. And its waters are to be the sign of the fulfillment of the promises contained in the Covenant.

When He descends into the Jordan's waters, Christ is in the midst of His own as one "whom you do not know" (1, 26). And yet "He who sent me to baptize with water said to me, 'He upon whom thou wilt see the Spirit descending and abiding upon him, he it is who baptizes with the Holy Spirit'" (1, 33). The Baptist knows that the life-giving and sanctifying reality of a veritable baptism is going to succeed the baptism of penance which he confers as a symbolic rite of purification; and this, because He has come who works out our salvation, and this has been revealed by the Holy Spirit. Henceforth there will be joined together in the waters of baptism the power which purifies and that which regenerates, the love which pardons and the love which gives life, the word which creates and the act which unites.

Soon Jesus will speak to Nicodemus of a birth through water and the Spirit (3, 5). It did appear incomprehensible to His interlocutor to see these two terms, water and the Spirit, set side by side when they were so distant from each other by nature and so unequally efficacious. In fact, it will seem to him absolutely impossible to be born again. "How can a man be born again once he is old?" (3, 4). At the Jordan however all becomes possible. To engender a new humanity Jesus takes upon Himself its burden, and going down into the waters He silently offers Himself to His Father's will. The latter has united to His will all the power of His love and mercy. And the Spirit, "as a dove," descended and abode' upon Jesus (1, 32).

This meeting of the Three at the dawn of the mission of Salvation gives a solemnity to the scene, and it gives effective power to the water with which it will be henceforth invested; flowing from the side of Christ it will have become the holy water which will make of the old man a new "child of God, through the merits of Christ's passion and the effusion of the Holy Spirit."

Christ comes forth from the waters of the Jordan as the Head of a new humanity upon which the Holy Spirit rests. A race blessed by God rises up and the heavens thrill with joy. The mystery which surrounds every divine manifestation is always great. We sometimes perceive certain traits of this mystery but its real depth escapes us. In the Jordan scene the entire mystery of God is given to us to measure.

A light seems to be thrown upon the plan of salvation, the redemption from sins, and our spiritual regeneration. The realization of this plan is conjointly the work of the Three; it is due to a perfect unanimity in the divine will and flows from a common love which is both merciful and life-giving. "The three are one" (1 Jn. 5, 8), John will say of the water, blood, and the Spirit. At the Jordan this unanimity is manifest. Each of the three Persons expresses in His own way His share in the work of salvation: the Son by conformity to the Father's will, the Spirit by descending upon Him, and the Father in declaring, "This is my beloved Son in whom I am well pleased" (Lk. 3, 22; Mt. 3, 17; Mk. 1, 11).

Though John is silent concerning this declaration reported by the Synoptics, he sets aside only what is outwardly striking about it; he emphasizes the totally interior characteristic of profound conviction and certitude that results from it in the soul of the witness: "I have seen and I have borne witness that this is the Son of God" (1, 34).

Election and dilection are the two terms which best describe the great revelation God makes at the Jordan. Election first: Christ is the Elect of God, the one whom God has chosen for the redemption. John the Baptist does not hesitate a moment upon the meaning of this mission. In fact, it is from this day on that he designates Jesus as: "Behold the lamb of God who takes away the sin of the world" (1, 29). Thus Christ's baptism under the effusion of the Spirit is the announcement of the sacrament which will definitely remove all sin and restore divine life, for Jesus is really "The one who is to come" (Mt. 11, 3).

Matthew and Luke will point out certain perplexity and persistent anguish regarding this in St. John the Baptist. (Mt. 11, 3; Lk. 7, 18). John, on the contrary, will report only the Baptist's exultation, and accentuates it with a conviction which is not misleading: "This my joy, therefore, is made full" (3, 29). These are the Baptist's final words of testimony.

"He who comes from above is over all. . . . He who comes from heaven is over all. And he bears witness to that which he has seen and heard . . ." (3, 31). John the Baptist did not know Christ according to the flesh. "And I did not know him" (1, 31), but he knew Him in the Holy Spirit. "But that he may be known in Israel, for this reason have I come baptizing with water" (1, 31). God's testimony is not misleading, but true. The

Spirit of God is "the Spirit of Truth" (14, 17; 15, 26; 16, 13). No earthly argument holds up when God designates His Elect. Now it is not only a man who has been chosen among other men for a divine mission, but one who, although man, has come forth from God, has "come from on high" (3, 31).

"I saw the Spirit descending and abiding upon him"

As great as the mystery of Christ's election is, it is deepened even more by the mystery of dilection that accompanies it. In fact, there is no question of some kind of investiture like that of the kings, judges, prophets of the past, but of the revelation of an election, at the very commencement of Christ's life, of His life as Son of God. And this divine election is unveiled here as the object of an inexpressible love. While the other evangelists make this understood by using the term "beloved," or by declaring of Christ that the Father "was well pleased with him," John uses the terms he prefers over all others, when it is a question of expressing this divine love which is at once the fullness of repose and of activity: "abide." "I saw the Spirit descending from heaven and abiding upon him" (1, 32). That instant has infinite extensions in heaven. And John the Baptist, in his very last confession filled with a certain joy, will state: "The Father loves the Son, and has given all things into his hands" (3, 35). Dilection confirms the choice, for election proceeds from dilection. We would dare to say of John's cry following the baptism, "And I have seen and borne witness that this is the Son of God" that it might also have been expressed in the Baptist's soul by the words: "Yes, I have seen and testify: this is the Beloved of God."

In the plan of salvation it is not a matter of small importance that the revelation of this election and this dilection comes at the very moment when the realization of the promises springs forth in the baptismal water. It is the vocation of this new race, which the waters will bring forth, that is brought to light. To be born again and to be born of God means that we are born into that beatitude of which John speaks. It does not mean being born only to the crucified Christ who gives His life for us, but also to the Father who is well pleased with Him and to the Holy Spirit who abides upon Him and who is the joy and the love of both Father and Son.

To be born of God cannot be a "leap into the unknown," a step so burdensome as to weaken the human will. This testimony brings with it a confident abandonment and an enthusiastic "élan" towards the Life, Love, and Beatitude of the Three. The child of God is brought to the Holy Spirit, to joy and not to sadness, to life and not to death. In place of our sins and their empty pleasures the Lamb of God gives us the love with which He Himself is loved, viz., the Holy Spirit. The first-born of a new generation and standing under the effusion of the Holy Spirit, Christ welcomes His coming in the name of all His brothers.

The Word and the Spirit

The entire scene at the Jordan is "trinitarian." We must not find in Christ's words, "Unless a man be born again of water and of the Spirit . . ." two successive principles of action. For this would give us the impression there are two separate principles, or two principles that are separable, whereas this is inadmissible with reference to God. Though He is three in Person, He is one in nature and in His external activity.

If Christ has employed this expression, it is because there are two effective ways for God to reach man. He does so through His Word and through His Spirit.

To be reached by God's Word means that man is enlightened by Revelation and adheres to it through faith. "I am the light of the world; he who follows me walks not in darkness" (8, 12). "This is my beloved Son in whom I am well pleased, hear him" (Lk. 9, 35). "The Word thrusts Himself upon us from the outside; He is active and penetrating, and more piercing than a two-edged sword; He lays all bare. He helps us to know and fully understand. He is the light of revelation."[7]

But man is born also of the Holy Spirit, and the Spirit is "fluid." Though the Spirit too is penetrating, it is after the manner of a liquid that enters in, like a gentle breeze that infiltrates without anyone being able to hear or see it. The Word is Revelation and the Spirit is interior transformation. The Word makes Himself heard, the Spirit springs up silently in the innermost depths of the soul. The Word enlightens minds and the Spirit enters hearts, transforming them and opening them up to the reception of the Word. And though distinct these two actions are inseparable, or would have to be,[8] since the Word never comes without the Spirit.

In the Old Testament this bond between the Word and the Spirit is perceptible. Whenever God revealed His word to the prophets, He took possession of them through His Spirit. "The word of Yahweh seemed to be carried to them on the wings of the spirit of Yahweh."[9]

---

7. L. Guillet, Thèmes bibliques.
8. In practice it often happens that Christians are born only of the Word, i.e., they content themselves with baptism of water and neglect completely to be born of the Spirit. The apostles themselves experienced before Pentecost this imperfect state in which they believed in Christ, but did not live in "his spirit." "You do not know of what spirit you are" (Lk. 9, 55).
9. L. Guillet, op. cit.

In the new economy we have this in an infinitely higher degree since the Word and the Spirit, though two distinct Persons, proceed one from the other and are united in a oneness of nature.

The Son has come to reveal His Father; He is the living Word of the Father in such a way that His Revelation is identified with His Father. "He who sees me, sees the Father" (1, 18). "If you had known me, you would have known my Father. And henceforth you do know him, and you have seen him" (14, 7).

The Word reveals the Father and the Son inseparably. But His mission being fulfilled, as the Son is the Word He can only return to the Father. And it is for this reason that he sends the Spirit who brings it about that the Word now penetrates hearts. This will not be done by a new revelation and by a new word. The Spirit has nothing else to say which is different from what Jesus has said. And as long as He has not come into hearts, the words of Jesus strike against closed hearts and unhearing ears.[10] The Son has come to speak of His Father. "The Spirit will speak of one thing only, viz., Jesus; and He will have one single motion: towards the Father. Such is the secret He discloses in His inexpressible confidences. The Old Testament awaited Him with all its desire; but it is only to the children redeemed by Christ and restored to life that the secret of this invisible and intangible presence of the Spirit will be given."[11]

Born of Water and the Spirit

It was necessary that the mystery of the Spirit be made explicit and be progressively revealed to men. The interview with Nicodemus introduces the teaching in a very abrupt fashion: "Unless a man be born again of water and the Spirit, he cannot enter into the kingdom of God. That which is born of the flesh is flesh, and that which is born of the Spirit is spirit. Do not wonder that I said to thee, 'You must be born again.' The wind blows where it will, and thou hearest its sound but dost not know where it comes from or where it goes. So is everyone who is born of the Spirit" (3, 3-9).

"Unless a man be born again of water and the Spirit. . . ." The continuity with the baptismal scene of Christ is evident. However, there will be no question in this interview of a clear allusion to an event which already has its historical and theological import. Rather it is a question of an initiation which, as abrupt as it appears for carnal man, yet proceeds

10. L. Guillet, op. cit.
11. L. Guillet, op. cit.

cautiously, through the repetition of simple words full of meaning, and through the use of known symbols, for they have already been used in the Scriptures: wind, breath, and water.

By comparing the Spirit to the gentle breeze and the wind, Christ brings His listener back to the beginning of time. He brings to his mind Genesis and the image of the Spirit hovering over the primordial chaos bringing order and life into it. He reminds him too of that breath of Yahweh which He "breathed into the nostrils of man and man became a living soul" (Gn. 2, 7; Wis. 15, 11). But Christ enlarges on these by referring the spiritual riches already contained in the "ruah Yahweh"[12] to the Holy Spirit.

What characterized this "ruah" was that it was a sharing in God's Spirit. The ruah is a kind of introduction to God, a participation in the divine. It is in man what is not from man but from God. This "breath" makes man vibrant with the divine, makes him breathe God. It is that door in man opening upon the invisible, the ineffable, and the unknown.

However, the spirit of Yahweh is also sovereign wisdom, intelligence, and foreknowledge. It guides all things to their end with an absolute surety (Wis. 1, 7; 7, 25). Likened to Wisdom, the Spirit of Yahweh is the "breath of the divine power" (Wis. 7, 22), and is endowed with numberless perfections which help man understand that what appears mysterious to him is sovereign wisdom in God. As the biblical author expresses it: "And hardly do we guess aright at things that are upon the earth. And with labor do we find the things that are before us. But the things that are in heaven, who shall search out? And who shall know thy thought, except thou give wisdom from above?" (Wis. 9, 16-18).

Christ will soon announce the coming of this Spirit to His disciples. But at present He teaches this "teacher in Israel" that man cannot enter "the kingdom of God unless he be born of the Spirit" (5, 5). This is a birth as mysterious as it is divine, for the wind can be heard by us, but "we do not know where it comes from or where it goes" (3, 8). His voice is not perceived as a word. The word is understandable and is expressed in a distinct manner. The divine breath is without words; it is interior, invisible in its coming as well as in its effects. Nevertheless, the

---

12. The *ruah* (translated "pneuma" in the Septuagint, and "esprit" in French) opens up a new dimension in biblical anthropology. In man the biblical pneuma is his supernatural part, it is what makes him a sharer in the supernatural order. The spirit of man is that part in him which renders him capable of a meeting with God's spirit, His pneuma. And it is this part in man through which the indwelling of God's spirit is not a strange intrusion, but something prepared and desired. (Rm. 8, 16). There is a permanent and substantial invitation in man to a transformation and a supernaturalization which enables him to take part in the uncreated life of the Creator. The pneuma is already something of the supernatural, it is the means by which we pass into another order other than that of nature. This passage and this participation in the Creator's life is something proper to man and his "spirit" constitutes its first-fruits. (Trestmontant, Essai sur la pensée hébraïque, pp. 109,110.)

Spirit never brings man into conflict with what the Word has taught him. There is a secret continuity between His teaching and Christ's. This does not prevent the Spirit having his own proper way of making the divine life enter into us, viz., in a manner that is likening, transforming, secret, and continuous.

While "being born of water" is reduced in time to a definite act demanding an adhesion of faith, "being born of the spirit" (3, 5) is a reality which is perpetually beginning, and it is characterized by the need of an endless renewal. It is in the Spirit that we must make of our status as "children of God" a reality that is in constant act and exercise, or an ever active reality.

In either case, there is a birth which takes place according to two very different forms. While one is a precise and definite act done once and for all, the other is always "in fieri," in the act of being done. This gives us a glimpse of the new depth of this life "in the spirit" which belongs to the child of God. We cannot say of it that it is a new "mode of being," as it is much more: it is the revelation and the actuality in us of the divine life itself, the "life of Life." Through our active participation in this Life we are progressively transformed into it. And there results for us an entirely new way of knowing, thinking, willing, acting, and suffering. In a word, it is a new way of "living" simultaneously "under" and "from" the breath of God.

We can easily understand how the symbol of "breath" leads to that of "water" and blends with it. For water, besides being a symbol of purification and regeneration is already in the Old Testament and even more so here the symbol of a slow penetration and a mysterious control over souls. It visits them, opens them, and renders them fruitful. It makes them grasp interiorly through a sort of impregnation what remained exterior to them. It makes them permeable. Water is gentleness in strength, and vice versa. It is that irresistible wave which rises and bathes everything equally. The soul was prisoner to a multiplicity of attachments, and behold, without knowing what has taken place, she finds herself enveloped by this Presence insinuating itself everywhere and reducing everything in the soul to a certain unity and simplicity.

Water is also the milieu proper to life; it is its preparation, germination, and expansion; its maternal womb. And it is not forbidden us to think that Christ, when descending into the waters of the Jordan and coming forth from them, willed to make men understand that they could henceforth realize that secret aspiration which urges them to go back to their origins, to flow back towards the source whence they came.[13]

13. The meeting between the supernatural and the psychological plane, even psychoanalytical, is not only chance.

What is not possible in the natural order: "Can a man enter a second time into the womb of his mother and be born again" is possible in the supernatural order. As children of God, we have to come back to Him in Christ, to hide ourselves in Him, to flow back towards Him as towards our eternal origin, eternally in the act of filiation. He is our spiritual Jordan and we must be "in sinu Christi" as He Himself is "in sinu Patris." Nicodemus, ironically asking whether it is possible for a man to re-enter his mother's womb and be born again, did not suspect that he was voicing a universal aspiration to which baptism and life in the Spirit would afford an answer, and that henceforth the power would be given to men to experience an eternal birth in God.

It hardly seems possible then to separate these two symbols: breath and water, insofar as they signify the action of the Spirit in souls. This water seems to enjoy a certain preference in John's writings. Not only at the Jordan (1, 31-34), at Cana (2, 1-11), with Nicodemus (3, 4), does it appear as the instrument of salvation to be used in the future sacrament, but it is also the element which figures in the miracle at Bethsaida (5, 1-9) and the miracle of the walking upon the waters by Christ (6, 16-21). Finally, it is the theme of the teaching given to the Samaritan woman (4, 5-16), as well as the teaching given to the disciples at the washing of the feet (13, 2-17). It is expressive of the spiritual life when it springs forth from the pierced side of Christ (19, 34), and it is a symbol of the milieu in which the "fishers of men" will exercise their apostolate (21, 4-14). John seems to have seen in water the bearer of life and of God's gift.

Gift of the Spirit and thirst for God

He alone receives the gift of God who feels a thirst and a desire for it. The Spirit is not only the water, but, if we may so express ourselves, he is the thirst which He rouses in us in order to quench it. The scene at Jacob's well is an admirable illustration of this.

Christ seizes upon the most opportune thing to reach this woman who is filled with an ironical attitude simply because she is not clearly conscious of the thirst she is experiencing; she has forced it to the background, but Christ is about to free her. "If thou didst know the gift of God and who it is who says to thee: 'Give me to drink,' thou perhaps wouldst have asked of him, and he would have given thee living water" (4, 9). He continues: "Everyone who drinks of this water will thirst again. He however who drinks of the water that I will give him shall never thirst;

but the water that I will give him shall become in him a fountain of water springing up unto life everlasting" (4, 14).

On the Feast of Tabernacles He cried out: "If anyone thirst let him come to me and drink. He who believes in me, as the Scripture says, from within him there shall flow rivers of living water" (7, 37,38).

For the Israelites who were listening these words brought to their mind their own arid country and the surrounding desert. They reminded them also, in that past in which every Israelite was deeply rooted, of that long journey through desolate solitudes and the bitter waters drunk in the rebellion. Those to whom Jesus spoke knew that thirst infallibly brings on death. Eden was for them that country where four rivers flow (Gn. 2, 10), and the Temple, that edifice which will be traversed with a current of flowing water (Ez. 47, passim). The psalmists had sung of the just man's happiness, planted as he is like a tree beside the running waters (Ps. 1, 3). Finally the prophet has warned against the "broken cisterns that hold no water" (Jer. 2, 13).

Thirst, for the man who has experienced it, is the mirage in the desert and the agony of death. Jesus raises up this haunting picture in the minds of His listeners in order to promise them, along with the quenching of their thirst, a gift that is inexhaustible. The woman of Samaria cried out: "Sir, give me this water that I may not thirst" (4, 15). In these words in which this thirst after living water is manifested, is it not life in the Spirit after which she longs though she does not yet know it?

Thirst and water, these elementary words like those of death and life are sufficient on Christ's lips to bring the soul to the summits of a mystery. But in biblical perspectives, thirst and water are eminently evocative of the time of the Exodus, of that march through the desert, of that passage towards the Promised Land, images of human destiny. Christ Himself, coming into the desert of this life, allows us to make this passage. He takes the lead in humanity and He traverses through life tracing out a Way which He actually is Himself, inviting us to follow after Him.

Here on earth is the desert, but it is also the time given by God to man to cultivate in the depths of his soul that thirst for eternal realities. "I have led thee into the desert" (Os. 2, 16), the prophet had said. The desert is likewise the time of "espousals" (Os. 2, 21).

We may say too of this time when Jesus came among His own that He lived there alone. It is in a desert of divine dimensions that He effects His great passage. He too experiences thirst, but it is the thirst of making known to souls the "gift of God," souls who run the risk of dying of thirst and don't even realize it; His thirst is to make them discover it, to teach them to have this thirst for God; this is what He will attempt to do during that three years period of teaching. Then "the land that was desolate and impassable shall rejoice and shall flourish like the lily" (Is. 25, 1), and men "shall draw waters with joy out of the Savior's fountains" (Is. 12, 3).

Each of Christ's words is poured out upon the cracked and parched earth and life is restored little by little. Humanity is still unaware that in its midst it has "the rod come forth from the root of Jesse. . . . And the spirit of the Lord shall rest upon him: the spirit of wisdom and understanding, the spirit of counsel and of fortitude, the spirit of knowledge and of godliness" (Is. 11, 1) and already the earth commences to "be born again of water and the Spirit" (3, 5).

How often during these days did not Christ have to whisper to Himself: "The needy and the poor seek for waters, and there are none. Their tongue hath been dry with thirst. I the Lord will hear them. I the God of Israel will not forsake them. I will open rivers in the high hills, and the fountains in the midst of the plains. I will turn the desert into pools of waters, and the impassable land into streams of waters. I will plant in the wilderness the cedar and the thorn and the myrtle and the olive tree I will set in the desert the fir tree, the elm, and the box tree together" (Is. 41, 17-19).

"The hour is coming . . ."

At Jacob's well Jesus says the hour and time has come when everyone's thirst would be quenched. "But the hour is coming, and now is here, when the true worshippers will worship the Father in spirit and in truth" (4, 23). "If you but knew the gift of God" (4, 10). Jesus bears within Himself this gift and He actually is this gift in Person. Upon Him the Spirit has descended and abode. God gives Him the Spirit "without measure" (3, 34). Is not Christ the Anointed of the Lord?" (Os. 6, 3).

Already His word is poured forth. But there still remains the price of His life and death, in order that this gift spring up as a torrent. Through Him men "will know Yahweh" (Os. 6, 3), and their life will receive a definite orientation and expansion. And this is not a question of choice. Man is actually drawn towards God and eternal life by vocation or calling. Through the Spirit who will be given to him, he will know this life in the Anointed and there he will quench his thirst. He will adore the Father "in spirit and in truth." The true life of the child of God is not an independent life, but one of loving dependence on Another Life which nourishes this life and keeps it close to its sources. If Jesus is the Shepherd, the Spirit is the Fountain at which the flock quenches its thirst, and the sheepfold is eternal life itself, for there is no other for the child of God.

"The hour is coming when neither on this mountain nor in Jerusalem will you worship the Father" (4, 21). Adoration "in spirit and in truth" will no longer recognize any other Temple but the very Heart of the Crucified.

" 'He who believes in me, as the Scripture says, from within him there shall flow rivers of living water.' He said this, however, of the Spirit whom they who believed in him were to receive; for the Spirit had not yet been given since Jesus had not yet been glorified" (7, 38).

The hour of Christ's death, that hour so long awaited, is also the hour in which His glorification begins. "But I have a baptism to be baptized with, and how distressed I am until it be accomplished" (Lk. 12, 49). The fire will actually descend upon the apostles in the Cenacle, and Jesus thirsted for this living fire which was going to enkindle the apostles and for this Spirit who would come to "make them love Love."

"He came among his own and his own received him not. But to as many as received him he gave the power to become the children of God" (1, 12). Between this refusal and the coming of the Spirit who will strengthen the faith of those who received him, there is a death of Christ. This would have been only the death of a crucified man like all other such deaths, if He had not "given up the spirit." He said: " 'It is finished.' And bowing his head he gave up the spirit" (19, 30).[14] Again, it would have been a death like others, if from his pierced side there had not come forth "blood and water" (19, 34). This is the baptism He longed for so ardently; it is the baptism of water, blood, and of the spirit, as John points out in his Epistle: "This is he who came in water and blood, Jesus Christ; not in the water only, but in the water and the blood. And it is the Spirit that bears testimony that Christ is the truth. . . . And there are three that bear witness on earth: the Spirit, the water, and the blood; and these three are one" (1 Jn. 5, 8).

These three are one. The death of the Lamb of God upon the Cross follows the baptism on the Jordan as night follows day. Directly from the Heart of God transpierced the Spirit passes into men's hearts in order to bear witness. But from Christ's Heart, the Spirit re-ascends to the Father, while from the Cross upon which Jesus remains nailed Love will burst forth upon the earth from one age to the next.

The Help of the Holy Spirit

Every road henceforth that leads to God is through the Cross, and the way followed by Christ is the way that the Spirit will give to men.

---

14. Cf. note to Jn. 19, 30: Bible de Jérusalem: "The Greek expression is singular. Literally, 'he gave up the spirit.' This is not without design. For the evangelist the last breath of Jesus is a prelude to the effusion of the Spirit."

They too must confront the scandal and the folly of the Cross in order to attain to wisdom. Insupportable to the Jews and disciples alike, the Cross stands at the crossroads where faith trembles and hesitates. Where would faith be without the Spirit's help? Something else besides reason and feeling is necessary for our spirit in order that we be rallied to the Cross, and so that it will be our hope and our joy, that our faith be nourished, comforted, and enlightened in the night. This help that is given us in our weakness comes from the gift of God, the Holy Spirit.

On two occasions Jesus has gently reprimanded the apostles for their sadness. "If you loved me, you would rejoice because I go to the Father" (14, 28); "And now I am going to him who sent me, and no one of you asks, 'Where art thou going?' But because I have spoken these things to you, sorrow has filled your heart" (16, 5). He not only gives His distracted apostles the assurance that they will not be left alone and orphans (14, 18), but that they will find Him again in the one whom He will send them to aid them with His presence.

True, under a different form, but in a very real one, the Spirit will be to them "everything" that Christ had been for them, viz., defender, counselor, protector, support, and with regard to the Father whom Justice has taught them to love, He will be Advocate and Intercessor.

To show Him to them Jesus Himself takes the title of Paraclete which He has given to the Holy Spirit. "And I will ask the Father and he will give you another Paraclete to dwell with you forever" (14, 16).

The Spirit will give life to Christ's teachings. He will reveal what still escapes them in those teachings, but will not introduce them to something new, for He will not speak on His own authority (16, 13). "But the Advocate, the Holy Spirit, whom the Father will send in my name, he will teach you all things and bring to your mind whatever I have said to you" (14, 26).

A traditional belief would be a small thing. "And no one can say 'Jesus is Lord' except in the Holy Spirit" writes St. Paul; and to be content with what we have learned from Dogma would be really despising it. "I have many things to say to you, but you cannot bear them now" (16, 12). "But when he, the Spirit of Truth, has come, he will teach you all the truth" (16, 13).

"Therefore, if you, evil as you are, know how to give good gifts to your children, how much more will your heavenly Father give the good spirit to those who ask him" (Lk. 11, 13). Rather than ask the Spirit who would give them to us, do we not justify our negligence by pretending they are too great for us? How can we be ignorant of the fact that the Spirit has no other preoccupation, no other desire than to "receive of what is Christ's and declare it to you" (16, 14). He will do nothing else but manifest, explain, and bring to light the inexhaustible riches of Christ. As a faithful executor of a will, He will put His followers in possession of this gift of God which Christ bequeathes to them, but the value of which they would not know how to appreciate or use. Coming to them and revealing Himself to them, the Spirit will show them its hidden meaning. Thus, not only will nothing of what goes to make up Christ's heritage be taken from them, but the Holy Spirit alone will have the power to help them benefit fully from it. (Cf. chap. 20 below).

Thus would Christ really draw attention to what merits attention, viz., His return to the Father, life in God, and the gift of the Spirit which follows upon His return.

The sending of the Spirit

Jesus promised the Paraclete to His apostles. This is "His" Spirit (14, 26; 16, 14), but the Spirit is no less united to the Father in an intimate way. He proceeds from Him (15, 26) and He is the Father's gift. "I will ask the Father and he will give you another Paraclete" (14, 16).

In a word, it is in union with the Father that Christ sends the Spirit (15, 16), as the following words of Christ help us understand, "When the Paraclete comes, whom I will send you from the Father" (15, 26).

Christ has His apostles enter into the mystery of the Trinity which is likewise the mystery of the unity between the Father and the Son when, at the Last Supper, He speaks of the Spirit and promises to send Him.

The mutual possession of all things by the Father and the Son is stressed during the discourse after the Supper. Possession of goods: "All things that are mine are thine, and thine are mine" (17, 10). An even more essential ownership is expressed in that mutual indwelling and giving of one to the other. ". . . that they may be one, even as thou, Father, in me and I in thee" (17, 21). But are we dealing here with a necessity of nature which would oblige God to share the divine life and its riches among the Persons? The fact that this nature is spiritual sets aside the question. The divine will is such that it is never subject to anything that takes on the nature of a "duty." Necessity, in the Trinity, is not constraint, but it is freedom and that freedom is expressed in an eternal act: the procession of the divine Persons. The Father begets the Son who is eternally in the bosom of the Father.

The Spirit is the mutual bond expressing this unity, the love of the Father for the Son and the Son for the Father. "The Father and I are one"

(10, 30). "The Father is in me and I in the Father" (10, 38). Here we have inexpressible generation and unity.

In the words of Jesus we perceive the equality of the Three is absolute in the complacence which the Father and the Son take in each other. "I do always the things that please him" (8, 29). This shows the conformity of wills. We see it again at the baptism and on Mount Thabor where this complacence is emphasized. "This is my beloved Son in whom I am well pleased" (Lk. 3, 22).

Jesus will make use of this love to state that whatever they ask the Father in His name they will receive (16, 23); and in the sacerdotal prayer at the Supper He says: "Father, I will..." (17, 24).

As for the Spirit, He will "receive of what is mine and declare it to you" (16, 14), not as a servant with regard to his master, but as an equal to an equal. Sent as "another Paraclete," the Spirit will complete the work which they both agreed upon in one will.

The Spirit of Love

Such as it has been presented by St. John to us, the mystery of the Trinity is made explicit and is expressed under the form of the mystery of love which is without comparison and as eternal as God Himself.

"God is love" (1 Jn. 4, 8) and the proof is that "God has given his only-begotten Son" to save the world, but with the baptism at the Jordan we have the Spirit as the supreme testimony of this love. The Spirit is the flame leaping up from the furnace of the love of the Father and the Son.

The Spirit is in Himself eternally just as are the Father and the Son. What we know the best about Him perhaps is what we already had a presentiment of on the banks of the Jordan: the dilection of the Father for the Son and of the Son for the Father. The entire discourse after the Supper is filled with the sweetness of the Son's return to His Father.

"But now, Father, I am coming to thee; and these things I speak in the world, in order that they may have my joy made full in themselves" (17, 13). He informed his disciples that there still remained the giving of the Spirit. From the world they would receive persecution and hatred; from God in whom "they abide," the very joy of the Son will be given them "in its fullness" (17, 13). Joy and the Spirit are one and the glorification which Jesus has received will be in them also: "... and all things that are mine are thine, and thine are mine; and I am glorified in them" (17, 10).

The glorification of the baptism, as that of Thabor, had consisted in the testimony given by the Father of His infinite complacence in His Son, and of the joy found in loving Him and in the Spirit resting upon Him. This "glory" which the Son had "with the Father before the world was made" (17, 5) He will find at His death as supreme glorification of Love Who is pleased in His work.

Glorification is always the work of the Father and the Son, of the Principle that creates and the Word who makes. "I have glorified thee" (17, 4), "Father glorify me." But it is the Spirit who bears witness of this glorification and fulfills it. The humble testimony of our faith which glorifies God through the Holy Spirit is addressed to all Three, as a cry of joy in their infinite beatitude.

Outside this unity and blessedness of God, there is nothing but shadows. His love has become man's real earth. The Holy Spirit is our fatherland, and as Christ He is always "with us" (14, 17). He teaches us how to enjoy divine things and when the silent hymn of faith re-echoes in our hearts we can say with St. John, "And in this we know that he abides in us by the Spirit whom he has given us" (1 Jn. 3, 24).

CHAPTER 11

FAITH

The author of the Epistle to the Hebrews, wishing to invite his readers to approach Christ with faith, sees no better way than that of citing the example of their ancestors in the faith. "It was through faith that Abel presented a sacrifice agreeable to God . . . that Henoch was raised to heaven, . . . that Noah became heir to justice, . . . that Abraham, called by God, obeyed and left for a country he knew not; when put to the test, he offered Isaac, . . ." And he continues until the moment when he cannot go on citing all those who gave "testimony of their faith" in their life or death, and then he cries out: "Therefore, let us also, having such a cloud of witnesses over us, put away every encumberance and the sin entangling us; looking towards the author and finisher of our faith, Jesus" (Heb. 11, passim, 12, 2).

The Gospel of Faith

It seems that St. John extends a similar invitation to us when he places us face to face with Christ in his Gospel, for Christ cannot appear in his Gospel without the problem of faith immediately coming up. Faith is man's response to the one who reveals Himself to him, a response from which no man can separate himself. Wherever Christ is, there faith is proposed to men. Faith comes to them with Christ; it is, so to speak, His shadow borne over us, a luminous shadow, true, but it accompanies Him everywhere. There is not a single scene in the fourth Gospel of which Christ is not the center and focal point. In fact, why should not the problem of faith present itself from the very beginning of the Johannine Gospel?

Already in his Prologue, the apostle had made faith the path through which men welcome and receive the Word who gives them the power of being born to a new life. "But as many as received him he gave the power of becoming sons of God, to those who believe in his name" (1, 12). "The Word was made flesh and dwelt among us. . . ." He has come to walk our paths, and, while He advances, faith rises on His very steps. The fourth Gospel is inseparably this road of Christ and this faith which must accompany Him.

Christ passes along the Jordan's banks; the Baptist gazes upon Him and says: "Behold the lamb of God" (1, 29). Hearing him speak, his two disciples follow Jesus. "They came and saw where he was dwelling; and they stayed with him that day" (1, 39). "Now Andrew, the brother of Simon Peter, was one of the two who had heard John and had followed him. He found first his brother Simon and said to him, 'We have found the Messias'" (1, 41). "We" have found, for the other disciple was none other than John.

And from the first encounter with Christ faith is born in the apostle's soul as it had been in that of Andrew, Peter, and Philip. The last mentioned had not only followed Christ as soon as he was called (1, 43), but upon meeting Nathanael he says: "We have found him of whom Moses in the Law and the Prophets wrote, Jesus the son of Joseph of Nazareth" (1, 45). Nathanael, little inclined by nature to commit himself, finally admits: "Rabbi, thou art the Son of God, thou art the king of Israel" (1, 49). And Jesus answers, "Because I said to thee that I saw thee under the fig tree, thou dost believe. Greater things thou shalt see" (1, 50).

Faith is likewise the fruit of the miracle of Cana. "He manifested his glory, and his disciples believed in him" (2, 11). The interview with Nicodemus is oriented towards the birth and development of faith. Jesus said to him: "For God so loved the world that he gave his only-begotten Son that those who believe in him may not perish, but may have life everlasting" (3, 16).

Undoubtedly we must see a real profession of faith in the Samaritan woman's words to her fellow-citizens, "Come and see a man who has told me all that I have done. Can he be the Christ?" (4, 29). At least, faith had made progress in her soul and it is through it that many inhabitants of the village come and listen to Christ. They will be able to say later, "We no longer believe because of what thou hast said, for we have heard for ourselves and we know that this is in truth the Savior of the world" (4, 42).

It is with an act of unreserved faith that the royal official at Capharnaum responds to the miracle of his son's restoration to health. His entire family makes this act of faith with him. "He believed and his whole household" (4, 53).

To the Jews' question, "What are we to do that we may perform the works of God?" Jesus answers, "That is the work of God, that you believe in him whom he sent" (6, 28,29).

In the discourse on the bread of life, Jesus comes back to the necessity of faith. "Amen, amen, I say to you, he who believes in me has everlasting life" (6, 47).

He demands this faith from His apostles and He expects them to direct it towards His Person. Peter understood this so well when hearing Christ's words, "Will you also go away?" that he answers, "Lord, to whom shall we go? Thou hast the words of eternal life, and we have come to believe and to know that thou art the Christ, the Son of God" (6, 68,69).

If the eyes of the man born blind are opened to the light, his soul is opened to the light of faith. " 'Dost thou believe in the Son of God?' He answered and said to him, 'Who is he, Lord, that I may believe in him?' And Jesus said to him, 'Thou hast both seen him, and he it is who speaks to thee.' And he said, 'I believe, Lord.' And falling down, he worshipped him" (9, 37).

The works accomplished by Christ are directed towards faith. "If I do not perform the works of my Father, do not believe me. But if I do perform them, and if you are not willing to believe me, believe the works, that you may know and believe that the Father is in me and I in the Father" (10, 37).

Lazarus' death and resurrection are also directed towards faith. "Lazarus is dead. And rejoice on your account that I was not there, that you may believe" (11, 15).

Men will be judged according to their faith or their unbelief. "I have come a light into the world, that whoever believes in me may not remain in darkness. He who rejects me and does not accept my words, has one to condemn him" (12, 46).

Christ's teaching, miracles, prayer, thanksgiving, all these firmly implant in the apostles' souls (13, 19) this faith which later they are to communicate and spread. "Yet not for these only do I pray, but for those also who through their word are to believe in me" (17, 20).

The saving mysteries of the Passion, Death, and Resurrection must arouse in these who are to be their witnesses faith in His Person and His mission. "I tell you now before it comes to pass, that when it has come to pass you may believe that I am he" (13, 19).

The closer this event approaches the more Christ exalts faith. He speaks of it now without any qualification, as an absolute which has God as its object. "Believe in God" (14, 1). But He Himself is the object of faith since He is always with the Father. "Believe also in me" (14, 1).

As source of salvation, Christ's death is likewise the source of the grace of faith, and John who had a revelation of it when seeing the water and the blood come forth from Christ's side, cried out: "And he who saw has borne witness and his witness is true, and he knows that he tells the truth, that you may also believe" (19, 35).

As a counterpart to his first chapter in which the apostles receive the call to faith, the last pages of John's Gospel show how the sight of the empty tomb for John and Peter (20, 8), and the sight of the Risen Christ for Magdalene and Thomas and the other disciples will succeed in transforming their wavering faith into a strong one.

The one and only beatitude of this Gospel, "Blessed are those who have not seen and have believed" (20, 29), has faith as its object. And the last of Christ's apparitions to His apostles will be hailed by John, the first to recognize the Savior, with a cry from the heart which is also a cry of faith, "It is the Lord!" (21, 7). Hearing these words, Peter throws himself into the water in order to meet Christ the sooner.

Who could doubt the place faith holds in this fourth Gospel? It has been really written in order that "we may believe" (20, 31).

Revelation and faith

To lead men to believe is the real goal of the Word's revelation. He offers us Life, Truth, and Light through His teachings and miracles. A revelation cannot be separated from those to whom it is addressed, nor from the welcome they reserve for it. Faith is not only linked to revelation, it is one with it. Between revelation and faith there is a sameness of object and a similarity of traits. Thus, revelation comes to us through Jesus Christ and He is its object; faith comes to us through Jesus Christ and He is its object. "And to all who received him he gave the power to become the sons of God, to those who believe in his name" (1, 12).

From the Prologue itself faith appears as "men's response to the Incarnation" says P. Mollat. And, as Fr. Bouyer puts it, "Believing is receiving the Word." In the fourth Gospel, faith is not a particular aspect of man's religious activity, rather it is this activity in itself. And this activity is not man's deed alone. God, the source of this activity, shares in it in a most constant, intimate, and effective manner. Christ's words as reported by John show that in faith God and man work together. "This is the work of God, that you believe in him whom he has sent" (6, 29). In fact, there is no supernatural act of faith in man which does not proceed from God's grace. St. Paul had already taught this to the Corinthians: "And no one can say 'Jesus is Lord' except in the Holy Spirit" (1 Cor. 12, 3).

A grace of God both in its origin and its activity in the soul, faith is man's essential religious activity; faith is also the fruit of the encounter of God and man and it is their mutual knowledge. Hence, we can understand why faith is to be found throughout a Gospel which sets out to be God's living revelation in Christ Jesus. But we see too how necessary it is, before following the development and effects of faith through this Gospel, to seek out its structure and to discover its inner nature.

Personal structure of faith

As numerous as are the teachings about faith in the fourth Gospel and as many as are the lights which this Gospel sheds upon faith, one thing is certain from a reading of the Prologue: Faith appears endowed with a "personal structure."[1]

When writing "No one has seen God at any time. The only-begotten Son who is in the bosom of the Father, he has revealed him" (1, 18), John does not only liken Christ's mission to a knowledge, but he clearly indicates the object of this knowledge; it is neither a body of doctrine nor a particular truth, but a Person, that of the Father, "The only-begotten 'Son' who is in the bosom of the 'Father,' he has revealed him" (1, 18).

Thus, in this revelation which supplies the substance of faith everything is "personal." "God has spoken only one Word and that is His Son" writes St. John of the Cross.[2] When expressing Himself and when making Himself known through the Incarnation, this Word makes the Father known.

God's appearance then to humanity is expressed in a way that is supremely personal. God speaks "through" His Son. It is in Him that He confides His secret to us. Man responds properly to God's desire and receives the divine gift simply by listening to the living Word of the Father, by adhering to His teaching, by attaching himself to the Person of the Word made flesh. "For God so loved the world that he gave his only-begotten Son, that those who believe in him may not perish, but may have life everlasting." (3, 16).

There is not a passage in the fourth Gospel which makes reference to the faith that does not confirm the above statement. To believe does not mean simply to adhere to a body of truths, but rather to recognize in Christ's Person the Son of God sent by the Father to reveal the Father and save the world. To believe means to recognize that every truth is con-

---

1. This expression is from M. Mouroux. Cf. notes on "The personal structure of Faith" in the volume entitled "Je crois en Toi."
2. St. John of the Cross, Ascent of Mount Carmel, Book 11, C. 23.

tained in Christ, that it is one with Him, that He is the living Truth; that he is "in Person" the true Revelation of God, for "He who sees me, sees the Father" (14, 9).

Also, through Christ's words, John invites us to unite ourselves to the one who has spoken them and transcends them, viz., the Word. In St. John faith is not directed so much to Christ's words as to Christ the Word. It is to Him, much more than to His words, that we must give faith, and it is in Him that we must believe.

When dealing with Christ we are dealing with an indivisible Reality that cannot be expressed in human words. It is a question of a living Reality and a totality.[3] "I have said everything to you in my Son" St. John of the Cross will write when commenting on the Father's words at the Transfiguration.[4]

In Christ the Person of the Son of God comes to man. Addressing each He says: Do you believe in Me? Do you know Who and What I am?[5] Do you believe in My name? i.e., in my Person? Have you that confidence and faith in me that one gives to God alone? (14, 1).

And when He produces titles so clear, so powerful, and so divine, and asks your confidence, no other answer can be made but an act of absolute faith. This act of faith is a personal and unconditional act of self-surrender. "Follow me!" (1, 43). "And leaving all things, he arose and followed him" (Lk. 5, 27,28).

Faith in John's mind is then: the revelation of God in Jesus Christ His Son, the absolute confidence due to Him, and our dedication to His service. It appears as the encounter of two persons, drawing one towards the other in a fullness of presence and a totality of surrender.

"Believe in me"

Johannine faith cannot be reduced to a purely intellectual assent. In the fourth Gospel to believe is essentially a disposition towards a Person and not so much towards a revealed truth. That is why the Johannine expression is not: believe some thing, but believe "in someone." This is a meaning in full conformity with the usual signification of the word in the Bible where "to believe" has the meaning of "trusting someone, confiding in someone."

The idea of stability and fidelity included in the word "believe" strengthens the "personal structure" of faith still more. Faith seals the

---

3. "To believe" means to be open towards a Person and make oneself submissive to his teaching.
4. "This is my beloved Son in whom I am well pleased. Hear him" (Mt. 17, 5).
5. "I am": Cf. Jn. 8, 28,58. These words are allied to those by which God in the Old Testament concludes many statements announcing an intervention of His power (P. Mollat, Ev. de saint Jean).

relationship between two persons. To believe is to depend upon someone with full confidence, to trust his statements, to give him absolute credence. Such is exactly the meaning of Peter's answer to Christ's question: " 'Do you also wish to go away?' Simon Peter therefore answered, 'Lord, to whom shall we go? Thou hast the words of eternal life. And we have come to believe and to know that thou art the Christ, the Son of God' " (6, 68,69). From words, Peter immediately ascends to their author, Christ's Person. In a word, it is upon Him that faith rests and is founded.

In Isaias the word "believe" has the meaning of stability, constancy, firmness. "If you will not believe, you shall not continue" (Is. 7, 9). In other words, if in the midst of dangers which assail you, you do not remain firmly attached to Yahweh, fully confident of the protection of the one who has chosen you, your God who alone can save you, you will perish.

There is another example of this "confident firmness" in Chapter 28: "Therefore thus saith the Lord God: Behold I will lay a stone in the foundation of Sion, a tried stone, a cornerstone, a precious stone, founded in the foundation. He that believeth, let him not hasten" (Is. 28, 16).[6]

Israel's strength rests upon "perfect confidence" in Yahweh (Is. 30, 15). It is in this that faith must consist. "Blessed is the man that trusted in the Lord, and the Lord shall be his confidence" (Jer. 17, 7).

From the idea of holding firm, of leaning upon the only one who cannot fail or deceive, viz., God, we easily come to the idea of having "faith" in Him, of "believing" Him.

There does not exist an equivalent in ordinary language of this expression which will be reserved for God. When applied to Christ, John does not only consecrate its religious value, but he practically makes of it a recognition of Christ's divine nature. "You believe in God, believe also in me" (14, 1). Son of God and God Himself, Christ can demand of us that "we believe in him," i.e., that we have absolute and personal confidence in Him.

Finally, we must place side by side with the expression: "believe in Jesus Christ" or "believe in me," that other expression typically Johannine: "believe in his name"[7] which underscores the personal character of faith.[8]

6. Is. 28, 16. Let him not hasten, etc.: let him expect Christ's coming with patience.
7. Cf. Jn. 1, 12; 2, 23; 3, 18; 20, 31; 13, 23; 5, 13.
8. It seems from John's time baptism was given in the "name of Christ." If this is really so, the passage of the Prologue: "But to those who believed in him he has given the power of becoming the sons of God, to those who believe in his name," would refer not only to faith, but to baptism, that act through which the Christian becomes dependent upon Christ and His possession, contracts a real relationship and promises Him absolute fidelity.

Faith appears clearly in St. John as a personal adhesion made from a sentiment of confidence, attachment, and dependence with regard to God who reveals Himself to us in Christ.[9] It brings with it an unconditional surrender on our part to His Person.

"I believe in thee"

The revelation of God as Father in the Person of His Son Jesus Christ does not suffice to explain that faith has a personal structure. This structure is strengthened by the fact that faith is demanded by and given to "persons."

"I" believe because God speaks to "me" and gives me the grace to answer: "I believe in thee."

Insofar as faith is a vital act, it is inseparable from those in whom it is received and in whom it is active. Whether we consider grace accompanying it, or the adhesion of the mind, or the act of the will, its personal structure is evident throughout. God, having placed it in the intimate depths of a being, it does not become effective if this being does not assume it personally, and make it its own and say: "I believe." Only then is there faith.

Faith is not only personal, but it also is "personalizing." God calls each being by name. When answering this call through faith, the being truly is born to itself, for it begins to realize the divine designs upon it. By calling it by its name, God comes seeking it in those depths into which the being has not yet entered and of which it is still unaware. Faith, revealing God to its being, reveals the being to itself. "That I may know thee and know myself."[10]

The grace of faith is always "unique" in its nature. The light, certitude, love, feeling of a presence which accompanies faith, show themselves in a way that can be only personal, since it reveals each person to himself while revealing God to him. That is why the Good Shepherd can say: "I know my sheep and my sheep know me. . . . My sheep hear my voice, and I know them and they follow me" (10, 14, 27).

In faith a Person who is the source and center of all light and love reveals Himself and communicates Himself to another person who is poor, miserable, famished. The former brings to the latter His "Reason" and His "way" of life. By uniting a being to God, faith gives it the means of fulfilling itself as a person. Otherwise the person runs the risk of remaining enclosed within itself and of taking self as the measure of all things.

9. It is clear that the "personal" character of faith is not opposed in any way to its "objective" value. To the "sentiment" of confidence is joined certitude for the mind, for God "is" truth.
10. St. Augustine.

Through faith a dialogue is entered into between a Person who has all to give and a human person who has everything to receive. "If you but knew the gift of God . . ." (4, 10). Faith brings man to a door opening out upon the Absolute.

This personal call and personal response which is faith bear in germ a friendship and postulate a union. "Because it was he and because it was I . . .", these words so rich in meaning even on the plane of human encounter and friendship are even much richer when applied to God and man. They give us a glimpse of the transcendent value and that sense of accomplishment of this encounter which goes to make up faith.

Because ordinarily speaking faith is given to us at a time in our life when we don't even have the the use of reason, we do not realize that it contains a personal calling; we tend to identify faith with something pertaining to the Church, with an adhesion to a body of truths which this Church has received. We risk the danger of forgetting that the personal call of God demands a personal response, and, when this is lacking, faith would be missing one of its constitutive elements.

It fact, even today for each of us as formerly for John and Paul, faith requires a personal calling and a personal response. It must be a living encounter with Christ. The external differences between the vocation to the faith of a John or a Paul and our own Christian vocation must not make us forget that there exists between them a deep-seated identity. Whether it is perceptible or not, God's call to the faith still remains necessary, as also our response. To us also Christ says, "Do you wish . . . ? Follow me. . . ." And He has no need to make His voice heard as He did to Paul on the Damascus road or to John on the shores of Lake Tiberias. As for our own response, we should make it as soon as possible. The response made for us at baptism does not dispense us from it.

Faith does not require that we see or hear in a sensible way. "Blessed are those who have not seen but have believed" (20, 29). It leans upon testimonies and is founded upon "knowledge" which God gives of Himself through grace.

That God "makes Himself known" and that we "know Him," this is the important element in faith and what makes faith a grace. Without this grace faith could neither be born nor develop in us.

Faith as "knowledge"

We too frequently tend to reduce faith to its human elements, viz., adherence of the intellect and surrender of the will, whereas it is initially a divine step and the manifestation of grace. Faith is a gift of God, and it

is this gift manifesting itself to man. To believe, according to John's way
of expressing it, is to have knowledge of God's gift to His creatures. Faith
is God making Himself known in His Son and making Himself known
effectively. True, it is eternal life rather than faith that John will specify
in terms of knowledge: "Now this is eternal life that they may know thee,
just Father, and Jesus Christ whom thou hast sent" (17, 3). But there is
more than a relationship between faith and everlasting life. Not only does
"he who believe have everlasting life" (3, 15,16), but the knowledge of
God is, though in a different manner, at the basis of one as well as the
other.

As long as revelation remains a reality exterior to man, even when it
is a very deep abstract knowledge in him, it is still not faith. To be
acquainted with revelation is not to have "a knowledge of God," and still
less to be known by God. John places the knowledge of man by God in
the foreground when speaking of faith; and in so doing he is following
both his own personal experience and the most traditional biblical data.

The grace of the knowledge of God does not produce its effect unless
it is consciously received. "But to as many as received him he gave the
power of becoming the sons of God . . ." (1, 12). Those who misunderstand the gift of God by stopping at the human element of faith change
John's thought in an essential way.

To form an idea of this gift of God without which faith can neither
develop or even exist, it would be well to pay close attention to the repeated expressions of the apostle everytime there is question of "believing." These expressions help us enter into his deep thought regarding the
problem of faith.

To believe, receive, and know

In John's Gospel and Epistles the words closely associated with the
expression "believe" are "to receive" and "to know." The last expression
is used more than fifty times in the fourth Gospel and always with reference to faith. It appears as one of the keys enabling us to enter more
deeply into the mystery of faith. This study is important, as this word,
when used in the Gospel of St. John, takes on a much different meaning
from its actual acceptation.

The Johannine and biblical concept of knowledge is clearly distinct
from that which is current in the Hellenistic world of the apostles' times.
The Hellenistic concept was that knowledge proceeds from the contemplation (theoria) of an object. An attempt is made to extract from the
object its essential and unchangeable qualities, those which constitute

its essence. Anything that would tend to hinder this vision of the essence because of mutation, etc., or anything that would be marked with any subjectivity is to be cast aside. Thus we arrive at the apprehension of the object as it is in itself, attaining its genus and specific difference.

When the Alexandrians, heirs to Greek thought, utilized these data to apply them to the contemplative life (bios theoretikos), which they realized was supposed to be transforming in its effects, they were led to a reconciliation with another form of knowledge, that offered by biblical tradition of which John had made use.

This form of knowledge is expressed in terms of a relationship, a sympathy, and an experience. I know in proportion to my own deep and vital relationship to an object. Likewise, there is true knowledge only between persons, for only persons can enter into this relationship with one another and acquire that experience called "sympathy." The more frequent, intimate, and deep is this relationship, the more real and rich is this knowledge. Thus we shall know a sickness, not because we are able to give an exact diagnosis of it or explain its evolution, but because we have been personally affected by it, we have suffered it in our flesh. Again, we shall understand the suffering of one mourning the loss of a dear one only when we ourselves have undergone the same experience. Is it not this form of knowledge to which the Word made flesh laid claim when He willed to take on our frailty (Heb. 5, 2) and have actual experience of our human condition?

Such knowledge, however, does not develop only with regard to suffering and trial. It can also refer to an intimate grasp of the divine presence and action in the soul. "Taste and see that the Lord is sweet" (Ps. 33, 9).

It appears, then, that whenever the Old Testament and St. John say "know," we would say instead: support, suffer, be visited by, be inflamed by, experience. This knowledge stems from a series of personal and dynamic relationships of the subject with the object.

To know is likewise to be conscious of this relationship which we entertain and to be affected by it in one way or another. This knowledge is not only on the theoretic level or on the level of concepts, but on that of affectivity, the will, life, and love.

While for the Greeks the word "know" signifies the contemplating of a reality in its unchangeable essence, for the Hebrews this word means the entering into contact with this reality through its manifestations; and if it is a question of a personal reality, e.g., God, it means to listen to His calls and answer them, to enter into intimate contact with Him, "convivere." The highest form of knowledge of God is expressed among the Greeks in pure contemplation, but among the Hebrews it consists in entering into communication, into communion with Him, in experiencing His designs upon each of us, in knowing and in doing His will, and on the mystical level "in loving divine things."

Though John remains faithful to this Hebraic concept of knowledge, we can see that his numerous contacts with Hellenism have enriched in an admirable manner a conception in which the experience of God is united to the "look"; and the desire to see, to the thirst for a "communion" in love.

God's knowledge of man

A question necessarily arises: If knowledge demands contact and a relationship, how can man possibly know Him who infinitely surpasses him, the one who is the Unknowable? This difficulty did not escape the Scripture writers and John makes their answer his own. It is a simple answer and has never varied.

Man could not know God if God had not taken the initiative of "making Himself known" by man. This mysterious visitation of man by God is a grace without which all knowledge of God by man would be impossible. Man knows God only in virtue of this coming, of this incorporation of God into him. We come upon that relationship already pointed out between revelation and faith. The initiative comes from God who reveals Himself to the soul and makes Himself known by her, but man must not undergo this divine visit passively. It is demanded of him that he actively welcome God, i.e., open himself to His coming, receive it. The "knowledge of faith" springs from this receptivity, this welcome, it is identified with this encounter in which man is at once known and knowing.

This is exactly what John wishes to make understood when he wrote in his Prologue: "But to as many as received him he gave the power of becoming sons of God; to those who believe in his name" (1, 12). That absolute priority on God's part in the matter of knowledge and the necessity on man's part of receiving the divine visit are clearly pointed out in this statement.[11]

11. This notion of coming, visit, descent, is perceptible throughout the Johannine work. Linked to the idea of the Incarnation: "The Word was made flesh and dwelt among us" (1, 14) as well as to the divine indwelling in the soul: "If anyone love me he will keep my word and my Father will love him and we will come to him and make our abode with him" (14, 23), it allows the spiritual life to develop: "Behold I stand at the door and knock. If any man listens to my voice and opens the door to me, I will come in to him and will sup with him and he with me" (Apoc. 3, 20). Love alone accounts for this divine conduct, and John will reveal in his Epistle, "As for us, let us love, for God first loved us."

Furthermore, the depth at which man is known by God, the richness of this visit of the Word in us, these are so great that the notion of "sonship" alone can express them. For God "to know" is "to create" and to create according to His own image and likeness. Knowledge here, i.e., in God, generates the most intimate relationship, the most profound and living that can be in existence: the relationship between father and child. Such a relationship leaves all others far behind, but it comprises them all while surpassing them. Between the Father and this child "born of God," there will be a community of thought, of sentiment, of mind, of life, everything will be shared, all will be in common. The infinite richness of participation which the Johannine Gospel will develop throughout finds its source in this very relationship.

In a movement of incomprehensible and merciful love God has known man and has made him capable of returning this knowledge through the gift of faith. An encounter is brought about in which God communicates the fullness of the divine "gift" to man. "All that is mine is thine" (17, 10). This fullness is expressed in the word "divine filiation," promised and offered to those who "receive the only-begotten Son" given to the world through love (3, 16), and to those who believe in His name.

And concerning this filiation, Peter has not hesitated to say it is a sharing in the divine nature itself.

"For indeed his divine power has granted us all things pertaining to life and piety through the knowledge of him who has called us by his own glory and power. Through which he has granted us the very great and precious promises, so that through them you may become partakers of the divine nature, having escaped from the corruption of that lust which is in the world" (2 Pet. 1, 3,4,). Such is the fruit of grace and faith in us.

Known by God, man can know God in his turn. This knowledge is at once the condition and the fruit or result of faith. This twofold exigence never ceases to be brought to light in the Bible.

Yahweh knows there (in the Bible) a chosen community, Israel: "You only have I known of all the families of the earth" (Am. 3, 2). But this election is the consequence of a choice going back to the time of Abraham. It is Abraham whom God chose and knew; and it is with him that He has set up His "Covenant" which He has tied with intimate bonds, and Abraham's response to the divine visit was faith. "Abraham believed God and it was reputed to him unto justice" (Gn. 15, 6).

If we wish to understand the personal structure of faith, we must examine closely the account given in Genesis where we are presented with the patriarch's vocation and his response. What is this "Covenant" between Yahweh and Abraham if it is not faith? Nowhere can we find such an intense degree of faith as in Abraham on this occasion; and first from the fact that it is a "birth." Abraham's fruitfulness is not only God's response to his faith, it symbolizes likewise the filiation which is realized in him—and which is realized in us after him—through faith. Abraham, before becoming the father of a "multitude," must first be born to God through faith. With him, paternity flows from his divine filiation and that is why, in spite of appearances, it is essentially spiritual. The faith which made Abraham the father of many nations, made him first the father of the chosen people. The birth of this people, which never ceases considering Yahweh as its Father throughout the Bible, is then completely dependent upon that act of faith of the patriarch.

And it is a birth which is announced as the term of this filiation: that of the Messias, the fruit of the Promise, and this Promise which is attached to the Covenant is dependent like it on faith.

Thus, when we are face to face with that statement in the Prologue where the new Covenant opens with the fulfillment of the Promise: "To all those who received him he gave the power of becoming the sons of God to those who believed in his name" (1, 12), it is impossible not to bring back to mind that first Covenant concluded with Abraham "our father in the faith" (Gn. 17, 4, 6). It is impossible too not to see that in each case this generation and this filiation are the fruit of faith. (Rm. 4, 16).

Man's knowledge of God

"And I will make of thee a great nation" (Gn. 12, 2). Yahweh who had "known" Abraham and the people born of him, and who had chosen it and attached Himself to it through faith, will know more particularly in this people certain individuals: patriarchs, prophets, and their faith in Him will be vivified. They will even have as their mission: giving an account of this divine knowledge of which they are conscious of being the object. They will present it very generally as the experience of an all-powerful, sweeping, penetrating, and irresistible presence. Yahweh has swooped down upon them and taken possession of them in a violent way. He has seized them as the lion seizes its prey (Am. 3, 5).

Man sets himself in opposition to this control and struggles against it. Thus Jacob struggles with the angel (Gn. 32, 29). And though victorious, he is still known and marked by God. A "new name" is given him symbolic of this intimate and creative knowledge. "Thy name shall not be called Jacob, but Israel" (Gn. 32, 29).

With regard to the prophets, they try to express this encounter of

God with man and the knowledge resulting therefrom in terms of love and passion. "Thou hast deceived me, O Lord, and I am deceived; thou hast been stronger than I and thou hast prevailed" (Jer. 20, 7).

Violence and the embrace of love are the symbols which the prophet judges least inadequate to describe this knowledge which takes on the meaning it frequently has in the Bible, i.e., "knowledge through love of two spouses."[12]

Thus, faith like knowledge is closely allied to the idea of Covenant in the Bible. And Covenant, the dialogue of man's heart which becomes the center of an encounter with God, is expressed in the Bible in terms borrowed from the realities of conjugal love and marriage.[13]

"The definition given by the prophets concerning the 'knowledge' of God has nothing to do with an intellectual preception of Him or moral progress. It is attached to the concept of the history of the universe to which they are accustomed, that great conjugal adventure between God and Israel, a history which they are conscious of living in their own private sphere. Revelation for them is not a gift but the discovery of a love. The encounter with the living God does not reveal to them a spirit or an idea but a partner."[14]

Love's encounter

In the Bible knowledge of God, rather than being a knowledge "of" God, appears to be knowledge "by" God and is closely related to the idea of election or choice. Applied first to the people of God and His servants, the prophets, this idea will be extended to the personal relationship between the faithful soul and God (Ps. 138, 1,4). Knowledge gives rise to election, to choice and salvation. We are not only at the origin of biblical thought, but of Pauline and Johannine thought as well (Rom. 8, 28-30).

---

12. "Knowledge accorded by the Spirit of God taking possession of man and communicating to him an experience of God is not only intimate and penetrating. Being a question of an encounter between the human and the divine this knowledge is of the conjugal order and its symbol covers two notions: to the constant fidelity of two beings differentiated by their sex, there is added the bond, also constant, of two beings whom space or the discordance of their sentiments can temporarily separate. Conjugal love differs from simple sexual love by its persistence after the act of encounter. Even when separated by the infinity of time and space, the spouses know each other by the same force of love. And even when the sentiment of love happens to waver in one of them, it is enough that this love remains intense in the other in order that the relationship of love remain secure." (A. Neher, L'Essence du prophetisme).
13. In the Bible the term "yadoa" expresses both the union of man and woman, that apex of love and source of fecundity, and the knowledge of God.
14. Neher, op. cit.

This knowledge "by" God which introduces a choice of love and a calling, also brings with it a demand for a response and a return of love on man's part. We grasp here why, in the Johannine thought entirely nourished on the Bible, faith is necessarily impregnated with love. It is because the act itself by which God knows us and communicates His grace will, when actually received by us, become faith as an election, a knowledge, and a choice of love. How can man's response, viz., faith, attain its purpose if it does not use the same language of love?

Is not love the only way of knowing deeply and of entering always more and more into this knowledge? God knows us perfectly simply because He loves us infinitely. "For those whom he has foreknown he has predestined to become conformed to the image of his Son . . ." (Rom. 8, 28). And St. John gives us Christ's words: "I am the good shepherd, and I know mine and mine know me, even as the Father knows me and I know the Father; and I lay down my life for my sheep" (10, 15).

If we ask: Why does God not content Himself with knowing man, and will that man know Him also?, we shall answer that one of the facts stressed in the Bible is that God not only loves man but that man is called upon to know and love God in return. God reveals to man that the relations between Him and man must be based upon an exchange of love to which free consent is given. That is His reason for entering into this Covenant which terminates in Christ's coming among men (3, 16). In this really new perspective, the necessity for man to know God is not destined simply to subsist. It actually becomes an exigency of love of God at work in him. Knowledge of God without love is an impossibility (1 Jn. 4, 8). Faith appears to be the response of love which God awaits. The freedom of this response is totally safeguarded since it consists not only in being known but in knowing. "To those who knew him . . . he has given. . . ." The freedom and spontaneity of man's response are as absolute as the first grace was gratuitous through which man was known by God. However if, in the genesis of faith as in that of love, priority always belongs to God, it is less of a succession than of an interaction and an exchange that we should talk. Provided that he does not shut himself off from God's coming but welcomes and receives Him, man knows God in the very act by which he himself is known by God. All is bound together in a living unity where receiving and giving make up one thing, and this is characteristic of love; where being known and knowing constitute one and the same act, one and the same living plenitude which fidelity buries deeper and deeper in man's being.

In the faith such as it is presented in the Johannine Gospel, the data received from the Old Testament are essential. But there is an element in John's faith which imprints upon it a character that is radically new.

Although it remains a knowledge of man by God and vice versa like that of the Old Testament, henceforth it is Christ who "knows" man and it is likewise to Him that man's faith must be directed. "You believe in God, believe also in me" (14, 1).

How could it be otherwise, Jesus being the "author and finisher of our faith" (Heb. 12, 2)? God is revealed to us and we are able to know Him only through His only-begotten Son (1, 18). And did not John write his Gospel in order that "you may believe that Jesus is the Christ, the Son of God, and that believing you may have life in his name" (20, 31)?

If Abraham's faith remains a model for Christians,—let us recall the praise given it by Paul as well as the author of the Epistle to the Hebrews (Gal. 3; Heb. 7)—it is because confidence in God and the patriarch's fidelity are admirable. Moreover, we must say of it what Christ said of the Baptist, "Amen, I say to you, among those born of women there has not risen a greater than John the Baptist; yet the least in the kingdom of heaven is greater than he" (Mt. 11, 11).

If our faith is conditioned by the way we know God and are known by Him, who cannot see the change since Christ's coming? The role of Mediator which He has because of the divine and human natures helps Him show how God loves us and will enable man to know God better than ever before.[15]

Christ's knowledge of man

Christ has a knowledge of man that is both human and divine. Having become man He is like us. He has a knowledge of us which stems from a likeness of nature and which John stresses repeatedly. He says that He knows "not only what is in man" (2, 24), but that He knew because He experienced Himself the sentiments that are the lot of humanity. St. John points out His fatigue at Jacob's well (4, 6), His sighs and tears at Lazarus' tomb (11, 33), His suffering when misunderstood by His disciples (6, 67), His tenderness towards them (13, 33), and His sadness (Mt. 26, 37). In other words, St. John emphasizes what the author of the Epistle to the Hebrews stated. "For we have not a high priest who cannot have compassion on our infirmities, but one tried in all things except sin" (Heb. 4, 15).

15. We should note here how essential this "knowledge" of God is and the degree to which it thrusts itself upon us, even over and above faith. Faith will cease, while knowledge will endure. It is because faith is a modality of our present mortal condition. Knowledge is the very substance of our beatific life, which enables us to understand how much it is informed by love which also will endure. In the measure in which we shall have worked here below to "know" God in the biblical sense of the term, i.e., with the aid of all the faculties of knowing and loving, in this measure we shall be favored eternally with a higher beatitude.

Christ's "human condition" is a reality of such depth that it is quite impossible to measure or perceive all its consequences. However, in what concerns faith it is possible and even necessary to glimpse certain consequences of it, since it is through Christ that our faith must pass and in Him it must be centered.

Although it is directed to the same God as the faith of the men of the Old Testament, the faith of Christians has undergone a transformation as it now encounters Christ, God made man (Col. 2, 9). Perhaps even the danger for many would be to see no longer anything but this humanity, and to disregard the divine transcendence of the Word made flesh. God has nevertheless willed this "incarnation" with all its consequences.

Now, in what concerns our faith, we cannot say to what an extent the certitude of being known by Him who, while being God, has willed to be born and to die like a man and a poor man, miserable and naked, modifies our relations with God and reveals Him to us in a way both new and infinitely more profound. Yes, "when the goodness and kindness of God our Savior appeared" (Ti. 3, 4) something changed in that relationship between God and humanity: our confidence, love, gratitude, and faith all grew immeasurably. And we have likewise perceived that this "knowledge" of man by God cannot fail to have an infinite and admirable mercy in it. How could it fail to be penetrated through and through with compassion and pity when exercised by one who was made our own and who underwent death for us? It is because He knows "what is in man" that the Word made flesh cries out "I have compassion on the multitude" (Mk. 8, 2), and again, "Come to me all you who labor and are heavily burdened" (Mt. 11, 28); and that on the Cross when about to succumb to the blows inflicted upon Him by those whom He has come to save, He cried out to His Father, "Father, forgive them for they know not what they do" (Lk. 23, 34).

If faith demands that before knowing God we are known by Him, and if this divine knowledge draws light from love, what must be the depth to which Christ's merciful and compassionate glance descends into our souls! (Mk. 10, 17). Christ is our Judge and He is also our Savior, and as much as the soul fears being known by her Judge, she still is reassured and calmed when she realizes that she is known by Him who has been "sent into the world not to judge the world, but that the world may be saved through him" (3, 17).

And if faith demands that we know God, how easy will this knowledge be made and how much more intimate and comforting when it has as its object the one who has assumed our own nature and "has dwelt among us" (1, 14)?

The more we examine the effects of the coming of Christ upon faith, the more we understand it must be considered in the light of this coming. The faith that John proposes as the ultimate reason of his Gospel (20, 31), is faith in Christ. He is the one that claims it from us and it is to Him that it must be directed. He is the Author of the Revelation upon which our faith is established, hence there is a link between the nature of this faith and the means Christ employed to reveal its object to us.

Furthermore, nowhere as much as here is it true to say that the Person and the message are identified in Christ. If faith, because of its personal structure, confers such an importance upon the Person of Him who is its Author (Heb. 12, 2), it is likewise of primary importance to discover the economy and the pedagogy which Christ used to reveal and communicate it to us.

Finally and above all, this economy will bring out the fact that the structure of faith is more personal than we can even imagine. In fact, what is it that Christ has revealed if not one God in three divine Persons? To have faith will no longer be simply believing in God and trusting in Him; it will be becoming true children of the Father in heaven, in the Son and through the Holy Spirit. We grasp the distance between the faith of the Old Testament and that which we call Christian faith. The latter will not only be a knowledge by man of the three divine Persons, but it will first be knowledge of man by the Father, the Son, and the Holy Spirit. To discover the personal structure of faith there is no other means than that of examining attentively Christ's message such as it is transmitted by the Johannine Gospel. Its author states that he has written "in order that you may believe that Jesus is the Christ, the Son of God, and that believing you may have life in his name" (20, 31).

Faith in the Trinity

Faithful in presenting all things in a concrete unity and living totality (a method which makes the fourth Gospel an edifice in which everything "is compact" as in the holy City), John does not propose faith as stemming from a definition. It is made specific little by little on the occasion of definite personal situations, and advances progressively towards its fullness without ever ceasing—and we touch here upon one of John's miracles—to manifest itself as an absolute, an unbreakable unit with regard to both its object and its subject.

The object of faith is none other than the holy Trinity. True, Christ does not reveal this object to His listeners from the outset. There is no mention in the Gospel made of "persons" or of a "Trinity." And yet, from the Prologue on we see that the faith required of those who listen to Him or are present at a miracle must be directed to Him "who sent (Christ)" (5, 24) at the same time as it is directed to Christ.

The Father is never absent from the thought or the discourses of Christ. It is impossible to forget, even for an instant, this Father whom the only-begotten Son has come to reveal (1, 18). Christ calls the Temple "the house of my Father" (2, 16); He tells Nicodemus that God "has sent his Son into the world, that the world may be saved through him" (3, 17); and He states that "the Father loves the Son" (3, 35). It is to the Father that prayers of adoration from true worshippers must go (4, 23), and it is the Father's will that Christ came to do (4, 34).

As for the Holy Spirit, He is present in the first chapters of the Johannine Gospel, e.g., at Christ's baptism (1, 32), in the interview with Nicodemus (3, 5,6,8), and again in that statement of Christ, "For he whom God has sent speaks the words of God, for not by measure does God give the Spirit" (3, 34).

As the Gospel scenes and discourses succeed one another, we find the persons of the Father and the Spirit more frequently and more clearly being proposed as the object of the faith of those who intend becoming Christ's disciples. In the discourse after the Supper, Christ finally succeeds in "speaking plainly and uttering no parable" (16, 29).

There is a totality no less personal, viz., the subject called upon to believe, corresponding with the personal character of faith considered in its object, viz., the divine Persons.

And faith in the subject is not directed towards any particular faculty but to his entire being. It is love as well as knowledge, or rather faith is knowledge in the biblical sense of the term, i.e., a knowledge demanding a total surrender in the one believing. Therefore, to believe in Christ means to listen to Him, to place one's trust in Him, to love, obey, and follow Him; it means being united to Him. There is no room left for indecision, half measures.

The fourth Gospel, as far as faith is concerned, does not have us take part in interior debates presenting reasons for believing. At the most this is discreetly pointed out. Neither is Christ's teaching compared with other teachings, and not for an instant does it come to the mind of the listeners to discuss Christ's statements on the doctrinal or philosophical plane. The problem of faith is indeed presented on the doctrinal plane, but it is presented to us, before all else, in this Gospel in terms of surrender of a person with regard to another. And if this is done in the name of Truth, this Truth presents itself as a Person. Thus, everything takes place on the personal level. "Do you believe in me? You . . . follow me."

Will the obstacles to be overcome for answering such a question be surmounted? And in this struggle, where light and darkness themselves appear as persons and not as abstractions, which will outweigh the other? This is the question to be solved.

The apostle never supposes that one can place the absolute value of Revelation in doubt. Since we are placed before the Son of God, before Him who is the Life, the Light, and the Truth, there is no place for any hesitation.

Does this imply that John is unaware of the struggles of a soul presented with such a choice? By no means. The necessity of believing in the Son of God does not go against realism or the psychological make-up as far as John is concerned, as the scenes bear witness in which the sentiments of the participants are so accurately noted and pointed out. But the unique problem remains always that of the welcome given to the Person of Christ.

For the listeners it is a question of accepting or rejecting, not truths, not a doctrine, but a Person who is there before them and who asks that they believe in Him.

"Dost thou believe in the Son of Man" (9, 35-37)? Asked this direct question, man can answer "yes" or "no"; and he cannot answer "yes" without immediately being presented with the consequences of this faith, viz., that total surrender accompanying it. "Leave your father, mother, nets . . . come follow me" (Mt. 4, 20,22).

Though the problem of faith is reduced to this choice, it does not mean that it is presented to all in like manner. The contrary is true, since it is a question of a personal surrender. For each one it is necessarily a unique and absolute giving; and it is such as he is, and with his entire self that he approaches, for he hears himself called out by name. It is then personally that he must answer.

The Johannine Gospel notes down the diversity of these responses as carefully as it notes the different forms of the calls.[16] That is why, from the viewpoint of the types of responses, we would look in vain for any kind of gradual progress in the various scenes reported by the evan-

---

16. Such a renunciation is asked of one, such, of another. Nicodemus' call is unlike that of the Samaritan woman's or like that of the apostles'; the Lord takes into consideration the temperament and vocation of each one. Of St. John He asks that he remain until He comes (21, 22), in such a way that the faith of this disciple "will remain" of the same nature as his first call, "Come and see." It will continue to develop into contemplative love. Whereas to Peter who was invited to leave his nets, the Risen Christ will say again, "Follow me" and will make him understand that his faith will set him on the ways of renunciation and service. "When thou art old thou wilt stretch forth thy hands, and another will gird thee, and lead thee where thou wouldst not" (21, 18).

gelist. To each the problem is presented in the form of a choice from
which there is no escape. In these Johannine accounts there is room only
for acceptance or refusal, for light or darkness, for the "world" or for
belonging to the group which Christ calls "his own," for Satan or the
children of God.

Does this mean that faith has neither a birth or a development in it?
Must we content ourselves with stating it "is" or it "is not," and give up
trying to discover any principle of development? Certainly not.

Faith undergoes a development (Mk. 9, 24) as John's Gospel testifies
in many places, but the apostle's admirable spiritual sense enables him
to grasp the fact that this development follows certain supernatural
principles. In other words: if conversion, "metanoia," the soul's welcome
of God, if these condition faith, this faith in its birth and development is
constantly dependent on the action of the three divine Persons.

Action of the three divine Persons

As important as are the favorable dispositions of the soul, its "good
will" especially, the development of this faith remains essentially dependent upon the progressive action and the indwelling in the soul of the
Father, Son, and Holy Spirit. The three Persons act conjointly in the soul
and when God comes into it He does so in His entirety.

We can state also that the fact for a man to pronounce the words:
"I believe" is a grace the mystery of which no one is in a position to
fathom. There is no reason that is humanly sufficient for making an act
of faith. If intellectual preparation and good will have an important role
to play, they do not account for faith. Frequently in the Gospel and in the
accounts of conversion we see faith "rising." Some kind of preparation,
a rational foundation, even a miracle could have played an apparently
decisive role. In reality, however, nothing accounts for faith which remains always an absolutely gratuitous gift. It happens that it is something
desired all through one's life and never possessed; it can be given to
one who apparently has never sought it or even desired it. God is the
absolute Master of faith and it is as Master that He gives it. He has to
give an account to no one and He keeps the secret of faith's advances
just as He keeps the secret of His own visitations.

Undoubtedly faith demands total dedication of a man once it has been
given him; it will suffer no division, or looking back (Lk. 9, 62). And yet
it still remains true that it appears as the result of the continued action of
the three divine Persons, and that the influence of each Person is discerni-
ble. The spiritual sense and experience of the beloved disciple allowed him

to grasp better than anyone else in what manner and in what direction this unique and threefold action is exercised.

If the Father did not "help" the soul by making it experience a secret attraction for His Son, no one could come to Christ. In His turn, Christ as author and guide and finisher of faith, presenting Himself to the soul, enables its good will to become effective. In Him faith finds its object and also its principle of development and progress. Faith deepens in a soul in direct proportion to this soul's belief in Christ. "To believe" and to "grow" in Christ are two realities advancing in the same step.

Faith also needs the Holy Spirit if it is to live, to realize full development, and attain its fullness and ultimate fruition. He must be constantly at work in the soul, for He alone is the one who effects that intimate and inexpressible knowledge which develops into union and a lived experience of God.

The fourth Gospel bears testimony in an unqualified manner to this visitation and indwelling of the Trinity that constitutes the substance and the principle of the life of faith. And to St. John goes the credit for having placed the mystery of faith under this light and those who meditate upon his work receive some rays of this light.

CHAPTER 12

DIVINE ATTRACTION AND HUMAN RESPONSE

In many places in the Johannine Gospel we see Christ attribute to His Father the first grace of faith. "All that the Father gives to me shall come to me" (6, 37). "No one can come to me unless the Father draw him" (6, 44). "No one can come to me unless he be enabled to do so by my Father" (6, 65).

This attraction which the Father places in the soul turns the latter towards the light and the truth, but the soul is still unaware that these are called: Jesus Christ.

Through what ways and under what forms does this attraction manifest itself? This is the Father's secret from whom "descends every perfect gift" (Jas. 1, 17). We can only say it is extended to all souls and placed in each. "It is written in the Prophets, 'And they shall be taught of God.' Everyone who has listened to the Father and has learned comes to me" (6, 45).

When does this attraction bring about its fruit in the soul? The Master's words show that the divine gift demands an active response from man in order to develop. "Everyone who has listened and has learned" (6, 45). However everything here is mysterious, for to the mystery of God is added that of our freedom. Man can always allow himself either to be drawn or to place an obstacle to the divine attraction.

John respects the secrets of hearts, but he shows this attraction at work in many places. Few problems held his attention more than this one and it merits ours. In our own days we fail to give it proper attention. For the greater number of Christians no conscious life precedes their baptism. And in the greater number of cases faith is not distinguished from baptism. And yet who could deny that not only an act of personal faith is necessary, but also a faith that is active?

Baptism acts "ex opere operato," but it does not dispense with the profession of faith. The child being incapable of this, others express it in his place and he is to make it himself when he is in a position to perform a personal act.[1] Must he not be "born from on high" (3, 7) which demands that baptism be "of water and the Spirit"? And how would baptism operate without a conscious participation and a positive spiritual reception on the part of the baptized?

The fourth Gospel helps us understand all this since it describes a different state of affairs. Attachment to Christ, acts of faith in Him are the deeds of adults who, though they did not know their paths would cross Christ's one day, were nevertheless for a long time responsible for their actions. Through a grace from the Father, an attraction turned them unconsciously towards the Messias-to-come and asked them not to sin against the light. How did they answer?

John has pointed out two possible attitudes in his Prologue (1, 12). He has also shown that if, before this encounter, they habitually followed their conscience and acted "in the truth" (3, 21), i.e., if they were motivated by "good will," the grace of faith found a prepared terrain. Between this attraction and good will there exists an intimate bond which, far from interfering with adhesion to faith, remains necessary for its existence and exercise. This is something John brings out forcefully, judging it to be of vital importance for the faith.

That is the reason baptism appears as a sharing in a reality perpetually in act. Faith is not only an attachment to Christ, it is our incorporation in Him; it is a sharing in his life through an ever renewed fidelity in Him and a preference for Him manifested continually in our actions. It is an ever deepening knowledge, an exchange of love becoming ever more intense. Such a reality cannot be lasting unless "good will" is ever active.

When bringing peace to men on Christmas night, the angels made it understood that Christ's coming offered their good will the object towards which it had been groping in an obscure manner. To the first grace which is presupposed in their very attraction, the Father has now added a still greater grace, viz., the coming of His Son. The initial grace had the purpose of conducting anyone to Christ who freely allows himself to be turned by God to the true light (6, 65; 3, 16).

It is very easy to imagine the use man would have made of his freedom if left to his own resources. Thanks to this secret calling which echoes in the heart, he can freely advance towards that faith which will give him eternal life (1, 12; 6, 40).

This faith sustains the soul by uniting it to Life, Truth, and Light, which are henceforth explicitly identified with Christ on condition that

---

1. Such are the role and meaning of the renovation of baptismal vows and the profession of faith. This is necessary for the life of faith.

man's good will remain cooperative. If it happens that God mercifully allows faith to remain in a soul no longer possessed of good will, this faith is dead since it is no longer vivified by love.

Good will

Good will remains necessary for man, not only to attain faith, but also to keep it once attained. The fourth Gospel gives proof of this. That it is necessary for arriving at faith, John shows us in those scenes where an act of faith is demanded of these men placed suddenly face to face with Christ and constrained by that fact to make the main and decisive choice of their existence. (Cf. Lk. 1, 76). Through His simple presence, in fact, Christ puts them to the test. This test is the principle of discrimination and of a judgment which men make themselves (3, 19). Now the former conduct of these men has a very great influence upon the position they take which becomes an adherence to Christ in virtue of a grace.

Have these men in the past been faithful in acting in the truth and the light? In other words, have they been of "good will"? They will very likely then recognize the Son of God in Christ. Have they, on the contrary, "loved the darkness more than the light"? They will remain blind (9, 39).

This fourth Gospel shows us in a concrete but tragic manner what can become of a faith not vivified by good will. John lived for three years in the company of men who had answered Christ's call and tried to remain faithful to Him despite their weaknesses. Among them and like them, having heard the same call and having received the teaching and marks of love, was the man Judas. Under what secret influence, through what strange paths did it happen that he refused this grace of light and love, closed himself off from the Spirit's inspiration, and finally performed that incomprehensible act of delivering up with a traitorous kiss his Master, Savior, and God?

Judas' case is tragic because faith had not become extinct. Had it been stronger, he would have rejected the idea of betraying his Master as a monstrous temptation. And had he lost it entirely, he would have been immune to despair, for he would not have believed that he had delivered up to death the Son of God. In fact, his faith had become incapable of hope as well as charity because it was paralysed by the absence of good will (6, 64, 70).

All the more mysterious since it not only implicates God and man, but also Satan, and since it bears upon the Person of the Redeemer, Judas' case is not unique, in this sense that John had often seen around him other men (6, 66) whose faith, for lack of good will, gradually closed itself to the light which had been welcomed at first with joy. Sought out by the Father, but later tempted by Satan, they "had preferred the darkness to the light" (3, 19).

Good and bad faith

Scenes reported by John show us in what good will consists and what sentiments go to make it up. It is composed essentially of good faith, detachment, generosity, and it is rooted in the heart. By the term "heart" we mean the sum total of the profound dispositions of a man.

God sounds the heart and really knows it. It hears His call. If the heart is "good" it reacts favorably when the grace of faith is offered it. If the heart is "bad," it closes itself to the divine advances. As the aged Simeon had prophesied, Christ's coming into the world shows what each one is in the intimate depths of his soul. "Behold this child is set for the fall and rise of many in Israel, and for a sign that shall be contradicted. And thy own soul a sword shall pierce, that the thoughts of many hearts shall be revealed" (Lk. 2, 34).

Nathanael's heart is good. Though timidly setting out upon the path of faith, he will merit this praise from Christ, "Behold a true Israelite in whom there is no guile" (1, 47). The hearts of the apostles are good, for they answer Christ's call with generosity and leave all to follow Him (1, 35-44). The man born blind is another example of good faith. His attitude is a contrast with the Pharisees' bad faith, for they do not want to see and deliberately blind themselves. To give themselves reasons for not drawing the inevitable conclusions from an undeniable miracle, they say of Christ, "We know this man is a sinner" (9, 24).

As for the cure of the royal official's son at Capharnaum, eloquent in its directness, the account permits us to see in this man not only a perfect uprightness of intention, but also the habit of regulating his conduct upon his convictions, and also having confidence in others whose intention he judges to be good. "And there was a certain royal official whose son was lying sick at Capharnaum. When he heard that Jesus had come from Judea into Galilee, he went to him and besought him to come down and heal his son, for he was at the point of death. Jesus therefore said to him, 'Unless you see signs and wonders, you do not believe.' The royal official said to him, 'Sir, come down before my child dies.' Jesus said to him, 'Go thy way, thy son lives.' The man believed the word that Jesus spoke to him and departed. But even as he was going down, his servants met him and brought him word saying that his son lived. He asked them therefore the hour in which he had got better. And they told him, 'Yesterday, at the seventh hour, the fever left him.' The father knew then that it was at that very hour in which Jesus had said to him, 'Thy son lives.' And he himself believed, and his whole household" (4, 46-53).

This path along which this father advances in confidence and already in faith is symbolic of the necessity of uniting to good faith a detached generosity and the desire of surrendering our entire being. Good will is not real unless it is given through a surrender of self filled with confidence. If there is no dedication, there would be no faith.

John has insisted much on the necessity of developing such dispositions in the heart and has revealed the obstacles such dispositions meet. Two Gospel accounts bring these out clearly, viz., the paralytic at Bethsaida and the man born blind.

When he recognized Jesus in the Temple as the man who cured him, the paralytic told the Pharisees and the Doctors of the Law. The latter, determined to rid themselves of a man who was undermining the established order, take the violation of the Sabbath as pretext for refusing to listen to the healed man. Jesus sees through their hypocrisy and says: "You search the Scriptures because in them you think you have life everlasting. And it is they that bear witness of me, yet you are not willing to come to me that you may have life" (5, 39).

Christ understood hearts. He knows that this so-called love of the Scriptures, laudable and salutary in itself, is nothing but a false front in these men. They are not awaiting, or rather they do not really desire, the Messias announced in the Scriptures. Men in office, well satisfied with themselves, very unwilling to listen to the solicitations of grace which would effect curtailment and changes in their lives and even a moral conversion which they fear, they examine the Scriptures and search them, but desire to find nothing.

Thus Christ directs these avenging words at them: "But I know that you have not the love of God in you. I have come in the name of my Father and you do not receive me. If another come in his own name, him you will receive. How can you believe who receive glory from one another, and do not seek the glory which is from the only God?" (5, 42-44).

In the scene of the man born blind (9, 1-41), prejudice and hypocrisy are even more evident if that is possible. Unable to deny a miracle witnessed by all, the Pharisees again use the Sabbath as pretext against Christ. "This man is not from God because he does not keep the Sabbath" (9, 16), say some, while others in whom there is still a spark of good faith ask, "How can a man who is a sinner work these signs?" Their protests were counteracted by the narrowness of those who "did not

believe of him that he had been born blind and received his sight . . ."
(9, 18), and they did not hesitate to say of Christ "We know this man is
a sinner" even after the miracle had been proven. In order not to lose
face they insult the healed man: "Thou art his disciple, but we are
disciples of Moses. We know that God spoke to Moses; but as for this
man we do not know where he is from" (9, 28).

This brought upon them that ironic answer: "Why, herein is the
marvel, that you do not know where he is from, and yet he opened my
eyes. Now we know that God does not hear sinners; but if anyone is a
worshipper of God and does his will, him he hears. Not from the beginning of the world has it been heard that anyone opened the eyes of a man
born blind. If this man were not from God, he could do nothing" (9,
30-33).

The Pharisees' bad faith and self-sufficiency do not only close them
against the faith, but bring upon them Christ's absolute condemnation.
" 'For judgment have I come into the world, that they who do not see
may see, and they who see may become blind.' And some of the
Pharisees who were with him heard this, and they said to him, 'Are we
also blind?' Jesus said to them, 'If you were blind you would not have
sin. But now that you say, we see, your sin remains!' " (9, 39-41).

Is this absolute condemnation? It appears so. We must realize to
whom it is addressed. It is a fact that the evangelist who has transmitted
to us these fearful condemnations against the Pharisees leaves at least one
of them outside the general condemnation, Nicodemus. "Now, there was
a certain man among the Pharisees, Nicodemus by name, a ruler of the
Jews" (3, 1).

If a man deserves credit for taking a stand against the milieu in which
he finds himself and to which he owes everything, his situation, fortune,
etc., there is none the less need of great courage to have an independent
opinion and to stick to it in the face of many difficulties.

Weighing down upon the individuals that compose it, a milieu ends
up by forcing them into a conformism and even by falsifying their judgment. It was often the case with those whom John throughout his Gospel
calls "the Jews," a word which aims at all those undoubtedly who opposed Christ, but more particularly the Pharisees, Scribes, Doctors of the
Law. Each was strongly influenced by the ideas of the time which had
taken on the force of law and by the weight of insurmountable traditions.

The pride, self-sufficiency, narrowness, attachment to their own views
of a great number of them were notorious. And we feel that among
Christ's fierce antagonists, the opposition frequently stems from established social positions, from interests to be safeguarded, from advantages
hard to give up, from honors, riches, etc., to which they are attached, and

attachment to Christ would bring about their loss. Their lack of good faith and loyalty is striking and the reasons they advance are for the most part pure pretexts. This is why they merit the reproaches directed at them by Christ.

However, it seems that their attachment to the religion and the institution of Israel and to the social order flowing from these, which Christ came to change, could have been a really sincere conviction in some of them.

In our own times if we admit that a capitalist cannot be necessarily suspected of partiality in defense of capitalism even when his own interests are bound up with the system he defends, with even greater reason, perfectly understandable was the persuasion of the Pharisees to defend a traditional, religious "order" which was extremely worthy of respect since it was revealed and set up by Yahweh and consecrated by a line of prophets and the entire history of Israel. In either case, we see how it is practically impossible for a milieu not to fashion and deform the judgments and sentiments of those who form part of it.

Personal and collective responsibility

We may consider Christ's condemnations as being directed as much to an "order" disfigured by abuses enjoying free rein as well as to the individuals composing that order. There are collective situations which constitute a formidable obstacle to the advance of truth in souls. Each epoch, on one point or another, experiences this state of collective sin, in which those who uphold an order close their eyes firmly to what brings to many of them distinct advantages, though intrinsically evil in itself.[2]

If this fact leaves the responsibility of the individual intact, it explains at least why it was more difficult for the Pharisees than others to arrive at faith. When reading St. John, we see in each case that the attachment of the "Jews" to their deformed religion was very often the obstacle to faith in Christ. But we see also that Christ's role was not limited to bringing truth to individuals; it was likewise to society as such and even to the world that He revealed a new "order," or at least the principles of life which would reduce external obstacles to justice and charity if it would not eliminate them entirely. They would henceforth be able to develop more freely. Christ had warned His disciples that difficulties and scandals would always remain in the world. "In the world you will have affliction" (16, 33) He says on the night of the Supper. And faith will always be the victory that will overcome the world according to St. John (1 Jn. 5, 4).

2. We could compare Paul with John (Rom. 10, 19 to John 11, 18).

As for individual responsibility, this remains God's secret. Aware of the mystery of the call or the rejection of souls, a Paul, who sets up the new order in opposition to the old, proposes first a justification for God's conduct or he attempts an explanation (Rom. 10, passim). But he finally comes to the truth that God's ways are unfathomable (Rom. 11, 33).

John offers no such consideration. He confines himself to presenting the problem as it is and to stating that all those who bear the name of "Jews" and more universally those who come under the name of "the world" (10, 26; 8, 41-46; 17, 9) are opposed to Christ. Their responsibility really appears to be entire for "now they have no excuse for their sin" (15, 22).

The weak and the pusillanimous

Although the world designates those whose pride, hardness, and lack of good will separate them from the faith, there is an entirely different category of souls in whom good will is present, but it meets with obstacles which run the risk of destroying this good will totally. In these souls the difficulty comes from weakness and not malice. The influence of the senses and the sins stemming from these senses hold them in slavery, substituting for the divine attraction another which is both tyrannical and overpowering.

These souls, however, have not voluntarily shut themselves off from the divine inspirations which they are still capable of hearing; they are incapable of following them. Good will is still not absent though it is ineffective and that is why God has an influence over them. These have an advantage over those that are proud and self-sufficient; they have the advantage of knowing themselves and of recognizing their culpability. They have not built an impenetrable wall between themselves and God. It is through human weakness and even with regret they have allowed it to rise up gradually. God, taking into consideration this weakness and their avowed misery, will trace out a path to them. Knowing better than they do themselves their desire to detach themselves from what holds them captive against their will, He will allow the occasion to arise which will bring them grace and deliver them.

Such is the case with the Samaritan woman, the Magdalene, the woman taken in adultery; thus does He act with each soul that is weak but of a good will.

John, who has reported to us in terms of formidable severity the condemnation of the Pharisees by Christ, makes use of extreme delicacy in order to show us the first glimmering of a return to the dawn of faith awakening under the influence of divine mercy in these souls, apparently badly prepared, but still so little removed from God.

He shows us Christ as more severe with pusillanimous souls whose good will is practically neutralized and destroyed by the fear of dedicating themselves and through an insufficient generosity. These souls appear incapable of making the step. This was the case with the many witnesses of the multiplication of the loaves. These "disciples" of Jesus, full of enthusiasm and an apparent generosity, cried out, "What are we to do that we may perform the works of God?" When faced with the necessity of adhering to Christ's words and making an act of faith that was difficult, they withdraw and refuse to dedicate themselves to Him. "This is a hard saying. Who can listen to it?" "From this time many of his disciples turned back and no longer went with him" (6, 66).

Faith and the slavery of sin

When bringing to light the obstacles to good will and faith, John does not fail to seek out the cause. Undoubtedly the inclination to evil of our fallen nature would be enough to explain why the attraction to the light and the truth is so frequently attacked. The same goes for those who are attached to the "world" and are its prisoners. However, the obstacles would not be so strong and so terrible without Satan's incessant attack.

He seeks to ruin good will in souls, seducing and holding them captive. If they do not free themselves from him who is "a murderer from the beginning" (8, 44), they will never come to know the truth. Rather they are given up to death. "I go, and you will seek me, and in your sin you will die" (8, 21). Jesus does not specify the sin about which there is question here, because all sin tends to produce the same effects in souls, to raise the same obstacles between them and God.

"Amen, amen, I say to you, everyone who commits sin is a slave of sin" (8, 34). This slavery prevents the soul from hearing God's voice, from listening to His calls and following them. "My word takes no hold among you" (8, 37). "You cannot listen to my word" (8, 43). Enslaved by sin, the soul can no longer set itself up in the truth and the light even when it has the desire to do so. His action "who has not stood in the truth" and who is "a liar and the father of lies" (8, 44) has gained mastery of that good will which could have still remained in the soul and had as its purpose the preparing of the paths of faith.

The obstacle to good will resides then in sin, in all sin, those turning us from the light and those subjecting us to the allurement of our senses.

By making slaves of us, these sins place us in Satan's power. Christ will go as far as saying of those who subject themselves to sin: "The father from whom you are is the devil, and the desires of your father it is your will to do" (8, 44).

To become a "child of God" through faith, or "to have the devil for a father," this is what is at stake in the choice to be made between good and bad will.

Modesty and good will

It would be unsound to make Satan alone responsible for the failure of our good will. He does exercise an undeniable influence over it and this influence is constant and varied. But the difficulties encountered by our good will come even more from our fallen nature and from our reaction to divine graces.

It seems that good will leans upon a more hidden and intimate disposition demanded of those whom the Gospel presents to us: the proud Pharisees, souls weak and enslaved in their sin, pusillanimous souls who hesitate to make the final step, finally upright and generous souls, e.g., the royal official at Capharnaum, the man born blind, and the apostles themselves.

This disposition appears to consist in a will of benevolent attention, and also in an acceptance of God, both of which are governed by true humility and "poverty of spirit." But since the fourth Gospel does not employ this word, we should speak rather of "modesty," either intellectual or spiritual.

The possessor of this modesty realizes his limitations. He does not shut himself up in his own little world, but accepts the fact that others exist as good as his own, still unknown to him and which his neighbor will aid him in discovering.

In this Gospel those who have refused the light appear as prisoners of their own treasure, their possessions, their privileges, their own will or their own universe, even of their own religion, considered as a good of which they have exclusive possession and usage. The more self-centered a rich man is, the more he reacts against whatever threatens to overreach him and deprive him of his goods, and the less capable he is of "good will." On the contrary, the humble and the modest man, even when possessing much materially speaking, retains a sense of his limitations and uncertainty and he is always ready to leave them for other values of a higher and more universal nature.

The invitation to the faith directed to each one takes him where and how he is. It asks of him only one thing: not to consider himself as an absolute, but to be willing to see attitudes called into question. This demands that he have confidence in another and advance into the unknown.

The fourth Gospel illustrates this state of mind admirably and helps us see how this modesty is still lacking in its beginnings on certain levels, while it is evident on others. Thus, in the Samaritan woman no notable change of attitude is apparent though grace is already working in her soul. The Gospel account presents her to us when immodesty of habits and mind run the risk of setting up an irresistible barrier. But her banter and her seemingly careless attitude soon appear as only a shield behind which she hides herself to defend herself against a control she fears. When she is pursued by Christ beyond her defenses, she finally acknowledges defeat. It is because in spite of outward appearances, her soul had never really set up any real opposition to the divine advances.

In this, her actions reveal much more to us than her words. They show her to us accepting the fact of being placed face to face with herself, of admitting her weakness and misery (4, 29), and not setting herself against what this "Prophet" (4, 19) is trying to break down in her. She also allows Him to place that Absolute before her for which she unknowingly thirsted, but whose demands upon her she feared. From then on the ways were opened up through which grace is going to progress and finally lead her to faith.

As for the sinful woman, it is, we would say, through her state of life that she is immodest; she has for her trade the soliciting of attention and homage for her own advantage. Once converted, her attitudes retain their former "form"; and yet, beyond that immodesty—that persistent odor of perfume which her person was not able to give up all at once—we perceive the effort she is making to deny herself, her soul being captivated by another Beauty. If such deeds as pouring out the ointment remain similar to what they were before, the intention is different. Henceforth, they will no longer be controlled by the cult of self, but will be the object of self-denial.

She is not disturbed at seeing the means mocked and sneered at which only recently she had employed for other purposes. What does it matter if the same human grace emanates from her entire person, from her gestures, etc., (Lk. 7, 38), and if the odor of the ointment fills the house, since she is no longer seeking herself and since everything is renounced and offered up to God?

Here we have modesty and good will in a soul while outward appearances remain the same. God alone can judge an interior transformation and He alone judges the heart. The secret advances of good will remain hidden to men and are known only to Him (Lk. 7, 29). The Savior's words, admirable for both their depth and gentleness, enable us to understand how Christ places His divine knowledge of "what is in man" (2, 25) at the service of His mercy. The words spoken on this occasion were: "Her sins, many as they are, are forgiven her because she has loved much" (Lk. 7, 47).

Other examples of good will are easier to interpret. The royal official at Capharnaum and the man born blind need no explanation. They surrender themselves confidently to the Master's words. Both accept the fact that Another takes their destiny in hand and, making an entrance into their life, modifies its course according to His own dispositions.

The modesty of the future apostles is more noteworthy. What is astonishing, some will say perhaps, about Christ exercising an influence over simple fishermen of Lake Tiberias, over men of little worth? The argument should be rather: If He revealed Himself to them, if He found a way to their hearts, it is because He knew them to be humble, open, permeable to the light and the truth.

In fact, unless we see in their vocation and their response a very strong stroke of grace trampling their liberty under foot, we must really admit that in them the rapid victory of faith is explained by their deep-seated modesty. If they answered Christ's call, it was because their soul was that of the truly poor in spirit, it was because they were not attached to themselves. These souls of hope, expectation, and desire, were not in any way whatever "proprietors."[3] Thus, when the Master's path crossed their own, it was easy for them to follow Him.

The Secret of hearts

Keeping souls like this in mind, the attitude of the Pharisees, the Doctors of the Law, of the "wise and prudent," appears as filled with self-sufficiency and closed against all intrusion. Their pretended modesty hides a deep pride and a determined will to accept nothing, even Truth itself, that would upset their little world. In such an atmosphere the divine attraction remains powerless as it knocks at closed doors. Full of themselves and sure of themselves, the Pharisees view everything from a high vantage point. "We ourselves know . . ." (9, 24). They have taken a final stand on all matters. For grace to reach them they would have had to consider Truth as an absolute towards which all men tend, renouncing themselves and their own lights, and submitting to a loving dependence on Truth.

3. This is St. John of the Cross' expression, Ascent of Mount Carmel. 11, 25.

Such an attitude, impossible for the "wise and the prudent" (Mt. 11, 25), is easy and acceptable to the humble and the little ones, those true "children of God" in whom we can almost perceive a reflection of Paradise. If sin has taken hold of them as of all men, at least it does not seem to have separated them from God and set them in opposition to Him, such as it has done in the case of those who have closed themselves in and have formed the habit of receiving only what their judgment has passed on. They raise barriers around themselves and gradually become their own prisoners.

Humility, renunciation, and a generous acceptance of the Truth and His demands would allow them to recapture that freedom which Christ offers and which they do not want because it is too burdensome. " 'If you abide in my word, you shall be my disciples indeed and you shall know the truth, and the truth shall make you free.' They answered him, 'We are the children of Abraham, and we have never been slaves to anyone. How sayest thou, 'You shall be free'? Jesus answered them, 'Amen, amen, I say to you, everyone who commits sin is a slave of sin. . . .If therefore the Son makes you free, you shall be free indeed. . . . Why do you not understand my speech? Because you cannot listen to my word. . . . My word does not take hold among you. . . . The reason why you do not hear is that you are not of God' " (8, 31-47).

Renunciation and faith

John sees the secret of good will and the condition for progress in this freedom obtained through dependence, humility, and renunciation. In fact, the true obstacle to good will in a man is not so much his weakness as it is his refusal to renounce in himself what is opposed to faith and above all a refusal to renounce himself.

Renunciation is the universal and necessary means without which the divine work in the soul cannot be accomplished. This renunciation appears tied in with the divine attraction, i.e., with the grace of faith taken in its initial steps as the means is related to the end. Now no one answers a call without leaving the place where he is; and no one follows a grace which draws him except by knocking down, breaking, or avoiding the obstacles in his path. To answer God, even when His call does not have the clear and personal form which faith will later confer upon it, demands that we already place ourselves in a state which will make it possible to answer Him, i.e., that we free ourselves from what holds us prisoners to go where God calls us and where He awaits us.

Such was the teaching of the Old Testament. When meditating upon it, John did not fail to find the close ties joining renunciation to faith even in the first pages of the history of the People of God.

Yahweh's first words to Abraham the "father of believers" and "our father in the faith" were: "Go forth out of thy country and thy kindred and out of thy father's house, and come into the land which I shall show thee" (Gn. 12, 1). The first step on the road of faith was accompanied by this first and necessary renunciation.

A second renunciation, more difficult still, that of his hopes, must correspond with the second step. Abraham has burned all his bridges behind him; he now has to renounce his desire to survive himself. To Yahweh who promises him a great reward the old man without descendants can only answer: "Lord, what would you give me? I am going without a child." Bringing him outside Yahweh will say to him: "Look up to the heavens and number the stars if thou canst. . . . So shall be thy seed." Abraham believed God "and it was reputed to him unto justice" (Gn. 15, 6), for the old man, renouncing his own lights, threw himself into God's hands with absolute confidence.

However, a third step was necessary that Abraham's faith reach the zenith of its purity and perfection. This could not be made without that final act of renunciation which was both painful and incomprehensible. And did not this renunciation touch Abraham in his very flesh, and was it not killing the present, after having taken away from him both the past and the future? "Take thy only-begotten son Isaac, whom thou lovest, and go into the land of vision; and there thou shalt offer him for a holocaust upon one of the mountains which I will show thee" (Gn. 22, 2). Abraham obeyed and this heroic renunciation established his faith in the perfection of love.

Such were Yahweh's demands to set Abraham's faith upon an unshakable foundation. And the demands were not less for John the Baptist, the beloved disciple's teacher.

What an example of renunciation was given by the Baptist! He had been given the office of tracing out the paths of faith for Israel and he himself was a giant in the faith. He completely renounced all personal glory. "Who art thou?" "I am not the Christ." "Art thou Elias?" "I am not." "Art thou the prophet?" "No." "Who art thou, that we may give an answer to those who sent us?" "I am the voice of one crying in the desert" (1, 19-23).

Then there is the renunciation of all personal influence. "And looking upon Jesus as he walked by, he said, 'Behold the lamb of God,' and the two disciples heard him speak, and they followed Jesus" (1, 36).

There is total self-effacement. "I am not the Christ, but have been sent before him . . . He must increase, but I must decrease" (1, 20; 3, 29).

This will all end in martyrdom, but he is filled with joy because it is a renunciation of love. "But the friend of the bridegroom, who stands and hears him, rejoices exceedingly at the voice of the bridegroom. This my joy, therefore, is made full" (3, 29).

But was it necessary to seek examples in the past? His own personal experience would show John that his faith had followed similar paths: renunciation of his father, his fishing trade, his master John the Baptist (Mt. 4, 22; 1, 27). And the words, "Come, follow me" (1, 39,43,46) which appear at the commencement of his Gospel are linked in his memory to the birth of faith in his companions: for them as for him, faith had sprung up from the soil of renunciation, a renunciation that was essential and entire.

True, the call is always first and divine love precedes our response and our renunciation. But renunciation is bound up with the call itself and faith does not spring up except from a detached soul, just as certain flowers open up in the forest only when the woodcutter has felled the high trees which cut off the rays of the sun.

Repeatedly, John makes it understood that failure to practice detachment paralyses in us this grace of attraction which would have ended up in faith had it been followed. "How can you believe who receive glory from one another and do not seek the glory which is from the only God?" (5, 44).

There must be renunciation of egoism, pride, and vanity; renunciation of the lights we believe we have, of esteem, of human hope; renunciation of sin under all its forms. "Everyone who commits sin is a slave of sin" (8, 34). "For everyone who does evil hates the light and does not come to the light, that his deeds may not be exposed" (3, 20).

There must be a renunciation for gain and personal possessions which John stigmatizes in Judas, the "thief," a desire which must have strongly contributed towards his downfall.

There must be renunciation of the threefold concupiscence which holds men enchained and from which there is no deliverance except through true detachment, the condition for that "victory which overcomes the world, our faith" (1 Jn. 5, 5).

Finally, there must be renunciation of self and this contains within it all the others and accomplishes all these renunciations. "Amen, amen, I say to you, unless the grain of wheat falls into the ground and dies, it remains alone. But if it dies, it brings forth much fruit. . . . He who loves his life, loses it; he who hates his life in this world, keeps it unto life everlasting" (12, 24,24).

Such appears to be the demands of Him who comes to offer faith to us. However, renunciation and good will are necessary not only on the road leading to faith; they remain necessary even after the divine call has been answered and man has received the grace of faith from Christ, if he desires to progress in faith and to live according to its inexhaustible riches.

CHAPTER 13

CHRIST AND FAITH

In the Johannine Gospel of faith Christ's role is preponderant. "Because thou hast seen me, thou has believed. Blessed are they who have not seen and yet have believed. . . . But these are written that you may believe that Jesus is the Christ, the Son of God, and that believing you may have life in his name" (20, 29-31). We see likewise that faith is man's response to the revelation Christ made of His Father and His own Person (1, 18; 8, 19; 14, 9).

It is not surprising that this response takes on different forms. This diversity depends not only upon the different dispositions of men, but also upon the manner in which Christ presents Himself to them. Christ is the Life, the Light, the Truth, and the Way. What is each one's attitude with regard to this Life, this Light, this Truth, and this Way?

As the Life and the Way, Christ will not be received by men unless they renounce their own life and their own ways. As Light and Truth He must extend His influence over their faculties, intellectual as well as sensible and moral. Faith is the response of our entire person to the Person of Christ, and as such it will always entail our entire being: intellect, will, mind, heart, all will have to make an unreserved surrender.

Furthermore, since it is a response to the living God, faith must always be in act, it must have a continual development and exercise a constant victory over the obstacles presented to our interior and exterior powers.

As necessary and decisive as is the "act of faith," it is really "faith in act" that counts. This act is simple since it is the surrender of our being and its total surrender. It is complex, since it must assimilate and penetrate all the faculties of our being in order to be true.

Christ alone can give us birth in the faith. In faith everything comes to us through Him, and in faith everything must pass through him in order to be united to the Father.

In Him we are able to know and love God and gradually our faith is transformed into love through fidelity to Him. It is entirely determined by Him and it exists by the very fact that we are born to Christ. "But to as many as received him he gave the power to become the children of God, to those who believe in his name" (1, 12).

If faith in Christ is a sharing in God, it is also, in Him and in Him only, the thing that makes our encounter with God and our communion with the Trinity possible. Such is God's will. "This is his commandment, that we should believe in the name of his Son Jesus Christ" (14, 6).

If "no one can come to me unless the Father who sent me draw him" (6, 44), it is likewise true that "no one comes to the Father except through me" (14, 6).

Christ's role is precisely to give birth to all those whom the Father has given to Him, to generate in them a new life, the chief characteristic of which is faith.

Many other aspects would have to be considered if we wished to point out the pre-eminent place occupied by Christ in our faith. To be convinced of this we have only to recall those words which seem to give faith a new object: "You believe in God, believe also in me" (14, 1). Or again, that statement made at the last Supper which appears to make knowledge of Christ the object of faith here below and an essential condition for eternal happiness: "Now this is eternal life, that they may know thee, the only true God, and Jesus Christ whom thou hast sent" (17, 3).

And yet this Gospel which shows us Christ as the author of our faith and the one who assures its development, warns us that He is likewise a stumbling block to this faith. Many who believed in God did not succeed in believing in His Son Jesus Christ. This is the reason why many of the "children of Abraham" and the children of Israel did not become "children of God" (8, 33; 1, 14).

Certain questions arise when we consider these things in the fourth Gospel: Is the act of faith in the Person of Christ necessary in order that faith be worthy of the name? Are not the men of the Old Testament who received a share in the faith still looked upon as models for Christians? (Heb. 11, passim). How is this possible? Is it a question of the same faith in both the Old Testament and the New? If we answer in the negative, how can we give the same name to different things? If we answer affirmatively, how can Christ be called the Author of our faith, how can faith in Him be a condition of eternal life? And if faith in Christ is the only true faith or perfected faith, what are its specific elements and its demands?

Meditation upon the fourth Gospel helps us to perceive the extraordinary richness and the great complexity of the act by which a man coming in contact with Christ says: "I believe."

Undoubtedly these are not new. Already Abraham had put them into practice and has been praised "for having believed Yahweh" (Gn. 15, 6). But between faith in God "whom no one has ever seen" and faith directed towards the "Word made flesh" what a distance there is to travel and what a step there is to take! (1, 14,17). The richness of a faith in a God whom one can "see with his eyes and touch with his hands" is not less great than the problem posited by the Incarnation.

We can say then that if the act of faith as such remains a mystery, it becomes an even greater mystery when it is applied to Christ. Far from removing mystery, the Incarnation increases its depths. However, faith in Christ is necessary and He has even made it a condition of salvation. "He who believes in me has everlasting life" (6, 40,47).

From the Old Testament to the New

And this is so, because the newness which faith in Christ introduces really has within it an essential continuity. True, the coming of the Word here below confers a new character upon faith. However, the presence and action of this same Word have never ceased to operate in the faith of men of all times, though they did not know it. Thus, it was always towards His Son that the Father was attracting them. "Everyone who has listened to the Father and has learned comes to me" (6, 45). "Abraham saw my day and rejoiced" (8, 56). There is a real continuity, then, between the faith of the Old Testament and faith in Christ. And yet who would not sense the progress from one to the other?

Undoubtedly this progress is more perceptible if we consider those who in the Old Testament had a faith that was limited to belief in the existence of God and in His rewarding omnipotence. This already was a faith which was supernatural. However, the Old Testament does offer examples of a faith that is more advanced and more perfect. We have an excellent example in the person of Abraham who did not only believe in the existence of Yahweh. His faith is a personal faith in a personal God. Also we find in this faith all the elements characterizing Christian faith: confidence, surrender, personal structure.

And yet it is true that to say "I believe" to a hidden God or to say it to a man who claims to be the Son of God constitutes two entirely different steps.

Christ's contemporaries experienced this difference more than we do, for we Christians do not have to break down our faith into two phases: one and the same act permitting us to attain God in Jesus Christ.

It was not the same for those of whom Christ asked that they believe in Him when they already believed in God. Only a grace emanating from

Christ Himself could have made them grasp and admit that their faith in Yahweh was to be accomplished through faith in this man who had the name Jesus Christ.

Christ's divinity

Conscious of this difficulty and desirous of not compromising His mission by a premature revelation of His divinity, Christ proceeds gradually.

He begins by presenting Himself as the one sent by God, the Christ or the Messias (4, 25) whom John denied he himself was (1, 20), or as the "prophet" expected by Israel (1, 21).

Despite appearances, Nathanael's statement, "Rabbi, thou art the Son of God, thou art the king of Israel" refers to a messianic title (1, 49).

As for Nicodemus, he contents himself with this prudent statement, "Master, we know thou hast come a teacher from God . . ."(3, 2).

It is the Messias who awaits the Samaritan woman and it is under this title that Christ reveals Himself to her. "I know the Messias is coming (who is called Christ). . ." "I who speak to thee am he" (4, 25).

Jesus confines Himself at least in the beginning of His ministry to answering the general expectation of a Messias and the teaching He gives, along with the miracles He works, enables them to recognize Him as such.

A further step is taken when Christ begins calling Himself the "Son of Man." This expression which He seems to have loved and which is repeatedly used in the fourth Gospel is comparable to that of Messias, but it stresses the mysterious grandeur of His mission. It is to be found in the vision of the prophet Daniel (Dan. 7, 13) and it carries, in germ, faith in Christ the Son of God which alone in the fourth Gospel appears as the true faith and the one into which Christ intends to lead men gradually.

Peter gives us an example of this faith. To Christ's question "Who do you say that I am?" Peter answers, "Thou art the Christ, the Son of the living God" (Mt. 16, 17).

But in order for the apostle to add to the simple messianity a recognition of the divine sonship a very special grace was necessary. We can say that we have here authentic and full faith.

This is exceptional even among the apostles. It is explained by the function with which Peter was going to be invested. This exception will be destined to become the rule. Henceforth, faith demands of every man that he see in Christ, not only the Messias, but the Son of God Himself.

The path leading to such a faith is traced out in the fourth Gospel.

We have just seen that the gradual revelation of Christ's divinity, so evident in the Synoptic Gospels, is found also in the Johannine Gospel. What characterizes the latter is its constant reference to the Father. Rather than declare Himself "Son of God," Jesus speaks about His Father and it is in His Father's presence that He would place men. He does always the will of His Father who sent Him (6, 38). He is the one "whom the Father has marked with his seal" (6, 27). All those whom the Father gives Him come to Him (6, 37).

These allusions to the Father are so numerous, Christ declares so frequently that He is alone in knowing the Father, in having seen Him, in being intimately united to Him, in glorifying Him, that it is important to know the reason for such insistence.

And first, speaking of God as His Father permits Christ to reveal His own divinity in a more veiled and hidden way, less abrupt, than if He declared directly that He was the "Son of God" or "God."

But it is also because faith, in making us children of God, must orient us towards the Father by following Christ. That is why the sentence that closes the Prologue, that sentence which is so essential and so characteristic of the whole Johannine Gospel: "No one has seen the Father at any time. The only-begotten Son, who is in the bosom of the Father, has declared him" (1, 18) does not only give Christ His place, but it also gives us ours. We are not children of God unless we know the Father, and this cannot be done except through the Son. Jesus answers Philip's request, "Lord, show us the Father," in the words: "If you had known me, you would have known the Father also . . . Philip, he who sees me, sees the Father also" (14, 7).

We have here the real object of faith: God known as Father and Christ as Son of God. Before the soul enlightened by such revelations there unfold boundless horizons of realities contained in the mystery of the Trinity. On the eve of His death, projecting the vision of eternal life before the disciples' eyes, Christ will set up no other object of faith (17, 3).

It is in this way that the fourth Gospel never separates the Son from the Father. Faith never ceases uncovering in Christ the mirror in which we can glimpse the Father. The more our faith in Christ increases, the more it increases in the Father. Knowledge of one is intimately linked to knowledge of the other.

The God-Man

He who presents Himself as having God as His Father is a man, or at least He appears as such to those who hear him speak and who see Him, and so true is this that His contemporaries really believe they know the identity of the "Word made flesh." "Is this not Jesus, the son of Joseph, whose father and mother we know?" (6, 42).

This point which made difficulties for His contemporaries, makes it and will make it so for men of all times. They find themselves stumbling not so much against God as the object of faith, as against Jesus Christ, this man who calls Himself God.

True contemplative that he is, St. John is drawn by the object of faith: God known in His Son. However, he has understood that Christ's humanity constitutes the true difficulty in this matter. The following scene brings this out clearly.

" 'What my Father has given me is greater than all; and no one is able to snatch anything out of the hand of my Father. I and the Father are one' (10, 29,30). The Jews therefore took up stones to stone him. Jesus answered them, 'Many good works have I shown you from my Father. For which of these works do you stone me?' The Jews answered, 'Not for a good work do we stone thee, but for blasphemy, and because thou, being a man, makest thyself God.' Jesus answered them, 'Is it not written in your Law, I said you are gods?' If he called them gods to whom the word of God is addressed (and the Scripture cannot be broken), do you say of him whom the Father has made holy and sent into the world "Thou blasphemest," because I said, "I am the Son of God"? If I do not perform the works of my Father, do not believe me. But if I do perform them and if you are not willing to believe me, believe the works, that you may know and believe that the Father is in me and I in the Father' " (10, 31-38).

This scene alone, in which the necessity of an act of faith in "the man" appears with its full impact, suffices to show that John fully perceived the difficulty. It is interesting to note that this difficulty does not take on the same importance with John as it does with Paul.

Is this because Paul did not live with Christ, or rather that his faith in Him is the effect of a conversion which appears as a rough reversal, whereas John becomes the Savior's intimate little by little and that from the first moment Christ's humanity was an object of attraction for him? The fact that the Word was made flesh never seems to have been a scandal for John as it was for Paul before his conversion. On the contrary, faith in the Word Incarnate whom the apostle has "seen with his eyes and touched with his hands" (1 Jn. 1, 1) appears to have always been for him the principle of strength and light and the source of joy and expansion.

The union of the humanity and the divinity in Christ, far from being an obstacle to the apostle's faith, seems to give him a support and a kind of supernatural confirmation. "I write of what was from the beginning, what we have heard, what we have seen with our eyes, what we have looked upon and our hands have handled of the Word of Life. And the Life was made known and we have seen, and now testify and announce to you, the Life Eternal which was with the Father, and appeared to us. What we have seen and heard we announce to you" (1 Jn. 1, 1).

On the one hand, the Word of Life and Eternal Life; on the other, "what our hands have touched." One could not possibly better express the opposition of the two natures in Christ. What is quite evident in the Johannine Gospel is the joy coming from that glance upon the Word made flesh, that glance which contemplation has fully unified. Man or God, Jesus is for St. John supremely attractive. It does not seem that his faith had to undergo any kind of rending or tearing, and that is why in him it always seems to show itself as an essentially positive reality. If it still remains difficult and burdensome to nature, and it does, it is for other reasons: Because man has preferred darkness to light because his works are evil; because the act of faith is inseparable from the plan of renunciation and a change of life; or because the powers of seduction and false-hood, of the world, the flesh, and Satan keep man in a state of illusion, and hinder him from discovering the worth of sign and testimony included in Christ's miracles and works.

In St. John's mind one of the difficulties in making this act of faith and in living the life of faith, which is the end result, lies in the necessity of a "victory over the world" (1 Jn. 5, 4). Thus, he congratulates those who have gained this victory thanks to which their faith is now a living one: "You are strong and the word of God abides in you, and you have con-quered the evil one. Do not love the world, or the things that are in the world, because all that is in the world is the lust of the flesh, the lust of the eyes, and the pride of life; which is not from the Father, but from the world" (1 Jn. 2, 15).

John does not consider, however, that, once these obstacles are over-come, faith imposes itself upon us with the gentle force of a love to which it is enough for us to surrender ourselves. The difficulties are found not only on the road, but also in faith itself; St. John's faith was not a reality definitely implanted in his soul from the moment of his en-counter with Christ. Even on Easter morning he was still hesitant in his belief.

In him, as in every man, faith appears both as a grace and as a meritorious act, and John's Gospel helps us understand where the dif-ficulty lay which he had to surmount. Two words express it clearly and these words flow spontaneously from his pen when he describes the scene at the tomb.

Though he arrived first at the tomb, he did not enter. "Simon Peter therefore came following him, and he went into the tomb, and saw the linen cloths lying there, and the handkerchief which had been about his head, not lying with the linen cloths, but folded in a place by itself. Then the other disciple also went in, who had come first to the tomb. And he saw and believed" (20, 6,8). It was not because he saw, but because he saw an "empty" tomb, that John's faith now became forever unshakable.

"Seeing" and "Believing"

The true problem of the faith seems to be contained in the two words "seeing" and "believing" used by St. John and they seem sometimes to complete one another. "For this is the will of my Father who sent me, that whoever beholds the Son and believes in him, shall have everlasting life" (6, 40); at other times, these words seem to be opposed to each other. "Because you have seen you have believed. Blessed are they who have not seen but have believed" (20, 29).

In fact, they are the constitutive elements of faith, and they account for the tension contained in faith by its very nature. Furthermore, they bear within themselves the secret of its development. John is not unaware that faith consists in "believing without seeing," the conclusion of his Gospel is proof of this. But that he holds the fact of the Incarnation as of absolute importance in the genesis of faith can no longer be denied.

The links between "sight" and faith" are constantly brought out in the Gospel and the first Epistle. Even in his concept of eternal life where the predominance is given less to love than to knowledge, i.e., to the alliance between vision and love, vision seems to remain for John the dominant element about which he speaks with a sort of enthusiasm. "We will see him as he is" (1 Jn. 3, 2) he cries out, encouraging his followers to keep themselves pure against the day of the "manifestation" (1 Jn. 3, 2).

There is in St. John a thirst for vision which is a supernatural replica of that desire to "see" of which his Gospel so often speaks. The word "see" is one of his favored words. It often happens that he transfers it from the material realm to that of the spiritual, and even to us it seems to express realities which stem from the faith. It is thus he cites Christ's word: "He who believes in me, believes not in me but in him who sent me. And he who sees me, sees him who sent me" (12, 44,45). And again: "If you had known me, you would have also known my Father. And henceforth you do know him and you have seen him" (14, 7,9).

The Incarnation is necessary, but one must look beyond the material "view" of Christ in order to attain the view of faith: this is what these texts try to suggest to us.

But here we should make the following observation: The problem of faith must be viewed from two different aspects. It presented itself in one way to Christ's contemporaries; it presents itself in another way to generations unborn. The first have "seen" Christ and the gospel accounts present them in this perspective. The second class have knowledge of Christ only through testimonies and these testimonies furnish objective bases for the faith. John did not simply understand this, but to him goes the credit for having given an account of Christ's miracles and teachings in their relationship to this twofold perspective.

Where was the difficulty for their faith for the eye-witnesses of Christ's work and miracles? In this, that it was infinitely more difficult for them than for us to recognize the position of Son of God in this man who was like them and even their compatriot, and who did not flatter their desire for glory, power, human domination, but rather applied Himself to living in a humble and hidden way.

To this difficulty, which as we have seen was not the greatest for St. John, there is added another which the apostle stresses in those words of Christ to Thomas: "Because you have seen me you believe. Blessed are those who have not seen, but have believed" (20, 29).

What is reproved in Thomas is that he wished to "see" what he should have "believed." Now, the other disciples, eight days earlier had also "seen" and even upon the express invitation of Christ. "When it was late that same day, the first of the week, though the doors had been closed for fear of the Jews, Jesus came and stood in the midst and said to them, 'Peace be to you.' And when he had said this, he showed them his side" (20, 20).

Is it not likewise when going to "see" and when entering the tomb, that John finds there not the risen Savior, but what was much more important: faith in the risen Savior? "He saw and he believed" (21, 8). Did not Mary Magdalene also attain faith when recognizing Christ in His voice, His look (20, 16)? It is not then for having wished to "see" which meets with reproach in Thomas. Christ will even satisfy this desire. "Bring here thy finger and see my hands; and bring here thy hand, and put it into my side." It is true He immediately adds, "And be not unbelieving but believing" (20, 27). Upon what exactly does the reproach fall, and what precisely was asked of Christ's contemporaries?

They could see and they even had to "see"; what they saw served as the point of departure for their faith. Had not Christ said to His disciples: "Blessed are the eyes that see what you see! For I say to you, many prophets and kings have desired to see what you see, and they have not seen it; and to hear what you hear, and they have not heard it" (Lk. 10, 23-24). And John shows the inestimable value which he sets upon the knowledge of Christ in the flesh and the intimacy it allows. The beginning of the first Epistle speaks of this grace which he received of hearing, contemplating, and touching the Word of Life, of seeing the manifestation of Life, "this Life Eternal which was with the Father, and has appeared to us" (1 Jn. 1, 1-3).

Undoubtedly the apostle continues in this strain (and his words are very important) : "I write of what was from the beginning, what we have heard, what we have seen with our eyes, and now testify and announce to you. What we have seen and have heard we announce to you" (1 Jn. 1, 1) indicating the exact function sight filled in the Christian economy. It is directed towards "testimony."

And nevertheless this sight for the witnesses themselves will not become the source of faith unless it is a "sight of faith." What does this mean? It is here that we must remember what has already been pointed out and what Chapter 12 of St. John brings to light.

In the crowd that sought out Christ following the news of the raising of Lazarus: "There were certain Greeks among those who had gone up to worship on the feast. These therefore approached Philip and asked him, saying, 'Sir, we wish to see Jesus.' Philip came and told Andrew; again Andrew and Philip spoke to Jesus" (12, 20,22). And what answer does Jesus make to this legitimate request? " 'The hour has come for the Son of Man to be glorified. Amen, amen, I say to you, unless the grain of wheat falls into the ground and dies, it remains alone. But if it dies, it brings forth much fruit. Now is the judgment of this world. And I, if I be lifted up, will draw all things to myself.' These things Jesus spoke and he went away and hid himself from them" (12, 23,24, 31,33,36).

Thus, Jesus does not show Himself to those who wished to see Him merely with the eyes of the flesh. He offers them the testimony of His works and especially that of His Passion and Resurrection. Such was the answer already given to the Jews. "When you have lifted up the Son of Man, then you will know that I am he" (8, 28). This is likewise the meaning of the quote from Zacharias recalled by John: "They shall look on him whom they had pierced" (19, 37; Zach. 12, 10).

Signs and faith

John would have us understand that there are two ways of seeing: a material and a spiritual way. The first, purely sensible and carnal, is incapable for many reasons of passing from "miracles" to "signs," from material realities to their spiritual signification and import which alone trace out the path to faith. At the wedding of Cana, the miracle, unperceived by the greater part of the guests, was verified as a material fact by the steward and a few servants and it was perceived by the apostles alone as a "sign" revealing the glory and, to a certain extent, the identity of Christ. This first of his signs Jesus worked in Cana of Galilee; and he manifested his glory, and his disciples believed in him" (2, 11).

The same material fact brings with it, then, different reactions and brings about different results. Now, it is to this capacity of perceiving spiritual realities included in a fact, and especially in a miracle, that faith in Christ is allied as far as His contemporaries and witnesses are concerned. This capacity is itself linked to their good faith, their good will, and subjective dispositions.

Christ's "works"[1] and especially His miracles are not an end in themselves. They are signs indicative of a presence and an activity that are divine, and they say: "God is here." That is why John, while recognizing both their necessity and import in the building of the faith, is more attentive to what they show than to their intrinsic value. They are directed towards something very definite, and they are the revealing elements of this something. It is not necessary to report a great number of them, but rather to choose those which shed a more living light upon the important spiritual teachings being imparted. That is why there are only seven in his entire Gospel, even though the apostle knew many others. "Many other signs Jesus worked in the sight of his disciples . . ." (20, 30). In those he does relate, the miraculous element itself is always set forth with great reserve, pointed out in a few well chosen words. The "sign," contained in the miracle, is brought into the light. Why is this, if it is not because faith is destined to be nourished not on the miracle as such, but from the miracle in so far as it is a sign. This alone helps us approach the spiritual reality which the miracle has the purpose of uncovering for us. Though the miracle is necessary to draw our attention, it is simply a door and helps us enter into the mystery. Now, is there any necessity of pointing out a door whose entrance we have found and of multiplying keys with which to open it? John does not think so. "Few are necessary." To the one who has understood that the real miracle is the Word made flesh and that this miracle is also the sign which contains all the others, there is no need for "wonders." John has recorded Christ's words of sad complaint: "Unless you see signs and wonders you do not believe" (4, 48), because they appeared to him to reveal the mystery of faith. In the spiritual realm

1. 5, 36; 6, 29; 7, 21; 9, 3; 10, 25-32, 37-38; 14, 12; 15, 24; 17, 4.

material facts have no meaning. His Gospel retains only the most significant miracles, those which make the underlying substance of the facts clearer and allow the divine light to filter through.

The Johannine accounts develop on two planes: that of the miracle and the sign. Today as always, carnal souls feed themselves on the former, but advance no further for they stop at externals. Spiritual souls, more interested in signs, enter upon the mystery of faith. Thus, there is a division brought about between two worlds: the first is a material world in which signs reveal nothing, it is a dull and sluggish world in which even miracles themselves finally lose their significance; the second is entirely spiritual, in which faith becomes more and more revealing, where the import of signs never ceases to grow, where Christ holds the central place and all converges on Him and takes on meaning only in Him. "It is the spirit that gives life, the flesh profits nothing. The words that I have spoken are spirit and life. But there are some among you that do not believe" (6, 63,64).

Faith and testimony

In a word, faith is tantamount to seeing in or through what is materially perceived, what is invisible and not perceptible except through "its eyes." It is going "through the visible to the invisible." In other words, it is introducing "testimony" with regard to sight, for Christ will take care to point out repeatedly that "testimony" is not limited to words reported by witnesses. Words also give testimony. "If I do not perform the works of my Father, do not believe me. But if I do perform them, and if you are not willing to believe me, believe the works" (10, 37-38). And again, "The witness that I have, however, is greater than that of John. For the works which the Father has given me to accomplish, these very works that I do, bear witness to me, that the Father has sent me. And the Father himself who has sent me has borne witness to me (5, 36,37). And likewise: "You search the Scriptures, because in them you think that you have life everlasting. And it is they that bear witness to me, yet you are not willing to come to me that you may have life" (5, 39,40).

Christ's contemporaries, the witnesses of His miracles and the hearers of His words, were expected to pass from the material level to the spiritual; this was to be done by means of "testimony" which enables one to see in a material fact the sign of a spiritual reality. This sign sets other faculties to work besides the sense faculties. In fact, it is one thing to abide by what the senses give us, but something else when we confide in someone who has seen and gives testimony of a fact. It was precisely for this that St. Thomas was reproached by Christ for his incredulity, for being incapable of "believing" what was reported to him by witnesses "worthy of faith." In fact, the other apostles had seen and had made him part of the apparition of which they had been witnesses. St. Thomas was blamed because he answered their unanimous testimony, "We have seen the Lord," with the words, "Unless I see in his hands the print of the nails and put my finger into the place of the nails, and put my hand into his side, I will not believe" (20, 25). He was saying: Unless I have visual proof, direct and personal, instead of your testimony, which proof alone has value in my eyes, I will not believe.

True, for carnal creatures such as we are, materially verified facts are necessary to give a basis to our faith, but on condition that through them we reach spiritual realities. Men were necessary, viz., the apostles, evangelists (in other words Scripture and Tradition, i.e., the Church) in order to affirm and testify to the facts of which they were witnesses, and among them no one insists as much as John upon the value of his testimony which is "true and authentic." But not one of them would dream of stopping at the facts themselves that he reports; all strive to extract the hidden meaning and the symbolic value in order to lead us to the spiritual place upon which faith rests.

Men's capacity to "believe" is then tightly linked to their faculty of perceiving this other plane which places them in contact with God through the external facts. And this faculty is not so much intellectual as spiritual and is itself linked, as we have seen, to their moral dispositions, their good will.

The statements of those whom we might call "bold men" and "honest men" are indicative of this. The spontaneous reaction of the man born blind will be to declare straight out: "If this man were not from God, he could do nothing" (9, 33). And among the Jews there are two lines of thought resulting from the miracle: "Again there arose a division among the Jews because of these words. Many of them were saying, 'He has a devil and is mad. Why do you listen to him?' Others were saying, 'These are not the words of one who has a devil. Can a devil open the eyes of the blind?'" (10, 21).

If we keep in mind that faith has a personal structure we can see that testimony enters into this structure normally. The one who desires to depend solely upon his senses and who wishes to "see" in order to believe, descends from the personal (spiritual) level to the material level. He sets himself on the level of "things" and gives them a kind of preference. The man, however, who does not deny the validity of material reality but accepts testimony sets himself upon a "personal" level. In other words, he does not place his confidence as much in things as in a person. This is an attitude that is only apparently imprudent, especially when we consider how much man is susceptible to error, but it is in fact full of good sense, for testimony leads us higher than external deeds and helps us reach a certitude much more essential: one which depends upon a statement of God Himself, or upon the understanding God has of divine realities, an understanding in which He allows us to share in Christ.

What disturbs us in testimony is the margin of error which can be in the witness. But it is impossible for man to believe in any other way besides testimony. The greater part of the facts and truths man knows, he knows solely through testimony. He "believes" those who know or who have seen, even though they are only men. The Gospel also has recourse to witnesses, but it chooses them because God Himself has commanded them to bear this witness, and besides the assistance of the Holy Spirit protects them from error. Besides, as astonishing as it appears at first sight, the number of intermediary witnesses between God and us is infinitely less in the order of religious and spiritual realities than in that of the physical or historical sciences. John has "seen" Christ and he has heard Him and it is his testimony, as well as that of the other evangelists which, preserved and transmitted by the Church, remains through the centuries the source of our faith.

Christ, Witness of the Father

Furthermore, the testimony to which we refer is not the testimony of man but of God. Christ insists continually that He has been sent by God, by this Father whom "no one has seen at any time" (1, 18). He is the Father's witness and our obligation to believe in the Father is reduced to believing in the testimony of Christ. "Amen, amen, I say to you, we speak of what we know, and bear witness to what we have seen, and our witness you do not receive" (3, 11).

In what concerns the ultimate signification of the miracles and identity of the one who claimed to be the Father's envoy and the Son of God, the apostles were then obliged as we are to subscribe to the testimony of a "man." This man laid claim to the position of witness, and it is to this testimony about God that faith owes its contemplative value. And it is this that prepares us for vision.

In fact, Christ Himself does not believe, He "sees," and He is the only one that "sees." When accepting His testimony we "believe," true, but in such a way that our faith is a sort of "sight" for through Christ we already see in a way what He sees and what He testifies. "I speak what I have seen with the Father" (8, 38).

We see with Christ's eyes, just as a short man turns to a taller man in a crowd and receives from him an account of what is going on. Our faith becomes a sort of anticipated vision, in direct proportion to the confidence we have in the one who sees. If this confidence is absolute, which is the case in supernatural faith since God can "neither deceive nor be deceived," we share through faith in the vision that Christ Himself actually enjoys.

The depth of John's faith in Christ helps us understand how he so often brings the two words "seeing" and "believing" together. "He who believes in me, believes not in me but in Him who sent me. And he who sees me, sees him who sent me" (12, 44,45). The problem of faith with John is less in believing than in having eyes for seeing.

Seeing God in Christ

To become capable of "seeing" we must "know" the object of our faith: Christ. This knowledge Christ demands of His disciples. Though confidence makes up an integral part of faith, this does not mean it must be blind. On the contrary, a "knowledge," stemming from "light" and from a light rendered more living through love, must be applied by us to the object of our faith.

The world was especially reproached for not having "known" the Word (1, 10). And this same reproach will come again at the end of His mission to strike the world and this time it will be final: "Just Father, the world has not known thee" (17, 25) because it has refused to know "him whom thou hast sent, Jesus Christ" (17, 3). To refuse to know, to receive, and to believe have the very same meaning in St. John (1, 12). The trials inflicted upon the disciples will come from those who "have known (and did not want to know) either the Father or him" (16, 3). Those will be saved, on the contrary, who have been docile to this knowledge Christ tries to communicate. It is a knowledge of what He is. "Just Father, the world has not known thee, but I have known thee, and these have known that thou hast sent me" (17, 25); it is a knowledge of what His Father is, "If you had known me, you would have known my Father" (14, 7). This knowledge communicated through Christ is neither limited nor partial.

It is God in His entirety that we are expected to know in Christ and through Christ. In Christ we know the Father. "All things I have heard from my Father and I have made known to you" (15, 15). And we know too the Holy Spirit in Christ, since He "will receive of what is mine and declare it to you" (16, 14) and "he will teach you all truth" (16, 13).

It is as an object of knowledge that Christ has been given to us by

His Father, and it is still in knowing Him that we shall find a source of life in Him: "If anyone thirst, let him come to me and drink. He who believes in me, as the Scripture says, 'From within him there shall flow rivers of living water' " (7, 38); a source of light: "He who follows me does not walk in darkness, but will have the light of life" (8, 12); a source of joy: "These things I have spoken to you that my joy may be in you, and that your joy may be made full" (15, 11); source of love and glorification: "As the Father has loved me, so also I have loved you" (15, 9); "And the glory thou hast given me, I have given them" (17, 22). This knowledge is already the seed of eternal life in us since: "This is eternal life: that they may know thee, just Father, and he whom thou hast sent, Jesus Christ" (17, 3), and "He who believes in me has eternal life" (6, 40,47).

The fact that God became man allows this knowledge to be intensified and deepened and to take on traits it never before possessed. Faith in Christ constitutes a priceless grace from this very fact. It makes it possible for the divine life to be revealed and communicated to us through His human life and the sentiments that dwelt in His Heart (Phil. 2, 5).

John's faith is nourished from contacts that he has with this humanity of Christ. He has heard His voice and he has discovered when living in His presence who He is. His confidence, love, admiration were aroused at the same time as he became aware of what was more than human in this man. And yet the human element never ceased to come under his gaze. Never did Jesus cease to be man for John. Must not faith, in order to be Christian, even while contemplating the divinity in Christ, still nourish itself on confidence, friendship, and intimacy?

It is in this atmosphere that Christ's words and teachings reached the apostle asking him to model his life upon Christ's life, to love Him to the point of sacrifice, to renounce all to follow Him. Christ had become for John more than a friend and brother, and still He no longer revealed Himself to him as the Master and the Son of God.

When saving him with His Blood and nourishing him with His flesh, Christ was going to render the bonds which united Him to John even closer, more intimate still, for He was going to dwell in him forever.

Faith is not something added as an extrinsic reality to these truly vital and supremely personal divine and human data. Faith is only the response of the being in whom all this takes place and who is conscious of it; faith is this being's total confidence and entire surrender to one who is all and gives all. These bonds which Christ's humanity had woven, these sentiments which it had permitted and developed and which, thanks to it, had taken on more intensity, compactness, all these faith had taken hold of. It is made of them, they nourish it, sustain and give life to it.

So the question presents itself: Would it have been possible without the Incarnation and without God's having become man and having lived among us to find anything which resembled even distantly this faith which was born in the soul of a St. John, and which is destined to be born in the soul of every faithful Christian?

This reciprocity, this ensemble of relations stemming from confidence, respect and love, woven between two beings; this glance placed upon the object of our tenderness, these words which he spoke and which, coming down to us, bear fruit; these numerous bonds woven between the soul and Christ, thanks to which our faith is a warm reality, a living tissue in which the blood flows and beats, would all this have been possible without "the Word made flesh"? (1, 14).

John's faith in Christ's person went to the man and then to God. Afterwards it came back upon the man; and this so perfectly that it was impossible for John not to envisage, at the same time as faith, the sentiments of love which accompany it and these in their turn are not separated from a desire of union with Him in whom one believes and whom one loves.

Without Christ men would never have known the Father as the Father, for only the Son could express Him with words containing His own experience and love of the Father. Christ's actions alone were able to show what a true Son is when filled with love for His Father. Only Christ could reveal to us our divine filiation and the Father's love for us. Without Him men would never have realized what divine adoption and filiation are. Never would they have experienced in the secret depths of their being the Spirit's presence and action. Never finally would they have perceived how living faith is perfected in love and how one act allows them, in Christ, to know God and to believe in Him and love Him.

Christ brings faith to perfection

What has struck John is the new dimensions faith draws from the coming of Christ; but it is also with Him that the mystery of the hidden God already inscribed in the Old Testament henceforth takes on all its compactness and reveals God and His fullness.

"Make me see thy glory" (Ex. 33, 18) Moses had asked of Yahweh. God answered this request through His Son. His baptism at the Jordan and His transfiguration on Thabor correspond to Sinai. And yet, resplendent as it is, the glory of God has never been as hidden as it is in the humanity He assumes.

"He has come among his own and his own received him not" (1, 11). He has spoken and their ears have remained shut against His words. He has performed signs such as no man before Him ever performed and small is the number of those who saw the Son of God in Him.

If God is hidden to such a degree in Jesus Christ, how can the Incarnation nourish and enlighten our faith? How does this mystery confer new dimensions upon faith? Precisely in this that the Word made flesh is a God so hidden that He is able henceforth to become infinitely close to us, because He is truly within us.

The manifestations of God's power and transcendence speak for themselves. But the marks of His merciful love and unfathomable humility teach us much more about Him. The more God hides Himself, the more He reveals Himself. In the crib, at Calvary, in the Eucharist, God enables us to penetrate more deeply into His mystery. Without Christ, without His human life and death on the Cross, who would have revealed such depths in God? "In this have we come to know his love, that he has laid down his life for us" (1 Jn. 3, 16).

"I know my sheep"

What depth Christ has conferred upon the two terms "to be known" and "to know" which already expressed the two aspects of knowledge and hence of faith! Thanks to the Incarnation, man can know God in Him who has conducted Himself as man, in Him whom he sees in everything like himself except sin, and so close to himself that He is his own flesh and blood.

John helps us know these realities repeatedly, but especially when he reports the words through which Christ gives Himself to us as the Good Shepherd. Having known us with a human and divine love, He enables us to know Him both as Man and as God. "I am the good shepherd, and I know mine and mine know me, even as the Father knows me and I know the Father, and I lay down my life for my sheep. . . . My sheep hear my voice, and I know them and they follow me" (10, 14,15,27).

John never tires of contemplating the new condition in which men are placed through the coming of the Word into the world: Faith does not have to go far to search out and find God. He is close, and much closer than in the time of Moses when he could say: "But the word is very nigh to thee, in thy mouth and in thy heart" (Dt. 30, 14). And this "Face of God," so often invoked by the psalmists, is now turned towards the world and even identified with the Man whom the apostle "has seen with his eyes and touched with his hands" (1 Jn. 1, 1).

"The Word was made flesh and dwelt among us" (1, 14). He has come to all men: the poor, the simple, the little, sinners, to those also who have a proud mind and a hard heart; He has spoken to them and since He has spoken, a dawn has risen over the world. Something has changed because Jesus is in the world, and because men and women, without knowing it, are face to face with God and God speaks to their heart, and they contemplate God Himself in this Man who is like other men.

What Christ's Person brings to faith is the presence of God without an intermediary. The mystery of God acts through Him in an immediate manner. Hence, for upright souls, how could that current fail to pass through them, how could life fail to be born in them, and how could their eyes not be opened when there appears the light that is the true Light? The Light comes to the blind man and he sees; Life comes to him already four days dead and he springs forth from the tomb, bound hand and foot. "The Master is here and calls thee" (11, 28).

Those spiritually dead feel a silent, pure, and irrepressible life spring up in the depths of their being. This life casts aside all obstacles, it traces out a passage, and finally it springs up unto eternal life. Yes, "the Life was made known . . . , the Eternal Life which was with the Father, and has appeared to us" (1 Jn. 1, 2). Behold what Christ's presence brings to faith!

And it is not only certain ones, and not even all men, but it is nature itself and the entire earth which stir under the breath of God who has come to pay a visit. An unexpected and unbelievable springtime has been born in souls, and it causes unknown flowers to germinate over those wide expanses so long given over to death and enveloped in darkness. Without dispersing the cloud which hides God from us in this life, the divine Sun comes to us; it illumines and warms us and awakens within us what has been wrapped in a death-like sleep. "Awake, sleeper, and arise from the dead, and Christ will enlighten thee" (Eph. 5, 14). "Now it is the hour for us to rise from sleep, because now our salvation is nearer than when we came to believe" (Rom. 13, 11).

"The goodness and kindness of God our Savior" have accomplished this miracle (Ti. 3, 4). Under the veils of a humanity, the fruit of divine love, and "in which dwells the fullness of the Godhead corporeally" (Col. 2, 9), faith is communicated to us in its totality and Christ's glory shines forth in direct proportion to His abasement, misery, and poverty; but it does so only for pure hearts.

Henceforth, on this earth where, up until now, men were born of flesh and remained of the flesh, a man born "according to the flesh" is born also entirely of the Spirit. How can a reality of this order, as hidden as it is, not act upon the souls whom the Father has prepared? And how would the faith not find in such an event matter upon which it may increase and purity itself? Pure divinity is communicated to us through pure humanity. This is what sets faith on its real foundations and gives to it wings with which it may fly directly to God.

Undoubtedly for John this divine presence, hidden and buried in the humanity of Christ, confers upon faith a very definite dimension and an unfathomable depth and makes it an adorable and living mystery. God present and yet hidden in Christ: before such a mystery John's faith becomes luminous and acquires eyes and it feels itself invaded by love. It sees, it loves, and it lives.

"My sheep know me"

But though faith lives, it carries within itself the exigencies of life which consist in receiving and giving oneself. This mutual relationship entails for faith exigencies that are all the greater as this knowledge is a knowledge of love, of a love from which the sheep are born and upon which they are continually dependent for this life.

The following are the demands faith makes upon us: that we do not refuse the attraction the Father makes the soul experience (6, 45), that we listen to the call of the Good Shepherd's voice (10, 16) and answer it by coming to Him (6, 35,37), and following Him (10, 27); all the movements and attitudes necessary for a faith which is living are transformed since Christ's love animates them.

Also, faith is not simply a "coming" to Christ. It is walking in His light (12, 35) and abiding in Him (6, 56; 15, 4); it is knowing the truth (6, 31) and welcoming it into the depths of one's being (12, 48), and while keeping it, making it truly one's own (12, 47). While adhering with all our being to the truth revealed by Christ (1, 17), we shall know from experience its fullness; we shall be visited and filled with it (1, 16) and, our communion with Christ becoming more intimate, we shall approach life which has no end (5, 24).

All this is said in these words, so meaningful and so gentle, "I know my sheep and my sheep know me" (10, 14). And there is no question here of a simple response but of an actual reciprocity as the text implies. Man's knowledge of faith and love for Christ flows necessarily from this human and divine knowledge with which Christ has first visited him. It is because they were first "known" that the sheep in their turn are able to know. Faith is a grace which comes entirely from Christ. Thus John stresses that receptivity which demands that in order to believe in Christ, we must welcome Him. Without this welcome, which the Prologue already gave as the secret of faith, "To those who received him...," faith remains sterile and it cannot give birth in us to "the child of God" (1, 12).

This receptivity, far from rendering the soul passive, stimulates the response of love in her which makes her faith living and fruitful. The soul's faith in Christ will be in proportion to the welcome she extends to Him. When she actually and lovingly allows herself to be known by Christ, the soul is drawn to turn towards Him with a look and a movement of faith which conduct her along the paths of intimacy and union. "My sheep hear my voice, and I know them and they follow me" (10, 27). They follow because they feel and know themselves to be known with a loving knowledge. This love penetrates them through and through. Then their knowledge too is impregnated with this love and it gives rise to a fidelity which no longer fails.

Christ has told us: this fidelity will meet with obstacles and it will experience many trials. The world will hate and persecute us (15, 18). And we shall not only suffer from the world, but our faith will go through painful hours, darkness, and will ever run the risk of being seduced and misdirected by bad shepherds.

Satan will let loose his fury against us, trying to overcome the light within us with his darkness and to lead us astray with his illusions, since he is the father of lies (8, 44). But Christ is there watching over us and repeating, "take courage, I have overcome the world" (16, 38). "I have not only judged the world, but I have cast down the prince of this world" (12, 31).

The apostle also insists upon the difficulties to be encountered by our faith. To preserve it we shall have to break with sin by remaining in the truth (1 Jn. 2, 4), by obeying the commandments, especially that of fraternal charity (1 Jn. 2, 10), by guarding ourselves against the world and all that is in the world (1 Jn. 2, 15), by being victorious over the evil one (1 Jn. 2, 14). Then we shall be faithful, we shall be of God (1 Jn. 4, 6), we shall be "born of God" (1 Jn. 4, 7).

"All that is born of God overcomes the world; and this is the victory that overcomes the world, our faith. Who is there that overcomes the world if not he who believes that Jesus is the Son of God?" (1 Jn 5, 4,5). Having experienced and overcome all obstacles, our faith takes on its true sense, it becomes "fidelity."

Thus we find, henceforth inscribed not in tablets of stone or external laws but in the depths of the heart, that true and definite Covenant which faith seals between the soul and God. The entire discourse after the Supper shows the union and the unity which is promised as the outcome of a living faith; it shows that mutual love between the Bridegroom and the bride.

As long as we have not known "Love" (1 Jn. 3, 16), as long as God has not succeeded in making Himself known by us, in making Himself welcome, our faith remains inefficacious, sterile, and without an object. But from the moment in which, under pressure of divine love, we welcome the Son whom God has sent into the world, our faith becomes dynamic and living. In Christ we know love and the fidelity we vow to Him is the proof that faith is born in us, for the soul has found her Spouse.

Does John present any examples of this fidelity in faith? In a Gospel in which faith appears so often as timid, uncertain, and in which its imperfection and weakness shine forth even in the best of souls, as we are given to understand by that sad question, "Will you also go away?" (6, 67), or that prediction, "Do you believe now? Behold, the hour is coming, and has already come, for you to be scattered, each one to his own house and to leave me alone" (16, 32); in a Gospel where the best examples of faith are given by pagans or very humble folk, the faith of the apostles does not present much of a figure. Little is required to shake them (6, 68) and for their presumption to shine through (18, 17,27). Their outbursts of faith, generous as they are, are frequently without stability and contradicted by their actions. It will be necessary to await the coming of the Holy Spirit in order that the true faith put in its appearance and become rooted in their hearts.

If we make an exception of the Blessed Virgin, the fourth Gospel furnishes us with only one example of a model faith, viz., that of John the Baptist. He is the witness of faith par excellence. "This man came as a witness to bear witness concerning the light, that all might believe through him" (1, 7), and this testimony definitely manifests the necessary conditions for the development of faith. The Baptist's character appears to be filled with an unfailing humility and an absolute detachment (1, 20; 3, 30), and his humble faith is regarded with the highest revelation ever to befall man, viz., the revelation of the Trinity on the banks of the Jordan (1, 32). His unfailing fidelity brings him to martyrdom (Mk. 6, 29). And he was not spared painful uncertainties and trials. "Art thou he who is to come, or shall we look for another?" (Lk. 7, 19). The witness, herald, and martyr of the faith seems to dominate the entire fourth Gospel; he stands guard over its entrance as a giant who has measured and known the depths of faith, all the demands of fidelity, all its lights and visitations. And Christ will praise him as no man has ever been praised: "Amen, I say to you, among those born of women there has not risen a greater than John the Baptist." He was the "lamp burning and shining" (Mt. 11, 11; Jn. 5, 35).

And yet Christ has said something with regard to John which is all the more mysterious as it follows upon what He has just stated. "Amen, I say to you, among those born of women there has not risen a greater than John the Baptist; yet the least in the kingdom is greater than he" (Mt. 11, 11). What does this mean, if not that in the Christian economy the gift of faith is linked to Christ's death and the coming of the Holy Spirit? This does not mean that John the Baptist did not have a faith so great that its equivalent is not to be found in the New Testament; but there is in Christian faith so new a reality, and it transforms this faith so radically that it explains this apparently disconcerting statement. This reality which makes something very special of Christian faith has struck John the apostle so deeply that we should give it our attention.

"Christian" faith

If we attempt to measure the distance separating faith such as the Old Testament knew it and "Christian" faith such as it is proposed in the fourth Gospel, there are two texts which immediately come to mind. On the one hand, the one appearing in the prophet Habacuc: "My just man lives by faith" (Hb. 2, 4), and on the other, the text of the Prologue: "But to as many as received him he gave the power of becoming the sons of God; to those who believe in his name" (1, 12).

As filled with spirituality as is this "justice," as great as it is since it generates life, nevertheless as confident, constant, and intimate as we may suppose it to be, it still cannot lead the just man to "a life with God."

On the contrary, in the Johannine Prologue, faith is given to us as procuring a share in the very life of God. Thus, the fourth Gospel opens upon this certitude which is both joyful and marvelous: faith makes us "children of God." And it is upon this certitude that this Gospel is built.

Since this is so, how then would the Christian faith not introduce us into a realm in which the air we breathe is entirely renewed, and in which everything has become new because of that condition brought about by faith: "Son, thou art always with me, and whatever is mine is thine" (Lk. 15, 31)?

"My just man lives by faith." John knew this statement as one of the jewels of the Old Testament; and it seems that he suddenly discovers in the light of Christ the distance that separates it from what has been given to us in Him. That is why he recalls it at the very moment in which he is about to sing of the condition of the Chrisian and the filial life of the child of God. "He who confesses the Son has the Father. If you know that he is just, know that everyone also who does what is just has been born of him" (1 Jn. 2, 23,29). "Behold what manner of love the Father has bestowed upon us, that we should be called the children of God; and such we are. This is why the world does not know us, because it did not know him. Beloved, now we are the children of God, and it has not yet appeared what we shall be. We know that when he appears we shall be like him, for we shall see him just as he is" (1 Jn. 3, 1,2).

Faith of the just

"My just man lives by faith." "To those who believe in his name he has given the power to become the children of God" (1, 12). Christ's entire mystery is contained in these two sentences. Through Him the Christian passes from one order over into the other, and that is why he must be born again in order to approach this other order.

We could ask why a baptism, expressly qualified as a "birth,"[2] is necessary for people who have belonged for centuries to God. If Jesus comes among those who had been chosen from the beginning, and from whom the Messias was to be born, and if this Messias comes to accomplish what had been prepared in the bosom of this people, we could ask why did His own have to be born again? And yet the necessity is very clear: "Amen, amen, I say to you, unless a man be born again of water and the Spirit, he cannot enter into the kingdom of God" (3, 5).

St. John's eighth chapter shows us the fierce opposition raised by the Jews against this rebirth. Are they not the children of Abraham? His children in the faith? "Abraham is our father. We have not been born of fornication; we have one Father, God" (8, 29,41).

Was it not insulting them when the rights of the legitimate children were called into question? And was it not inflicting a deep wound upon them by inviting them to "be born again" in order to enter their Father's house? Yet this is what Christ asks of them. Everyman must be "born again," even the true Israelite and the true son of Abraham. Christ has not come merely to set a seal upon all the preparations of the Old Testament, to ratify and sanctify a faith already orientated towards its fulfillment, to confirm the inhabitants of the house in their right to occupy it; He has come to announce to all without any exception the necessity of a new birth.

2. The word "birth" or "to be born" is used eight times at the beginning of the interview with Nicodemus, whereas baptism is not used once.

Life of the children of God

In the interview with Nicodemus stress is placed upon a "birth" and not a "baptism"; and it is this term "birth" that arouses his surprise and skepticism. "How can these things be?" (3, 9). And undoubtedly he asked himself why Christ did not content Himself as all prophets before Him with simply asking a change of life, a purification of heart. But a new birth! As though Israel were not a vineyard planted by Yahweh Himself!

Nothing can legitimize this pretention of Christ as long as faith does not enlighten His contemporaries, and as long as it does not enlighten us concerning His position as God's Envoy and Son of God. But if He is truly God and if He has come to bring us in His own life eternal life, then a "birth" to this Life is imperative as there is no proportion between it and our natural life.

This new life is for us first a regeneration, a purification, because it comes from Christ the Savior and because it has made His sacrifice necessary. We are washed and purified in the Blood of Christ. But this "regeneration" strikes the apostle less than the "generation" which is inseparable from it. What Christ brings us is not so much the fact of having snatched us from Satan's empire as the power of entering into the divine Life itself. This aspect is the all-important aspect for John and it brings out the word "birth."

A God communicating to men His own life and having him approach this life through a birth is a reality which had been unknown in the Old Testament. And it is this, much more than the notion of redemption, pardon, or purification which makes the "Christian" faith something specific.

In St. John the orientation of his thought is towards "life." "Birth, source of life, living water, child of God...." And these terms seem to try to tie together the essential reality, the fruit of our union with Christ. Through Him and in Him we are born to the very life of God; He is the Door that opens out upon this life and makes it possible for us to enter upon it.

Undoubtedly there are certain exigencies introduced by this birth which are negative in character and John is aware of them. We have already emphasized them in our last chapter. In particular, faith demands of us that we leave our former way of living, that we withdraw from the threefold concupiscence, from the world and Satan, and that we practice self-denial. Undoubtedly too there is a permanent tension, a struggle between light and darkness, and a man must engage in it valiantly till the end of his life. But is it not significant that John speaks even of this combat as a victory?

While Paul invites us to leave what is behind us, to fight the good fight, to struggle generously, John, whose perspectives are on a more contemplative plane, is taken up with the realities that are promised and already in our possession, rather than with the necessity of the struggle itself. For him the faith is before everything else a victory because it is a life in Christ, and this life is already possessed by us. "Who has the Son has the life" (1 Jn. 5, 12).

With a kind of predilection which betrays the bent of his interior contemplation, he comes back constantly to that ineffable reality according to which faith permits him to live and which makes of him and us "children of God" (1, 12). He has set it in the beginning of his Prologue with regard to the coming of the Word in the flesh, showing that in his eyes, it was the fruit par excellence of this coming. He returns to this thought in his Epistle, but not without having again and repeatedly insisted upon that beautiful title of "born of God" (1 Jn. 5, 1,4), and not without singing of his gratitude and astonishment at being a child of God. "Behold what manner of love the Father has bestowed upon us, that we should be called children of God, and such we are" (1 Jn. 3, 1).

Better than all others, this text or rather this cry reveals to us John's basic thought concerning faith of which Christ is the source, object, and perfection. "Everyone that believes Jesus is the Christ is born of God" (1 Jn. 5, 1).

Once placed in us, the divine life does not cease to grow and transform us. It conducts us towards that reality still hidden in germ, but which will develop until its "manifestation."

"Beloved, now we are the children of God, and it has not yet appeared what we shall be" (1 Jn. 3, 2), but what we shall be, we are already, for everything is contained in that title and that reality of children of God: not only the assurance of an eternal love or the part of Him who is "our Father"; not only the assurance of an intimate union with Christ in whom and through whom we share in the title of sons in this divine life, but also the affirmation that faith is truly the seed of glory and vision in us.

"What we shall be has not yet appeared" (1 Jn. 3, 2); but "we know that when he appears . . ." faith which will have worked in us and will have transformed us into Christ will let fall the scales; and that chrysalis, the child of God, will come forth transformed into a son of light and connaturalized with God. "We shall be like him . . ." From faith will come forth what it has prepared, what it has already woven within us: that vision which will allow us "to see God as he is" in the glorious radiance of eternal truth, and in the very light of Christ in which we shall be transformed.

Is it not this final development which Christ envisions when, turning to His Father, He says: "Father, I will that where I am they also whom thou hast given me may be with me; in order that they may behold my glory, which thou hast given me . . ." (17, 24) ?

Thus, the work His Father sent Him to do will have been completed on earth and also the mission given to the apostles: "But these are written that you may believe that Jesus is the Christ, the Son of God, and that believing you may have life in his name" (20, 31).

CHAPTER 14

THE PASSOVER

Jesus gave a striking confirmation of the revelation He made of Himself as Life and Light when He raised Lazarus from the dead. This event was to arouse faith in Him more than any other. " 'Father, because of the people who stand around I spoke, that they may believe that thou hast sent me.' When he had said this, he cried out with a loud voice, 'Lazarus, come forth!' " Jesus demands this faith of Martha even before He works the miracle. " 'Whoever lives and believes in me, shall never die. Dost thou believe this?' She said to him, 'Yes, Lord, I believe that thou art the Christ, the Son of God, who hast come into the world' " (11, 25,27). It is also the fruit which its witnesses draw from the miracle. "Many therefore of the Jews who had come to Mary, and had seen what he did, believed in him" (11, 45).

The reaction of the high priests and the Pharisees was immediate and violent. "If we let him alone as he is, all will believe in him" (11, 48). Caiphas has no trouble convincing them they should rid themselves of Jesus. " 'You know nothing at all; nor do you reflect that it is expedient for us that one man die for the people, instead of the whole nation perishing.' From that day forth their plan was to put him to death" (11, 50,53).

The raising of Lazarus is not only an event of capital significance and importance; it is likewise loaded with consequences. With it begins the final period of Christ's life.

Christ's Hour

Jesus "withdrew" (11, 54) with His disciples "to the district near the desert, to the town called Ephrem," and there He awaited His hour which was to be that of the Passover and His death.

John has repeatedly stressed the conjunction of these two events so long foreseen and carefully prepared for by Christ. He makes the remark that "the Passover of the Jews was at hand" (11, 55), and that "six days before the Passover" (12, 1) Jesus leaves Ephrem and comes to Bethany. The meal He ate with Martha, Mary, and Lazarus gives Him the opportunity of bringing up the subject of His approaching burial (12, 7). References to His hour are multiplied. Now we know that in St. John this hour ordinarily means His death. Evidently this death is very close and Jesus allows this to be clearly understood.

"Yet a little while the light is among you" (12, 35). "The hour has come for the Son of Man to be glorified. And what shall I say? Father, save me from this hour! No, this is why I came to this hour" (12, 23,27). "Now is the judgment of this world; now will the prince of this world be cast out. And I, if I be lifted up from the earth, will draw all things to myself" (12, 31,32).

These clear words, which remind us of the interview with Nicodemus (3, 14), John accompanies with this precision: "Now he said this signifying the death he was to die" (12, 33).

Jesus has resolved that this death coincide with the Passover. That is why He comes to Jerusalem at the approach of the Passover feast. "Now the next day, the great crowd which had come to the feast, when they heard that Jesus was coming to Jerusalem, took branches of palms and went forth to meet him. And they cried out, 'Hosanna! Blessed is he who comes in the name of the Lord, the king of Israel!' " (12, 12,13).

In that year of the Redemption, there were then two Paschs at Jerusalem. While one unfolds according to the usual custom, the other is celebrated in the Cenacle and on the Cross which seals the eternal Covenant between God and humanity. It is a Passover in which Christ "passes" from this world to the Father, and begins to have His followers "pass" also.

"Before the feast of the Passover, Jesus, knowing that the hour had come to him to pass out of this world to the Father, having loved his own who were in the world, loved them to the end" (13, 1).

Christ's Will and Testament

This final period of Christ's life is marked with a certain number of new characteristics which John's Gospel reveals to us. We could qualify the ensemble between the second to the thirteenth chapter, which has been called "the book of signs":[1] a "history of Christ's rejection" by the Jews. The Prologue has already given us a glimpse of this conclusion of

1. C. H. Dodd, op. cit.

that sad history: "He came among his own and his own received him not" (1, 11).

This history is taken up again in Chapter 13, in that passage which places the finishing touch to Christ's ministry and preaching among the people. "Now though he had worked so many signs in their presence, they did not believe in him; that the word which the prophet Isaias spoke might be fulfilled, 'Lord, who has believed our report, and to whom has the arm of the Lord been revealed?' This is why they could not believe, because Isaias said again, 'He has blinded their eyes and hardened their hearts, lest they see with their eyes and understand with their mind and be converted and I heal them.' " (12, 37,40). And John follows up the prophetic text with the words: "And yet among the rulers many believed in him" (12, 42), and he adds Christ's own words which ring out as an announcement of His departure from the world: "I have come a light into the world, that whoever believes in me may not remain in the darkness . . . for I have not come to judge the world, but to save the world" (12, 46,47).

John makes it understood that the history of salvation remains what it always has been: on God's part, a universal salvific will, and on man's part, a response which is the fact of that small number called to become the "children of God." It is to them henceforth that Christ's words will be directed, and herein is the first new characteristic of these chapters which form "the book of the Passion."[2] These children of God are today the apostles, that little group of eleven surrounding Christ at the Cenacle, and tomorrow "those who through their word are to believe in me" (17, 20).

Setting His revelation upon miracles, Christ has manifested Himself to the world as the Life and the Light. From now on the teaching He must impart takes on a more intimate character; and an audience, not in complete accord with it, could not understand it and much less accept it. Even to this small group to whom He is directing it, this teaching appears new and will be understood only later on. But Jesus cannot hold back any longer the moment for revealing the secrets of His Heart. He can no longer withhold His last will and testament from His "little children" (13, 33).

This testament may be expressed in the one word "love." Until then rarely used, it is constantly introduced by John into the discourse after the Supper and even in the introductory words to this discourse it appears twice. "Before the feast of the Passover, Jesus, knowing that the hour had come for him to pass out of this world to the Father, having 'loved' his own who were in the world, 'loved' them to the end" (13,

2. C. H. Dodd, op. cit.

10 ST. JOHN

1). This word, those many allusions to His approaching death, this feast of the Passover so long awaited by the Master are all so many elements characterizing this supreme period of His life, a period marked with a note of finality. There is a clear indication in all His actions of a desire to build the future with the present which is being lived this evening in the Cenacle and tomorrow in Gethsemani and on the Cross.

Until now, Christ has worked to gain belief in Himself and His message. And now, surrounded by His disciples, by those who have admitted He is the Son sent into the world by God (17, 8), He is preoccupied with leaving them certain "rites" which will give life to the Church and develop it.

These rites, as in all other things Christ has come on earth to realize, do not destroy those of the Old Testament but they "fulfill' them, for the latter have been willed and ordained by God from the beginning as a preparation for this one which fulfills them all.

God alone could choose a rite which would both convey and express His salvific plan, and which would manifest most profoundly the Covenant formerly realized between God and His people and which Christ came to render new and eternal: the Passover.

The celebration of the Passover, a figure of the new Passover, contained in germ the elements upon which Christ confers a transcendent meaning by fulfilling them. The celebration of this feast gives full meaning to His life not simply by chance, but because the religious character of its institution is in full agreement with what Christ has set out to realize.

In fact, when Jesus pronounces the words of the ancient blessing and the act of thanksgiving to Yahweh, Liberator and Savior of Israel, these words are no longer simply hymns and vows ascending from a human soul but the Divine Word praising the Father. And the body He bequeathes to the disciples, along with His soul and divinity, remains God's living Eucharist among His disciples.

For Christ, celebrating the Pasch is offering thanksgiving for divine favors and what favor will be ever more complete than the total gift Jesus makes to men of His own Person!

However, as long as the Resurrection has not taken place, the Passover remains incomplete. "If Christ is not risen, vain is our preaching, vain is your faith" (1 Cor. 15, 14). The Passover does not only solemnize what has been given to us but also what restores us to God: the entire work accomplished by Christ for His Father's glory. The last Passover celebrated by Jesus does not have in view only what is going to happen that night or the next morning in Gethsemani and on the Cross, but also the day after the great Sabbath: the glory of the Resurrection.

In the Cenacle Jesus anticipates His death. He knows that after three days, as first among His brethren, He will go forth living from the tomb and will return to His Father. That is why His praise is the act of the definitive Passover, of joy without end, where everything is summed up in God in stability and peace. His "Hallel" springs up from the distant past and with the present it covers the future. It resounds throughout eternity. Christ's Passover is the Passover of all passovers, *the* Passover of the world.

Ever present Memorial

The continuity between the old and the new Pasch, already evident on the level of "thanksgiving," is even more so if we consider the deep meaning of the divine initiative and of redeeming love which gives life to this Pasch. Drawing an immense "parabola" which embraces that night in Egypt and that in the Cenacle, one sole act of salvation develops through time under the figure of the Paschal Lamb.

As a remembrance and summing up of the mercies of the Lord and His great deeds performed in favor of Israel, the Passover was first and foremost a "memorial."

In order that this signfication be never forgotten, the father of each family, when celebrating this feast, was to comment on the text of Exodus which reported its institution and recalled its original circumstances. It was invested with the character of a "thanksgiving," a "eucharist," celebrated by the whole people gathered together. For was it not the entire nation that God had delivered from slavery and conducted "with a strong hand and outstretched arm" towards a land "vast and rich" and "flowing with milk and honey" (Dt. 7, 19; 11, 9)? Each year Israel gave thanks for these wonders and this miraculous protection, and it did so by renewing the deeds which Yahweh commanded it to carry out at the time of the Exodus.

A Memorial forever in act

The new Passover must also be lived as a memorial. It turns us towards what was once realized in the Cenacle, on Calvary, at the Resurrection. But grace remains present in it for us, forever living. We carry its actual renewal and sacred testimony in our hearts which are "born of God" (1 Jn. 4, 7). For us also the Passover is a memorial, but a memorial that is forever living and actual.

It does not seem at first glance that the Passover had the characteristic of "memorial" for Christ by whom all things were about to be renewed. And yet if we consider the fact very attentively which gave rise to it, we will understand this memorial was and remains the basis of the Passover for all times.

On the night of the Passover, God had His people leave Egypt and delivered them from slavery. He commanded the Hebrews to paint their doorposts with the blood of the lamb so that their firstborn may be spared by the exterminating angel; and also, their loins girt, they were to eat the entire lamb and the unleavened bread with the bitter herbs. He prescribed that this rite be forever "renewed" (Ex. 12, 14). Israel obeyed, more resigned than consenting as the days of the revolt which followed testify. Moses alone perhaps had a real knowledge of the implications of God's will and His mercy which came to succor man. The first act of the Redemption was played in this liberation of the Chosen Race, from which the Savior was to be born. God committed Himself irrevocably to the fulfillment of the promise made in Eden, and contained in the blessings given to Abraham and the patriarchs. Manifestly and symbolically, the Passover was the announcement of the new era, making a free nation of an enslaved people, composed of the children of God living under His just laws.

God had committed Himself alone; He had gone first before men and His love for them was first (1 Jn. 4, 19). And it is in this that the Passover was for Christ the memorial par excellence. Were not His love and His sacrifice alone going to be committed for man's salvation, incorporating themselves in the line already traced out by God whose designs are unchangeable?

He alone was aware of the intensity of God's desire to accomplish man's redemption and He was going to carry it out. And that is why He alone could really celebrate the Pasch, and He only could give it its true dimension, that of a memorial of love, extending into the past and the future and forever (Ps. 89, 2).

In the Passover all initiative comes from God. And that is why it is not initially a sacrifice, that act of religion which has within itself a voluntary offering from man. When prescribing the immolation of a lamb, it is rather a net which God casts over man, thus taking him in the first meshes of what is going to become through Christ a voluntary and truly sacrificial oblation, an act which binds God and man together in the bonds of a fully reciprocal love.

In fact, the Jewish Passover asked of man no other participation but that of obedience expressing itself in an immolation which was neither expiatory nor sacrificial; it reminded him that innocent blood of a victim had spared the people of God and saved it. The paschal lamb is not even identified with the numerous sacrifices prescribed by the Law. If it prefigured a sacrifice, we could say it did so for God alone. It will not become an expiatory victim, a victim of praise, until Jesus Himself will freely anticipate immolation by men.

Lamb of God: it is thus John the Baptist salutes Him at His baptism, and it is thus John will designate Him in his Apocalypse. If it is probable that the title given by the Precursor literally corresponds with Isaias' prophecy rather than with the paschal lamb, it is certain at that hour the Baptist is prophesying. God's inspiration through the centuries ties all together. Through events, prophecies, figures, reality takes form and is fulfilled. "Behold the Lamb of God who takes away the sin of the world" (1, 29). Like the paschal lamb, Jesus will be immolated for men's salvation; and God is alone here in realizing His work: "Father, forgive them for they know not what they do" (Lk. 23, 34).

A victim without spot, innocent, of little value in the eyes of those who immolate it: such was the paschal lamb in this ancient Passover; such also will Jesus be. It is only at the price of blood shed that men will understand that salvation has been given to them and "they will wash their robes in the blood of the lamb" (Ap. 7, 14).

The new Passover instituted by Jesus is not simply a characteristic rite of a feast of commemoration. Christ inserts into it the act of religion par excellence when offering Himself to His Father for all men. His oblation is an oblation of Himself and of all His brothers in Him; and His sacrifice is the sacrifice in which all human sacrifices take on value and meaning. The Paschal Lamb is henceforth "the victim of propitiation for our sins" (1 Jn. 2, 2).

The Passage from the "rite" to the "sacrifice" in the heart of the Passover is perceptible in the Synoptics, with the recital of the eucharistic hymn; and in St. John, with the discourse after the Supper. Christ delivers Himself up with total abandonment to His Father's will, and He bequeathes to His disciples all that belongs to Him. The Cross will "accomplish" what is already realized.

Christ's sacrifice has two complementary aspects: total spoliation accompanied by a violence that inflicts death; and the gift of His life to those whom He loves. It is an act of supreme piety with regard to those whom the Father has confided to Him, but it is an act of religion also towards the Father who sent Him. In His sacerdotal prayer, Christ dedicates His whole work to His Father.

The Passover becomes the unique sacrifice with Christ, the unique act of worship of the people of God. The ancient prescriptions take up this unique road towards God. Praise or expiation, prayer or oblation, sacrifice or reparation: the many forms devotion towards God takes will have no other end but Christ's sacrifice offered to God for men.

Because it is unique Christ's Passover effects a unanimity. In fact, Jerusalem is the choice place for every Passover: the ancient Jerusalem of the Promised Land, but also the new Jerusalem, viz., that holy city shining with the virtues of the saints, "the Spouse of the Lamb" John will call it (Ap. 21, 9).

If the first Passover signified the choice and the building up of a people to whom salvation is promised, the first celebration of the Passover in the desert of Sinai emphasizes, as the text of Numbers points out, the community character and the communion with which it was invested: "He will be cut off from his race who omits to celebrate the Passover" (Nm. 9, 13). Even in Egypt Yahweh has established the celebration of it "forever" as the rite by which His people will be distinguished from others.

The eating of the flesh of the victim is a rite common to different religions. It takes on its meaning of approbation from the victim by the god invoked, and from the divine favor which this victim contains and communicates to those who feed themselves on it. This favor can go so far as to identify the eater with the god.

For Israel, the eating of the paschal lamb remains the memorial of a famous miracle of God which both brings deliverance to the people and sets up this people as a people; it "personifies" it, establishes it in a very special relationship of belonging to God and of having a mission. The Passover creates a definite community very much present to its God, dedicated to Him. It binds the members of a same race, more spiritually than carnally, and binds them to God. Indeed, Israel will become the beloved child of Yahweh and also His spouse, though faithless.

The Passover celebrated by the Lamb of God retains the same meaning; but it is the limitless expansion of the ancient Passover. Deliverance, as it is realized in our days, is totally spiritual and it is definitive as long as man does not separate himself from God. It also creates a race of children of God and joins them together among themselves and with God through the twofold commandment of charity.

The community and the communion are joined together in the paschal feast under the sign of Christ's victory, just as formerly they were joined under the sign of the triumphal departure from Egypt and from the passage through the Red Sea. But the physical and spiritual dimensions of this community are radically different, and the communion among the members of this community and God depend henceforth upon a reciprocity of love.

It is a group of friends that surrounds Jesus the night of the Supper, and it is to friends that He hands the morsel of bread. It is no longer servants but friends that Jesus calls to know eternal life with Him (15, 15). It is no longer a question of a people among other peoples, but of those who are not of this world while remaining in the world (17, 15); of those who will return love for love. "Love one another as I have loved you" (13, 34). The new Passover gathers together all the sheep in a unity, "all the children of God dispersed" (11, 52); it creates the city of saints.

And it is in this sense that the Passover realizes in Christ the integrity and the full significance of its name: "passage." The ancient Passover did not simply gather a people together on the memory of the past, but it had within itself a certain dynamic quality stemming from its messianic and eschatalogical mission. The Jewish Passover was something else besides a memorial and commemoration; it held out the hopes of a very definite liberation to be brought about by the Messias.

"All Israel's longings and desires since the first Passover of Exodus, and even since the promises made to Abraham, all its dissatisfaction in its history of trials, sufferings, captivities, drew from the Passover it celebrated each year renewed reasons for hoping that the hour of that mysterious passage inaugurated by the Passover would finally be realized."[3]

Begun with the departure from Egypt, this passage continued each day "until he comes" Paul will say (1 Cor. 11, 26), wishing to point out that Christ, and He alone, would fulfill what Moses had begun. Passing first through the Red Sea, Moses had remained standing on the opposite bank until the entire people had made the crossing. Thus, the Messias will make the people of God cross, but this time in a definitive manner from captivity to freedom by introducing them forever into the Promised Land of the kingdom of God.

On the night of the first Passover, the angel of Yahweh had "passed," delivering His people at the price of the blood of the lamb. On the night of the new Passover, the Lord passed Himself and there is no other passage to await, for He passes once and for all.

God, the divine Ferryman, had made Israel pass into the Promised Land. Jesus, the divine Ferryman made man, leads them on this night from darkness to light, from death to life, from ignorance to love.

The name "Passover" attests to Christ's victory as it bore testimony to the triumph of the Hebrews over the Egyptians. The Red Sea is crossed, the people of the children of God is liberated, and it "passes" henceforth with Christ "from this world to the Father" (13, 1) and thus enters into eternal life.

3. P. Feret.

Communication of the Mystery of Salvation

"Before the feast of the Passover, Jesus knowing that the hour had come for him to pass out of this world to the Father, having loved his own who were in the world, loved them to the end" (13, 1).

John's merit lies in having succeeded in recalling to us in this compact statement which opens the account of the Last Supper that the figure of the ancient Passover was about to be fulfilled in the new Passover, making of the latter the veritable and definitive Covenant.

To fill this role it would not be sufficient, however, for the new Passover to fulfill the old. The Covenant projected by God postulates that other realities be set to work. Christ must find a means of pouring His own presence, love, and life into this Covenant. This Passover must become a sort of spiritual womb which, receiving these realities in proportion as they are lived, gives to the total gift of Christ, His love, His passion, and redeeming death, a real survival which remains the life of His followers right to the end of the world. It is necessary that these realities, escaping in some manner from time in which they are nevertheless incorporated, become communicable to men and assimilable by them. It is necessary, and this is impossible with men but possible with God, that a new order be created in which "the whole mystery of our salvation is contained,"[4] and that this new order remain forever actual so that it can always be shared in. It is necessary that through this Passover, Christ's life, grace, and love be able to pass from His disciples and be transmitted through His Church.

Communion in Christ's Life and Love

It is necessary that the human and divine realities of the Redemption become henceforth "sacramental" realities. And it is because he had understood this that John's account proceeded along two parallel lines: the historic, i.e., the one in which actions unfold, words are spoken, in which Jesus continues to speak and to accomplish deeds, in which we see Him suffer and die; and the mystical and invisible, in which these same realities are gathered together as in a crucible and which the divine will and omnipotence are going to transubstantiate into sacramental realities.

Undoubtedly it is the entire Christ who is communicated to us in the sacraments. And yet we may say that the one who comes to us in the sacraments is Christ as the source of life, as the principle of grace and

4. St. Thomas.

pardon; and it is Christ with whom the soul is destined to be united in love and in which she is invited to be transformed.

There would be no need of the sacraments were there only question of communicating Christ's teaching or bringing us in contact with His miracles. The Gospel data and faith would be sufficient for this. But the Christian religion would then be a religion of the word of God, taken in the sense of a teaching which the Book alone would transmit to us. Now such is not the case, and what Christ has decided to communicate to us is His own life, His own love, and in these, the fruit of a redemption and a freedom from sin which were acquired through His own Blood. That is why the Christian religion is inseparably the religion of God's word and the religion of the Word made flesh, delivered up for our sake, and remaining with us through His Spirit. Nowhere is the Spirit's activity as great as it is in the sacraments which communicate Him to us along with Christ's life.

It is not without reason, then, that Christ made His revelation of love and the institution of the sacraments coincide. In fact, this love accounts for the sacraments, and it is the same love they have the mission to communicate to us along with divine life. Instituted during the Last Supper, in that atmosphere where death becomes an instrument in the hands of Love, the sacraments can be nothing else but a manifestation and a communication of divine love and this is what they really are. This love which comes to us in the form of a sacrifice, as the principle of union, as a means of passage from this world to the Father: behold what Christ revealed to men and what John transmitted to us in those chapters where the events of the Passover are narrated.[5]

5. John, Chapters 13 to 17.

CHAPTER 15

THE SACRIFICE

I. SACRIFICE OF LOVE

The apostles were troubled when they sat down to the banquet of the last Passover. Certain forebodings crowded their minds. And how could it be otherwise since the Master, far from reassuring them, had recently made so many allusions to His coming departure, and death?

The chief priests and the Pharisees had also given the order "... if anyone knew where he was, he should report it, so that they might seize him" (11, 57). No apostle could be unaware of their designs on the Master's life.

The atmosphere, then, in which the meal was begun was heavy and agonizing and Jesus did nothing to dispel the gloom. An unforeseen event took place which evidenced the special character of this Passover. When the supper had just begun, "Jesus rose from the supper and laid aside his garments, and taking a towel girded himself. Then he poured water into the basin and began to wash the feet of his disciples and to dry them with the towel with which he was girded" (13, 2-5).

Washing of the feet

This episode, narrated by John alone, surpasses the notion of service, or at least gives it a particular tonality which makes a true "sacrifice" of it, in the sense of "sacrum facere."

At the moment the apostles saw in it undoubtedly a gesture relative to ritual purifications, and Peter urges: "not my feet only, but my hands and my head" (13, 9). Christ answers, "He who has bathed needs only to wash, and he is clean all over. And you are clean, but not all" (13, 10).

"You are clean . . ." It is, then, a gratuitous service and a useless one, in a sense, which Christ renders His apostles and it is precisely as such that it is exemplary.

True, the custom in Palestine of the master of the house extending this service to his guests after the hardships of the journey was familiar to the disciples. They know what they should see in the act, viz., deference and esteem, testified by the welcome filled with courtesy. It is no small matter that, among so many other customs, Christ has chosen this one as exemplifying what He expects henceforth as the conduct of His disciples, their mode of action towards each other.

There is no question here of a service rendered to one in need or of an act of compassion dictated by necessity. As a gratuitous, free, and spontaneous act it implies all the forms of assistance, but it goes beyond affability and at the same time excludes condescension and servility. It has within it all the nuances of respect and solicitude. In a word, this gesture of Christ is much less an act of "devotedness" as it is an act of "devotion," hence a "sacrifice."

In this gesture Christ is offering Himself to His apostles, He is offering His own person; He is making an oblation of it under the form of a service. Apparently this action humbles Him; in reality it renders Him great and it exalts His apostles too.

It exalts Him, not because when performing it He lays claim to the title of "Master and Lord" (13, 13), but because He transforms the apparent humiliation into humility. It exalts the apostles, because it reveals to them what the Master sees in them: friends whom He is honoring.

Now, He is about to confer the dignity upon them which He sees in them and which His action emphasizes. After having chosen them, He is about to make them His friends (15, 15), and those who have been made children of God through faith in Him are about to be nourished with His body and redeemed with His blood. He is about to open His own kingdom to them and introduce them into it as one welcoming strange guests into his own home and placing all his possessions at their disposal (15, 7,23). He brings them to His repose and His banquet. These are the ones given Him by the Father as His "body" and it is as such He is honoring them.

All Christ's actions bear the stamp of truth. Furthermore, all His actions are creative. What He accomplishes at the beginning of His Passion is definitive and He realizes it. What Judas will do in a few moments will be all the more terrible.

Thus, beyond these actions of Christ, as exemplary as they are, there is what He is doing for His disciples, the homage He is rendering them. What He places at their feet is all the fervor, all that can be disposed of, and all the love He is about to set at work for them. Seriously and joyfully

He bends down before them, recognizing in them those for whom He was sent and those He will render worthy of His Father's love. He does not play the role of servant, for He is the Servant, with all the devotion, fervor, and piety of one offering sacrifice to God.

When we consider this scene, we cannot help bring back to our minds what John reports just a little earlier in his Gospel: Mary pouring her ointment over Jesus' feet and wiping them with her hair.

What a poor woman has done from the tenderness of her heart, that delicate and fervent act of homage rendered to the Master, Jesus Himself does for His disciples. And He does not hesitate to perform it towards the one who will betray Him and the other who will deny Him, thus erasing their stains in advance and beholding in them nothing but the dignity to which the Father has called them. All Christ's actions are merciful and redemptive and also gratuitous, as mercy itself is through definition, for it comes from love and is directed to nothing else.

What is unique about this act of humility of Christ and the sacrifice of Himself which it manifests, is that it offers us a vision of having been redeemed in advance and worthy of being honored. What it has about it that is forever imitable for the disciples is that attitude of deference due to one whose true name is written in heaven, that attitude of total self-surrender, and that attitude of mercy: "If you know these things, blessed shall you be if you do them" (13, 16). Yes, for all the beatitudes are included in mercy which is accomplished under a thousand forms which love inspires. "If, therefore, I the Lord and Master have washed your feet, you also ought to wash the feet of one another. . . . Amen, amen, I say to you, no servant is greater than his master . . ." (13, 14).

Not only do all actions of humility and devotedness, but even all "sacrifices" till then impossible, become possible. For it is a question henceforth of discovering in our brothers the divine image, of uniting our love to the love with which Christ has looked at them, and of honoring them as He has honored them. Sacrifice takes on the nature of the supremely gratuitous act and becomes, in the hands of love, a choice instrument for manifesting love.

Taking His place again at the table and having drawn out the lesson contained in the act just performed, Jesus reveals His inner feelings to His disciples in the statement, "Amen, amen, I say to you, one of you is about to betray me" (13, 21).

These words upset the apostles who "looked at one another uncertain of whom he was speaking." Making a sign to John who was seated beside Jesus, Peter says to him, " 'Who is it of whom he speaks?' He therefore leaning back upon the bosom of Jesus said to him, 'Lord, who is it?' Jesus answered, 'It is he for whom I will dip the bread, and give it to him.' And when he dipped the bread, he gave it to Judas Iscariot, the son of Simon. When therefore he had received the morsel, he went out quickly. Now it was night" (13, 22-30).

The last act of the drama begins. Jesus is aware that death approaches inexorably at every passing instant. And still how different is His reaction from what we would expect. "Now is the Son of Man glorified, and God is glorified in him. If God is glorified in him, God will also glorify him in himself, and will glorify him at once" (13, 31).

Freed at last by the traitor's departure and being surrounded by loving hearts, despite their weaknesses, Jesus is about to set the mystery of His sacrifice and death in their real light, rendering their meaning clear.

"It is expedient for you that I go"

Christ does not hide from them the fact that this sacrifice and death will bring about a painful separation for them as well as for Him. They will seek Him, and "where I go you cannot come" (13, 33). However, He shows them a way immediately afterwards, not of overcoming their sadness, but on the contrary of living with it in a fruitful way: "Love one another as I have loved you" (13, 34).

In other words: You ardently desire that death does not separate us; then keep me present in your midst by what is still truly my presence, by what gives me to you and vice versa, viz., my love which abides with you and in you. "This love which you will have for one another" (13, 35) will bring about my presence among you, and it will bear testimony of me to those who do not even know me.

Christ's death is not an absence. Because it is a sacrifice of love, it permits His spiritual presence to be multiplied indefinitely, and it permits a nearness which grows according to the fidelity and depth with which each loves his brothers with the very love with which Christ loved him.

Christ's death must not then disturb the apostles (14, 1), and not even the separation resulting from it; supported by their faith in Him, they are going to discover the positive aspects of that death.

Not only does the exercise of love make Christ abide among us, but even His departure gives Him the opportunity to prepare efficaciously for a definite reunion. "And if I go and prepare a place for you, I am coming again, and I will take you to myself; that where I am, there you may be also" (14, 3).

Christ thus has them understand that the real place of life is not where they are, but where He is going; Christ's victorious power transforms death into life. "He who believes in me, even if he die, will live" (11, 25). "Whoever lives and believes in me has everlasting life" (13, 16).

For Christ death means a return to His Father's house, that house in which there are "many mansions" (14, 2) and where He is going to prepare a place for His disciples.

Soon, He will say to His apostles, "If I do not go, the Holy Spirit will not come to you" (16, 7). But here he gives them to understand that without this death to which He is going to deliver Himself up, there would be no place for them with His Father.

Christ's death is generally considered from its expiatory aspect; but here Christ places His disciples before the positive fruits of this death. Through it He is able to open heaven which our sins have closed against us, but also, in an act where all the solicitude of His love is apparent, "to prepare a place for us" (14, 2). Who will express what Christ places under these words and what attention and love enter into this gesture on His part? It is only when we finally occupy this place in eternity that we shall understand Christ's tenderness for those whom He loves.

However, besides substituting the image of the home He is preparing for the sad picture of His departure, Jesus further adds the assurance of His speedy return: "And if I go and prepare a place for you, I am coming again, and I will take you to myself" (14, 3).

If He deprives them of His physical and passing presence, it is to give them the power of sharing His spiritual and definite presence.[1] And this is not all. This death of Christ will likewise give them the power to do "greater works" than the ones He performed. "Amen, amen, I say to you, he who believes in me, the works I do he also shall do, and greater than these he shall do because I am going to the Father" (14, 22).

Setting the apostles on the plane of faith, Christ's death will enable them to possess the Master in a spiritual way, i.e., interiorly, immediately, constantly, livingly. "Yet a little while and the world no longer sees me. But you see me, for I live and you shall live. In that day you will know that I am in the Father, and you in me, and I in you" (14, 19,20).

Finally, faith will give them the power to know Christ's person, no longer as they enjoyed it in His mortal life, but by discovering in it the Son of God. If the grace of Christ's presence is limitless, what must we say of the grace which flows from the coming of the Trinity into the soul? "If anyone love me he will keep my word, and my Father will love him, and we will come to him and make our abode with him" (14, 23).

1. It is not a question here as it is in 16, 16 of the transitory presence of the Risen Christ, but rather of the definitive presence which the elect will enjoy at the Parousia and at the second coming of Christ which the author of the Apocalypse calls upon with his prayers "Come, Lord Jesus," an event upon which the whole expectation of the Church rests. (1 Cor. 4, 5; cf. also: 1 Cor. 11, 26; 16, 22).

Christ's departure and the giving of the Spirit

However, this promise is made dependent upon Christ's departure and death. And it is likewise the case for the sending of the Holy Spirit. "For if I do not go, the Advocate will not come to you; but if I go, I will send him to you" (16, 7).

The apostles must cease "being troubled" and being filled with fear; they should understand: "It is expedient for you that I depart"; and if they really loved Him, they would rejoice that He is returning to the Father (14, 1,28,30). Both their own spiritual advantage as well as their love for Him should make them understand that His leaving them is absolutely necessary.

However, the assurance given by Christ to His disciples that His departure will benefit them and be spiritually fruitful for them does not give them the real reason for His death. Are these graces and supernatural benefits, certainly of inestimable value, necessarily linked with His death? Is the divine omnipotence restricted to this manner of communicating sufficient to cleanse the entire world of its sins and assure its salvation. itself to men? Nothing in the Gospel texts would force us to think so.

True, the necessity for the Lamb of God to bear in Himself and "to take away the sin of the world" by means of an expiation proportionate to the gravity of our innumerable sins already accounts for Christ's death. Nevertheless, it is a fact that this death was not demanded in any way. What the Church has us sing in the "Adoro te": "Cujus una stilla salvum facere, totum mundum quit ab omni scelere"[2] is rigorously exact on the theological plane, and Christ's least action, because of the dignity conferred upon it by the hypostatic union, would have been more than sufficient to cleanse the entire world of its sins and assure its salvation.

Thus, Christ's death is demanded neither by the benefits it confers upon us nor by the rigor of divine justice. There must be a reason from another order for this death. Christ makes it known to us and John has transmitted this knowledge. Pointed out at the end of this first part of the discourse after the Supper, ". . . that the world may know that I love the Father, and that I do as the Father has commanded me" (14, 31), it is resumed again in the second part and made more explicit, "Greater love than this no man has, that a man lay down his life for his friends" (15, 13). And John comes back to this thought in his first Epistle, proof that he considered it of capital importance. And it does nothing else but take

2. "O loving Pelican! Lord Jesus dear!
Cleanse with thy blood my unclean soul within;
One single drop whereof sufficed to clear
The world from guilt, and save it from all sin."

up and carry out the idea presented at the very commencement of His teaching: "Yes, God has so loved the world as to give his only-begotten Son . . ."(3, 16).

Death through love

"Christ's death, far from being the result of sin, was caused by His love, with sin as the occasion, and this is not the same thing."[3]

Love then is the real reason for Christ's death and the only one that makes it a necessity. It is because there is no greater love than the giving of one's life (15, 13) that Christ desired to die for us, and it is because the Father has loved the world that He has given His only-begotten Son for it. This reality is so central, so basic, and our religious and spiritual life is so essentially bound up with this truth that we should examine carefully what St. Thomas Aquinas expresses in these words: "Christ accepted death through love, and the Passion is a sacrifice by reason of the love of one who suffers it."[4]

Undoubtedly the statement, "Greater love than this no man has, that a man lay down his life for his friend" is clear, and yet to understand its spiritual meaning it is good to look at it in its context.

Christ has just asked His apostles to keep His commandments, for they will abide in His love in this way. Then He immediately adds: "This is my commandment, that you love one another as I have loved you. Greater love than this no one has, that one lay down his life for his friends" (15, 12,13). And He is even more precise when He states, "You are my friends if you do what I have commanded you" (15, 14). What He has commanded them is "to love one another."

Love is then the all-important commandment, but this commandment has a supreme manner of being put into practice, viz., "by laying down one's life for one's friends" (15, 13).

At the summit of the commandments, love; at the summit of love, death through love. Such is the truth set before our eyes and which speaks for itself, for man has never doubted that giving his life is the sign and proof of the "greatest love."

However, if we understand this, we do not grasp very well that love justifies death and how it does so. We keep in mind God's prohibition of immolating human victims. Remembering how He arrested the arm of Abraham ready to sacrifice his son Isaac, we cannot see why what was

3. Philip of the Trinity, in "Love and Violence."
4. St. Thomas.

prohibited in one era, in which the customs rendered such an act less surprising, becomes in another era the means God chooses and utilizes, since He delivered His Son up to the death of the Cross.

Now it is a fact that this "death" occupies the central place in the mystery of the Redemption, and this "blood" holds in John's mind, this evangelist of the Lamb of God and the pierced Heart, a place of primary importance. How can John be simultaneously the evangelist of the God of love and of God's Son delivered over to a bloody death? If we consider "love" and "death" with human eyes, there is no answer to this problem. If, on the other hand, we admit, as our point of departure, that God modifies, transforms, and veritably transubstantiates a reality once He enters into it, then we can give an answer to the problem.

Love changes death into life

Until the coming of Christ, death was a human reality; and human too were the sentiments, even when most generous and detached, with which a man was able to face death (Rom. 5, 7). With Christ, we are in the presence of the death of a God-Man, and in the presence even of divine love. The fact that this love is at the very core of Christ's sacrifice on the Cross really changes everything. However, just as divine grace does not destroy nature, God, when taking hold of a human reality, neither disfigures it nor alters its nature. This reality does not only retain its outward appearances, but its deep inner sense and value. God takes these as His point of departure; He sustains them and brings them to perfection.

Christ's death is the true death of a real man. Jesus dies as truly and His blood flows as realistically as the blood of any man whose hands and feet and side had been pierced; and this sacrifice brings with it sufferings as atrocious as any man placed under similar circumstances would suffer.[5] And yet, what Christian enlightened by faith would say when face to face with the Crucifix that there is nothing more here than a human death and a pouring forth of human blood?

Christ is God, and the plenitude of divine love, taking possession of a human death, can confer upon that death a meaning and a value which transcend those of any human sacrifice whatsoever. Again, Christ's blood is not the blood only of a man, but of God, and that is why its value and power cannot be compared to those of any other blood. What the blood of other victims could signify and obtain only at the price of a

---

5. It is not forbidden to think that because of Christ's inner sentiments and the perfection of His love, even His physical sufferings were incomparably greater than those of any other man that has suffered.

legalistic fiction, viz., expiation, pardon, Christ's blood signifies and obtains this in truth. His blood seals and ratifies the Covenant of the entire human race with God.

We always have a tendency to consider life as having an absolute value, whereas even for man this value is relative. The same goes for the human life of Christ if we compare it to that to which it is ordained and sacrificed. As precious as is His human life, it is not as precious as His death, at least in view of salvation, since the latter, in realizing the "greatest love," gives His life its ultimate meaning, fulfilling it and conferring upon it its plenitude and fecundity.

We begin to glimpse the real aspects of the problem to be solved. When a man offers his life in sacrifice, he cannot prevent this sacrifice from bringing on his death. When God, in the Person of Christ, offers Himself in sacrifice, His divine power brings it about that His death is converted into life. God is Life, and everything He touches, even though it be death itself, comes to life. The more an apparently negative reality contains love, the more it is capable of becoming positive, i.e., a bearer of life, through the change God brings about when taking up this reality.

Now, if God is Life, He is also Love, and He is this entirely and divinely. Consequently, when entering into death, He not only transforms it into life, but also into love. Such is the case of Christ giving His life on the Cross through love. Here we have the greatest act of love of His entire life. "It is the fruit of His most free human will and of an incomparable communication to this will of the mystery of God as Love. In this act, God's infinite and eternal love breaks into His creation and history. This love demands the sacrifice of everything He is able to sacrifice and finally the sacrifice of His very life. In God there is such love for men that He goes even to the limit of sacrificing His Son for them."[6]

Death as love's demand

And if love goes to the limit of sacrificing everything it can sacrifice, it is because love is by nature indivisible. It is at one and the same time a totality and an exigency. It has no other choice but that of being itself, i.e., without limit, end, extreme. "Having loved his own . . . he loved them to the end" (13, 1), to the very extremity of love. And if we dare so express ourselves, there was no other way of being faithful to love even for God. Love saves only by being itself, i.e., absolute. If it did not go to the limit, to the extremity of sacrifice, to death, it would not be love.

6. P. Feret.

It was not, then, the necessity of adjusting the reparation to the enormity of the offense (though Christ's death does help man realize something of the infinite malice of sin) which made God choose death on the Cross for His Son; but the will to reveal divine Love to men, while manifesting it to them under the only form which would not betray it. Hence, the Cross can be envisaged in no other way but as the summit of love. All Christ's love, all its manifestations, all its powers are enclosed within this; and if Christ willed that His Heart be pierced on the Cross, it was in order to set free divine and human love at one stroke, for this love was contained there and it longed to pour itself forth over the whole world: "I have come to spread fire on the earth, and what will I but that it be kindled" (Lk. 12, 49).

We can understand now how, taking what comes from man, viz., death marked with the negative sign of sin, God, when making it His own, marks it with His positive sign.

In a certain sense at least, it is just as true to say that on the Cross there is a death and there is no longer death.[7] In the hands of God death becomes life and the source of life. Springing forth from the furnace of love, blood becomes the principle of union and eternal alliance.

Thus, where we see death, God sees life. Where we see sin, God sees at the same time love which triumphs over sin. Where we see blood shed, He sees in this same blood, the unifying principle of the Covenant. Blood and death are what Christ receives from men in the bosom of the mystery of the Incarnation and the Redemption. He pours into these His own love and offers them to us transubstantiated in an Alliance and in Life.

We understand from this why Christ's death cannot be compared to the other bloody sacrifices and why, forbidden in all other circumstances, this sacrifice is permitted here. Divine love has not only transformed everything in itself, it converts death into life and absorbs death into its victory. It has found in Christ's sacrifice a possibility, which will no longer ever be reproduced, of a communication that has no limits. For never again will divine love have at its disposal a humanity that assumes this love and expresses it in its fullness. Never again will the infinity of love, "the greatest love," encounter in a human nature a possibility of containing it and living it without betraying it, without holding back anything whatsoever.

When St. John wrote in his Epistle, "In this we have come to know his love..." (1 Jn. 3, 16), it is this that he is trying to express. The revelation of divine love in Christ crucified is doubly miraculous: it supposes first that the fullness of love, like the fullness of the divinity, dwells

---

7. This theme is used in the Liturgy during Passiontide and Holy Week.

in this man whose name is Jesus; and again, that through this act through which He "has given his life for us"[8] the fullness of divine love is both revealed and communicated to us.

If, meditating upon these matters, we understand why God, having so loved the world, has "given his only-begotten Son," we perceive also how other realities included in this sacrifice retain their importance and value.

In fact, John, when recalling the Master's words which shed light upon death from the angle of love, has seen also in this death sacrifice for sin (1 Jn. 2, 2). The bloody sacrifice retains its value in his eyes and the meaning it always had. If Christ's death is a sacrifice and a death of love, it is also a sacrifice and a death for sin. "Jesus Christ the just . . . is a propitiation for our sins" (1 Jn. 2, 2; Cf. 1 Jn. 4, 10).

II. SACRIFICE FOR SIN

The notion of punishment linked to sin, born in man from the sentiment of culpability, is not the result of an aberration reducible to some kind of masochism. Punishment is actually a law enunciated by God Himself and applied to man expelled from Eden immediately after the rebellion; this punishment appears under the form of the suffering and pain substituted for the happiness he formerly enjoyed. Rejected from communion with God because of Adam's "no" which separates him from his Author, the child of Adam finds himself banished from the great joys of Paradise. The serpent is cursed. The woman sees the glory of her fertility destined to become her burden and her shame. The man is given hard work as a chastisement. And to both, death.

But does a punishment repair the offense? Will it be sufficient for man to live this hard life and to die in order to experience again, at least beyond death's portals, communion with God? The entire Old Testament testifies that such was not the belief of the patriarchs, and that their hope was buried in the very distant future; in the promise alone God made to the serpent: "I will place enmities between thee and the woman, between her seed and thy seed; she shall crush thy head and thou shalt lie in wait for her heel" (Gn. 3, 15).

Man must undergo the law of punishment, but he will not know rest except with the termination of the conflict between him and Satan. However, work and death have set man right now during this life in a certain

---

8. We shall notice that in St. John it is almost always in terms of "life" that he speaks of Christ's death. He does not "die" for us, He "gives" or "offers his life" for us.

state of just punishment: not that God might find in this a means of appeasing His "anger" as was later believed, but because He agreed to sanction the state of things created by Adam's fall, to make of it a sort of temporary order.[9]

"Jesus Christ the Just" and Satan's defeat

A long historic, messianic, and sapiential tradition courses through the Scriptures with regard to the "just one." Abraham is set up as his model. In Job, we have the living embodiment of the moral virtues described by the psalmists and the sapiential authors as belonging to this "just one." And finally in Isaias, we come upon the prophecy of the "suffering servant."

Now St. John does not hesitate to recognize this "just one" par excellence in the person of Jesus. Frequently in his Epistle he designates Him as such, intending not only to place emphasis upon the exceptional integrity which gives Christ a perfect liberty and intimacy in His Father's presence, but he also wishes to qualify Christ's mission itself.

This mission comes at a time when justice is identified with the fulfillment of the punishment due to sin. This justice left unsatisfied those longings for happiness and immortality inherent in the depths of the human soul; but it did develop the hope that God would come to remedy this miserable condition which was being lived out in a recognition of God's rights and the creature's duties.

In Jesus Christ the hope of the just was not in vain, for when becoming man He fully espoused their condition. Jesus said to the Baptist who would refuse to baptize him, "Let it be so now, for so it becomes us to fulfill all justice" (Mt. 3, 15). And it is rather significant that Jesus wished to characterize His entire life by this "justice" rendered to God through the state of labor. Having been born among poor artisans, Jesus submitted to their condition and became a perfect observer of the Law in this, the "just one" par excellence. And He was servant to this justice through His death, desiring to sacrifice Himself totally to the "human condition." But it was with Him that was to rest the fulfillment of the Promise which was going to put an end to chastisement by bringing the conflict between Satan and man to a successful issue.

But Satan was lying in wait for this "man born of woman" to meet Him on the battlefield of perfect justice rendered to God, and it was his hope to surprise Him and crush Him.

---

9. We could call it an order in the midst of disorder, or again: a provisional state of things, but sanctioned by the divine will.

Who will ever know how the "just one" was tempted by Satan during those years when He came to fulfill His mission? We have an idea of how he tempted Him at its commencement during His retirement in the desert (Mt. 4, 1-11; Mk. 1, 12,13; Lk. 4, 1-13); afterwards in His death, that final combat of justice in which Jesus provoked Satan (Cf. John, chap. 8). Christ's agony, which is reported by all the evangelists including John, is proof of this. Far from simply expressing the weakness of a man, it speaks to us of the combat fought between the "Word" and His adversary. It speaks to us of God struggling for man against the prince of darkness. And as soon as the trouble disappears, as soon as the agony recedes, we already are assured of victory (12, 27,28).

In St. John the dawn of the glorification appears as early as the Supper, as early as Judas' departure, the instrument in Satan's hands. "Now is the Son of Man glorified" (13, 31), and from then on Jesus does not lose His majestic bearing or peace. On the other hand the Synoptics show us the combat and struggle continuing right to Gethsemani, until the last moments of Christ whose last words signifying the combat, "My God, my God, why hast thou forsaken me?" (Mt. 27, 46) are a prelude to victory: "It is finished" (19, 30), i.e., all has been fulfilled.

Jesus fought alone. Undoubtedly, as He said in Gethsemani, He could have been furnished by His Father with "more than twelve legions of angels" to repulse the adversary. However, He preferred to gain the victory with the strength of His soul alone united to His Father, with the strength of the soul of a man, just as formerly the first man Adam was vanquished; but it is a soul in which the superabundance of the Spirit, the Father's will, and the Word, His Son, are all one and the same omnipotent reality.

Such is the fulfillment of justice in God who is not an executioner, but a Father who comes Himself through love to deliver His lost children from their bonds. Human justice demands that expiation be equal to the offense, that it re-establish a certain equilibrium, erase and repair the damage caused. It pays blood with blood.

Although God was not obliged to buy our salvation with Christ's blood, Satan, whom He had to vanquish, had received permission to persecute Christ even to the total exhaustion of His human life offered in ransom for us. He had all power to tempt Him in His humanity, as the different temptations described in the Synoptics prove.

St. John says nothing of these temptations, but he does not conceal the trouble and anguish of Christ, external signs of His struggle against the one who can bruise Him but cannot enter into the sanctuary of His soul. Satan has no power over what belongs to God. Just like the hunter who misjudges the prey and sees it escape and must return empty-handed,

Satan fails. Having grasped at the bait offered him in Christ's humanity, so some of the Church Fathers express it, he was able to fatigue it and exhaust it to death. But Christ's death brings about Satan's defeat who remains prisoner of the divine Fisherman.

In fact, it is even to blood that Christ combats to deliver us. If one drop of this blood was sufficient for the expiation of our sins, divine love judges that the death of Christ is necessary so that we be not only justified but freed. Sacrifice and the fulfillment of justice extend to the entire life of Christ and this life comes to an end through the most difficult of sacrifices that can be asked of men, viz., a violent death.

Thus, Christ's blood is not only pardon poured forth upon all human crimes; it is the price, the only price Satan was finally to demand to consummate his hatred. But while allowing him to take all, Christ sent him away vanquished. "What you do, do quickly" (13, 27). Such is the "bloody" sacrifice offered by Christ to redeem us from our sins and such is our victory. St. John explains it at length in his first Epistle: "The son of God appeared that he might destroy the works of the devil..." (1 Jn. 3, 8).

The devil is powerless over one who abides in God as Jesus did. In Him there was no compromise with sin. Already Jesus had said: "Take courage, I have overcome the world" (16, 33). And John will later on say: "You are of God, dear children, and have overcome him, because greater is he that is in you than he who is in the world" (1 Jn. 4, 4).

Although the words of Genesis still stand and death continues to be the penalty for sin, yet it opens up a road upon which it is possible for men to discover once again friendship with God, and to enter into life even here on earth. "Amen, amen, I say to you, the hour is coming, and now is here, when the dead shall hear the voice of God, and those who hear shall live" (5, 25).

The "sense" of sin

Christ, the Lamb of God, was made "the victim of propitiation for our sins" (1 Jn. 2, 2; 4, 10) St. John tells us as also St. Paul (Rm. 3, 25). We cannot remove this reality from our personal sins, for it is placed in the very bosom of Christ's sacrifice.

This notion of sin is to be found on the most universal plane of human sentiments; but in Christ this notion is joined to one of the most mysterious characteristics of sin which escapes men, viz., the sense of sin.

"What is a man that thou shouldst magnify him? Or why dost thou set thy heart upon him? Thou visitest him early in the morning, and thou provest him suddenly. How long wilt thou not spare me, nor suffer me to swallow down my spittle? I have sinned. What shall I do to thee, O keeper of men? Why hast thou set me opposite to thee, and I am become burdensome to myself? Why dost thou not remove my sin, and why dost thou not take away my iniquity? Behold now I shall sleep in the dust; and if thou seek me in the morning, I shall not be" (Jb. 7, 17-21).

In truth, man is nothing "but a herb which withers away," and it seems to him also that his sin cannot diminish God's grandeur nor take away anything from Him. Many men believe themselves justified by the insignificance of their sin against the divine transcendence. On the other hand, does not Scripture itself in Job's discourse point out the poverty, the insufficiency, even the uselessness of reparation, since in the final analysis just and unjust are treated alike (Jb. 9, 22)? Finally man is not able to come up to the demand of purity God makes since "He finds fault even in the angels" (Jb. 4, 18).

And even the Cross does nothing else but emphasize even more man's ineptitude of matching his justice with that of God, since Another has suffered for him and taken his sins upon Himself. Man's misery appears even more profound when he is judged incapable even of bringing his tribute to the just reparation that had to be made. Had not the psalmist already said this? "Yet in no way can a man redeem himself, or pay his own ransom to God; too high is the price to redeem one's life" (Ps. 48, 8,9).

Why then does God even bother about such abjection and misery? And why does He raise it to the honor of a divine sacrifice? St. John answers this agonizing question: "God has first loved us" (1 Jn. 4, 19). More profound than his sin, there is in man a heart whose depths remain hidden from him, blinded as he is by his own weakness and misery.

It is true and false simultaneously that man is simply a being incapable of any good. We find throughout Scripture a continuous testimony of God's respect for His creature and the esteem He has for him in spite of everything. In fact, God's respect is one of the most moving and beautiful aspects of the sacred text. Whatever be his sin, God does not despise His creature and never treats him like a slave. If He pushes His creature aside, it is because He Himself has been rejected first. From the beginning He enters into contact with His creature, not as a Master only, but as a Father and Friend.

It is the blindness of our sins and the discouragement of our weakness that veil these realities. Outside of God we cannot experience love, we do not know that God loves us. But He never stops loving us and seeking His creature. His merciful designs are eternal. He never ceases desiring the creature. Christ's sacrifice, though it shows us the extent of our misery, gives us an estimate of the love God has for us and of what our soul is in His eyes when it is bathed in His brilliance.

"Create in me a pure heart, O God!" David begged, a heart capable of joy, truth, and love. What we had lost Christ's sacrifice restores a hundredfold. And the manner in which He does it confirms the respect and tenderness already poured forth in the Old Testament.

God could have extended pardon and reparation in an act that was less costly, while it remained an act of infinite grace. But the facility of this act would have revealed to us the divine omnipotence much more than the kindness of our Savior. That is why He desired to come into the very heart of our misery, to make Himself like us. "There is no beauty in him, nor comeliness. We have seen him, and there is no sightliness, that we should be desirous of him" (Is. 53, 2,3). "Behold the man!" (19, 5).

He came not to share our shame but to wipe it out; not to overcome us but to be overcome for our sakes and thus lift us up. If the ignominious death of the Cross was chosen by Him, it is because of this very ignominy that we become conscious of what our own really is. If He shed His blood for us, it is because we cannot even take the initiative of shedding our own without adding a sin to our sins, since our life does not belong to us, while His life belonged to Him.

Victim of Propitiation

As Victim of propitiation for our sins and Lamb of God, He renders to God the honor of His love which we have misunderstood. We sing: "Christ our Passover has been sacrificed" (1 Cor. 5, 7). And after this we too should immolate our own heart. "My sacrifice, O God, is a contrite spirit; a heart contrite and humbled, O God, you will not spurn" (Ps. 51, 19). And St. Paul has declared that Christ: ". . . who though he was by nature God, did not consider being equal to God a thing to be clung to, but emptied himself taking the nature of a slave and being made like unto men. And appearing in the form of a man, he humbled himself, becoming obedient, even to the death of the cross" (Phil. 2, 6-8).

John, in his own way, admirably expresses how Jesus changed things in order to come among us, how much He made Himself our own even to the point of espousing our cause with God as though He has ceased to look upon us as God but only as man, burdened with the obligation of defending us and pleading our case. "But if anyone sins, we have an Advocate with the Father, Jesus Christ, the just; and he is a propitiation for our sins, not for ours only but also for those of the whole world" (1 Jn. 2, 1-2).

Eucharist, fruit of sacrifice

At the moment when the Passover began Christ had desired to give the disciples, in the washing of the feet, an example of service which would be a true sacrifice performed out of love. In the very heart of the Passover He realizes another sacrifice of an incomparably superior value by instituting the Eucharist.

True, this sacrifice cannot be dissociated from the Cross, since the Eucharist is the fruit and the communication of it: "This is my body broken for you . . . This is my blood shed for you" (Lk. 22, 19-20). However, sacrifice takes on so permanent, essential, and characteristic a form that it deepens our understanding of the sacrifice of the Cross.

Even though John does not relate the institution of the Eucharist, it is not because of any indifference regarding this action, whose significance he understood better than anyone else. It is enough to re-read Chapter 6 of his Gospel to convince ourselves of this.

Here Jesus announces distinctly: ". . . and the bread that I will give is my flesh for the life of the world," and "Amen, amen, I say to you, unless you eat the flesh of the Son of Man, and drink his blood, you shall not have life in you." Further on He will say, "As the living Father has sent me, and as I live because of the Father, so he who eats me, the same will live because of me" (6, 51,53,57).

John has pointed out in advance the fecundity of this eminently oblative state to which Christ willed to reduce Himself in the Eucharist, and this in a permanent way and not only momentarily as on the Cross.

The life which the Host brings to us necessitates an eating on our part. Hence the sacrifice consented to on the Cross must not only be represented, but inscribed into the institution of the Eucharist, though under a sacramental and unbloody form.

Ordinarily speaking, a sacrifice fulfills its purpose when the death of the victim is effected. In giving one's life one gives everything and there remains no more to surrender. At the most this life that was sacrificed may still become a communion as it did in ancient sacrifices. And this even if it is not the will of the victim which is at the basis of this eating, but simply the will of the participants. And this eventuality being excluded when it is a question of a human victim, it is on the moral or spiritual level only that this prolongation must be sought and the fruits of the sacrifice gathered up.

However, these limitations which are imposed on men cannot be imposed on God. Thus, it is really that this flesh of Christ, become nourishment through His sacrifice, communicates life to those who nourish themselves upon it. It is then in all truth that this Eucharistic bread is called a "living bread."

When Jesus speaks the words, "This is my body," He is not satisfied with making His body really present and giving it to us in food, as the fruit of His sacrifice, but it is Himself as a gift and as sacrificial offering who comes to us.

The Eucharist is Christ, but Christ as testament of love, i.e., He is not content with giving, nor even "giving Himself," but through this gift He renders us capable of becoming rich. During His final hours, Christ taught His disciples how to enrich themselves with the divine life, enriched both in living it and in communicating it.

Whereas in the evening of their lives men bring their work to perfection in order that it will outlive them, Jesus withdraws from His, casts it from Him, objectivizes it. This work is nothing else but Himself; it is Himself as gift and fruit of His sacrifice of love which He is about to offer up on the Cross in a few more hours. He makes a gift of Himself to His Father and also to those for whom He is making this sacrifice. He does even more: when delivering up this work, He makes it capable of being eaten, assimilated, and thus lived.

He is not satisfied with sacrificing Himself; He goes to the very end, to the very end of what He can give of Himself. Within the gift He makes of Himself, He still remains a gift. Within His sacrificed life, Jesus remains life given, in a total dedication to those who will receive Him, and in a singular fore-knowledge of the difficulties they will encounter on the road.

When coming into other humanities to whom He will give Himself through the centuries, He will continue His oblation and His sacrifice; and He will do this either by making of them "humanities in which He renews His entire mystery"[10] or He will come to take away the sins of these weak and guilty humanities. The action of the one who passes from this world to His Father continues in His children. "Do this in memory of me." He throws Himself into their hands.

On the morrow He will admit that those who lay hold of Him, lead Him as prisoner before Pilate, make Him climb Golgotha, nail Him to the Cross, these have power over Him. In the Eucharist too, in a certain way, He gives Himself over with a certain voluntary and infinitely loving abandonment to those who receive Him. He grafts His life upon other lives. Invisibly but really, His life is lived in theirs.

The soldiers and the high priests will believe they have finished with the Crucified on Calvary when at the end of His bloody sacrifice He expires. But Jesus escapes their hands, not only through His resurrection,

10. Elizabeth of the Trinity.

but also in the Eucharist where He lives forever in His children, and in His Church which He founded in His blood. He escapes them because the chalice of His blood which they are about to pour out is already filled and will be filled until the end of time, and already those sacred words have been pronounced over it: "This is my blood . . . do this in memory of me." He escapes them because all of us henceforth "partake of this same bread," "though many, we are one body" (1 Cor. 10, 17).

This Man of apparently modest origin and without carnal descendants and whose name his executioners and enemies thought they had wiped out forever becomes in reality, through His sacrifice, the Father of a multitude to whom He transmits His life. "The bread that I will give is my flesh for the life of the world. He who eats this bread will live forever" (6, 51,58).

Never was the fruitfulness of a sacrifice as boundless in space and time. Is it not because never before was a sacrifice so thorough, so total, so perpetually in act? And is it not also because no other sacrifice was as purely a sacrifice of love as this one? Love is fruitful by nature. Hence, why should we be astonished that the greatest act of love, and of divine love, bears until the end of time innumerable fruits and is of infinite value?

The Passover, sacrifice of divine love

The Passover reveals itself, then, as a sacrifice of love. But this sacrifice is no longer the immolation of a substitute victim; it is the sacrifice of divine love itself in the Person of the Lamb of God. If the Cross reveals "the greatest love" to us (15, 13), Christ desires that men discover in all the various forms of service, of humility, renunciation, gift of self, just so many sacrifices which, according to His example and in union with Him, will allow Love to live and be communicated.

In union with Him. In fact, if love entails sacrifice, it no less necessarily demands union. The one who loves longs to sacrifice himself, but he desires even more union with the one he loves.

The ancient paschal lamb created a bond among the guests while uniting them all to Yahweh. How much more will a union be effected between God and all those who will nourish themselves on the Lamb of God, sacrificed on Mount Calvary!

CHAPTER 16

THE MEANING OF UNION

The new Passover, revealing divine love to us in oblation and sacrifice, reveals it to us under the form of union. It assumes and perfects the ancient Passover which, when renewing Yahweh's Covenant with His people, gathered them together in the remembrance of God the Savior's merciful gifts.

Love demands union

Terms can undergo change, and the New Testament calls "union" what the Old Testament preferred to call "Covenant"; but the profound reality remains the same. Moreover, the Covenant of God with His people formed the condition of that more intimate union destined to be realized between each soul and Christ. After having been incarnated in the bosom of the people of the Covenant, Christ longs to be born in those whom He has acquired with His Cross (Acts, 20, 28), and who make up the people of the new Covenant in His blood (1 Cor. 11, 25).

This union had been foreshadowed in ancient times even on the spiritual level and it was sung of in beautiful terms. And yet as ardent as were these aspirations they could make up only an approach to the great mystery. The Canticle of Canticles itself, which sings of the union of love between God and the Church in such an admirable way, between God and each soul, had to wait until it was bathed in the rays of Christ's love to reveal the real meaning of this union, its boundless fecundity and supernatural beauty.

With the Last Supper and its testament of love, everything is accomplished; realities, till then unknown, are brought to light, especially that "new commandment" which imposes on men the obligation of "loving one another as Christ has loved them" (13, 34).

Christ's love is always a revelation whether it is directed towards His Father or towards men, His brothers. Is it not divine Love itself? And we would not be able to transmit such love ourselves if we were not vitally united to Christ first. Union with our brothers in fraternal charity as well as union with God cannot be realized unless we are first united to Christ. Such is the revelation of the last Passover in which Christ, desiring to convince us that the commandment of love is "unique," does not cease joining and intermingling the themes of our union with God and with one another. Thus the commandment of "loving one another" (13, 34) precedes the invitation Christ extends to us of uniting ourselves to Him: "You in me and I in you," but it accompanies it: "Love one another as I have loved you" and follows it: "These things I command you, that you love one another" (15, 4,12,17). The same overlapping is evident in the actions revealing fraternal charity and those marking our union with God: the washing of the feet and the institution of the Eucharist.

Before such an intermingling of such rich and intimately united elements, it is not surprising that the light is a little late in showing itself. It is extremely important that everything end up in union and that there appear through Christ's actions and words that central revelation which the discourse after the Supper hides a unity of unheard-of richness. If we need not fear introducing some clarity into the text, it would be unnecessary however to substitute a logical order for this living richness which would only disfigure the divine message. The essential thing is never to lose sight of the fact that the two component elements of love, manifesting richness, testify even more to its unity.

The components of love

If we consider the two aspects charity must take on, viz., love of neighbor which entails fraternal charity and union among all those who are children of God, and love of God which brings about our union with Him, it appears that love of God holds the first place. Moreover, when inviting us to "abide in Him" as "He abides in us" (15, 5), Christ makes it clear that without union with Him love of the neighbor is impossible. "Without me you can do nothing" He will tell His apostles immediately after inviting them to abide in Him.

Before passing around the cup of charity, we must first drink it ourselves. Before communicating a love which is supernatural by definition to our brothers, we must first seek it at its source, Christ. We would naturally expect then that Christ's words and actions would set union with Himself in the first place, and afterwards love and fraternal union with our brothers in the second place and as a consequence of the first. And yet this is not what Christ did. With reference to His actions, first He performed the action of honor and devotion, the deed of service and humility which is what the washing of the feet was (13, 2-17). It is also at the commencement of the discourse after the Supper, even before proposing the similitude of the "vine and the branches," that He commands His disciples to "love one another." It is good to ask why Christ followed this order.

Union with Christ and fraternal charity

Christ placed the love He came to reveal to men on a realistic plane: total dedication which protects His followers from all illusion. Supernatural love is not a feeling but an act. Undoubtedly in God, who is "actus purus," acts are not necessary in order that love be fully "in act." But the same does not hold for us here on earth. Idealism and sentimentality have entered into the concept of love which is no longer based on total dedication.

"My dear children, let us not love in word, neither with the tongue, but in deed and in truth" (1 Jn. 3, 18). These words are the results of the apostle's own experience and his Epistle is insistent on the necessity of action. Besides, would we ourselves have "known Love" if Christ had not given His life "in one supreme act of love" (1 Jn. 3, 16)? John will write: "He who has the goods of this world and sees his brother in need and closes his heart to him, how does the love of God abide in him?" (1 Jn. 3, 17). He echoes St. James here for whom faith (love, for St. John) is dead without good works (Jas. 2, 17).

Christ's own life is lived out in this way. And the washing of the feet as well as the institution of the Eucharist is only a further reminder of this to the apostles. If Christ had said to them "I in you and you in me" (15, 5) without first having shown them in His own actions that only the surrender of our being in our brothers' service can realize union; if He had not begun by setting before them His own sacrifice as well as the many acts of devotedness in the service of others with which His life was filled, the apostles would have been exposed to the danger of being in the same frame of mind as the three companions on Thabor: "Lord, it is good for us to be here, let us make three tents . . ."(Mt. 17, 4).

11 ST. JOHN

But when asking them to love "one another as I have loved you" (13, 34), Jesus had given them to understand that His own love had to take on the form of fraternal charity if it was to be made manifest; without this, as divine as it was, it would not have been revealed to them. If Christ had not given Himself to men in the sacrifice on the Cross and in the Eucharist, His love would not have ended in union.

We can say then that if the apostles were led to "desire with a great desire" to participate in this union which the Master proposed to them, it is because His love had struck them by the ardor, purity, and delicacy of fraternal charity with which He constantly treated them.

All other practical ways of revealing divine charity to them would have run the risk of leaving the apostles an illusion, but would also have not given them a true notion of divine love such as it is in God and such as the union of the three divine Persons realizes among themselves.

I. UNION WITH CHRIST

In His last interview with His apostles Christ introduces the idea of union in the most natural manner. He was on the eve of His departure, already predicted on several occasions, and this was to be a farewell meal. The separation which hangs like a cloud over this final reunion is felt by all, for the love uniting Jesus and the apostles is true and profound. It gave rise in the Master to the showing of a real tenderness towards those whom He was about to leave. "My little children" was His mode of address after Judas went out into the night.

His kindness towards them and the words He speaks all serve to tie the bonds between Him and them even tighter. The apostles actually feel how much He loves them, for the Master has just given them unmistakable proofs of this love. Was He not only a few moments before on His knees washing their feet and was He not ready to give His life for them? How then could the prediction of His impending departure be otherwise than cruelly felt? How could they not be in such a state of anguish? He had repeated over and over again that He was about to leave them, but they don't want to believe what they fear and they convince themselves that such a thing will not take place. And in Jesus' case, since He had manifested such astonishing power on so many occasions, could they not hope that He would do so again?

Knowing they had such feelings within them, He had to state again and even more forcefully that the hour has come and He was about to leave them. But seeing them so upset and so helpless, He tempers His words with a special note of tenderness. "Little children, yet a little while and I am with you. You will seek me, and, as I said to the Jews, 'Where I go you cannot come,' so to you also I say it now" (13, 33).

What follows shows how troubled the apostles really were and how difficult it was for Jesus to convince them of His departure and to strengthen and console them.

At the announcement of this separation, the impetuous Peter expresses the feelings of his companions: "Lord, where art thou going?" Despite the Master's answer, "Where I am going, thou canst not follow me," he insists "Why can I not follow thee now? I will lay down my life for thee" (13, 36,37). He draws upon himself that answer which fills him with pain and bitter confusion: "Wilt thou lay down thy life for me? Amen, amen, I say to thee, the cock will not crow before thou dost deny me thrice" (14, 1-3).

This anwer was far from lessening their anguish, and Jesus had to console His disciples again: "Let not your heart be troubled . . .I go to prepare a place for you. And if I go and prepare a place for you, I am coming again, and I will take you to myself. . . ." This time Thomas inquires, "Lord, we do not know where thou art going, and how can we know the way?" If he is resigned to the coming departure, he will not settle for a long separation. And Philip asks: "Lord, show us the Father and it is enough for us" (14, 1-8).

Thus begun, the interview is about to be directed towards its essential object, viz., union with Christ to be realized and kept and intensified. This is not done, however, until assurances are given that this separation will not last. It is true He is leaving them, but they can ask the Father anything in His name and they will obtain it. He will send them the Paraclete and will not leave them orphans. He Himself will come back to them, and He will see them soon, and if they remain attached faithfully to Him, "the Father and I will come and make our abode with them" (14, 14,19,23,28).

For the last time He repeats as to those lost in their anguish and not concentrating on what is being said: "You have heard me say to you, 'I go away and I am coming to you.' " And then He speaks those reproachful words to draw them out of a sadness in which they are so immersed that they are thinking only of themselves: "If you loved me you would rejoice that I am going to the Father . . ." (14, 28).

Why did John dwell so long on these parting words if not because he felt this coming separation more than anyone else? And again, because through the centuries union will have as its purpose the aiding of Christ's friends to enjoy His presence and to abide in His love. If our faith is "the victory that overcomes the world," then our union with Christ is what surmounts this separation (1 Jn. 5, 4) .

Love as the principle of union

This union which corresponds with the thirst of the apostles not to be separated from the Master as well as His ardent desire to "abide" with them, does not simply make up the object of the last interview; it is also going to be effectively realized. Where men are capable only of using superficial means of doing away with separation and forgetfulness, Christ, because He is God and Man, realizes or brings about union between Himself and those whom He loves, and this union is "in God" and "in man" simultaneously. In God, because it is a real, divinizing and transforming union. In man, because it is effected with this Jesus whom the apostles have known and loved; with a Person who still retains for them His name, physical appearance, and personal love; with one who, having shared their human nature and lived among them, manifests to them both a human love as man and a divine love as God.

Never does the Incarnation lose its claims in all Christ's actions on earth. But here more than elsewhere, this mystery is about to develop its full consequences. Union with God which Christ has come to effect among men will be realized through Him and in Him or it will not be realized at all.[1] Even before we have made an attempt to discover the nature of this union, the "Person" of him who procures it for us has already set us upon the way; and the action through which Christ realizes it, when giving His apostles the power to nourish themselves on His flesh and blood, brings us light.

The Eucharist and union

It is certainly not the apostle of the Word made flesh, the evangelist of the discourse on the "bread of life," who would ever forget the degree to which the flesh and blood of Christ are to be instruments of His union with us. "Unless you eat the flesh of the Son of Man, you will not have life in you." ". . . he who eats me, the same also shall live because of me" (6, 52,57). It will be a personal bond in which His humanity is united to us as really as His divinity.

---

1. This does not mean that men will not be able to come to a union with God even when they are ignorant of Christ, but only that it is through Christ that they will pass to go to God, even when they do not know Him.

Besides, the words taken up again by Christ in the discourse after the Supper and which express this union with Him in the most formal way, "You in me and I in you" (15, 4), appear exactly in this way in the announcement of the Eucharist: "He who eats my flesh and drinks my blood abides in me and I in him" (6, 56).

And Jesus gives immediately afterwards this precise statement which is so expressive of the nature of the union realized: "As the living Father has sent me and as I live because of the Father, so he who eats me, he also shall live because of me" (6, 57).

"To live because of God," of the very life with which "the Son lives because of the Father," this is what union with Christ's blood and flesh is destined to procure for us.

Thus, the Eucharist unites our flesh, blood, and soul with Christ's. It unites us in a personal way with the one who received His human nature from the Virgin Mary and who on Holy Thusday night gave Himself to His apostles. And at the same time the Eucharist unites us to the Word substantially present and gives us the power to share, in and through Him, in the divine life, just as the Word lives because of the Father in a union of inexpressible love.

Through the Eucharist is realized this union, the depth of which Christ is now about to elucidate; it is a union which was going to accomplish humanity's desire from the beginning in a way that is as wonderful as it was unforeseeable.

Man's most profound desire has been to be united with God. At the epoch in which John is writing, this desire of union was being presented especially under the form of pantheism: The world was considered as being "in" God since it had God as its cause. As origin of all things, God contains them all in Himself. Besides, the divine Logos, the spirit of God, is shared by the spirit of man. The latter is therefore "filled with God." This pantheism, quite common in the Hellenistic localities in which John was moving at the time, did not exclude a belief of an authentically religious nature and mystical signification which was at the basis of a communion of man with God by means of the universe. Entering into communion with the universe, man enters into communion with its Author. This communion with God through nature generated certain mystical states, which the Greek expression "enthousiasmos" best expressed. In this expression is found the root "theos." The one who is "in God," "en theo," or rather whom God possesses, enters into ecstasy like the prophets or into a state of sacred furor like the followers of Dionysus. However, this expression never meant anything more than a transitory state and the result flowing from it relating to the divinity remains extremely vague and indefinite.

"Abide in my love"

It is much different when we consider Christ's words to the apostles. "You in me and I in you" (14, 20), or "abide in me and I in you."[2] In fact, on the lips of Christ this word "in" takes on a meaning and expresses a reality that is entirely new, and we should try to fathom its meaning since our life of union with God rests upon it.

If the Eucharist appears as a privileged form of this union, the humanity of Christ being present along with His divinity, other forms of union are brought forth in the fourth Gospel. Nothing, for example, permits us to think that the similitude of the "vine and the branches" has meaning only with reference to the Eucharist. When Jesus declares: "I am the vine and you are the branches. He who abides in me, and I in him, bears much fruit . . ." (15, 5), He is not directing His words to the Eucharist, but also to the truth that the Christian is intimately united to Him through sanctifying grace. The same must be said of expressions like: "Abide in my love" (15, 9,10). It is likewise the case when Christ, promising His disciples not to leave them orphans and telling them He will come back to them, says: "In that day you will know that the Father is in me, and you in me, and I in you" (14, 20).

The Johannine Gospel has also expressions which, at first sight, could appear very close to those we have been examining. Thus, "I will ask the Father and He will give you another Paraclete to be with you forever."[3] The difference is certain between "come to," "abide with," and "be" or "abide in," as we see in these words of the discourse after the Supper: "If anyone love me, he will keep my word, and my Father will love him, and we will come to him and make our abode with him." Evidently there is here a progression, for "to make our abode with" means more than "to come to."

That is why, when Christ repeatedly states: "You in me and I in you" (14, 20), or "Abide in me as I in you" (15, 4), He is expressing by these statements the most profound union that can be realized, and this

---

2. Cf. 6, 56; 14, 20; 15, 4; 15, 5,6,7,8,10; 17, 21,23,26. To grasp the meaning of this expression it is necessary to quote here all those which aim at union with God in the Johannine Gospel. A privileged form is given by Christ with reference to union with His body and blood: "Unless you eat the flesh of the Son of man and drink his blood, you shall not have life in you" (6, 53). "He who eats my flesh and drinks my blood abides in me and I in him" (6, 56). "I am the vine and you are the branches; he who abides in me as I in him bears much fruit . . ." (15, 5). However, union is not necessarily confined to the Eucharist. "In that day you will know that I am in the Father, and you in me, and I in you" (14, 20). Christ says the apostles must abide "in his love" (15, 9,10) so that his words abide in them (15, 7). We then proceed to that other use of the word "in," linked to the verb believe as "believe in" (1, 12), (12, 44), or "to adore in spirit and in truth" (4, 24).

3. In his Epistle John wrote: "And he who keeps his commandments abides in God, and God in him. And in this we know that he abides in us by the Spirit whom he has given us" (1 Jn. 3, 24). Cf. also: 1 Jn. 2, 27,28. The same Paraclete who abides with us (Gospel) abides in us (Epistle).

is all the more convincing since He compares it to the union existing between Himself and His Father.

Besides, if we consider what the Bible and especially the Johannine
Gospel would have us understand by the term "know" and its equivalents:
"welcome," "receive," etc., we realize it has reference to a knowledge of
love, accompanied by an experience which already supposes the object
known interior to the one knowing. When knowing us, God is totally
interior to us, He is "in us" much more intimately than we are in ourselves. But can we say that our "knowledge" of God gives us the power
of being in Him? The entire Johannine Gospel lets it be clearly understood
that this is precisely what the virtue of faith is. Through faith we know
God and we are in Him, through a movement which is the fruit of faith
and love in us. Faith, like love, makes us interior to the object of our faith
or our love; it is one and the same thing in John's mind. To believe, be
known, and know, to love and be loved, to abide in Him and He in us, all
these are realities linked one to the other.

But since it is not possible to love without knowing, faith is the condition of our abiding "in" Jesus and of Jesus abiding "in" us: "You
believe in God, believe also in me" (14, 1), He says to the apostles at
the beginning of the discourse after the Supper, wishing to teach that
faith is the root of this mutual indwelling.[4]

We understand then that the one who is the "author and finisher of
our faith . . ." (Heb. 12, 2), and who declares: "I am the way, the truth,
and the life. No one comes to the Father but through me. If you had
known me, you would also have known my Father. And henceforth you
do know him and you have seen him" (14, 6,7), is likewise the only one
in whom and through whom the union of love with God is realized.

Mediator on the plane of faith as on the plane of knowledge, Christ is
mediator necessarily on the plane of love and union. We must then be
in Him and "abide" in Him. But what does this mysterious word really
mean? We shall have an idea of its meaning when we examine the
Johannine text with great attention.

The demand of a reciprocity in love

There are two dangers to be avoided: (1) to remain on a material
plane where there is question of spiritual realities; (2) to wish to attribute
such a learned meaning to this expression, that the greater majority of
Christians will not be able to attain it. We must remain on the level of
simple notions without forgetting that: "But the hour is coming, and is

4. As it is the principle of their birth to the supernatural life and their status as children of God.

now here, when the true worshippers will worship the Father in spirit and in truth" (4, 23).

Although the word "in," drawn from the vocabulary pertaining to the senses, suggests an idea of "place," we must not evidently represent God in us in a local sense, the one containing the other. The fact of saying successively, "You in me" and "I in you" renders all mental representation impossible. Does this mean that for evoking "interiority," the word "in" does not retain anything of a material significance? It would be imprudent to deprive oneself of such an aid, especially when we remember that Christ did not hesitate, when instituting the Eucharist in which He becomes our nourishment, to strengthen the impression that He came "into" us. "He who eats my flesh and drinks my blood abides in me and I in him" (6, 56). But this expression which suggests a localization goes beyond it at the same time. "It is the spirit that gives life . . ." (6, 63).

The expressions will be more revealing which use the word "in" with reference to light, truth, or even faith, for these expressions give us to understand that there is question of movement, progression, life. The idea of interiority has no meaning when it is a question of spiritual realities unless it gives rise to the idea of a mutual penetration through a knowledge of love which deepens continually and through a life which becomes ever more "intimate."

The idea of reciprocity has this that is special about it, viz., that it is an absolute need when it is a question of love between two spiritual substances. Materially speaking, two objects cannot be interior in relation to one another. But reciprocity and mutual indwelling are necessities between spiritual substances of like perfection.

That Christ can say: "I in you and you in me" (15, 4) proves that we are dealing with a spiritual reality; but the equality in the reciprocity which this statement manifests demands likewise that His love has raised us previously through grace to this equality.

It would be contradictory that Christ invite us to this union of love and not give us the means of rendering it true. But without this reciprocity there is no true love.

We often have an inexact idea of the love of charity. We imagine it is not pure and perfect except in constantly giving, without ever receiving. But a "one-way" love would not be a fully perfected love. It is enough to consider love at its source and in its perfection, viz., in the Trinity, in order to convince ourselves of the above statement. In the bosom of the Trinity, love is perfectly reciprocal and it is impossible to talk about any kind of anteriority, for from all eternity the Father and the Son love one another with a mutual love.

Undoubtedly when we pass from the Trinity to the love Christ has for us, we do find ourselves in the presence of an absolute anteriority of divine love. "God has first loved us" (1 Jn. 4, 19) and this "even when we were sinners" (Rm. 5, 8). Why did God love us? Was it simply in virtue of a diffusive power of love which could not help pouring itself out? Undoubtedly this is so, but it was not only to give free course to "His" love that God loves man; it is also and mainly to render him capable of loving in return.

God loves man in order that love become in man what it is already in God; a possibility of giving love and not only of receiving it. It is on this condition that love can "live" and "breathe." Christ has said: "Without me you can do nothing" (15, 5), and the apostle: "What have you that you have not received?" (1 Cor. 4, 7). But it is precisely because the love diffused into our hearts by God has been diffused through the Holy Spirit, i.e., by the same Person who is this living reciprocity of love in the bosom of the Trinity that we have become capable of a love of reciprocity with God. If God loves Himself in us, He can then be loved by us as He loves Himself in the bosom of the Trinity. It is through grace alone that we are placed in this circuit of love, but, since we are in it, it is necessary that love have the same characteristics in us as it has in God, for it is His own love.

St. John teaches us not only that man can give God a "return" of love, but that he must do so: "Let us therefore love, because God has first loved us" (1 Jn. 4, 19). It seems that this return of love is not a simple "rebound" as the ball bouncing on the ground tends to return to its point of departure. Our will must be taken up with the love God has placed in us, and there is room in this return of love for all the efforts of fidelity, attention, and desire of which we are capable. If this is not true, then what is St. James' meaning in the statement: "Draw near to God and he will draw near to you" (Jas. 4, 8); and in Christ's words: "If anyone love me he will keep my words and my Father will love him and we will come to him and make our abode with him" (14, 23)? Although divine love is a free gift and it is "first," it must, as soon as it is placed in our hearts, find an activity in them which is grasped by it and turns this love towards God. That is the reason there is place for the free love of God and for the efforts we must make to welcome it and return it to its Author.

Christ has told us how this love is to be returned. "If you love me, keep my commandments" (14, 15). Fidelity to the commandments seems to be the condition of love and the proof that this love is living in us. Whatever be the necessity of our having received love from God in order to love Him in return, it still remains true that the words of Christ: "He who has my commandments and keeps them, he it is who loves me. But he who loves me will be loved by my Father, and I will love him and manifest myself to him" (14, 21) underscore what we "give" to God. The words of the Apocalypse: "Behold I stand at the door and knock. If any man listens to my voice and opens the door to me, I will come in to him and will sup with him, and he with me" (Ap. 3, 20) enable us to understand in what this gift consists. It is a question of an overture and a welcome and these are active. "To those who received him he gave the power of becoming the children of God" (1, 12). And it is in this same sense that we are able to respond to the invitation Christ extends to us of "abiding" in Him as He abides in us.

The vine and the branches

Reciprocity is one of love's demands, but when we are dealing with the love of God and ourselves it is necessarily going to be of a special nature. On the one hand, it seems that we are reduced to the state of returning what we have received; on the other, it appears that we must also personally and actually give something which is "ourselves" if this union is to be really accomplished. The similitude of the "vine and the branches" elucidates the nature of this reciprocity and the form it must adopt.

The first idea introduced by the similitude: "I am the vine and you are the branches. He who abides in me and I in him bears much fruit . . ." (15, 5) is that of such an intimate union that it is better to speak of a vital unity. However, the fact that we are the branches and Christ is the vine does not permit the following statement to be reduced to a simple equivalence: "He who abides in me and I in him. . . ." If the branch is "in the vine" and subsists because of it, the reciprocity is not absolutely valid. It is the branch that is grafted on the vine and not vice versa. The vine exists first, and it is from it the branches spring, and it is also in it that they are united one to the other. The vine is and remains unique. The relationship of the branches to the vine is a vital and necessary one. A vine may be the bearer of more or less branches without its existence being in any way affected. It is even deprived of them in the winter time, and its development in the spring is unimpaired. "For as the Father has life in himself, even so he has given the Son to have life in himself" (5, 26) because each possesses life as proper to Himself. In a word, the branch cannot live unless it is attached to the vine. Separated from it "it can do nothing" (15, 5). If the branch does not abide "in" the vine, "it withers, and they shall gather them up and cast them into the fire, and they shall burn" (15, 6).

However, the vine itself is also "in the branches" through the sap which circulates through them and without which they will bear "no fruit" (15, 4). Also, in order to allow them to ripen, it is necessary that the branch "abide" in the vine.

The action of the vine is of the "vital order." Not only is it from the vine that the branches spring, but their fruitfulness comes from the fact that the vine never ceases imparting its life to them. The life of the branches and the fruits they bear come from the vine. They are in the state of continual dependence for life from the vine. This dependence does not exclude an active role on the part of these same branches.

In fact, though the sap comes from the vine, it is the branches that bear the fruit and not the vine; and the vine is not truly entire unless it bear many branches. Far from exhausting the vine, the branches make it more vigorous. If everything comes from and depends upon the vine, there is room however for a reciprocity which leaves to each its individual role: life-giving for Christ, a dependence upon Him for us.

If we wish to understand in what this mutual indwelling consists which Christ's words express: "I in you and you in me" (14, 20), we must set the image of the vine side by side with Christ's words on the bread of life. The bread of life is called the "living bread" by Christ (6, 51) and this helps us grasp the truth that this bread does not only bring life to the one receiving it, but it sustains and develops its own life in the recipient because it possesses life in itself. "It is no longer I that live, but Christ lives in me" (Gal. 2, 20) writes St. Paul, and John recalls Christ's statement: "He who eats me the same also shall live because of me" (6, 57). Thus, the soul can bear supernatural fruits, just as the fruits of the branches are referred to the vine and bear testimony of its nature. In either case, the divine indwelling is not static but dynamic, efficient, and transforming.

Union, the principle of filial life

However, this efficiency is not the only aspect under which this union with Christ is to be considered. It is not even the most important. If it is true that Christ repeatedly insists that union with Him is necessary in order to produce fruit, it is likewise true that the union can and must be considered in itself without prejudice to the fruit resulting from it. Union of the soul with Christ is the source of this life about which the Prologue speaks: "To those who received him he gave the power of becoming the sons of God . . ." (1, 12). When Christ states, "I in you," He has this life in mind which is communicated to the "children of God." The "I in you" makes it possible for them to live this filial life, and it is on this plane that this reciprocity in love is to be sought. In fact, to say "child" is to say "Father." These bonds thus created are necessarily mutual. The fruits are the consequences of Christ's presence and action in us; but the filial life is the very reality of grace which He communicates to us when giving Himself to us. Now this filial life, this truth that, born of Christ, we are sons in the Son and by this fact children of the Father in heaven, enables us to understand that we are "in Him" and also "in His Father" who is likewise "our Father." The Son is "in the bosom of the Father," we also are "in Christo," and Christ is "in sinu Patris," "in the Father's bosom." This "life in God" is not only at the basis of our own life; it is also its exigency and term, in this sense that if God carries us in Himself in His love, we are called upon to refer everything back to God in whom we find our subsistence and our life. The child goes to his Father who is the divine, living, and nourishing milieu of which the child is in absolute need. The "You in me" is not only a return of love on our part, it is also a vital necessity.

It is extremely comforting that Christ gives us the assurance that His love draws Him to us and makes of Him the "living bread" which comes to us. But this truth is in conformity with the truth that divine love is self-diffusive. Omnipotence at the service of merciful love suffers no ill effects from "being in us." But the "you in me" is something else entirely. For this to be realized it is necessary that Christ give us the power of loving in our turn, and that we ourselves set about making this a reality. Thus He repeats: "Abide in my love" (15, 9). When we "abide" in His love, we allow divine love to live in us and to bear fruit. Only the branch vitally united to the vine and "remaining" attached to it is capable of bringing the fruit it bears to maturity. And he alone who "abides" in Christ can hope to see this union of love with Him brought to fulfillment.

We understand this all the better when we consider that reciprocity is an essential characteristic of love and that Christ has compared our union with Him to the union existing between Him and His Father.

"I in them, Father, and thou in me"

Between the Father and the Son there is no question of seeking "fruits" in the sense that we employ the word. In other words, it is quite evident that with regard to them we have the most perfect mutual indwelling and reciprocity. "Do you not believe that I am in the Father and the Father is in me" (14, 10)? "Whatever is mine is thine and whatever is thine is mine" (17, 10). Here the essential thing of the union is not fruits as such, but this mutual indwelling, this reciprocity in love. Now, John seems to compare our union with Christ to Christ's union with His Father. If this is really so, reciprocity in love and mutual indwelling which are essential in God would have to be found likewise in us.

This relationship established by Christ, on the one hand between the Father and the Son, and on the other between the Son and us is substantiated by several statements which uphold one another: "If you keep my commandments, you will abide in my love, as I also have kept my Father's commandments, and abide in his love" (15, 10). The love with which the Father loves the Son is also the same love with which we are loved: "As the Father has loved me, I also have loved you" (15, 9). "And I have made known to them thy name, and will make it known, in order that the love with which thou hast loved me may be in them" (17, 26).

Thus, the expression "I in you and you in me" draws its meaning from the relationship which Christ formally established between our union with Him and the union He Himself has with His Father. "But if I do perform them, and if you are not willing to believe me, believe the works, that you may know and believe that the Father is in me and I in the Father" (10, 38). Just as the Son is in the Father and the Father in the Son, so also the Christian is called upon to live in Christ and Christ in him.

If Christ employs expressions of the same nature to designate on the one hand His immanence in the Christian and vice versa: "I in you, and you in me" (14, 20), and on the other, the Father's immanence in the Son and the Son's in the Father: ". . . that the Father is in me and I in the Father" (10, 38), it is because a comparison can be drawn between them, as is evident in the following passages: "I and the Father are one" (10, 30).". . . that all may be one, even as thou, Father, in me and I in thee; that they may be one in us . . ." (17, 26).

The secret of this comparison or likeness is to be found in the concluding words of the discourse after the Supper: "And I have made known to them thy name, and will make it known, in order that the love with which thou hast loved me may be in them, and I in them" (17, 26).

It is then love, this same divine love which unites the Father and the Son, which is the principle of our union with Christ, and also—as we shall see—of our unity with our brothers. It is uncreated Love itself, which is in us the principle of the realization of the most intimate love which can be conceived between God and His creature, and among all the children of God.

The mutual complacence of love

When inviting us to consider our union with Him in the light of His union with the Father, Christ invites us likewise to confer upon it a characteristic which is repeatedly insisted upon by the Gospel: mutual complacence. The Father's love for His Son and the Son's for His Father appears to be marked with this trait: "This is my beloved Son in whom I am well pleased" (Mt. 3, 17; 17, 5). The Father says this twice, viz., at the Baptism and the Transfiguration when identifying His Son, and the latter states: "I do always the things that are pleasing to him" (8, 29). And to His apostles He reveals His happiness at being reunited with His Father.

Mutual satisfaction and reciprocity are the essential traits of love. Without them, there can be no perfect love. The Canticle of Canticles already intimates this, and to the Bridegroom's admiration for the bride: "Behold thou art fair, O my love," there is that corresponding cry of admiration: "Behold thou art fair, my beloved, and comely" (Cant. 1, 15,16).

We can understand this complacence when it is a question of the creature's remaining in loving and transforming contemplation of God; but how can this be in God as far as we are concerned when we are but misery and sin? It is this complacence that is pointed out in the Johannine Gospel. All through the Gospel text we see how much God desires a return of His creature's love, and that union be marked with the sign of reciprocal love. When Christ reveals "God has so loved the world as to give his only-begotten Son . . ." (3, 16), He is not only setting before us divine mercy, but pointing out the pleasure God takes in the work of His hands. As sinful and soiled as we are, we still remain His children; and God cannot be resigned to the fact that His children are not the object of His love. Even though it would be necessary for Him to deliver up His Son to the death of the Cross, the Father will have no rest till His creature be returned as the object of His grace and complacence, that the guilty and pardoned spouse be loved again because of the beauty with which the divine Bridegroom has adorned her.

We shall never be able to say often enough that divine love, because it is the perfection of love, knows not how to limit itself to an attitude of condescendent generosity, to a love willing to give but not desirous of a response. On the contrary, God wants men to realize the degree to which divine love desires to develop into a mutual complacence. When inviting us "to abide" in Him, Christ brings to light this complacence which is accompanied by admiration, rest, and joy; that "look" which is never finished resting upon the beloved object whose perfection eternity itself will never exhaust but rather always reveal more.

The Spirit sent into us by Christ has our purification and transformation as His main role; He is to infuse divine love into us so that the Father, looking upon His child, may find in him His Son. For the Spirit is to transform us into His image and His living love. God then takes His delights in His creature. Ezechiel has already sung of this when He has Yahweh say to Israel His spouse: "And thy renown went forth among the nations for thy beauty; for thou wast perfect through the beauty I had put upon thee, said the Lord God" (Ez. 16, 14).

John the Baptist contemplated this beauty when he said: "He who has the bride is the bridegroom; but the friend of the bridegroom, who stands and hears his voice, rejoices exceedingly at the voice of the bridegroom. This my joy, therefore, is made full" (3, 29). It is of the bride John sings in his Apocalypse when referring to her beauty, coming not from what she has in herself but from the presence of God's glory in her: "And she has been permitted to clothe herself in fine linen, shining bright . . ." (Ap. 21, 23).

The mystics alone have been able to understand that divine love and union, its fruit, are the cause of this complacence. It is not only man who "abides in God," but God who "abides in man" (1 Jn. 3, 24) and God as the entire Trinity. "If anyone love me, he will keep my word and my Father will love him and we will come to him and make our abode with him" (14, 23). The word "to make our abode" or "to dwell," echoing as it does the words of the Prologue: "And the Word was made flesh and dwelt among us" (1, 14) emphasizes an essential aspect of love. And we would understand nothing if we were to neglect this mysterious aspect of the divine attitude with regard to the creature, once again a "child of God."

Already Wisdom, the prefiguration of Christ, desired "to dwell among us" and in this she placed her joys and her delights: "And my delights were to be with the children of men" (Pvb. 8, 31). And how much more is this true of Christ, eternal Wisdom and uncreated Word!

Equality of love

When Jesus gives us the commandment of "love one another as he has loved us" we should have in mind the qualities of this love. It is not to be a love only of service and sacrifice: "In this we have come to know his love, that he laid down his life for us; and we likewise ought to lay down our life for the brethren" (1 Jn. 3, 16), but it must be a love of union.

Yes, God loves us with such a love that if not one man till the end of time loved God in return, God would nonetheless have offered His Son and the latter would have offered His life for us. But God loves us with such a love that He looks upon this love as attaining its purpose only if it elevates those whom He loves to the dignity of friends, i.e., being capable of returning this love. Thus, there is an equality of love established between us and God through the Holy Spirit, allowing God to take His delights in the soul as the soul takes her delights in God.

And it is only by keeping in mind what these relationships of union between God and the soul imply that we shall be able to envisage the second aspect of this union of love: what concerns the relationship among men themselves, and fraternal charity which makes them "one."

II. UNION WITH OUR BROTHERS

If the new Passover is a Covenant of souls with Christ, it is likewise a Covenant of souls with each other "in Christ." The apostles find in the Passover celebration not simply an invitation to love one another and a model to imitate: "Love one another as I have loved you" (13, 34), but also the origin of this mutual love and fraternal charity which Christ communicates to them by uniting them to Himself.

Union with Christ comes first

Christ's own teaching shows that union with Him is most important in acquiring union with others. Whereas ordinarily, when we think of love of neighbor, union and fraternal charity, we tend to consider the externals, "acts of charity" to be performed, as well as the material form this charity must take on, Christ insists much more on the necessity of our being closely united to Him if we really wish to love others with a supernatural love.

Thus the similitude of the "vine and the branches," far from being simply the charter of our personal union with Christ, is also that of our union with others. In the absence of this union with Christ there cannot be any fraternal charity just as there cannot be any personal spiritual life. "Without me you can do nothing" (15, 5). The "abide in me as I in you" is as indispensable here as it was before. If Christ gives His apostles and all men patterns of fraternal charity to be imitated, these patterns demand that the first condition be fulfilled: "Abide in me." The "new commandment" cannot be demanded or accomplished without this essential condition from which all flows: ". . . that the love with which thou hast loved me may be in them, and I in them" (17, 26).

"A new commandment I give to you, that you love one another: that as I have loved you, you also love one another" (13, 34). We see these words of Christ have two complementary elements. The first presents love as an absolute: "Love one another . . . By this will all men know that you are my disciples, if you have love for one another . . ." The second element specifies this love, giving it as a pattern what Christ has done and what men have come to know: ". . . as I have loved you." In either case Christ is both the source and the goal of this love. For men to love one another they must seek this love in Christ, and that is why they must be in Him and He in them; and they must abide in His love.

Union with Christ is accompanied by a knowledge of Christ as model of love. When we wish to set this love to work we must consider what He has done and find in that the model of our conduct. "If, therefore, I the Lord and Master have washed your feet, you also ought to wash the feet of one another. For I have given you an example, that as I have done to you, so you should do" (13, 14). "In this we have come to know his love, that he has laid down his life for us; and we likewise ought to lay down our life for the brethren" (1 Jn. 3, 16). "If anyone serve me, let him follow me; and where I am there also shall my servant be" (12, 26). John reduces these two ideas to a single statement: "He who says that he abides in him, ought himself also to walk just as he walked" (1 Jn. 3, 6). Christ shows the degree to which union with Him remains essential in fraternal charity, not only as a means but as an end. And what He emphasizes in it is the testimony He himself renders of it. The love we have for each other will allow others to recognize Christ's disciples in us. "By this will all men know that you are my disciples, if you have love for one another" (13, 35).

Fraternal charity as the fulfillment of love

Without union with Christ there can be no fraternal charity since He is its very source. However, if the same road leads to love of God and neighbor, this does not imply that love of neighbor does not have its own special virtue. The same St. John, who has just reminded us that fraternal charity originates in our union with Christ, writes: "If anyone says 'I love God,' and hates his brother, he is a liar. For how can he who does not love his brother whom he sees, love God, whom he does not see?" (1 Jn. 4, 20). This question is not only a proof of Christian realism, but it helps us understand that love of neighbor alone is capable of revealing supernatural charity in its final dimensions. Not that love of God and love of neighbor are realities of a different essence, but love does not reveal itself except in act. This is how Christ showed it, and this is why "we have come to know Love" (1 Jn. 3, 16). The words of John at

Ephesus in his old age were significant when he repeated over and over again: "Little children, love one another." To those who wondered at this, he said: "Because it is the commandment of the Lord, and it alone suffices." These words do not mean that love of neighbor can replace love of God, or that they contain a perfection not contained in the latter. Since love of neighbor demands love of God as its basis, it is always love of God which is manifested and fulfilled in it. But it gets its whole meaning only when its possessor is engaged in acts which concretize the gift of self which must be made.

In God love is perfect without acts being necessary since God is act and pure Act. We can easily see that, when coming into us and living in us, this love has no need of acts in order to be "in act." It does not seem that St. John considers the thing possible since He reminds us of the necessity of loving in "deed and in truth" (1 Jn. 3, 19).

True, the expression "to love in deed" does not necessarily imply "acts of charity." Prayer, renunciation, accepting the divine will are also acts and very often more pure than other acts. However, it still remains true that John has in view "acts of charity" when he invites us to love our brother "whom we see" (1 Jn. 4, 20).

But the question arises: Is it because of our own nature or the nature of charity that acts are necessary? When stating: "In this we have come to know his love, that he laid down his life for us" (1 Jn. 3, 16), it would seem that it is of the very nature of love to manifest itself in "acts." However, when Christ, after washing his disciples' feet, declares: "For I have given you an example, that as I have done to you, so you also should do" (13, 15), we may ask ourselves if He performed this act as an example, for to perform actions onerous by their nature constitutes the best way for sinful man to express his love.

Meditation upon the Scriptures leaves no room for doubt: Christ performed acts not only as examples of charity but because of the very nature of charity. Whether they take on different forms or bear different names depending on whether these actions are in God or in man, these still remain nonetheless linked to the life of love. It matters little whether we call these actions: mutual self-giving, reciprocal indwelling, surrender, devotedness. The Father "gives his Son for the world" (3, 16), the Son "comes to do the Father's will" (6, 38) and "to give his life for those he loves" (15, 13). The Spirit of love is none other than this mutual gift of the Father to the Son and the Son to the Father. In their highest and most perfect expression, these acts intermingle with God's very nature which is that of "Love." Refracted upon the human plane they still keep their meaning. Thus the actions performed by Christ have a twofold significance: they are exemplary and they reveal the true nature of divine charity.

Unity through charity

Undoubtedly we could consider this love under other aspects, and we have done it when considering "sacrifice" through love in divine love. However, when thinking over Christ's ultimate goal as expressed by John ". . . but that he might gather together into one the children of God who are scattered abroad" (11, 52), it is possible to reduce everything to the notion of union and unity. Just as our love for God terminates in union with Him, so our fraternal charity or love of neighbor terminates in unity of all in Christ. And it is practically to this central viewpoint that John has confined himself in his Gospel. We must read the first Epistle if we would know in what way love of neighbor commits us or in what manner "the love of God is perfected in us" (1 Jn. 4, 12) through the practice of fraternal charity.

In this Epistle John, enlightened by his experience and his office as Patriarch of Ephesus, extends his evangelical teaching through pastoral material. And we get a glimpse of what he means by love which must be exercised in favor of others.

He begins by reminding us that we must love and that we can love, for "God has first loved us" (1 Jn. 7, 19) and "love is from God." Then he insists upon the realism of this love and upon the demands it makes. Following the example of Christ "who gave his life for us," we too "must give our life for the brethren" (1 Jn. 4, 16), these brothers "whom we see" and whose needs furnish the opportunity of exercising this love which is practical and intelligent and at the same time social and supernatural.

"He who has the goods of this world and sees his brother in need and closes his heart to him, how does the love of God abide in him? My dear children, let us not love in word, neither with the tongue, but in deed and in truth. In this we know that we are in the truth, and in his sight we set our hearts at rest" (1 Jn. 3, 17-19).

With a sure instinct the "world" will recognize the true disciples of Christ in this charity. It will attempt to reach and persecute Christ through them. "No servant is greater than his master. If they have persecuted me, they will persecute you also. But all these things they will do to you for my name's sake" (15, 20,21).

While the Master warns His disciples of what awaits them, He traces out a program of life: True, "the one sent is not greater than he who sends" (13, 16), but he applies himself to the same work and uses the same means. What he will strive for then, after Christ's example, is the unity of all in charity. This charity will give those who are attached to the "world" the chance of withdrawing from it gradually. This charity will not attain this end except in setting out upon the road of self-surrender, sacrifice, service, and aid of the neighbor in all circumstances.

It appears that John sees in fraternal charity the power of communicating a deep experience of God. Is this not what he implies when, after having told us we must love one another, he adds: "Whoever loves is born of God and knows God. He who does not love has not known God is love" (1 Jn. 4, 6)?

Furthermore, if our love is to be like that of Christ, would not the apostle's words: "Beloved, if God has so loved us, we ought also to love one another" (1 Jn. 4, 11) mean that fraternal charity is a privileged means of working for the salvation of our brothers? Finally John states: "If we love one another, God abides in us and his love is perfected in us" (1 Jn. 4, 12). This passage sheds light upon the words attributed to the apostle according to which the commandment of fraternal charity "alone suffices." It allows us too to understand the deep grasp John had of the intimate unity existing between the two commandments.

In his Epistle he had not only emphasized the conditions and demands of love of neighbor, but he had also pointed out its beauty and fruits. If "one who does not love his brother whom he sees cannot love God whom he cannot see" (1 Jn. 4, 20), and if "one who says he loves God and hates his brother is a liar," on the other hand, there is no illusion to fear in our love of God if "we love one another" (1 Jn. 4, 7; 3, 23; 4, 12). The one who loves his brother "walks" and "abides in the light" (1 Jn. 2, 10,11). He experiences a spiritual joy which none can take from him. "What we have seen and have heard we announce to you, in order that ... our fellowship may be with the Father, and with his Son Jesus Christ. And these things we write to you that you may rejoice, and your joy may be full" (1 Jn. 1, 3). He has the assurance "of being in the Truth" and "he has passed from death to life."

In a word, the love of neighbor "perfects" love of God and aids us in discovering its true character. It gives us a faithful image of Christ's love and makes us walk in His steps who said: "Love one another as I have loved you."

Such then is the teaching of the first Epistle. As for the Gospel, it states that this commandment is "new," and it makes it a characteristic trait of Christ's disciples. It helps us in "knowing Love" (1 Jn. 3, 16) by setting before us Christ's example. But how can we fail to notice how this Gospel insists on bringing to light the goal towards which this love tends, viz., union and unity. The deeds which mark Christ's love: the washing of the feet, the Eucharist, as also the words of the discourse after the Supper—the vine and the branches—and especially the "prayer for unity" which terminates the interview are representative of this orientation.

We find here what we have already encountered regarding sacrifice, the fruit of which is likewise unity of all in Christ. "When I shall be lifted up, I will draw all things to myself" (12, 32; cf. also 11, 52). Union and unity are really the end sought through the sacrifice of the Cross and through the manifestations of charity; those which Christ testifies to in the Eucharist, and those which we must set to work in practicing the love of our neighbor. The Passion, opening with the washing of the feet and followed by the Supper and completed on this note: ". . . that they may be perfected in unity . . ." (17, 23), bears this sign. How can we forget when we try to discern the essence of fraternal charity, given by the Master as "his commandment" and taught by St. John as the "commandment of the Lord"?

Union with our brothers through the Eucharist

We have already said that the washing of the feet constituted an act of devotedness, humble service, respect, and "devotion." Christ is paying homage to His own body, His Mystical Body to which the Cross is about to give birth.

But the framework within which this act unfolds brings out the union between the Master and His disciples and of His disciples among themselves. Christ emphasizes this by saying to them that they must also "wash one another's feet" (13, 14). If we keep in mind that Jesus, through this act, has given proof of His love "to his disciples," we shall understand that the union among them does not stem from the simple fact that they are materially reunited; but that they are all Christ's disciples. The fact that they must manifest this charity among themselves implies no limitation to the extension of the love of neighbor: it is "all" men whom Christ would attract to Himself from the Cross, and it is then towards all that love of neighbor must be practiced. But Jesus wants to make it understood that it is in the measure that His disciples are really "his own" that men will witness a supernatural charity, since it alone is the source of the mutual love which they must bear within themselves.

Much better than the washing of the feet, the Eucharist underscores how much love of neighbor must effect this union. In themselves alone, the framework chosen and the act during the course of which the

Eucharist is instituted, testify to the union which this supreme act of fraternal charity must realize. Already united around a table for a meal—and a meal that commemorated the gathering together of the community of the people of God—the apostles are going to be infinitely more united when they will have shared in the "unique" bread and "all" have drunk of the same cup.

John does not recount the institution of the Eucharist; but when reporting the Master's words: "Unless you eat the flesh of the Son of Man and drink his blood . . ."(6, 53) he lays sufficient stress, leaving no possibility of doubt, upon the fact that there is only one body delivered for us and one blood becoming the source of eternal life (6, 54). The Eucharist, at the same time as it gives evidence to all men of the greatest love which consists in "laying down one's life for one's friends" (15, 13), brings about the most intimate union among them. Giving His body in nourishment and His blood in drink, Christ gathers them and unites them in Himself. At first sight the act by which Christ gives Himself to each appears to be "centrifugal," but this is only apparently so, since by allowing them to feed themselves on the same bread and to drink the same cup, He brings about a vital unity among them. He goes to them, He gives Himself to them, but it is for the purpose of binding them all together into a unity in Him. He places in each the same need of unity. How can we not see, beyond the gesture of love evident in the Eucharist, in this unity realized among His disciples, the supreme goal Christ has in mind?

When we analyze the similitude of the "vine and the branches" or glance over the general content of Christ's discourse after the Supper, we cannot fail to see a constant orientation towards union and unity. Taken on the personal plane, the similitude of the "vine and the branches" tends to promote an intimate union in each soul with Christ: "I in you and you in me" (14, 20). "He who abides in me bears much fruit" (15, 5). It is a union which effects the indwelling of the entire Trinity in the soul and the soul in the Trinity. "If anyone love me, he will keep my word, and my Father will love him and we will come to him and make our abode with him" (14, 23).

The same may be said on the collective level. Better still, the result of this personal union with Christ will be to realize a unity among all those united to Him. We must pay particular attention here, for our conception of fraternal charity and love of neighbor will not be true unless we consider it in the light of Christ's declarations.

First, Christ does not speak of the "vine-stock" but of the "vine." In fact, the Greek word "ampelos" is applicable, not to what we call the stock, i.e., the naked trunk as is seen in the winter months, but to a stock garnered with branches and these latter laden with fruit. In other words, the expression means "the vine." We should read then: "I am the vine and you are the branches" (15, 5), which gives fuller meaning to the words: "He who abides in me, and I in him, he bears much fruit, for without me you can do nothing."[5]

It seems that Jesus expects these branches united to Him to bear fruit and this is one of their essential functions. "Every branch in me that bears no fruit he will take away; and every branch that bears fruit he will cleanse that it may bear more fruit" (15, 5).

However, the fruit they bring forth is not only proof of their vital union with the vine, but of the vital communion of the branches among themselves, since one and the same vital principle feeds and renders them fruitful. The vital unity among them is found then at the source as well as at the goal. The branches live from the same vital sap, bear fruit of the same nature and life that dwell in them and are likewise the same in all.

"That they may be one in us"

Thus it is not enough for Christ that life go through the branches or even that they bear fruit. He wills that all the branches make up one entity and He has been careful to show how this unity will be realized: "I in them, and thou Father in me; that they may be perfected in unity . . ."(17,23).

The notion of vital unity which St. John brings to light in the similitude of the "vine and the branches" is found in St. Paul under the figure of the members of one body. Christ is the head of this body; but head and members form one being. Christ is the vine, but the vine-stock and the branches form only one vine.

However, the comparison is powerless to express that there can be progress in the union of the branches and the vine. For the more the

5. The greater number of commentators weaken Christ's words by explaining them as though He had said: "I am the vine-stock." He said: "I am the vine" and the insistence with which He speaks of the "branch which is in me" and not "attached to me" or "on me" would oblige us not to minimize His meaning. Jesus intends to declare Himself not only united with His disciples but one with them; He is not only the source of their life, but they themselves live only by being integrated to His being to such a degree as to no longer make anything but a living organism with Him. We can say that here Jesus no longer considers Himself as an individual, but as a "living" collective, and yet perfectly one, which comprises the entire regenerated humanity in Him. It is the same as Paul's teaching on the Church as the Mystical Body of Christ: Just as the body and the head do not make up two entities, so also neither do Christ and His disciples. But the similitude of the vine pushes the assimilation even further: In the expression: "I am the true vine" there is no longer a question of two complementary elements, but of one divine Person extending His incarnation from the stock which is the man Jesus right to the branches, the living unity of all forming, according to St. Augustine's beautiful words: "The entire Christ, head and members" (L. Bouyer, The Fourth Gospel, p. 204).

branches are united to the stock the more united will they be with one another. The more our union with Christ increases, the more we shall be "one" among ourselves. When Christ expresses that desire at the close of the Supper discourse that all be perfected in unity, He makes it understood this will not be effected unless they are united intimately with Him. How far can this union go? It is a reality which no word can express. What we can say is that "the unity of Christians among themselves will be a sharing in the mystery of the union of Jesus with His Father."[6]

We may add that this union among Christians is the conclusion of the discourse after the Supper and the supreme desire of Christ.

"That the world may believe that thou hast sent me"

If the teaching of the fourth Gospel on fraternal charity is not to be separated from that of the Synoptics and other Johannine writings, it is nevertheless clear that it presents us with the duty of loving one another before all else under the aspect of union and unity. It must be admitted that this perspective remains a great mystery for us. We are so far from union and unity, even among Christians, that it is very difficult to picture a world in which they have been realized. But Jesus, who knows the supernatural riches these would bring us and their great value as testimony, makes them the supreme object of His desires; He returns to the matter on two occasions: ". . . that they also may be one in us, that the world may believe that thou hast sent me. That they may be perfected in unity, and that the world may know that thou hast sent me . . ." (17, 21,23). Christ lives this unity with the Father in infinitely divine charity, and He desires to communicate it to us because it is the source of unity among Christians. It is the work of His Spirit in us. "One body, one Spirit . . ." (Eph. 4, 4).

We tend to see the highest development of charity in acts of devotedness and in the gift of ourselves. Indeed, when giving His life for us, Jesus shows us that this is one of the manifestations of charity and undoubtedly the highest. However, the entire discourse after the Supper proves that the expansion of charity is to be found in unity.

The summit of charity and what really reveals its essence is to be found in the Trinity. Now if love casts light upon the fact that the Father is in the Son and the Son is in the Father, it also shows that this mutual gift realizes unity. "The Father and I are one" (10, 30).

On the the human level the goal of supernatural charity must be

6. P. Mollat.

sought in the unity realized among the members of the Mystical Body of Christ, among the branches of the real vine. Unity in love furnishes us with the purest reflection of one God in three divine Persons, the most faithful participation in the Trinity here on earth. Such is then this "loving them to the end" that John has in mind when he assigns the reason for Christ's death, this gathering "into one of the children of God who were scattered abroad" (11, 52), and after opening the "Book of the Passion" with the words: "Jesus, having loved his own who were in the world, loved them to the end," he closes it with these words: "Father, I pray . . . that they may be one, even as thou, Father, in me and I in thee; that they may be one in us" (17, passim).

CHAPTER 17

CHRIST'S RETURN TO THE FATHER AND
PRAYER FOR UNITY

I. THE PASSOVER AS A RETURN

John makes it clear, when speaking of the Passover, that there is not only question of a sacrifice and a communion, but also that of a "passage" from this world. "Jesus, knowing that the hour had come to him to pass out of this world to the Father . . ." (13, 1).

The ancient Passover had commemorated Israel's passage from Egypt to the promised land, from slavery to freedom, being invited to pursue this freedom on the spiritual plane. Christ brought true freedom to men, and He is the "way" that every man is to follow to make a true "passover" of his own life. The Christian life demands this dimension which alone confers upon it its true meaning. The Passover introduces a principle of development for that reality Christ came to set up; it feeds the impetus that draws it towards its goal.

The divine Word is vivifying. "Lazarus, come forth!" (11, 43). "Rise, take up thy bed and walk!" (5, 8). "Follow me!" (1, 43). Whether it be a call, a cure, a raising from the dead, Christ reveals Himself as Truth and Life, and as the living Way and this Way leads to where He Himself has ascended: the Father's bosom.

If the Passover is the Christian mystery "par excellence," it is really because it is the mystery of salvation and it stirs up those participating in it. It brings into their lives a spiritual leaven, a movement which is the very soul of the Christian life, making of it a "passage." It is the way of return, as well as the way of salvation. "Father, I have manifested thy name to the men whom thou hast given me out of the world . . . I am no longer in the world, but these are in the world . . . But now I am coming to thee, and I will that where I am, these also may be with me" (17, 6,11,24).

The Passover is the way and the nourishment for the way; it is the passage and the strength necessary to make it, just as the food given to Elias by the angel upon his entrance into the desert was to sustain him in his walk towards Horeb, the mountain of God (1 Kgs. 19, 7). It associates us ever more closely even here below with Christ's body, for it makes us daily more and more the children of the kingdom. It sets us upon the road leading to glorification, the real reason for Christ's coming. "And the glory that thou hast given me, I have given them . . . Father, I will that where I am, they also whom thou hast given me may be with me; in order that they may behold my glory, which thou hast given me . . ." (17, 22-24).

When instituting the new Passover Christ brings three different planes in close relationship with one another: that of figures which He fulfills, that of reality, and that of a definite completion or fulfillment. The Passover celebrated by Christ really brings to complete fulfillment the figures of the ancient Passover. It brings us in Christ's Person the reality of sacrifice through which man finds and realizes again communion with God. It is the true road that leads men, united among themselves, to the Father and it does so by incorporating all in Christ.

Without this last dimension it could not be spoken of as the new and eternal Covenant. The Passover fully merits this name only because it is the Passover of the return of the entire humanity to the Father in Christ, and this is what makes it a Passover of unity.

"From the world to the Father"

"I came forth from the Father and have come into the world. Again I leave the world and go to the Father" (16, 28). The moment has come for Christ to bring these words to realization. The moment has likewise come for Him who has told His followers He is the "Way" (14, 6) to reveal where this way leads. Thus, to Thomas' question, "Lord, we do not know where thou art going, and how can we know the way?" Jesus answers that He Himself is the way and adds: "No one comes to the Father, but through me" (14, 6).

Jesus had announced His departure and necessary separation to His apostles. True, He had promised He would not leave them orphans but would send the Spirit, but in this He simply emphasized the reality of His absence. Now this absence had within itself a positive aspect which must be brought to light because something essential is linked to it. Every "passage" leads from one plane to another, from one state to another state, and the more important place is not the one left but the one at which one arrives, where one settles down, the state in which one is definitely transformed.

Jesus came into the world and now the hour has come for Him "to pass from the world to the Father" (13, 1). We see here how well marked out, between the point of departure and the destination, is the distance separating them, but also the bond uniting them.

Being made flesh, He obeys the laws of flesh. He permits time and death to take hold of Him. For a long time in advance He sees the "hour" of death advance. But if according to the flesh He must leave the world, divine power enables Him to remain in it. Spiritually present, He works in the world to aid us accomplish the passage He has already realized. The Passover and the Eucharist have exactly this function and make it possible for the body to join the Head, to follow where He already is.

When Christ speaks of His own "passing out of this world to the Father" and says to Him, "But now I am coming to thee; and these things I speak in the world . . .," (17, 13) the apostles must keep in mind that He is not of the world. He had already, under other circumstances, told them: "You are from below, I am from above" (8, 23).

But in the discourse after the Supper He speaks as though He has already returned to the Father. Also, He begs the Father that these men be united to Him again in the place of His glorification, which is considered as having already been attained. "And now do thou, Father, glorify me with thyself, with the glory that I had with thee before the world existed" (17, 5).

He does not say: "I will that where I shall be, they also may be with me," but rather, "I will that where I am, they also may be with me" (17, 24). It is in this frame of mind we must place ourselves if we are to grasp Christ's words and actions in this last hour.

Jesus has already referred to Himself as the way, the road. But in these last moments, what He wants to reveal to His apostles is that impetus of intense love that drives Him, so to speak, entirely "ad Patrem." The only way they themselves have of attaining this goal, is to allow themselves to be drawn by this divine road. Christ is not only the guide who lights up the road by His teachings, He is Himself this road which we must "follow." To listen to Him, to know and love Him, these are all ways of following Him.

Christ's revelation, such as it is proposed by John, tends to make us enter into Him and abide with Him. It likewise shows Him to us as desirous of coming to us and abiding with us. In each soul Christ is on the march towards the Father. And this not through roads that need space and time, but through roads that have no other dimensions but love of God for the soul and love of the soul for God. Through this road, Christ travels to the Father in us, and the Father comes to us through this same road and the meeting takes place.

The passing of each of us "from this world," under Christ's action, is a mystery into which He attempts to have His disciples enter. This is a mystery of love which bursts asunder all human limitations. It will not be fully accomplished in us and for all the children of God until that final re-union at the Parousia. However, even now the passage is being effected gradually, and the Passover is its instrument. Through it and in it, Christ advances towards us, gives Himself to us; through it we enter daily upon this "road" and we advance along it towards the Father.

"And you therefore have sorrow now"

For men who are not only "in the world" but of it, the world is the only reality of which they are conscious and in which they feel at home. It is not so with Jesus and His disciples. Christ is only in the world as one passing through and as an exile. "He has come into the world" (16, 28) sent by the Father, and He has accomplished what He has been sent to do; but once His work is completed, He leaves the world to return to the Father. "I have come forth from the Father and come into the world. Now I leave the world and go back to the Father" (16, 28).

These constant references to His Father as His origin, to His status as "one sent," to a mission He has to accomplish, and which, once terminated, will make it possible for Him to return to His Father, all these things create in the apostles' minds and in our own the vision in which the realities of time and eternity are in intimate communication one with the other. Time's realities resound in eternity, and those of eternity enter and transform those of time. However, passing from one to the other is possible only at the price of a struggle, a combat, a tension, for it is not natural to be in the world and not "of the world."

The entire Johannine Gospel is marked by this opposition between those who are of the world, of which Satan is prince, and those who are of God, born of God, children of God. This opposition is expressed in the Prologue in terms of light and darkness; they will be spoken of throughout the Gospel text.[1]

Man's state is presented in it under the form of a necessary and permanent struggle, a combat which only faith, God's gift, can transform into victory: "Everyone who is born of God overcomes the world. And this is the victory that overcomes the world, our faith" (1 Jn. 5, 4).

---

1. We might ask ourselves, in the light of the discoveries of Qumran, if the relationship of John the Baptist and perhaps even John with the Essenes did not lead the evangelist on to utilizing these terms in preference to others.

This tension does not cease with Christ's departure, but even increases, because the object of our faith, its author and finisher, is no longer here on earth but has returned to His Father. Having arrived on the other side, He draws us, calls us, and we seem to hear the voice of the "first-born of the dead" (Ap. 1, 5) in those words written by St. Paul: "... seek the things that are above, where Christ is seated at the right hand of God. Mind the things that are above, not the things that are on earth. For you have died and your life is hidden with Christ in God. When Christ, your life, shall appear, then you too will appear with him in glory" (Col. 3, 1).

John must have suffered more than anyone else at Christ's departure because He had lived in such intimacy with Him. Perhaps this is the reason he is so insistent upon the farewells of Christ and the coming separation, as well as the assurances given by Christ of His return, of sending the Spirit who will not leave His little children orphans (14, 18). That this separation weighs on him is to be seen in the conclusion of the Apocalypse which assures us of Christ's return, "It is true, I come quickly," and yet it ends with that cry of ardent longing, "Come! Lord Jesus!" (Ap. 22, 20).

John awaits Jesus' return and must struggle against a hostile world. He cannot have enough of the Master's promises in order not to be invaded by fear. But the divine words are there and they still resound in his ears.

"Do not let your heart be troubled, or be afraid. You have heard me say to you, 'I go away and I am coming to you.' If you loved me, you would indeed rejoice that I am going to the Father ..." (14, 27). "And you therefore have sorrow now; but I will see you again, and your heart shall rejoice, and your joy no one shall take from you again ... In the world you will have affliction. But take courage, I have overcome the world" (16, 22).

"Take courage, I have overcome the world"

The apostle did not forget these words. How great was that continued struggle against the world and its threefold concupiscence! How much the world hated those belonging to Christ! And in the evening of his life, John will make certain recommendations which will be filled with his memories of the discourse after the Supper: "And every spirit that severs Jesus is not of God, but is of Antichrist, of whom you have heard that he is coming, and now is already in the world. You are of God, dear children, and have overcome him, because greater is he who is in you than he who is in the world. They are of the world; therefore of the world they speak and the world listens to them. We are of God" (1 Jn. 4, 5,6).

And yet through all the struggles, trials, separation, joy fills the apostle's heart. Christ did not leave His followers exposed to the world, the flesh, and the devil without having told them of their true identity and status as "children of God." This certitude fills John's heart with a joy that already is evident in the Prologue and we see it again in the Epistle. "Behold what manner of love the Father has bestowed upon us, that we should be called children of God; and such we are. This is why the world does not know us, because it did not know him. Beloved, now we are the children of God, and it has not yet appeared what we shall be. We know that, when he appears, we shall be like him, for we shall see him just as he is" (1 Jn. 3, 1-3). And this is what transforms the perspectives of our life here on earth.

It is true that Christ leaves us while He returns to the Father, but He is simply preceding us into a house which is now ours, a house promised to us. A Father awaits us there, if we live as His children following Christ's example.

St. Paul made the attempt to conquer worldly attraction by substituting the attraction of Christ: "Seek the things that are above where Christ is seated . . ."(Col. 3, 1). St. John too feels this intense desire to be with Christ, but he stresses what has become our good fortune here below and what permits us to consider heaven with love and hope: God is our Father and we are his children.

"Born of God . . . children of God" (1 Jn. 3, 9; 1, 12). John sees this as a present reality; it bears fruit in his own heart and fills it with the divine presence. It allows him to remain in the world and work there according to the instructions given by Christ to his disciples.

Christ has never encouraged His disciples to escape from the world or to retreat from it. He has asked them, on the contrary, to work in the world and to raise it towards God. They will fulfill this work assigned them with the certitude that they are the children of God; with the certitude of rejoining Him who has preceded them and has gone to prepare a place for them. He will return to take them so that they will be there where He Himself is and they will be there as "sons."

Nothing will be changed here on earth as far as their present human condition is concerned. Not belonging to the world, they will be persecuted; the world loves its own; it will never pardon them and more so neither will this world's prince. He will not pardon them for being Christ's choice, the "children of light," trying to obey only truth. He will not forgive them for opposing his seductions and his falsehood with the barrier of their faith.

This is exactly what the Christian's position is. It is this combat and struggle forever renewed. Along with the notion of "passing," it is one of struggle constantly renewed. It is noteworthy that after promising them the Holy Spirit, after giving them the commandment of love and inviting them to be always united to Him, Christ judged it necessary to set before His disciples the image of their struggle with the world and the victories they must gain over it. His final directives are severe.

"Remember the word I have spoken to you: No servant is greater than his master. If they have persecuted me, they will persecute you also . . . But these things I have spoken to you, that when the time comes you may remember that I told you." (15, 20; 16, 4). "These things I have spoken to you that in me you may have peace. In the world you will have affliction. But take courage, I have overcome the world" (16, 33).

After announcing His departure for the last time, "I have come forth from the Father and have come into the world. Again I leave the world and go to the Father" (16, 28), and showing by His gesture (17, 1) that He intends to pray to the Father, Jesus commences the "sacerdotal" prayer, the great prayer for unity.

II. PRAYER FOR UNITY

The introductory words of the prayer, "Father, the hour has come! Glorify thy Son that thy Son may glorify thee . . ."(17, 1), as well as Christ's attitude when pronouncing them, seem to show that He is no longer interested in anything but eternal realities and entirely taken up with speaking to His Father. However, if Jesus had no other desire but this, His prayer would have remained unknown to others since it would have been entirely within His soul. The fact that He spoke it outwardly and brought it to the knowledge of His disciples is proof that this prayer concerns them and that they are to draw infinite riches from it.

In fact, men repeat the first petition of the Our Father in vain; they need someone to recall to them the primacy of the duty of sanctifying the divine Name. But that the Father be sanctified and glorified by the Son, it is first necessary that the Son Himself be glorified by the Father and that His entire work render glory to the Father, for it has been entirely offered up to Him. "I have glorified thee on earth; I have accomplished the work thou hast given me to do. And now do thou, Father, glorify me with thyself, with the glory that I had with thee before the world existed. I have manifested thy name to the men whom thou hast given me out of the world" (17, 4-6).

Only when men realize that in Christ all comes from the Father will the Father be glorified. "Now they have learnt that whatever thou hast given me is from thee . . . and they have known of a truth that I came from thee, and they have believed that thou didst send me" (17, 7).

Christ tells us in what the work accomplished for the Father's glory consists: "Glorify thy Son, that thy Son may glorify thee, even as thou hast given him power over all flesh, in order that to all thou hast given him he may give everlasting life." And everlasting life is: ". . . that they may know thee, the only true God, and him whom thou hast sent, Jesus Christ" (17, 2,3). The glory of the Father and the Son are identified in the accomplishment of the divine will of salvation, i.e., of bringing eternal life to men through the "one whom the Father has sent." Everything holds together. And Christ is not divided between His Father whom He intensely desires to rejoin and His disciples whom He is constrained to leave.

The glance of love He casts upon the Father does not distract Him from the care He has for His own. The glory His Incarnation, Redemption, and glorification procure for His Father does not hinder Him from being actively interested in men whom He has saved and who still need His help and intercession.

The mystery of His Person joined to a divine and human nature, which permits a complexity of sentiments only apparently opposed assures their unity. This accounts for that serenity and peace coming from Christ's prayer.

Everything is expressed in it: tenderness for those remaining behind, anxiety "to keep" them, the joy of glorifying the Father. One aspect of the prayer does no wrong to another, and there is no contradiction within it. Here also we may say, "All is consummated." Here is not the least of the proofs of the divinity of the one who goes to death with such serenity and detachment.

Our advocate with the Father

Christ has manifested His Father's name to His disciples, and henceforth all those who have kept His word know that everything that was given to Christ comes from the Father. They know He has given them the words of the Father. They have "known of a truth that I came forth from thee," and this so well that they are now in possession of eternal life which is knowledge of God and Christ (17, 3-8).

However, His work is not completed and He allows His anxiety for His disciples to be seen. While He himself is going to experience the glory of triumph, they will have to remain in the world. A troubled tenderness takes possession of Him. He does not leave them without having assured

Himself that they "know," have believed, and "have kept his word, and will keep it." He knows He has made "children of God" of them, but they remain in the midst of the world, exposed to its dangers. Though they are not "orphans," they are deprived of His visible presence and are weak (17, 6,8).

Though He envisions the return to His Father with great joy, He still will know no rest until the Parousia when the last sheep will have entered the sheepfold. That is why His prayer, while placing the flock in His Father's hands, asks Him to bring unity into it.

Thanks to the sacerdotal prayer we have the assurance that Christ is not only an impassible and glorious Head awaiting us in Heaven, but "a high priest who can have compassion on our infirmities" (Heb. 4, 15). He intercedes for us, and His prayer testifies that He does not consider His mission ended through the sending of the Spirit. What is more, He who ascends to the Father is no longer only the Word who descended; He is now the Word incarnate who brings back with Him that human nature which is forever associated with the only-begotten Son's glory. But the incarnate Word brings to heaven the stigmata of the Passion in His glorified human nature. These are the indelible marks of His passage among us, proof that He is forever our own, and that He may make Himself "advocate" with the Father; and this, not only with the omnipotence of the divinity, but with the appeal which comes from His humanity.

The incomparable intercessory value of His prayer comes from the fact that He not only prays for men but that He prays truly as "man." In Him a true man unites His prayer to that of the Son of God. Thus, we cannot imagine Christ returning to His Father and sharing His glory, and then simply becoming an onlooker at our combats or intervening through a grace granted us in answer to our prayers. The words of His sacerdotal prayer give us to understand that He actually helps us in our "combats" and that He gives us His support.

There is still another reason for his prayer for unity being heard, viz., Christ's glory is henceforth in the world as really as it is in His Father. It is "with his disciples" and in them really as it is in His Father. His position as Mediator confers upon His glory the power of developing on "earth as in heaven," in time as in eternity, and not only the power of throwing up a bridge between the two but of bringing about a unity.

Unity is not a grace Christ obtains for men, but to which He himself is a stranger. Unity is a reality interior to Christ and men cannot obtain it unless they are in Christ. It is not realized unless they are in Him and He in them.

"That they may be one"

Unity is the mark of His work. Christ presents this work to His Father, and it is so intimately united to Him that He is Himself at work in it, and His glory is no more separable from it than it is from His disciples.

Through the Incarnation He appears for the good of the earth, that earth upon which the "will of God must be done" and upon which the glory of God extends and can be found since the Son of God has come, and since His disciples are so intimately united to Him that they form one with Him. How could the Father separate in His own love, in His aid, and in the granting of His grace what is forever united with His Son? The sacerdotal prayer shows the beginning of this realization. Already God's glory is in those whom Christ has given to Him. The kingdom of God is not only in heaven, but in a certain sense upon earth. The preamble of the prayer is clear: "Father, glorify thy Son, that thy Son may glorify thee, even as thou hast given him power over all flesh, in order that to all thou hast given him he may give everlasting life" (17, 1,2).

Christ calls down upon Himself the glorification of the Father for two purposes: that He be glorified in the Son, and that this glorification allow the Son to give eternal life to those whom the Father has given Him.

We see how unity is a reality which cannot be sought or found except in Christ. In the measure in which men are united to Him will they be "one" among themselves. This is the meaning of these words: "Holy Father, keep in thy name those whom thou hast given me, that may be one even as we are" (17, 11). This is also the meaning of verses 23 and 24: "And the glory that thou hast given me, I have given them, that they may be one, even as we are one: I in them and thou in me; that they may be perfected in unity . . ." Again, in verse 26: "And I have made known to them my name, and will make it known, in order that the love with which thou hast loved me may be in them, and I in them" (17, 26).

And all this simply means that Christ must be necessarily invested with the glory which comes to Him, "put in possession" of what is proper to the Son of God, in order that the gift of eternal life be realized, and "the love with which thou hast loved me may be in them" (17, 26).

Hence, Christ praying to the Father says: "Father, keep in thy name those whom thou hast given me, that they may be one even as we are," i.e., have them abide in me through thy grace. Being united to me, they will be made sharers of the unity which exists in us, and this unity will make them "one" among themselves, with an entirely supernatural unity.

It is when meditating upon these words that we realize how the kingdom of God is in us. Our kingdom is "in God" and God is in heaven, but heaven is where God is. Jesus Christ as God is then destined to take possession of the Land. And this, not through the usual means of human power, but through charity which gradually penetrates the Land. This charity brings about union between Christ and us; and it enables this unity to develop because unity and charity are inseparable. Having within themselves the greatest apostolic strength, they draw hearts to believe and to be converted. "By this will all men know that you are my disciples, if you have love for one another" (13, 35), and in almost identical words He addresses the Father: "That they may be one in us, in order that the world may believe that thou hast sent me" (17, 21). And He adds: ". . . and thou hast loved them even as thou hast loved me." This seems to prove that if unity among them is the fruit of their union with Him, it testifies also to the divine love which "is" this very union. Charity and unity are the ways the kingdom of God enters among us since the Redemption effected by Christ.

True, Christ's departure tends to make the earth an exile where we await the moment when we may rejoin Him. However, when He speaks of having "descended from heaven" and goes on to say, "You are from below and I am from above" (8, 23), He has no intention of setting up opposition between two places, but He is speaking of two states of soul. He becomes more specific when He says, "You are of this world, I am not of this world" (8, 23). As soon as a man is no longer "of this world," he is no longer from below but from above. "I do not pray that they be taken out of the world, but that thou keep them from evil. They are not of the world, even as I am not of the world" (17, 15).

Christ did not desire to raise the veil which covers "the new heavens and the new earth" (2 Pt. 3, 13), but we should not consider the present world as a simple "place of exile" which must be left behind in order to enter the "promised land." This manner of looking at things is a temptation for the Christian, for it runs the risk of hindering him from embracing what is presented to him now, and it sets an obstacle to God's action. For God desires to lay the foundation stones of His kingdom even here on earth. This is as true of the relations of the soul with God as the unity realized among men through charity.

If union with Christ is not an illusion, and the entire Johannine Gospel proves that it is not, if faith carries the seed of vision and if charity is given to us (1 Cor. 13, 8), then Christ's words, inviting His disciples not to be of this world while remaining in it, open up wonderful vistas upon the realization of unity in charity.

In fact, charity is already here on earth what it will be in eternity. We are assured of bearing divine love in its eternal reality when we bear Christ within us. "I in them . . . I have loved them as thou hast loved me" (17, 23). ". . . in order that the love with which thou hast loved me may be in them, and I in them" (17, 26).

"That the love with which Thou hast loved me may be in them"

Thanks to Christ the "glory of God" and the will of God are on earth as in heaven; not that there is perfect identity between heaven and earth, but because one "unity" links them together, one presence inhabits both places, one divine love is active in each. But may we speak of a "here" and "there" when moving in the realm of spiritual realities? In His discourse after the Supper it is true that Christ constantly comes back to His return to the Father and He refers to it as a departure and a passage. He tells us He will come back to look for us and that ". . . where I am, there you also may be" (14, 3; 17, 24).

But what is presented to us as a passage (17, 11) must not be interpreted in a spatial sense, but of a different state. To pass from one to the other, neither displacement nor time are required. If there is "passage" from the state in which we are to that which God has prepared for us, it is only thanks to Christ. But this passage does nothing else but make actual what already is in us in "germ."

From faith which will have passed there will spring up "vision;" obscure certitude will be changed into face-to-face contemplation; and immutable charity will give us the power to possess in beatitude this same object which faith has presented veiled, viz., God. "I have revealed to them thy name and will reveal it, in order that the love with which thou hast loved me may be in them, and I in them" (17, 26).

Through these words we are reminded of those in the Epistle where John extends the thought expressed here and draws out its consequence: "Behold what manner of love the Father has bestowed upon us, that we should be called the children of God; and such we are. This is why the world does not know us, because it did not know him. Beloved, now we are the children of God, and it has not yet appeared what we shall be. We know that, when he appears, we shall be like him, for we shall see him just as he is. And everyone who has this hope in him makes himself holy, just as he is holy" (1 Jn. 3, 1).

What Christ asks for us and what remains to be realized is this passage from obscurity to vision, from this veiled light to the brilliance of the divine light which "will appear" and will be "manifested"; it will make us pass from love to the ecstacy of love and bring us to perfection in God (1 Cor. 13, 10-12).

"That they may be one, even as we are one"

The prayer for unity opens up wide vistas: a covenant definitely brought about between heaven and earth, unity between men and God, the glory which is God's becomes theirs, the unity of the Son and the Father communicated to men to enable them to form the Church, this spouse eternally united to the Bridegroom.

This prayer is a dialogue between Christ and the Father. If Christ has us present at it, it is that we may learn something of eternal life which is promised us. Eternal realities become more apparent through the veil separating them from us, for they are presented to us in Him who experiences them and who would share them with us. We experience them in anticipation in Him and He shares His joy with us: "...and these things I speak in the world, in order that they may have my joy made full in themselves" (17, 13). This joy remains with us while we continue to work for the coming of charity and unity in the world.

Charity and unity are the work of the Father through the Spirit. Men cannot accomplish it by themselves. The Father alone can gather together the members of the Mystical Body and that is why the Son prays: "That they may be one, even as we are one." To us He is content to say: "Love one another as I have loved you" (13, 34). Such is the way this unity will be realized on our part and such is what Christ expects of us.

Unity is the right side of a work whose wrong side we actually see and that in a very small way. For we perceive only misleading appearances and no one is able to say where the world is in its march towards unity.

A desire for unity is at work in it, but a power from on high must move it in order that what is now an aspiration may be transformed into a reality. For since Christ has come and since His sacerdotal prayer has been pronounced, humanity has the duty of hoping for this unity and working towards it. Though it is something elusive, it is nevertheless a reality already at work in the children of God.

We are speaking here of a unity which is not that which a Father would establish and maintain among His children, nor the perfect cohesion of all the members of a group; it is rather the unity of all in Christ, a unity realized by the fact that each and all believe in His Name.

Such a unity will not be accomplished except through our return in Christ. "And when all things are made subject to him ..." (1 Cor. 15, 28). Like the material creation, the spiritual creation is incomplete. In the spiritual world all things are perpetually becoming, and seek to be united. God is at work and never ceases to act in it and He draws it towards this unity in the depths of its being.

However, in the order of things on earth, fraternal charity alone is able to effect a bond among men, for it has as its origin their common belonging to God and His active presence in them which creates unity.

This is what Christ would have us understand in the closing words of His prayer. And this teaching is the highest revelation He could make to us, for it mingles with the very mystery of His love for the Father and His union with Him. This prayer teaches us that what makes our life and will make up our beatitude is the very thing that He lives Himself in the bosom of this divine unity. And at the very moment when He offers Himself for His disciples, when His Cross is being prepared, through which we shall share in this good, He unveils the riches which are reserved for them and which the Spirit will work to develop in them. And that is why the last words of Christ are to call down this Love upon them: "I have manifested thy name to them and will manifest it . . . in order that the love with which you loved me may be in them, and I in them."

CHAPTER 18

THE PASSION AND THE MOTHER OF
THE REDEEMER

I. THE PASSION

St. John, privileged witness of Christ's Passion since he alone of all the disciples accompanied His Master to Calvary, is nevertheless the one whose account is the shortest and the most unembellished.

He does not report the scene in Gethsemani at which he assisted, and is silent about many other colorful details reported by the Synoptics.[1] But, at each step, his account bears precise details which prove an eyewitness is at work. Thus, the remark, "Now the servants and the attendants were standing at a coal fire and warming themselves, for it was cold" (18, 18); and again, the details of Peter's denial, and that short reference made to the road that Jesus had taken from "Caiphas to the praetorium." "It was morning . . ." says St. John and we feel that this sad episode remained fixed in his memory to the sounds and familiar scenes of a day just beginning.

He remembered too that the Jews, having reached the praetorium, "did not enter, that they might not be defiled, but might eat the passover" (18, 28), and that the inscription placed over the Cross by Pilate's order was written "in Hebrew, in Greek, and in Latin" (19, 20). He saw and read it.

John discards everything that can overburden the text, details which would lend themselves to anecdotes: those two swords with which Peter armed himself in Gethsemani, or what concerns Barrabas. He goes straight to essentials, because in his mind all things are being directed towards a determined end. Already announced and prepared over a long period of time, these events are being fulfilled. If it is the end of Christ's life, it is

---

1. The scene before Herod, the episode of Simon of Cyrene, the daughters of Jerusalem, Judas' death, and the good thief.

important to point out that it is the "end of love," its supreme manifestation (13, 1).

The trial of Jesus

How explain, on the part of a witness, his rather surprising omissions and the choice he makes of certain scenes in preference to others? Besides the existence of the Synoptics which had already related the facts, many things are clarified for this reason that John advanced Jesus' agony to a time much sooner than the garden of Olives. John saw this agony all the time in the Master's look and discovered it in His many allusions to it. Even from the first meeting, was it not contained in the very name with which the Baptist saluted Him: "Behold the Lamb of God" (1, 29)?

No sooner is He baptized than He will accomplish His work. At Cana "his hour" has not come. In the cleansing of the Temple, He predicts His death and resurrection. He speaks to Nicodemus of His elevation on the Cross (3, 14), and to the Samaritan woman of salvation (4, 22).

After the cure of the paralytic at Bethsaida John apprizes us of the fact that the Jews "were most anxious to put him to death; because he not only broke the Sabbath, but also called God his own Father, making himself equal to God" (5, 18). From then on, death rises up to meet Him, it comes beating at His heels like the tireless waves constantly breaking into foam. His life is going to be cast between the rumors of an earthly glory by means of which the crowds try in vain to capture Him and the expectation of that "hour" which will be His last.

On many occasions, because that hour has not yet come, He steals away, hides Himself, escapes the hands of His enemies. But already in view of His death He prepares His means of survival: "The bread that I will give is my flesh for the life of the world" (5, 51). He knows He will be betrayed and He says it (6, 70). However, while the elements of His trial were accumulating (7, 45), He openly speaks of His death (7, 33,35). At every instant the incident which will bring an end to His preaching is on the point of bursting forth. It is held back in some inexplicable way, it cannot come forth until "his hour." John repeats this word endlessly.

With Chapter 8 the threat comes closer. Far from taking measures of security, from seeking some support, soliciting aid, Jesus faces up to His adversaries and even furnishes them with arguments, at the same time as He directs His own indictment against them. As for Himself, He lays claim to only one testimony, that of His Father (8, 18), only one origin, divine,[2] while He accumulates accusations against His enemies. The Jews hate in Him one who pretends to be God. Jesus hates in them Satan, their father (8, 44). He finally proclaims His judgment of condemnation against these perverse children (8, 47). Whatever happens henceforth, it is not a conquered man who will be judged and condemned, but the supreme Judge, the Conqueror.

Jesus' trial is begun in Chapter 8—and even before—and it is Jesus who conducts the debates. And while the Jews think of His mortal death, Jesus Himself places man face to face with eternal death and life.

The drama is played out on two levels. Each weighs the terms of the threat; each, the hour arrived, will ratify his decision.

The human and divine drama

Christ's death appears in the passion account according to John as an act already posited, a thing already judged which awaits nothing but its execution. Jesus seems to detach Himself from it in order to concentrate upon the life which will spring up from His sacrifice. From Chapter 10 on, He speaks and acts as one before whom a new phase opens up and death will be its completion only in external appearances.

In fact, not only does Christ look upon His death as an advantage, but He freely disposes of it as a good, assuring the salvation of those He loves; He considers it, as does John, in the light of the resurrection, i.e., in the light of what makes His death a point of departure for a new era. These perspectives lead Jesus to desire no longer to appear as an accuser and judge, but solely as the Good Shepherd who lays down His life for His sheep (10, 11).

True, unbelief continues to greet His words, and He is cast constantly against fierce opposition. He is completely aware of the plot against Him and what approaches Him in the shadows; but He is "beyond" it all. Condemned to death, Judge of eternal life and death, He lives in His kingdom already as king who disposes of life, as friend whose sole desire is to give life.

Having weighed and predicted the aspects, consequences, and fruits of His sacrifice (10, 28; 11, 52; 12, 32), He awaits His hour. This hour having arrived, the dramatic tension with which it was filled seems to abate in its "fulfillment."

John relates the unfolding of this drama as an objective witness, and this witness observes with his heart as well as his eyes. Many details noted

2. Cf. 8, 13,23,26,38,42,54.

down by him show how attentive he is to the Master's ever active love, of His desire to remove any trials from His apostles which they cannot endure, of His will to save all.

Thus, while the Synoptics relate that, "all the disciples left him and fled" (Mk. 14, 50; Mt. 26, 56) upon the arrival of the armed band led by Judas, John reports Christ's words to those who came to arrest Him, "If, therefore, you seek me, let these go their way" (18, 8). We feel that John was conscious of the Master's delicacy, anxious not to compromise His disciples and helping them in their weakness right to the point of giving them an opening to abandon Him.

Meditating upon this memory, John wrote: "That the word which he said might be fulfilled, 'Of those whom thou hast given me I have not lost one' " (18, 9). We see in this stroke of the pen how John was always attentive to the beatings of that divine heart upon which he had rested.

The exquisite reticence which surrounds these secret understandings, these unexpressed signs of tenderness, are found again at the Cross, in the intimacy of that Cross upon which John gazed with fixed eyes upon the transpierced heart.

There is the seamless tunic undoubtedly woven by Mary. This tunic had a story of its own, precious to the heart of those who were there surrounding the Crucified with their love and even crucified with Him. John casts to the side, after making a simple reference to it, the public and outrageous aspect of the crucifixion; he then recalls only the last moments lived between Jesus and those who loved Him and who followed Him to the bitter end; he confines himself to keeping in his heart nothing but the love Jesus gave testimony of by giving him to His Mother and vice versa.

It is sufficient to read, in order to feel that the degree of surrender of John's heart is entire, and yet what mastery he has over it; we see this in how attentive he is, in his account, in emphasizing the agreements between the actual unfolding of the drama and the prophecies which had announced it: "That the Scripture might be fulfilled" (19, 24,28,36,37).

Testimony rendered to truth

It is evident that Jesus knew "all that was to come upon him" (18, 4) just as he "knew what was in man" (2, 25). It is, however, in the context of social and political data, closely allied to the situation of a country occupied by the invader that John places the arrest and death of Christ, and gives the most plausible motive and official explanation for them.

True, the apostle was not unaware that the drama which is played out is essentially moral, religious, and spiritual; but he shows how it was stifled and camouflaged in order to circumvent the established order. Jesus is a menace to the peace and prosperity of Israel, and finally the empire itself (19, 12). Not that the Jews did not know better. They were able to despise Jesus as ignorant and unlettered, to insult Him as one possessed by the devil; they nonetheless experienced His strength when He criticized them, and His power as a miracle-worker: "This man is working many signs" (11, 47). In reality it was their interior security that was threatened and in immediate peril. "If we let him alone as he is, all will believe in him . . ." (11, 48). Already "the entire world has gone after him" (12, 19). The last resistance, the only possible one was the very falsehood of which Jesus had accused them.

If it had been question of a temporal power, there would have been men found to uphold Jesus against the present ruler; and many had sought to make him the king of their temporal ambition. The pretext remains good: ". . . it is expedient that one man die for the people, instead of the whole nation perishing" (11, 50). This was not the word of man, though it serves the designs of men, but a "prophecy" says St. John and it served God's designs.

From this moment ambivalence is complete. Everything which is accomplished according to men's will and which is falsehood and a negation of the divine work is accomplished according to God's order in truth and in an entirely positive manner for men's salvation. The parody of triumphal entry into Jerusalem was accompanied, says St. Luke, by the tears of Jesus (Lk. 19, 41). However, the whole abjection with which the the Passion is filled is illumined by Christ's calm, His serene gravity, majesty, and what we could term His detachment.

And Jesus sets aside this detachment, John points out, only in the presence of Pilate; not, indeed, to answer with greater eagerness than was fitting the questions of this timid functionary, but in order to proclaim for the last time with all possible solemnity His title and mission: " 'Art thou the king of the Jews?'. . .'My kingdom is not of this world' . . .'Thou art a king then?' Pilate therefore said to him. 'Thou sayest it; I am a king. This is why I was born, and why I came into the world, to bear witness to the truth. Everyone who is of the truth hears my voice' " (18, 33-37).

We feel that for John the incidents which followed converged towards this declaration which sums up the entire mission and vocation of the one sent from the Father. These words correspond to those which closed the interview with Nicodemus (3, 21), and with those Jesus had hurled at the Jews bent on His destruction. "If you abide in my word, you shall be my disciples indeed, and you shall know the truth, and the truth shall make you free" (8, 31). For the last time the true Light, come into the world to enlighten every man, recalls what He has come in person to bring and reveal, but the world does not care.

For Pilate it is question only of bringing to a successful issue an affair among the Jews. "What is truth?" This is the question full of scorn that Pilate asks of this meek one who would gladly have enlightened him.

In our own day he would have decided upon confinement pure and simple for this dreamer, this fool, with the purple cloak. But the Jews are right: One cannot be too careful with a man who claims to be the "Son of God." Besides, neglect on his part to take the necessary measures would lead this turbulent and revengeful people to take action into their own hands; they would not simply turn the matter into a grievance against him, but would misrepresent him in high places, accusing him of a lack of loyalty or of a coolness towards Caesar's interest (19, 12). "Then he delivered him to them to be crucified."

In any case, the interview of man to man had become impossible since Jesus had criticized the Jews. He was condemned in the minds of those whom He had condemned. For His disciples only He remained the one sent by the Father; He was the Master and the Friend. The whole affair had only served to reveal more of His traits and with what skill John bears witness to them!

"Shall I not drink the cup . . . ?"

No human construction could have been able to balance such a conglomeration of errors and truth, of errors accompanied by truth; of truths confounding error. John knows how to show us Jesus as human and overflowing with tenderness; and only a few strokes of his pen are required for Christ's face to appear in majesty, even though He is clothed in mock garments, for Him to completely dominate the debates, for Him to remain the infinitely great Master in the accomplishment of His father's will: "Shall I not drink the cup that the Father has given me?" (18, 11). When pronouncing these words, Jesus had already climbed the first steps on the road of ignominy, and until the end He seems to repeat them interiorly, as He seems to repeat those other words: "But I am not alone, because the Father is with me" (16, 32). Another glance besides that of men follows Jesus as He walks to His crucifixion. Another colloquy besides that of the earth fills the heart of Christ. We remember the words of the Baptist: "The friend of the bridegroom, who stands and hears him rejoices exceedingly at the voice of the bridegroom" (3, 29). John had heard Jesus ask: "Shall I not drink the cup that the Father has given me?" He knows Christ's thoughts. Without doubt, as he contemplates Jesus, it is not with a heart filled with the joy of the Baptist, but rather filled with sadness even to the breaking point. His Gospel only hints at this. At the most, we may divine a tremor in John as the soldiers seize His tunic, woven from top to bottom, to cast lots over it; or when Jesus says to him, "Behold thy mother," after having said to her, "Woman, behold thy son"; or finally, when He cries out in fulfillment of the Scriptures, "I thirst!"

"When Jesus had taken the wine, he said, 'It is finished.' And bowing his head, he gave up the spirit" (19, 30).

"They shall look upon him whom they have pierced"

For those who love, nothing ends with the loved one's death. The eyes, no more than the heart, cannot detach themselves from Him. They must remain there even though nothing will happen, and they must always come back to rest there.

The guards hustle about their work. In the distance, the sabbath approach sets the people busy. But John only continues to gaze upon Him. And then from the opened side come forth blood and water; and John's heart is torn. At the same time, it seems as though his life is renewed, his mind enlightened, his heart warmed and softened as in a great furnace. "They shall look upon him whom they have pierced" (19, 37). The whole Passion, the prolonged death of Jesus, that death which was threatening for months—behold it now suddenly delivered up to hearts. It no longer stifles, it no longer oppresses. It is no longer the death of one man for His people, but death in the heart of all those who loved Him and crucified Him. "Grant that I may bear about in my body the death of Christ; make me a sharer in His Passion, and make me mindful of His wounds," as we sing in the Stabat Mater. Each one, if a friend of Christ, bears this death in his heart: "They will look upon him whom they have pierced."

This look of faith, expanding and developing into love in John, is lighted for each of us in the furnace of the Passion. Christian love is not directed towards an impassible God; neither is it in eternal mourning. It knows that God is the Victor, but that being man He really died for us. And it takes this death into its heart. It carries it as its glory and pardon, its joy and humiliation. This death is a Christian's first good among others that have been promised. Nothing less than death would satisfy Him, and in spite of my sins, He loved me more than His own life. And if even He were not to give me heaven, I would still be the recipient of what cannot be replaced, His love unto death, His death through love. No one can say without blasphemy: What good is the death of this Galilean? This death concerns each one of us. "He loved us to the end" (13, 1), and the "greatest love," this death, must become the sign of Christian love, as it is already its source and object. In it, our faith finds a fire which will never cease to burn. Jesus died only after giving everything; and in His death He effaces Himself before His gifts.

"It is consummated"

The Holy Spirit alone was going to be able to reveal to John the infinite riches he was bringing with him from Calvary, and what the death of His Master, God, and Friend had accomplished for him. "Many things yet I have to say to you, but you cannot bear them now. But when he, the Spirit of truth has come . . . he will receive of what is mine, and will declare it to you" (16, 12,15). Everything weighed too heavily in the apostle's heart, and before his eyes there was always that Cross, that blood and water, coming forth from the pierced side. "I thirst". . ."It is consummated."

The hour would come when these events would reveal their true meaning, when the actions of that last Supper which had made of him a priest, and which had permitted him to offer this sacrifice of love with Jesus would be recalled: "But the Advocate, the Holy Spirit, whom the Father will send in my name, he will teach you all things, and bring to your mind whatever I have said to you" (14, 26).

II. THE MOTHER OF THE REDEEMER

"The soldiers therefore, when they had crucified him, took his garments and made of them four parts, to each soldier a part, and also the tunic. Now the tunic was without seam, woven in one piece from the top. They therefore said to one another, 'Let us not tear it, but let us cast lots for it, to see whose it shall be.' That the Scripture might be fulfilled which says, 'They divided my garments among them; and for my vesture they cast lots.' These things therefore the soldiers did" (19, 23,24). Mention of Christ's seamless tunic is not made here simply to suggest Christ's priesthood on the Cross, and perhaps also the mystery of the unity of which it is the symbol; it introduces us secretly to another mystery, that of the Virgin on Calvary.

While the soldiers retired a little distance to watch the crucified after having done their work, Mary advances to the foot of the Cross, and standing by was the disciple whom Jesus loved (19, 25). Right until the end Mary and John remained there, silent and motionless, their interest in nothing but that immolated form and that beloved face. Until the last word was spoken, "It is finished," until Jesus gives up the spirit, both remain there totally absorbed in the only object of their love. They were intimately united because of Jesus' words, "Woman, behold thy son... Behold thy mother" (19, 26), and it is with the same heart they live the death of Christ, that they join one another in the supreme sacrifice, that they welcome this great love into their own torn hearts. These few moments change the apostle's life and confer upon his Gospel a new depth and dimension.

If the entire fourth Gospel is directed towards love, the entire passion is directed towards that instant where Mary and John see the lance open a path into Love, whence flows upon the world the blood which redeems it and the water which regenerates it.

The Virgin of Cana

In John's eyes Mary is the Virgin of Calvary, the Mother of the Lamb of God, and she is also "his mother." Thanks to the fourth Gospel she remains forever associated with that "hour" in which Christ glorified His Father and saved the world.

We know how carefully John conceals many things that are in his heart; we do not find in his Gospel more than two scenes in which Mary makes an appearance: at the wedding of Cana and on Calvary. We shall now see how these two scenes complete each other in John's mind.

"And on the third day a marriage took place at Cana of Galilee, and the mother of Jesus was there" (2, 1). This Cana episode is rich in meaning. It contains many different signs. In particular we discover in it a kind of prefiguration of the Last Supper, as well as a prediction of Calvary, for we see Christ united for the first time at Cana with His disciples and, as at the Cross, Mary is present.

At Cana water is changed into wine, and at the Supper wine is changed into His Blood. The nuptials between Christ and the Church are prefigured at Cana and actually realized on Calvary, and in each instance, Mary is to be found as the first in the faith. At Cana the disciples needed this sign in order to "believe in him," but Mary believed before this sign was worked. Her confidence and faith did not only precede the miracle, but were instrumental in obtaining it. Mary's attitude enables John to understand and help us understand also that faith is the bond that unites souls to Christ, the unifying power of a Church whose Mother is Mary.

Mary's place at this wedding was the sign of another wedding, that of Christ to His Church.

Mary's role at Cana, however, is not limited to this act of faith, nor to inaugurating the nuptials of Christ with the Church; it appears even more profound still and in direct reference to the mystery of Calvary. In fact, her remark, "They have no wine" (2, 3) is answered by Jesus in a way that is rather disconcerting. "What would you have me do, woman? My hour has not yet come."

Whatever be the translation we adopt, the question does bring out the fact that Christ's submission to Mary in His hidden life is now changed. Jesus accedes to her desire, but in doing so gives her the title "woman" and states that His "hour has not yet come." We are introduced to a mystery here that is not cleared up until the Cross is raised on Calvary. Jesus will employ this same title again, strange on the lips of a son, when He gives John to her, "Woman, behold thy son." As for the "hour" which we know means His death, it is precisely in this hour that He will associate Mary with the redemption and make her mother of the disciple and of all men.

At Cana the public life of Christ begins. Jesus surrenders Himself to His Father's business and He invites Mary to withdraw. But when His "hour" has come, she will take up her place again by her Son and will be associated with Him in a very definite manner in His redemptive work.

It is a fact that in the fourth Gospel it is essentially with the mystery of the Redemption that the Virgin is associated. The absence of other references to Mary in other episodes in Jesus' life is explained perhaps by the fact that John speaks of only what he actually witnessed. In any case, it is certain that the time he best knew Mary was the period of Christ's public life and especially the hour on Calvary, the hour of the Redemption, and in events subsequent to this.

It is likewise certain that John says nothing of the Incarnation and yet, having received Mary into his home, he was in a better position than the others to obtain from her testimony of incomparable value concerning the birth and early years of Christ. But John, the evangelist of the Word made flesh, is the evangelist of the Lamb of God. In other words, he is the evangelist of the Incarnation considered from the aspect which terminates on the Cross, where Christ's flesh immolated on Calvary takes away the sins of the world and serves as food for redeemed men. It is also in this perspective that he considers the Virgin. In his eyes she is really the Mother of the Redeemer.

Undoubtedly Mary's divine and virginal maternity is at the basis of the mystery of the Word made flesh; it is a spiritual and physical link uniting her indissolubly to the Incarnation. But this fact once established, John considers its consequences in regard to the Redemption; and the silence with which he covers Mary in his Gospel until the day on which she appears at the foot of the Cross teaches us that she had need only of faith, silence, suffering, and love to prepare herself to live the word which would be one day addressed to her.

At Cana Jesus seems to make a "rendez-vous" with her in advance for that hour which would entail more than an encounter, more than an agreement of minds. Then there would be a communion so entire that the Virgin's spiritual fruitfulness would expand into the work of the Redemption itself.

The powerful intercession of Mary at Cana gives us another reason for referring this mystery to Calvary. In spite of an apparent unwillingness to listen to His Mother's request, Jesus still performs the miracle. He simply points out when answering, "My hour has not yet come," that He has no orders to take from anyone. Since this is so, He was all the more free to satisfy her request with His entire will and to condescend to her wish "before" the hour.

If the unusual character of the miracle is underscored, it is also to make it understood that once the hour has come, in the new economy prefigured by the change of water into wine—symbol of the passage from the Old Law to the Law of grace—the Virgin's intercession will be exercised in a regular manner. The hour of His passion and death is not only the hour in which Christ associates Mary with Himslf, but the hour when He constitutes her our Mother. It appears that the Virgin's function, once made Mother of us all, will be to obtain from her Son the wine of divine grace which is profusely given to those who take part in the nuptials of the Spouse and the Lamb.

The Virgin at Calvary

The Virgin's role at Calvary helps us to grasp how, in John's mind, this account and the scene at Calvary correspond with each other and are even complementary. His intention is evidently to recall at the close of his Gospel what he had announced at its beginning along with its fulfillment. Calvary gives him the opportunity to show the fulfillment of what was announced at the dawn of humanity's beginning.

It would be rather surprising if John, careful at all times to point out the fulfillment of the various prophecies concerning Christ, had not thought of placing the presence of the "Woman" standing at the foot of the Cross and the role she was called upon to play there side by side with the prophecy of Genesis known under the name of "Protoevangelium." And this is all the more evident since, immediately after Jesus confides Mary to John and vice versa, we read the words: "After this Jesus, knowing that all things were accomplished . . ." (19, 28). This is a statement in which John means the accomplishment of a prophecy. But which prophecy? Surely the one directed to Mary through Eve.

Yahweh had declared to the serpent who seduced the woman: " 'Because thou hast done this thing, thou art cursed among all cattle and beasts of the earth. Upon thy breast thou shalt go, and the earth thou shalt eat all the days of thy life. I will put enmities between thee and the woman, and thy seed and her seed: she shall crush thy head, and thou shalt lie in wait for her heel'. . . And Adam called his wife Eve, because she was the mother of all the living" (Gn. 3, 14,15,20).

If the woman in the text is Eve, through her it is Mary who is meant; for this "he" appears to designate one of the woman's sons, viz., Christ. The Protoevangelium announces a struggle between the serpent, Satan, and the woman, one of whose descendants will transform this struggle into a victory. And it is at the Cross that we find the protagonists of the drama of Genesis.

John says repeatedly that the devil is at the Cross. He is not only the great adversary against whom Christ struggles; we see him especially evoked when Jesus speaks of His death on the Cross. " 'Now is the judgment of this world; now will the prince of the world be cast out. And I, if I be lifted up from the earth, will draw all things to myself.' Now he said this signifying the death he was to die" (12, 31). In Jesus Satan recognized his great enemy, this "son of the woman" who would crush his head, and the struggle between them was to be to the death. At the Cross, the adversaries face each other: the serpent and the Son of the woman. That the conditions of the prophecy be realized, it is necessary to discover the woman of whom Genesis is speaking and to specify her role.

It would seem that it is Eve who is aimed at through the text of Genesis. Now, in the fourth Gospel, Eve does not appear at all, neither does Adam. But St. Augustine expresses the Johannine thought as well as that of the Fathers when he writes: "Mary was already present in Eve, but it was through Mary that what Eve was, was revealed."[3] The prophecy of Genesis designates actual personages: the serpent, the son of the woman. The woman to whom it alludes must also be an actual person and she too must participate personally in the final combat. It

3. St. Augustine, Sermon 102.

cannot be woman in general, but a certain woman, viz., the new Eve, Mary.

Perhaps for John himself the prophecy will not be fully brought to light except in seeing Mary at the foot of the Cross. He understands that at the hour when the Son and the Woman were going to crush the ancient serpent (12, 31), it was right that the woman be there so that the prophecy would be fulfilled.[4] And at the same time this word "Woman" applied by Christ to His Mother finds an explanation. Its strangeness disappears as soon as we see it has the purpose of evoking, over and above her relationship to Jesus, her role as the new Eve.

Mary cannot even receive this name "new Eve," if we intend through it to make her only an extension of the Old Testament. Just as Jesus, as the new Adam, does much more than simply extend or fulfill Adam's role, so Mary also does much more than bring Eve's role to perfection. She is Eve's substitute in such a way that it is not Eve that elucidates Mary, but rather Mary that elucidates Eve. Of the two women, it is Eve to whom the prophecy refers in a less perfect way. Also, while Eve, "the mother of all the living according to the flesh" tends to grow progessively indistinct, Mary, on the contrary, "mother of all the living according to the Spirit," does not cease to grow, since the time that her role at the foot of the Cross has been brought to light by St. John. This "woman," through whom the Messias has come, appears as the true Mother of all the living. She joins to the divine maternity, which was according to the flesh and the Spirit, a spiritual maternity of which John is going to be first beneficiary. But how are we to take this maternity?

"Woman, behold thy son"

Are we to see in these words a real spiritual maternity or simply an act of tenderness and spiritual piety through which Jesus confides Mary to John and vice versa? And if it is question of a maternity, is this to be limited to John alone or should it be extended to all men through him? And, in the latter case, what extension must one give Christ's words: Are they directed to His disciples, those constituted "children of God" through the faith or are they directed to all men? We can easily see the result of the answer in what concerns the Virgin herself. Following the

---

4. "A kind of connection unites these three complementary texts: the prophecy concerning the woman as enemy of the serpent (Gn. 3, 15), the Woman of the mysterious nuptials at Cana (2, 4), and finally, the Woman present at the foot of the Cross (19, 27). "Eve is implied in Mary and both are intermingled in the realization of one plan" (F. M. Braun, Mary, the Mother of God's People, p. 94).

answer given, we will see in her the "Mother of the faithful," or also the mother of all men, and the Refuge of sinners.

To answer these questions it is good to come as close as possible to Gospel realities and to consider what gave rise to what we look upon as the spiritual maternity of Mary. We have a tendency to give this notion, as also that of the Mystical Body, an abstract form.

Now there is nothing less abstract than the reality designated by the words, "Woman, behold thy son." In fact, as far as Mary is concerned, John was not only a very close relative whom she looked upon somewhat as her child from the beginning of their association with one another; and he was also in her eyes "the disciple whom Jesus loved" with a special love and who had been more faithful to Him than the others. Finally and above all, he was the one confided to her by Jesus in an express and very special manner.

If what characterizes John, viz., the love uniting him to Christ and making him His friend, if this union and love give him the right to become the son of the Virgin, it is nevertheless to one of Christ's words, His all-powerful and creative word, that Mary's spiritual maternity owes its existence and fruitfulness.

The concrete realism of the Gospel places us before a situation that is eminently personal (what could be more personal than Mary's feelings for John?), but since it is based not upon physical ties but upon Christ's word, it is capable of multiplying itself and renewing itself endlessly because of its spiritual nature.

John himself could not have understood and realized Christ's words except under their personal form. True, he already loved Mary with a deep tenderness and a great respect and Christ's words served to develop this even more. But these words were really effective in him. Henceforth they gave rise to a twofold current of supernatural love between them and this strengthened and deepened the sentiments of human tenderness already uniting them. Although in a different manner, Christ realized between these two souls something of what He had recommended and left in His last will to His disciples: "You in me and I in you" and "Abide in my love" (14, 20; 15, 9). When confiding them one to the other, Jesus gave their sentiments the power to develop into that mutual and common relationship that was to exist between them. "And from that hour the disciple took her into his home" (19, 27).

"He took her," i.e., he received and welcomed her. How can we fail to see a reflection in these words of John of that attitude we are supposed to have towards Christ? If He gives the power of becoming sons of God to those who receive Him (1, 12), how would He not give the power to those who, like John, welcome His Mother, of becoming like him "children of the Virgin"? If we may draw this consequence from the spiritual order, the material fact is this: The same roof henceforth sheltered Mary and John; and between them they lived a true life in common. And in this way, for the first time, the spiritual motherhood of Mary was exercised. Before asking ourselves if this spiritual motherhood extends only to the faithful or to all men in general, let us examine what it was precisely in John's case.

"The disciple took her into his home"

John was not Mary's child simply because he took her into his home. He was her child much more because he had received her as an inheritance from his Master as the most beautiful flower of His garden, as one who would make it possible for him to breathe in at each instant the good odor of Christ. This is a good time to recall the words of Origen: "No one can acquire the spirit of John's Gospel (the flower of Gospels) if he has not rested upon the breast of Jesus, if he has not received Mary for his Mother."

The Johannine Gospel owes much of its charm and depth and beauty to the fact that Mary lived in John's heart and John in Mary's. The first to recognize, through the Baptist, the Lamb of God and the promised Messias and first to recognize the Risen Savior on Lake Genesareth, John was also the first to receive the Savior's Mother into his home and his heart. He is a model for the Christian under this twofold aspect.

On her part, Mary came to John with this title of Mother, a title covering a living reality according to her Son's will; and she brought to him also all that she had received and kept in her heart since the day the angel announced her motherhood until the day her soul, in conjunction with the Redeemer, was offered for the salvation of men. She brought John her heart which was forever united to that of her Son and living its life. All Christ's mysteries, all His love and His thought and His presence, all this John discovered in Mary and it was this that enabled him to enter more deeply than anyone else into the redemptive mystery of Love.

Mother of pure love

"I am the mother of fair love, and of fear, and of knowledge, and of holy hope" (Sir. 24, 18). St. John's Epistles prove that he knew this *mysterious Mother* of Scripture and that Mary was this Mother of fair love for him. He was formed by her and received everything from her hands. An extraordinary "science of divine love" was within him when he contemplated, as an ecstatic child, the mystery. "Born of God" (1 Jn. 3, 9) : is this not the title he constantly employs to designate and single out the grace of this new generation of believers? And he will call them: "Little children."

In the presence of this "birth" he conducts himself as he would before a light which dazzles him. Each day he realizes the joy of being born and of perfecting himself in love. This perfection stems from the two commandments of love and John will never believe that he has insisted enough on fraternal charity; but the perfection of love is an interior perfection, the overwhelming certitude of being loved and of loving in return.

"In this is love perfected with us, that we may have confidence in the day of judgment; because as he is, even so are we also in this world. There is no fear in love; but perfect love casts out fear, because fear brings judgment. And he who fears is not perfected in love. Let us therefore love, because God first loved us" (1 Jn. 4, 17-19).

Years of union with Christ have given John this experience of divine things which makes him a teacher similar to the wise men of whom the Scripture speaks. In the young turbulent Church of his advanced years the words of this Epistle have a hidden meaning, a meaning which he alone perhaps understands. Although his teaching is entirely new, for everything is new now since all begins with Christ, we perceive that this teaching still remains connected with the ancient teaching of the Sapiential Books. And between the writers of these books and John there is a definite bond, a living person who never ceases calling men to the interior life and instructing them in love. There is a Mother, and John was to look upon her.

We would be forcing the Johannine text were we to try to discover the influence of the Sapiential Books and that of the Virgin upon it, just as we would be forcing the issue in attributing to Mary the sayings of the book of Wisdom. However, there is an uninterrupted current underlying things divine. The same spirit dwells within them and gives them a unity of emphasis. John has this spirit which comes to him especially from the Old Testament. The books of Genesis, Exodus, and the Sapiential Books mold certain lines of his Gospel. But it is impregnated with Christ's own words even to the point of borrowing their stress: "And his commandments are not burdensome" (1 Jn. 5, 3), John writes, while Christ says: "My yoke is sweet and my burden light" (Mt. 11, 30). In John there is no real division between old and new things, but the same current of redeeming and life-giving love.

Time and reason build up systems, not love; and love in St. John makes them come tumbling down. To time John opposes not only a future, but also a past and a present that will fill everything. "God has first loved us" (1 Jn. 4, 19). The explanation of all things is always placed farther ahead, always deeper into the mystery of God. John draws at the fountains of love.

We don't know if he would have done the same if he had not had Mary as model and teacher. We are not authorized to think that it is from Mary that he receives his simplicity and that unity of purpose which characterizes his closing years. But we can say that it seems as though Mary had been for him: "the mother of fair love, and of fear, and of knowledge, and of holy hope." If John received love and knowledge of divine things from her, he also received hope from her.

What a difference and transformation between the text of the above-quoted Epistle and that youthful trait described by Mark. How he had roused the fire of the other apostles at the request: "Grant to us that we may sit, one at thy right hand and the other at thy left hand, in thy glory" (Mk. 10, 37). Jesus was not so indignant: "Can you drink of the cup of which I drink, or be baptized with the baptism with which I am to be baptized?"..."We can!" True, this presumptuous boast was to become a more subdued reality after they had walked the Master's paths. "Whoever wishes to be great shall be your servant; and whoever wishes to be first among you, shall be the slave of all" (Mk. 10, 44).

John does not quote these words in his Gospel; they have actually become his own way of acting. He detached himself from his concerns in order to follow the Master only. But when he hears Jesus say: "Shall I not drink the cup that the Father has given me to drink?" (18, 11), does he not recall his own boastful claim? Has not the moment come for him to drink this cup, just as it has for Peter to lay down his life for the Master? (18, 37). However, he does not run to seize it, and it is from another that he receives it. "When Jesus, therefore, saw his mother and the disciple standing by . . ."(19, 26). His weakness and nascent humility have dictated this attitude to John. He has placed himself in her shadow who knew both how to approach and drink of the cup. He follows her who followed Jesus, and it is near her that he stands during the hour of agony.

Always in the background like a servant, Mary knew how to take the first place by Jesus' side in the dereliction and the glory of the Cross. A little one among all, she, who lays claim to nothing, is there where the ambition of the others has grown weak, where John's fervor has been covered with confusion. And it is through her, this silent one, this servant, that he is introduced into the mystery of the cup which he had desired to drink!

"Behold thy son ... Behold thy mother"

If John was finally able to raise his eyes to the Cross, it was with Mary's strength, her humility, and her grace; for this Mother less than any other mother was not able to allow the chalice offered to her Son to pass without drinking it with Him. John's secret story, and ours also, is written on these pages of the Gospel which are both eloquent and silent. It is Mary on Calvary who introduces us to the mystery of the Cross. Between the Cross and ourselves stands Mary our Mother.

The Cross, so uplifting in the distance, so heavy when actually present, is the chalice of our sufferings and the sign of our sins. We stumble against it, but we have no fear for our Mother is present. The assurance which shines through John's text testifies to the truth that he knew she was near him. "In this is love perfected with us, that we may have confidence in the day of judgment; because as he is, even so are we also in this world" (1 Jn. 4, 17).

Judgment day will come and has come already. For John the judgment Christ spoke about so much was that of the prince of darkness who has been cast out. But it was also the day of his own judgment as well as ours. That day was terrible to his once presumptuous heart which is now failing because of his weakness; but now that day is sweet because between the Cross and him there is a Mother who alone has been found worthy to drink the cup.

As the chosen daughter of God, preserved by the Cross, the "first born of Jesus," Mary is invested with His fruitful grace. While Jesus enters into His Father's glory as the only-begotten Son and the Savior, He confides this salvation to Mary. She becomes its Mother, and it is in her that humanity henceforth meets its Redeemer.

Thus, we can answer the question we asked above: Is Mary simply the Mother of the disciples whom Jesus seemed to represent in the person of John, the beloved disciple? Or is she Mother of all men, because she carries in herself the fruits of the Redemption acquired for humanity?

While acknowledging the fact that she is in a special manner the Mother of all those united to her Son through love and fidelity, it seems more in conformity with the Gospel to acknowledge with the teaching magisterium of the Church that in John's person "the whole human race was symbolically designated by Christ, and more particularly those who adhere to Him through faith" (Leo XIII).

Popular sentiment has always had it that all men, even sinners, must have recourse to Mary as their refuge. John, far from opposing this, confirms it. When all the others had fled, overcome by discouragement, fatigue, and human weakness, was it not "near Mary" that John stood to be present at the Master's death? And it is Mary whom Jesus, in His final act of detachment, gives to him. "Unless the grain of wheat fall into the ground and die . . ." (12, 24). The grain of our life here below must fall into Mary's earth; she is given to us so that she may accept, warm, and make it live and render it fruitful unto the eternal life of the children of God. John still has to be taught that "perfect love casts out fear" (1 Jn. 4, 18). Before the Crucified he was able to understand that the real and only chastizement of those who love is contained in the look of compunction cast upon the side wounded by the lance. "They shall look on him whom they have pierced" (19, 37). It is a look which makes one realize the infinite price of love, but which desires to realize it more and more.

In the short episode of the woman taken in adultery and brought to Jesus to be judged and then stoned, the Master pronounces the words: "Let him who is without sin among you be the first to cast a stone at her" (8, 7). All withdrew and when they had gone, Jesus said, "Woman, where are they? Has no one condemned thee?" "No one, Lord." "Neither will I condemn thee. Go thy way, and from now on sin no more" (8, 10).

There was one at the Cross who never sinned and who could have accused us of her Son's death, but she is silent. "Behold thy mother," says Jesus. "He who fears is not perfected in love" (1 Jn. 4, 18). Jesus has not opened for her the book in which all our sins are written and numbered, but in her heart she has experienced their bitterness. No Gospel presents her hastening with Joseph of Arimathea, Nicodemus, and the holy women to prepare and bury the body of her Son. None reports that she saw and touched that body after the resurrection, nor that Jesus said to her as to the Magdalene, "Do not touch me" (20, 17). After the Cross, Mary has no longer anyone else for sons but John and all men. Towards them she has turned once in the Gospel to speak and then it is to direct them towards her Son: "Do whatever he tells you" (2, 5; Cf. Gn. 41, 55). She has nothing else to say, but she remains with us to teach us how to do this. Thus is she also a witness. She tells us of the one in whom she has believed, hoped, and whom she has loved; the one who was her justification and glory, viz., the Word of God.

Mary, Mother of the Faithful, Refuge of Sinners

Is Mary "Mother of the faithful" or "Mother and refuge of sinners"? She is Mother of the faithful because of Jesus' love for those who believe;

but she is also "refuge of sinners," for she is given to us as a mother at the hour of judgment, at the hour when our hearts will be laid bare in the presence of Him who dispenses life or death.

Mary is refuge of sinners because she was given to us at the Cross. "For I have come not to judge the world, but to save it" (12, 47). Christ's last gift to us on the Cross is proof of His pardon and of the infinite tenderness of His Heart; for He offers to share with us His most treasured possession, Mary, His Mother.

We have only to look at His heart to understand the reason he had for giving her to us, viz., His love. But this love of Christ is never only a feeling; it is a power that acts, a grace surrendering itself and pouring itself out, and the entire activity of this grace is exercised in one direction, Christ's return to the Father, life in God.

If He gives us Mary for our Mother, if He makes her our Mother, it can be in no other way except by investing her with a love so that she is henceforth oriented actively, effectively, and efficaciously towards the return to the Father and life in God. If we find in her one who consoles us, one whose tenderness warms the most wearied hearts, it is not because of the pleasure we find in being loved, but because of the taste she will give us for the things of God, that intense desire for eternal life that we draw from her.

Already here on earth the task of a mother worthy of the name is to bring forth her children to this earthly life. The task of Mary consists in detaching us from the goods of earth to turn us towards realities which lead us to God.

Mary's total effacement in John's Gospel testifies to her effacement in her spiritual maternity for the sake of Christ's life in us. But all motherhood calls for a return of love. In these words: "Behold thy mother" we hear the call which assures us we are her children; it invites us to rest our eyes upon her, to place her in the center of our affections, and to pass through her in order to attain life.

Christ must have been very sure of His Mother when confiding us to her, in spite of our human attachment and our slothfulness in going to God. But He knows that the maternal action of Mary would work to free us from both these defects. John who points out the danger of misleading cults, "Little children, guard yourselves from the idols," has only one word when there is question of Mary: "And from that hour the disciple took her into his home" (19, 27). Not for a moment does he fear that his love and devotion to her will turn him away from Christ or withdraw any of his love for Christ. Mary has never been anything else but the Mother of God.

Mary's silent consent

This is the Mother the fourth Gospel presents in all its soberness. Nothing which concerns her personally is shown us, e.g., the youthful freshness of her virginity, her expectation and beauty as a young mother, her anxiety at the loss of Jesus in the Temple and the three days search. She appears only once with her Son at the beginning of His public life at Cana, and she is careful even then to turn us towards Christ. The second time is at the foot of the Cross, and Jesus turns her from Him in order to confide in her all those who will henceforth be her children.

These very conservative strokes of John's pen uncover the long and secret preparation of Mary for her maternity. The first picture presents her as being interested in the needs of those around her, full of assurance of her Son's power and the hearing she will receive, totally receptive to whatever He says. She does not stop at the apparent refusal of her request, for undoubtedly she is aware of the fact that this miracle will decide the faith of the disciples. Jesus had taught her long ago, as the other evangelists point out, that His main concern is His Father's business and she too already works at this by drawing aside in her own way.

Mary's reserve at the Cross is even more total. John does not tell us that Mary's consent to becoming our mother was required at Calvary, just as he says nothing of his own consent at becoming her son. Jesus' most constant teaching in the discourse after the Supper is that everything that belongs to Him is ours and that everything that we are becomes His. God respected Mary's liberty when asking her to become the Mother of Jesus. Was everything then contained in her first "fiat"?

The source of life originates on the Cross; that is why it was only at the Cross that Mary could become our Mother. "The baptism with which Jesus was to be baptized" was to make the fountains of grace pour out upon her; this grace was so abundant, so full, that it renders her forever fruitful. Thus, Mary becomes our Mother freely through the action of divine love. "All that is mine is thine" (17, 10). Everything I have, I give you to be transmitted and communicated to others. Her divine maternity is augmented then by her maternity with regard to humanity; and it comes from an infinite grace, from the love of God for her, and we contemplate in this mystery the manifestation of her union in the Spirit with the charity of Christ.

St. John places us at the foot of the Cross in the presence of Mary's crowning with grace; but he also places us before Mary who has finally arrived at the end of all those growths in intimacy with her divine Son, at the end, in some way, of all the "fiats" she gave throughout her life until that moment on Calvary. Mary's effacement in the presence of Jesus helps us understand that, far from being only passive, she never ceased giving herself actively to what was being demanded of her during the three years of the Public Life right up until that total stability of her union with Christ which was crowned by her spiritual maternity.

Mary's maternity was suspended at the death of her Son. Undoubtedly Jesus' life belonged to no one but Himself, but He had received it from Mary, from Mary's consent. The Father had once sent an angel to ask the child of Nazareth for her consent. Did Jesus have to act in like manner? No, for between Jesus and Mary, miracles are not necessary and words are useless. John tells us simply: "Now there was standing by the cross of Jesus his mother" (19, 25). Her attitude is a form of consent. If anyone had to say "yes" at the Cross, the Virgin to whom Jesus belonged as a Son was alone with God in having to say it; but undoubtedly she did not pronounce this "yes." Jesus was sure of her heart, united as it was to His own. She had been drawn there with the same desire that burned in Him of drinking this cup, of setting aflame that fire on earth. Mary, standing, is ready.

In what way and in what measure does Mary's consent to Jesus' sacrifice share in the Redemption? We do not know and it is not the object of our study here. Christ gives us the opportunity of drawing the fruits of it from John's writing. We know this consent was given for the spiritual maternity was the crowning of the espousals at the Cross. When making her mother of men, Christ reveals in her the highest marvels of His redeeming sacrifice: she is a creature in whom are strewn the sources of the spirit of charity and in whom flow the infinite waves of universal mercy.

No creature will ever be a daughter of God in the same way as was Mary for she was entirely God-centered. But in return God made a gift to her of what He loved with an everlasting love, viz., this humanity in whose favor He even delivered His Son up to death. And it is this grace of infinite love that St. John proposes as the object of our contemplation in Mary. It is because of this that it is good, it is infinitely beneficial to stay with Mary, to take her into our own home, to live with her as the disciple did; in a word: to be her child. For the child of Mary can be nothing else but the perfect lover of God and Jesus Christ.

Mary and the Church

After this mention of her at the foot of the Cross the fourth Gospel says nothing else about Mary. We know from the *Acts of the Apostles* that she was among the apostles when they, after a long and intense preparation in prayer, received the Holy Spirit. Through this we see the link that unites Mary to the Spirit on the one hand, she who conceived through Him, and on the other, to the Church whose Mother she is.

According to his customary manner, John invites us to consider these realities not in precise circumstances which he has not related but in a spiritual way. John's Gospel, as we have seen and shall see, is the Gospel of the Spirit. It is also an ecclesial Gospel, in the very measure in which the data he proposes are those with which the Church will be constituted and which will give it the power to live and develop: faith and the sacraments.

Now, we may ask ourselves if the long and profound influence of Mary upon John, of Mary the first in the faith and in whom the Church saw its beginnings, did not play a decisive role in the vision which St. John had of spiritual realities, and the manner in which he presented them in his Gospel?

When the rivers of living water began to flow from the side of the Crucified, who was actually there to receive this effusion if not the Virgin Mary? But these rivers of living water are inseparable from the blood, that blood which Jesus received from His Mother. Now Tradition has seen in this water and blood the symbol of the Spirit and the new birth, of baptism and the Eucharist, the symbol of the Church being born from the side of Christ.

Between Mary and the Church there exists much more than a comparison. Mary is the first link in that line of life which the Mystical Body of Christ will form through the centuries. But this link resembles no other, for it is she who gave Christ His body and, at the Cross, the entire Church is to be found concentrated and assembled in her, that Church whose foundations are to be strengthened a few days hence in the Cenacle and over whose cradle Mary will bend with maternal solicitude.

The Holy Spirit is to be found in her, at the origin of the Mystical Body of the Church as well as of its Head, of Christians as well as of Christ. Thus, we cannot reduce her maternity simply to the affective order. Her role is effective. She does not have as her mission the duty only of adopting us as her children and of forming Christ in us; she must work also to build up the Church, in us now in the Spirit, without whom our birth to the divine life and our position as children of God would not be realized.

These realities remain more or less implicit in the Gospel and we would ask ourselves if they really express the apostle's mind. He has explicitly pointed them out in the Apocalypse. There in fact the role of the Virgin is described under the traits of that woman: "clothed with the sun, and the moon was under her feet, and upon her head was a crown of twelve stars. And being with child, she cried out in her travail and was in anguish of delivery" (Ap. 12, 12). She struggles against the dragon who is ready to devour the child as soon as it is delivered. But while the child is raised up to God and to the throne, the Woman receives the two wings of the great eagle to fly into the desert. "And the dragon was angered with the woman, and went away to wage war with the rest of her offspring, who keep the commandments of God, and hold fast to the testimony of Jesus" (Ap. 12, 17).

She furnishes the Church with a perfect model for the children she must bring into the world over the centuries. The Church will conquer with Mary, through the Blood of the Lamb, and like Mary the Church will be a mother by remaining united to Jesus, source of divine life.

In the Apocalypse Mary appears as having arrived at the place destined for her and as reunited to her Child. In the Gospel she is before all else the one who accompanies the Church in its march here below. It is under these two aspects that she must be considered. Triumphant in heaven whose Queen she is, sharing the glory of her Son, she remains nevertheless occupied with her children on earth. She continues to recognize their need and she obtains it for them through her intercessory prayers. She never ceases bringing them forth to the life of heaven and guiding them to her Son. "Do whatever he tells you" (2, 5).

Spouse of the Lamb

On earth as in heaven Mary is the Mother as well as the Woman associated with the nuptials of the Lamb. At Cana, she was present at the figure of these nuptials; at Calvary, these nuptials were sealed in the blood of Christ offered in sacrifice. In the heavenly Jerusalem she is all at once: Mother, Spouse, and Queen, occupying "near Jesus" the place of honor at the eternal nuptials of the Lamb.

"And I heard as it were the voice of a great crowd, and as the voice of many waters, and as the voice of many thunders, saying, 'Alleluia! for the Lord, our God almighty, now reigns. Let us be glad and rejoice, and give glory to him; for the marriage of the Lamb has come, and his spouse has prepared herself. And she has been permitted to clothe herself in fine linen, shining, bright. For the fine linen is the just deeds of the saints ... Blessed are they who are called to the marriage supper of the Lamb" (Ap. 19, passim).

CHAPTER 19

UNDER THE HOLY SPIRIT'S GUIDANCE

If the Johannine Gospel is preceded by a Prologue which places us at the "beginning" and plunges, so to speak, into eternity, it does not come to an end until after opening the doors of the future upon the final Parousia.

The contrast is great between what may be termed the "body" of this Gospel which is so strictly limited to the time John lived with the Savior and which contains no scene John has not actually witnessed, and these two "antennae" which plunge, one into the distant past and the other into the future.

The Prologue brings us face to face with the Word who was "in the beginning and who was with God" (1, 1). The conclusion of the Gospel sets us before the Holy Spirit and the Church, those two closely associated realities which will henceforth be "Christ continued, diffused, and communicated." Or to be more precise still, these two realities will be: the Holy Spirit acting in the Church as a whole and in each individual soul, and the Church as the body of Christ governed and vivified by the Spirit.

Between the Prologue and the body of the Gospel lies that essential truth, the Incarnation. And between the body of the Gospel and its conclusion, there is likewise an event of primary importance, a capital truth upon which rests the structure of the faith, the Resurrection. With this resurrection, not only is the earthly life of Christ brought to completion, but a new era commences which will consecrate both Christ's return to His Father and the Spirit's mission to mankind.

St. John did not wait until the Ascension and Pentecost to present us with the coming of the new era with its essential characteristics. Undoubtedly the Cross already gives meaning to Christ's teachings and actions. Nevertheless, the Resurrection alone brings a consecration to them which actually changes this death into a victory and this "end" into a beginning. A new epoch begins in which a regenerated humanity is destined to live.

The Resurrection and its Witnesses

The fourth Gospel, as well as the Synoptics and the Epistles of St. Paul, assigned a conspicuous place to the event of the Resurrection. But following his usual mode of procedure, John spends no time recounting what others have already written about. Before extracting the effects of Christ's victory over death and especially over one of its consequences, viz., his return to the Father, John gathers together the testimonies of others, while not failing to note down details he has actually witnessed. These testimonies do not only bolster up those of John, but they also form a counterpart to the testimonies which honor the Messias at the beginning of his Gospel. This time, however, his purpose is to make a clear declaration concerning Christ's divinity and His title of "Son of God." The testimonies John brings forth are those of Peter, Mary Magdalene, the apostles in general, and St. Thomas.

These are all very definite testimonies upon which is to rest the new order in which humanity is called upon to live. The new order is the Church and the sacraments, the Christian faith, and the Holy Spirit since henceforth it is under His constantly guiding influence that men will have to "pass from this world to the Father" (13, 1).

The scenes reported by John which refer to the Resurrection are particularly vibrant and evocative. For instance, upon hearing the Magdalene, just returned breathless from the tomb, cry out: "They have taken the Lord from the tomb, and we do not know where they have laid him" (20, 2), Peter and John immediately hasten to the spot. "The two were running together, and the other disciple ran on before, faster than Peter, and came first to the tomb. And stooping down he saw the linen cloths lying there, yet he did not enter. Simon Peter therefore came following him, and he went into the tomb . . . Then the other disciple also went in . . ." (20, 3-8). The description of the tomb, the low opening necessitating one's bending down to peer inside, and those details concerning the bands lying on the ground and the shroud rolled up in a place apart, all these are truly the work of an ocular witness. And the words which follow give evidence of the emotion that seized him when, before the empty tomb, faith suddenly invaded his soul.

For John faith will always remain linked to the Resurrection. If he sees in the latter Christ's victory over death, he also is aware that this resurrection is to serve as the indestructible foundation of faith over the centuries.

To his own personal testimony and Peter's, he now joins that of the Magdalene. "But Mary was standing outside weeping at the tomb. So, as she wept, (a detail surely seen by John), she stooped down and looked into the tomb, and saw two angels sitting, one at the head and one at the feet, where the body of Jesus had been laid. They said to her . . . And when she had said this she turned round and beheld Jesus standing there, and she did not know that it was Jesus . . ." (20, 11-14).

Then comes that wonderful description, penetrated through and through with tenderness and bathed in a virginal light: " 'Woman, why art thou weeping? Whom dost thou seek?' She, thinking that it was the gardener, said to him, 'Sir, if thou hast removed him, tell me where thou hast laid him and I will take him away.' Jesus said to her, 'Mary!' Turning, she said to him, 'Rabboni!' (that is to say, Master). Jesus said to her, 'Do not touch me, for I have not yet ascended to my Father, but go to my brethren and say to them, 'I ascend to my Father and your Father, to my God and your God' " (20, 15-17). This is the dawn of a world created anew in grace and love, the first morn of a new humanity which realizes it is pardoned. God finds His children once again and calls to them. The Good Shepherd knows His sheep by name and they hear His voice.

John reports the testimony proceeding from the apostles as a group, first in the absence of Thomas, then with him (20, 24,26). These two very similar scenes, succeeding one another after a period of eight days, furnish a priceless testimony concerning the Resurrection and also concerning the quality of faith that greeted the Risen Lord!

Magdalene had recognized Him by the sound of His voice, and love opened her eyes. The apostles made use of their eyes to behold the Master's hands and feet and side (20, 20), after He had entered the room in which they were gathered together, the doors being shut. They give in only after they have seen the evidence, and then their joy is boundless (20, 20). Nevertheless, the unanimous testimony of his companions is not enough for Thomas. "Unless I see in his hands the print of the nails, and put my finger into the place of the nails, and put my hand into his side, I will not believe!". This incredulity, as well as that of the two disciples on the road to Emmaus, earned for us a priceless evangelical pearl which may be called the Johannine beatitude: "Because thou hast seen me, thou hast believed. Blessed are they who have not seen, and yet have believed" (20, 29).

This declaration which introduces us to the concluding words of the fourth Gospel seems to open up at the same time the doors of the future.

"Blessed are they who have not seen, but have believed," exclaims the Lord whose glance rests already upon an immense assembly "which no man can number" (Ap. 7, 9) of those who will become children of God by believing in the Risen Christ. These words place before us that new era into which humanity enters, the era of faith for which the fourth Gospel has just furnished the content, communicating the good news of salvation. "Many other signs Jesus worked in the sight of his disciples, which are not written in this book. But these are written that you may believe that Jesus is the Christ, the Son of God, and that believing you may have life in his name" (20, 30).

The Spirit at work in time

Faith, however, represents only one of this Gospel's dimensions. Destined for men living in time, this Gospel is not content with revealing simply the immutable, the eternal, and the divine, for these do not participate in time. The Gospel must give them the means of perfecting themselves in the time in which God has placed them, and it must teach them the road which, in Christ, leads to the Father, as well as the means of passing from this world to Him.

The notions of becoming and of time are interconnected and they bring with them the notion of an itinerary to follow. John has hardly insisted upon this itinerary, except to point out that it may be reduced to fidelity to the commandments, a fidelity of which love is both the soul and the lever. "If you love me, keep my commandments . . . He who has my commandments and keeps them, he it is who loves me" (14, 15,21). But John gives more attention to the fact that the Christian life must be realized inside time and through time.

Undoubtedly in the fourth Gospel Christ presents Himself as the Way, and the one and only Way to the Father. We cannot possibly envisage a code of morality which would not proceed from Him and terminate in Him. Indeed, since the mysteries of the Incarnation and the Redemption, moral life and ways stem from a fidelity to Christ, an attachment to His Person, whether this Person is manifest in our brothers or in Christ Himself. But salvation, individual or collective, is realized in the bosom of history and is inseparably linked to time.

If Christ had not taken into account the concrete conditions in which men have to work out their salvation, if He had not procured for them His aid and presence under a suitable form while they advanced towards God, He would have been unrealistic. But He is our Creator. "He is the Lord our God" (Ps. 94, 6) and "he knows what is in man" (2, 25).

He has fully shared in our human life and has experience of the many difficulties that beset us. The place given to the "world" in the fourth Gospel is proof of it and shows that, following the Master, the disciple was conscious of the obstacles presented by the world to man on his journey towards God.

This does not prevent the same Gospel from insisting on what is given us in the immediate present, and from reminding us that to possess Christ and to believe in Him means to be even now the children of God (1 Jn. 3, 2), and to have life everlasting (6, 47). We can say that God gave us everything in Christ Jesus.

Far from opposing one another, these two dimensions fulfill one another. That is why at the moment when, through the sacraments, the community of men with God commences to be built up, Christ merely envisages His departure as time which will follow. His actions and His words foresee and organize this time within the framework of which His life is destined to become theirs.

The words with which John opens the account of the Passover, "Before the feast of the Passover, Jesus, knowing that the hour had come to him to pass out of this world to the Father, having loved his own who were in the world, loved them to the end" (13, 1) take on their full meaning. While the sacraments and the Church are the means through which Christ's watchful love will be communicated to men "till the end of time," their faith, nourished by the sacraments, will have to overcome the world and manifest their own love for Christ (1 Jn. 5, 4).

There is another trait we must add to those already mentioned as characterizing the new era about to open. This one dominates all the rest. Christ explicitly linked the coming of the Spirit and His action to His own departure from the world. It is under His guidance that He placed humanity, and it is to the Spirit's all-powerful and creative action that the rites instituted by Christ will owe their efficacy and value.

Thus, it is upon this Spirit at work in this "time" which extends from Christ's departure until His return (as well as upon the nature and form of His action) that we must meditate, not without taking note of the following: John's Gospel shows us Christ on the point of leaving to His disciples a work which not only seems accomplished, but which He actually expresses as accomplished: "Father, I have accomplished the work that thou hast given me to do" (17, 4). "It is finished" (19, 30). And still this same Gospel appears entirely geared towards a reality which is only beginning, the foundations of which Christ was satisfied to lay. "Many things I have to say to you, but you cannot bear them now" (16, 12). Thus, John does not put less stress upon showing in Christ the unique foundation of everything that shall be, a foundation to which nothing can be added and from which nothing can be subtracted, than he does in turning us towards what must be realized, once Christ has returned to the Father.

The present is and remains then the foundation of the "future," while the future is the development of this present which, in a certain way at least, contains it. Between the one and the other we speak of a continuity and a unity that are vital. The present is forever "in act" and it is the present which, inside time, makes up the future.

The similitude of the "vine and the branches" sheds light upon these realities. We must recognize however that it does not account for one aspect of the problem: the one according to which being and becoming, time and eternity, which are on two different planes, have to be interpenetrated. The manner in which eternity takes possession of time in each of us is not envisaged in the similitude; neither is the manner in which the absolute and eternal Being is incorporated into a relative being, perpetually becoming, in order to permit the latter to perfect himself.

What the vine and the branch similitude does not explain is found elucidated by the revelation of the fourth Gospel concerning the Holy Spirit. And it is under this aspect that we would like to examine the Johannine work.

"He will glorify me, because he will receive of what is mine and declare it to you"

The coming of the Holy Spirit modified the spiritual perspectives of humanity. Undoubtedly even before Christ's coming the Holy Spirit was at work in this humanity. Men existed in the ancient economy (even aside from the sacred authors and those inspired) who were not obligated by the legalism of the Judaic precepts and observances. These men lived under the guidance of the Holy Spirit. However, this was still only an exception. The greater part of the people of God remained enclosed in the life which the Law marked with its imprint and literalness.

In the new economy of grace St. Paul vigorously opposes faith to the Law. It seems likewise that we can see rather an opposition than a progression in the words of the Prologue where John writes: "For the Law was given through Moses; grace and truth came through Jesus Christ" (1, 17).

Now the reign of grace is linked to the reign of the Spirit. The prophets already had some inkling of this. Ezechiel states when quoting the words of Yahweh: "I will put my spirit in the midst of you ..." and again, "I will put a new spirit within you" (Ezech. 36, 26,27). Joel announces that Yahweh will "pour out my spirit upon all flesh..." (Jo. 2, 28). St. Peter makes allusion to this text on the day of Pentecost: "But this is what was spoken through the prophet Joel, 'And it shall come to pass in the last days, says the Lord, that I will pour forth my spirit upon all flesh; and your sons and your daughters shall prophesy; and your young men shall see visions... And moreover upon my servants and upon my handmaids in those days will I pour forth of my Spirit'" (Ac. 2, 16-18).

This actual coming of the Spirit was effectively pointed out by St. Paul through the wonders and manifestations about which he speaks. While admitting their usefulness, he invites the Corinthians not to set too much emphasis upon these charisms, but rather upon charity and upon life in the Spirit (1 Cor. 12, 31; Ephes. 6, 18). And John also tries to make us understand this, having grasped the idea that the real revolution brought by Christ was not to be realized in the soul except in a very interior way by the Holy Spirit. He does not insist too much upon the fact itself of Pentecost, nor upon the visible effects in general of the Holy Spirit. The main idea in his Gospel concerning the Holy Spirit is to be found in Christ's declarations to Nicodemus and the Samaritan woman, as well as what He says at the Last Supper. If the facts contained in these declarations have already been meditated upon, it still remains to be seen how, under the guidance of this Spirit, each Christian and also the Church in general are destined to make that journey towards God and to pass from this world to the Father.

In the fourth Gospel the Holy Spirit cannot be reduced to such and such a manifestation. Neither the prophecies, nor the charisms, nor the gifts themselves, nor the spiritual realities which the symbols of the Spirit try to express, and not even the lights which souls can receive from Him, none of these is identified with the Spirit as such.

Though John does not speak of interior illuminations or of extraordinary gifts, it is not because he discards the possibility of these things or denies their accidental usefulness. What he is trying to do is unite himself to the Spirit on another level and at a greater depth. What interests him is the Person of the Spirit, living in us, penetrating our entire being, becoming the principle of our activity, and this in each of us as well as in the Church in general. At such a depth the specification of His action is very difficult and becomes at times hard to distinguish from that of Christ.

Undoubtedly it is precisely this that the apostle is trying to make us understand, for he goes to the heart of what Christ permitted the apostles to understand in the discourse after the Supper. Speaking of the Spirit, Jesus said to them that He would send "another Paraclete" (14, 16). It is then because He Himself already fufills this role towards them. From now on, the Spirit will pursue His action "in the same spirit and in the same direction."

He also tells them: ". . . the Spirit of truth whom the world cannot receive, because it neither sees him nor knows him. But you shall know him, because he will dwell with you and be in you" (14, 17). This seems to mean that having received the life of Christ, they will have in themselves, by this very fact, the life of the Spirit.

Christ repeatedly declares that the Spirit will come in His name, that He will teach them, recalling to their minds what He taught them (16, 13), that He will bear witness to Him (15, 26), that He will lead them to the truth with which Christ identified Himself (14, 5), and finally that He will not speak on His own authority, but whatever He will hear He will speak "because he will receive of what is mine and declare it to you" (16, 14). It could not be put more clearly that the Spirit's action is exercised in perfect continuity and in union with Christ's. The union is so close that the spirit of Christ cannot be separated from Christ. But if this is so, then what is the usefulness of the Spirit's action, what is its "raison d'etre"? Here we must try to understand as clearly as possible John's teaching, for our concept of the Christian life and its exercise will be influenced in a definite way by this proper understanding.

Envisioning the period opened up by Christ's departure and considering it in the light of the words: "But I speak the truth to you; it is expedient for you that I depart. For if I do not go, the Advocate will not come to you . . ." (16, 7), John makes us understand that Christ did not want His disciples to be deprived of a personal and living presence. His presence being withdrawn, He brings it about that another replace it.

It cannot be denied that the difference, at least in appearance, is great. His sensible and physical presence will be exchanged for the invisible presence of the Spirit. However, in the discourse after the Supper, the stress is placed not upon this difference but on the continuity and on the truth that a presence is maintained among the apostles. Although it is purely spiritual, it is nonetheless real and efficacious. For an action to be operative and reach its ends there is no necessity that it be sensible and visible. Christians had to be aware of the fact that the visible and perceptible presence of Christ could not of itself be anything else but transitory, exceptional, and linked to a very definite mission, viz., that of revealing the Father, communicating the Word, realizing salvation, placing the seed of divine life in the world, and finally laying the foundations of the Church destined to assure men the communication of this life.

But once this mission is carried out, Christ's physical presence is withdrawn from the world so that the normal order will be established by God. Christ points out certain things of this new order which He even presents as advantages to us. "But I speak the truth to you; it is expedient for you that I depart. For if I do not go, the Advocate will not come to you; but if I go, I will send him to you. And when he has come he will convict the world of sin, and of justice, and of judgment: of sin, because they do not believe me; of justice, because I go to the Father, and you will see me no more; and of judgment, because the prince of this world has already been judged. . . . But when he, the Spirit of truth, has come, he will teach you all the truth . . . and the things that are to come he will declare to you. He will glorify me because he will receive of what is mine and declare it to you" (16, 7-14).

These advantages, of course, are exclusively of the spiritual order. But this action is opposed in no way to the action of Christ. The latter on many occasions taught His disciples that "the flesh profits nothing" and that the "spirit gives life" (6, 63). He said His words were spirit and life; He underscored the degree to which each of the aspects of this life is marked with the sign of the spirit. It is in the Spirit that one must be reborn (3, 5), that one must adore God (4, 23), and that one must nourish oneself with His flesh (6, 63); it is in the Spirit that one must receive and communicate this life of which Christ is the source (7, 39). And it is still the Spirit received by the apostles who presides over the destiny and diffusion of the Church (20, 22). There is nothing surprising in all this since "God is spirit" (4, 24). The Incarnation was necessary, as without it the abyss between ourselves and God would have never been filled. But the Incarnation has taken away nothing of our need to be born to a veritable "life in the spirit."

The Holy Spirit's mission is to extract the meaning of Christ's teachings and bring them to light for us. He is to teach us why Christ has come into the world, viz., to give us divine life in all its purity. And the Spirit is to realize little by little this work in us.

"He will teach you all things"

But since the Spirit is the Spirit of Christ, this work cannot be carried out on other data but those furnished by Christ. The Spirit can do nothing else but receive of "what is Christ's" and draw out its spiritual reality for each soul. This is better expressed in Christ's own words: "When he, the Spirit of truth, has come, he will teach you all the truth" (16, 13). This does not mean that Christ is not the Truth also, but men cannot discover the ultimate reality of things which is of the spiritual order except through the Spirit. A work of maturation, purification, and spiritualization is necessary in those who have received this truth, and the Spirit alone will accomplish this.

This does not mean that He will lead us to revelations of a superior order reserved for the initiated, for the "spiritual," as some formerly believed. It means that the revelation brought by Christ, in order to be known "in truth," must be interiorly revealed by the Spirit. Then only will Christ's words to Nicodemus be realized: "that which is born of the spirit is spirit" (3, 6). The child of God will be an adorer of the Father "in spirit and in truth" (4, 23).

Not only does the Spirit's action in the soul not cast aside what comes to us through Christ, but the Spirit is unable to work on anything except what has been revealed and communicated by Christ to men. Those who are truly spiritual are not less desirous of the word of God and the reception of the sacraments than other Christians. It is just the opposite. And the only way they have of being born more profoundly of the Spirit is to keep themselves always more closely in contact with the source: Christ.

When making us know the Son, the Spirit reveals the Father also, for He proceeds from the Father and the Son as from one sole Principle. And the manner in which He reveals the Father consists essentially in transforming us gradually into Christ, making us similar in nature, in making us true "children of God" (1, 12). To succeed in this the Spirit must make us understand everything that pertains to Christ "in truth" (4, 23). Christ is the Way, the Truth, the Light, and the Life. The sole possibility we have of communicating with Him as such is to receive communication of Him through the Spirit. Christ is likewise love. In order that this love live in us "in truth," it is necessary that the Spirit, the uncreated Love of the Father and the Son, "Caritas Dei," reveal it to us by coming and living in us. Such are the basic truths and from them flow many consequences.

"But you shall know him, because he will dwell with you, and be in you"

The Spirit's action is by its very nature interior and constant, even though it can occasionally in its effects manifest itself in a visible manner. We should not be surprised then when Christ applies the word "dwell" to the Holy Spirit. "And I will ask the Father and he will give you another Advocate to dwell with you forever, the Spirit of truth, whom the world cannot receive, because it neither sees him nor knows him. But you shall know him, because he will dwell with you, and be in you" (14, 16,17).

Returning to these words, John speaks repeatedly in his Epistle of this "dwelling" of the Spirit in the soul. He does it in terms that merit consideration. In fact, he does not say, as in the preceding passage, that the Spirit dwells in us, but he assigns to Him the role of "bearing witness" that God dwells in us: "And he who keeps the commandments abides in God and God in him. And in this we know that he abides in us, by the Spirit whom he has given us" (1 Jn. 3, 34). Or again, in a very similar way, "In this we know that we abide in him and he in us, because he has given us of his Spirit" (1 Jn. 4, 13).

"Let the anointing which you have received from him dwell in you"

Nothing, it seems, can better account for this interior presence and constant action of the Spirit than the symbol of anointing applied by John to Him. "And as for you, let the anointing which you have received from him, dwell in you, and you have no need that anyone teach you. But as his anointing teaches you concerning all things, and is true and is no lie, even as it has taught you, abide in him. And now, dear children, abide in him" (I Jn. 2, 27).

We shall soon come upon this abiding when there is question of deepening the Spirit's action in the soul and the developments it imprints upon the faith. Let it be sufficient here to note how characteristic of the Spirit and His action is this constancy of presence.

The continued presence of the Spirit

Interior and continued, the Spirit's influence appears creative and transforming as a consequence. In a word, it is renovating. And this introduces the notion of time in a very direct way. This notion is certainly not absent from Christ's words: "Abide in me and I in you . . . Abide in my love" (15, 4,9). And He speaks here of a fidelity which can neither be proved nor tried except through the passing of time. However, what is stressed here is not so much time as the idea of the union and the intimacy of this union.

Since the same word "dwell" is applied to the Spirit, the notions of time and "becoming" take on a special aspect. If we consider the terms used in this passage relative to the Spirit, we may state that they do point out a reality which takes place progressively and demands time if it is to be realized. "Many things yet I have to say to you, but you cannot bear them now. But when he, the Spirit of truth, has come, he will teach you all the truth. For he will not speak of his own authority, but whatever he will hear he will speak, and the things that are to come he will declare to you. He will glorify me because he will receive of what is mine and declare it to you" (16, 12-15). However, it would be wrong to oppose the two meanings of this word, according as it is applied to Christ or the Spirit. In fact, the Spirit does nothing but confer on the union of the soul to Christ that dimension which comes from time.

When announcing the coming of the Spirit to His disciples, Jesus has in view what will be realized all through that long and mysterious time which will pass until the Parousia. He helps them understand that the Spirit is necessary as a Guide and a Light during this time. This Spirit's mission is to "teach the truth, to announce, to make known, to receive of what is Christ's in order to declare it to us": all realities having no meaning unless thought out and realized in time.

But before looking into the nature of the relationship between time and the Spirit who makes use of it to build up His work, it is good to be a little more precise about the form and nature of His action.

Nature of the Spirit's activity

True, the Spirit may act in a perceptible way, manifesting Himself exteriorly. However, the true form of His activity is interior. Similar to the leaven so intimately mixed with the dough that it is impossible to perceive its presence, He literally makes our spiritual being germinate and grow. To be effective the action of the leaven supposes an interior and prolonged contact with the matter to be transformed; its work of fermentation is progressive and continuous. The same may be said of the Spirit's action, interior, constant, and hidden. The Christian is to understand that the Spirit is not an extrinsic reality, but a presence perpetually in act. Closer to us than we are to ourselves, He cannot be dissociated from us nor perceived independently of us. Each time Christ speaks of the Spirit He makes use of expressions that lead us to such a conception of things. Thus, when Christ states: "If anyone thirst, let him come to me and drink. He who believes in me, as the Scripture says, 'From within him there shall flow rivers of living water'" (7, 37,38). St. John adds, "He said this, however, of the Spirit whom they who believed in him were to receive . . ." (7, 39).

This passage does have certain difficulties of interpretation, e.g., do the waters flow from within Christ or the one having faith in Him? It is nevertheless apparent that the activity of the Spirit is entirely interior and so intimately associated with our being that it constitutes the higher principle of what is for us the source and development of the divine life.

We can say as much also of the expressions used by Christ in the discourse after the Supper. It is from the interior that knowledge, comprehension, and understanding of the truths revealed by Christ come to us; it is from the interior that the Spirit takes these truths, develops them and brings them out into the light. It is then of a really supernatural maieutics that we must speak, not limited to the mind as in the Socratic method, but extended to everything which is accessible and permeable to the Spirit in one's being.

It has been said: John is not interested in bringing to light any manifestations of the Spirit when He takes possession of man, but in seeing what He effects with the Revelation, the grace, and life of Christ that have been placed in man. We seek in vain for anything else in the fourth Gospel.

If we intend to specify the Spirit's influence in us we are led little by little to exchange the word "action" for that of "Presence." Action, though it proceeds from a person, ends up by separating itself from its author even though his mark is upon it. The same cannot be said for this active Presence of the Spirit in the soul, for it is identified with the Spirit.

As we have seen, it is rather the Person of the Spirit than His activity that occupies John's mind. Or at least, if he considers His action, he considers it as the action through which God engenders us, as the "Virtus Altissimi" through which He makes us His children. In this case it is both action and presence, but an action which is nothing but a continued presence, imprinting the living likeness of God on the soul in whom He dwells. And it is in this way that the Spirit works in us.

"You must be born again of the Spirit"

Christ said to Nicodemus that he must be born again of the Spirit (3, 6). That which is born anew in us under His influence is the child of God, i.e., Christ Himself whose likeness the Spirit imprints on us. And yet this word likeness is inadequate, for it is not a question here of a likeness obtained from a copy that is faithful to the original, but of a "living" likeness, i.e., of the spiritual presence and life of Christ infused into us through the Spirit.

We understand then why it was that Christ had to leave us. Without His departure this spiritual regeneration would not have been realized "according to the Spirit" and our birth "in spirit and in truth" could not have taken place.

What is the nature of the fruits of this living presence of the Spirit in us? Two words express it: The Spirit is the guarantee of a "continuity" in us, at the same time as He is the source of a perpetual "newness," of an incessant renewal.

Perhaps we would say that He permits and realizes in us a "creative continuity." "You must be born of the Spirit," said Christ. Now there is nothing that gives a more evident proof of a vital unity between two beings as one to be born of the other. But in the natural order birth is effected once and for all; the child is dependent upon those responsible for its birth only for a limited time. Spiritual birth, on the contrary, goes on endlessly and is continually in act. To be born of the Spirit means to be in vital union with Him at every moment, it means to experience a development that is forever new.

In the physical order, the development of a living being, while obeying certain definite laws, allows of a margin of newness. It is even more difficult and positively impossible in the spiritual order to foresee with any precision what a being will be like in ten, twenty, forty years. Life, sicknesses, events, influences, personal impression and reflections, everything a being can receive, learn, see, assimilate, suffer, as well as all that is accomplished secretly in him and unknown to him, weighs on him, enters into him, imprinting upon his moral and spiritual evolution, and even his physical personality, certain definite characteristic traits which no one could ever predict or foresee. Day after day this being develops and undoubtedly he is more incapable than anyone else of knowing himself enough in order to get a glimpse of the paths along which he advances and of the general outcome. It is because a new being never ceases being born in him, although he feels himself to be always the very same.

Much deeper still is the mystery of the relations between the Spirit and our spirit. "What is born of the Spirit is spirit," said Christ to Nicodemus and He continues, stressing the mysterious traits of this relationship: "Do not wonder that I said to thee, 'You must be born again.' The wind blows where it will and thou hearest its sounds but dost not know where it comes from or where it goes. So is everyone who is born of the Spirit" (3, 7).

If the continuity between what will be in us, under the Spirit's influence, is more profound than we can imagine, since it is towards divine Truth that the Spirit of Truth is leading us; the newness too is more radical than we can imagine, for to the newness of the object better known each day is added the renewal of the knowing subject who too never ceases to be transformed. The Spirit renders us more capable of the Truth, and the Truth appears to us under a perpetually new light from the fact that we never cease to be born to the Truth. There is not only a living continuity, but a creative one.

While on the human level whatever lasts cannot escape a certain "wear and tear," or damage, or slackening of its powers, or it is even threatened by deformations and corruption; on the level of the Spirit, duration is creative, it is forever making new and more pure those who approach the Source. By telling us again what Christ has taught us, the Spirit, far from simply repeating, creates us, and this essential and vital fidelity is the principle itself of a true newness, an authentic and supernatural creation. "Send forth thy Spirit and they shall be created, and thou shalt renew the face of the earth."

Life in the Spirit

It is impossible to express these realities, or even to think of them otherwise than in the light of, and in relation to, time. It is, in fact, in utilizing the events of our existence woven into the framework of time that the Spirit fashions this new being in us; and these two realities, the Spirit and time, though unequally mysterious, work together to attain a result which is God's own secret.

The spiritual life draws from them not only a new dimension, but the principle of incessant transformations. Although every comparison, in such matters as this, is going to be necessarily imperfect, we may recall here the changes a plant undergoes when it comes forth from the soil. What a difference there is between the part that remains hidden beneath the earth and the part which grows and develops in the free air, producing eventually stem, leaves, flowers and fruit. The development, appearance, respiration, assimilation, everything is new and proceeds nevertheless from the original seed from which the plant draws its life.

It is by returning frequently to the notion of presence that makes it possible for us to grasp the Holy Spirit's role. If we keep in mind that, for St. John, the Spirit is a Person, a divine Person, the secret of His influence becomes more accessible to us and we open ourselves more to Him; at the same time, we perceive that "mode of being" which we call in human terms "a spirit" which gradually takes root in those in whom the Spirit dwells.

"... and they will be created"

We must take up again and meditate upon Christ's words to Nicodemus if we are to grasp in what this "spirit" consists: "What is born of the Spirit is spirit," placing them side by side with those of the Prologue: "For the Law was given by Moses; grace and truth come through Jesus Christ" (1, 17).

This new regime, to which Paul applies the name "Law of the Spirit" (Rm. 8, 2) to distinguish it from the Old Law, is effective on the collective level as well as that of the individual, in the relationship of men among themselves as well as their relationship with God; however it demands a radical transformation and a recasting of the entire being in order to bear fruit.

In order to create us anew "in the holiness of truth" (Ephes. 4, 24), the Spirit must cast aside, burn, destroy, sublimate, and transform whatever in us is of the carnal and natural order. This weighs us down. For this natural life He substitutes a supernatural life, endowed with a dynamism which places our being in a state of perpetual expansion and tension. We would have to find a better way of expressing ourselves, for here there seems to be too much stress placed upon the act of the will, a gathering of our energies.

The dynamism and tension placed in us by the Spirit have nothing of this about them, but are akin to the power that the being finds in its inmost depths of realizing and perfecting itself by uniting with its Principle; and this tension generates freedom, the lot of the children of God, and expansion. This interior freedom and this life bear within themselves an urgency to pass over into act. When living the life of the Spirit, we know God, we advance in the discovery of God and God advances in us. "But he who does the truth comes to the light" (3, 21). "If we live by the Spirit, by the Spirit let us walk" (Gal. 5, 25).

Thus man finds himself on the road where the breath of the Spirit draws him. But this work of continual renovation, discovery, transformation, and creation is inscribed in time and it remains dependent on or subject to the circumstances and conditions in which each being lives. To better understand the problems presented by this march of the Christian through time under the Spirit's guidance and in fidelity to Christ, we may have recourse to the account given in the Book of Kings concerning Elias' last moments on earth.

Accompanied by Eliseus the old prophet goes towards the Jordan river which he must cross. He realizes His work is completed and that God is about to call him. Eliseus realizes this too, but is filled with anxiety at succeeding his Master in his office as prophet. How can he do this unless he is invested in his "spirit"? He wants to make the request but does not dare do so. Elias anticipates his request. They have scarcely miraculously crossed the Jordan when Elias says to him:

" 'Ask what thou wilt have me to do for thee, before I am taken away from thee.' And Eliseus said, 'I beseech thee that in me may be thy double spirit.' And he answered, 'Thou hast asked a hard thing. Nevertheless if thou seest me when I am taken away from thee, thou shalt have what thou hast asked; but if thou seest me not, thou shalt not have it.' And as they went on, walking and talking together, behold a fiery chariot, and fiery horses parted them both asunder. And Elias went up by a whirlwind into heaven. And Eliseus saw him, and cried: 'My father, my father, the chariot of Israel and the driver thereof.' And he saw him no more. And he took hold of his own garments and rent them in two pieces. And the sons of the prophets at Jericho seeing it said, 'The spirit of Elias hath rested upon Eliseus' " (4 Kgs. 2, 9-15).

"It is the Spirit that gives life . . ."

A very similar problem presented itself to the apostles on Ascension day when their Master ascended into heaven, leaving them in time to live and work while He returned to His Father. But the problem was more formidable.

The apostles had to continue the work begun by the Master; they had to gather up and render fruitful the divine heritage left in their care. Had not Christ told Peter he was to be the rock upon which His Church was built? And all those with him who made up the Church. The apostles did not have only to keep a deposit, they had to transmit a spirit and spread and communicate a life: Christ's life. They had to face difficulties and possible divergencies in the interpretation and solution of the problems that would be presented.

As long as the Master was with them, they always had recourse to Him. He had enlightened, guided, and supported them. But now He had left them, leaving them in the world, in time, and they experienced the need of His living presence. They too would have liked to be "walking and talking" with Him and to possess "a twofold part of His spirit." But He had forestalled them and had resolved to leave them much more. He had promised them His Spirit in Person. When He came He would recall all He had told them and would teach them the whole truth; this Spirit would dwell with them and be in them. Thus they would not be orphans; they would be accompanied, guided, sustained, along the long road that was beginning. They would be able to "walk and talk."

This living presence alone would deliver them from that feeling of inadequacy and anguish which struck them all the more since it was not only a question of spreading a teaching duly regulated and codified, presented within a set of commandments like those of the Old Law; it was also a question of a teaching which, in spite of its unity and coherence, would take its meaning from and bear fruit only in the Spirit who gave it life. "It is the Spirit that gives life; the flesh profits nothing" (6, 63).

Furthermore, Christ had not traced out in advance any precise line of conduct. His instructions regarding the apostolate concerned the dispositions for undertaking it (Mt. 10, passim). For the rest, everything would have to be discovered and resolved from day to day, in the light of the Spirit, and thanks to an intimate union with Him. Here again those words of Christ would have meaning, "Sufficient unto the day is the evil thereof" (Mt. 6, 34). Detachment, confidence, constant recourse to God were to constitute the necessary dispositions for those who wished to live under the Spirit's influence.

"The wind blows where it will . . ." (3, 8) and the soul's sail must always remain in a state of readiness to capture the Spirit's gentle inspiration no matter when or where it comes. But, at the same time, this invitation God directs to us proves that He will never fail to guide us and lead us. "The Father works until now and I work" (5, 17). It can likewise be said of the Spirit that He is always at work in us. Insofar as He is "digitus paternae dexterae," He enters directly into us, dwells perpetually in contact with us. He never stops inscribing in our soul the mind and will of God, just as He always disposes events in such a way that God's designs are always manifested to the soul. With Christ's coming God has been revealed, the Son had made known the Father, but God's plan in each soul and in the Church still remains to be accomplished day after day. And the Spirit is there precisely to guide the progress, unfolding, and development of this plan.

Christ, the divine Sower, accomplished His task: "It is consummated!" (19, 30). He returned to His Father. Now begins the time of germination and growth. And the Spirit presides over this in a world perpetually being born and transformed. It would be vain to pretend to foresee and dictate in advance what conduct must be followed. Under penalty of falling into routine and death, or of acting according to our discretion which is just as bad, each Christian, as well as the Church at large, is supposed to place himself under the Spirit's guidance and advance this way. This is absolutely necessary. As burdensome as it may be, the promises of eternal life are dependent upon its fulfillment.

"Behold I am with you until the consummation of the world" (Mt. 28, 20), Christ declares to His apostles as leaders of His Church. And to each apostle as to each Christian He says: "Abide in my love." And through the evangelist He tells them that they will know, "That he abides in them, by the Spirit whom he has given them" (1 Jn. 3, 24).

Our guidance by the Spirit brings us a great security which is accompanied by the unforeseen. For we are always advancing into the unknown. "Put out into the deep . . ." (Lk. 5, 4). Advance out into the deep where soon there will be neither bank, nor lighthouse, nor signal of any kind; nothing but that mysterious presence of God in us, under the form of His Spirit invisibly guiding us.

God, who wills that men really live and face the dangers of life, has not cast them out to sea without any means of knowing themselves, or rather of remaining in vital contact with Him at all times, capturing the inspirations coming from Him and leading them to Him. For, whatever be the journey a soul must make through time, the Spirit will always lead the soul towards God just as He leads the Church. Originating with Christ, the project ends up in Him. The Spirit is Christ's Spirit and leads to Him as He traces out in each of us His living Image.

But at the same time the Spirit maintains in each soul, as in Christ's spouse, an ardent aspiration, an eschatological hope which confers upon the Christian life and the life of the Church their dynamic quality. It is not without reason that John terminates the Apocalypse with the words: "It is true I come quickly. Amen. Come, Lord Jesus!" (Ap. 22, 17). These are the concluding words of the New Testament and they express the expectation of the soul and the Church for Christ's coming.

In order to fill this time of expectation with God and realize His designs in it, to aid each child of God and the entire Church to accomplish their passage to the Father, Christ has sent His spirit. St. Paul states in his epistle that in the entire creation the Spirit groans in expectation of the Redemption (Rm. 8, 23). And nothing expresses what He brings to light, that intense desire for all beings to see the Parousia, that vision of the world on the march, nothing expresses all this better than the image of the woman in travail who is ready to bring forth a new being.

This image is used by Christ at the Supper: "A woman about to give birth has sorrow, because her hour has come. But when she has brought forth the child, she no longer remembers the anguish for her joy that a man is born into the world" (16, 21). This expresses the travail the Spirit accomplishes in the soul and in the Church; without this travail the life brought by Christ would not take hold either on the personal level or the ecclesial level.

The Johannine Gospel, and this is the last thing to be considered, is going to help us grasp in what the expansion the Spirit procures for each soul consists, and what life He communicates to the Spouse of Christ, the Church.

CHAPTER 20

THE HOLY SPIRIT AND THE SOUL

The Spirit's mission is exercised upon the Church as Christ's spouse and upon each soul in the Church. He takes their conduct in hand and assures a deepening of their lives, guiding them, revealing them to themselves, and bringing them to perfection in God.

St. John has shown the central and constructive reality around which the actions and the influence of the Spirit gather in the soul and that reality is Faith. How would this Spirit not bring this faith to perfection to which the Father draws souls and which has the Son as its author (Cf. cc. 11,12, & 13)?

His action is exercised over those whom the Redemption has made children of God and to whom Christ has sent Him upon His own return to the Father. Certain conditions were necessary for this action to develop and these conditions were not realized until Christ's departure from the earth, when the invisible presence of the Spirit was substituted for the visible and tangible presence of Christ. He had told us that such conditions were necessary in order that faith take on its true nature and that it accomplish and bear fruit in us. He said to His disciples: "But I speak the truth to you; it is expedient for you that I depart. For if I do not go, the Advocate will not come to you; but if I go, I will send him to you" (16, 7).

The Spirit "will teach you all the truth" (16, 13)), this Truth which they could not bear as long as Christ was in their midst. In the new Christian economy, marked by Christ's departure in view of His glorification and the sending of the Spirit, faith has as its mission the drawing of souls to the heights of "life in the spirit" under the Holy Spirit's guidance.

The Spirit, teacher of faith

For it is apparent that for St. John faith carries in itself the seed of the entire "life in the spirit," and from beginning to end of its development, there is no break in its continuity.

It is because for the apostle, as was seen when analysing the nature and structure of faith, this union between the soul and God brought about by faith exists from the very beginning. Without this union, faith would not exist. From the point of departure it is an alliance between the soul and God, and the bonds it weaves between them are personal bonds, even though the soul is aware of this only in a gradual way. Faith, from its beginnings, introduces a relationship based upon friendship, confidence, and love.

As a consequence, from the first word pronounced silently by the soul: "I believe in Thee, O Lord," right to the highest heights of the life in the Spirit, winning that victory over the world (16, 14), faith remains always the same in nature: that of union with God which is forever deepening.

From Christ's statements in the Cenacle it is evident that the Spirit's mission is not to communicate new truths, but "he will receive of what is mine and declare it to you" (16, 13), and "he will teach you all the truth and bring to your minds whatever I have said to you" (14, 26). We could not possibly have it more clearly stated to us that the Spirit's action and influence takes over from what Christ has given to us and placed in us. The "data" upon which He works owe their origin to Christ, and the first is faith which contains all the rest and permits their entry into our soul.

The Spirit gradually reveals the potentialities of this faith. He aids us to discover especially that this personal structure of faith brings about a "personalizing" reality. The lights the Spirit furnishes the soul allow the latter to enter into very intimate relations with each of the Persons of the Holy Trinity. When perfecting our status as "child of God," He makes us know the Father "as a Father." For is He not the "Spirit who proceeds from the Father" (15, 26)? And has not Christ said of Him that He is the "one whom the Father will send in my name" (14, 26)? Likewise, the Spirit cannot make us children of God unless He reveals the Person of the Son whose image He is to trace out in our souls.

But the Spirit's action is likewise personalizing in this sense that He works in our soul in such a way as to draw out and make our own proper spiritual personality appear. This He does very gradually.

While directing us interiorly towards God, He makes us gradually transformable under His influence; He forms us according to God's image through an increasing connaturalization which gives real meaning to the words: know, believe, and love, for each day they unveil a reality that is richer, more interior, more living.

The work to which the Spirit sets Himself in our souls and about which Christ's discourse after the Supper gives us an inkling appears as a real work of education. And it is sufficient to consider the great effort required, on the human level, when anyone desires to guide a being from the state of infancy to that of the mature "personality," if we would understand how much the Spirit's work requires even greater care and effort.

Rarely are teachers truly successful. And this success will be even more rare in the supernatural order even though the Teacher is divine. It is because the material upon which He works remains human. And it is why the education He undertakes demands an infinite understanding, patience, and love.

When He takes us in hand, if He finds us already united to Christ through grace, He must still reveal to us the riches which have been confided to us, and about which we are still very ignorant. He must teach us how to discover them and use them to our best advantage.

The Holy Spirit develops and deepens in us, which makes the faith in us a light, a force, a principle of attachment and union with God. But above all He reveals Christ to us who is the object of this faith. He does this in His own divine way which is both interior and spiritual. He makes a real instrument of "knowledge" out of our faith and for this He infuses into us the gifts of wisdom, understanding, and knowledge. He makes us more capable of understanding the object of our faith and of uniting us to Him. He reveals Him to us in His transcendent reality, i.e., not only as our God and Savior, but as the only-begotten Son of the Father. Thus our faith necessarily becomes a faith and a life of the children of God under His influence.

The Spirit of filial adoption

John reverts frequently to that title "children of God" (1, 12). We can sense that the reality he has in mind appears to him as the result in us of the Spirit's activity. It is the Spirit who accomplishes this filial adoption, which we owe to Christ's grace, and to the all-loving will of the Father. "Behold what manner of love the Father has bestowed upon us, that we should be called children of God; and such we are ... Beloved, now we are the children of God ..." (1 Jn. 3, 1,2).

The remainder of the text confirms the effective influence of the Spirit. "That is why the world does not know us, because it did not know him"

(1 Jn. 3, 1). In other words, since the world was not of the Holy Spirit's school, it will always lack that true knowledge of God, that knowledge of love which only children filled with the Spirit of adoption have of their Father (Rom. 8, 15).

We see in what sense the Spirit fashions our faith and in what manner He perfects it in loving knowledge of a God who is Father. Now this cannot be without a transformation of the entire being. After revealing to us our identity as children of God, the Spirit reveals our being to ourselves and this is brought about through incessant transformations which take the form of a succession of spiritual awakenings, awakenings which are one of the aspects of our life of faith and the advancements faith realizes.

In the natural order, the passage from infancy to adolescence and to an adult age is marked by a series of awakenings which stem from the discovery of interior realities as well as exterior circumstances. The person discovers the world outside himself, then others, and finally himself, and all this takes place amidst great difficulties, sufferings, and "growing pains."

The same may be said of the supernatural life; and nevertheless, because the Holy Spirit is the soul's Teacher, this succession of awakenings and the crises which accompany them take place according to a certain continuity. In fact, from the very beginning until the end is reached, the action of the Father, as well as that of the Son, and that finally of the Spirit whom they have sent to us, all is performed along the same line and in the same direction. It is an admirable continuity which God "as three Persons" can bring about and which makes us become what he has destined us to become from eternity. But, though in each soul everything is built upon the same faith and there is a constant development of this faith, yet all do not reach the same point or travel along the same paths.

All we have just said shows that for St. John the spiritual life (life in the Spirit) consists principally in an education and a deepening of faith. He, better than anyone else, had understood the spiritual heights for which faith had been promised and what were its inherent potentialities. But this brings us to another aspect of this problem of the Holy Spirit's action upon our life of faith.

Experience of God

When the soul gives itself over to the life of the Spirit through a "living faith" (John ordinarily envisages faith as such), it surrenders itself to a veritable "experience of God." Do St. John's Gospel and Epistles give us his thought about this experience and the stand he took with regard to it?

One point is certain: John was aware of this experience and he speaks of its existence. However, contrary to St. Paul who tells us about it and gives an account of it (2 Cor. 12), John does not dwell upon it even though his own mystical experience cannot be doubted. He is content to state: "And in this we know that he abides in us, by the Spirit whom he has given to us" (1 Jn. 3, 24).

It is true that under his pen the simple words "we know" take on a singular force. His certitude in the matter of an "experience of God" equals that certitude he had of the reality of the Word incarnate. "What we have seen with our eyes and our hands have touched" (1 Jn. 1, 1), and likewise the certitude of his position as "child of God" (1 Jn. 3, 1).

This threefold certitude, viz., that of the Incarnation, of filial adoption, and the indwelling of the Spirit, makes up that extremely rich Trinitarian atmosphere in John's soul simply because it was intensely lived and experienced. Such a certitude normally comes from the life of faith which is in us. But the Holy Spirit adds an "experience" to it, and John was its fearless champion because he was its most sure witness. He shows, however, a great reserve and prudence in the matter.

Though he is the Spirit's witness and has an "experience" of God, he is the apostle who has raised the faith to the level of a beatitude (20, 29) and has opposed faith to the sensible. This does not prevent him from stating that spiritual realities are perceptible in a certain interior "sense" which is above the natural senses.

Thus, the "light of God" is not seen and yet Christ demands that we "walk in the light" (12, 35). How perceive it if not through the aid of a spiritual sense, with "the eyes of faith"? The same goes for Truth which we must be capable of recognizing and for the Way which we must be able to follow.

John sometimes employs the verb "connaitre" and sometimes "savoir" in order to designate this interior faculty which helps us apprehend spiritual realities. He speaks also of the "testimony" God renders of Himself in the depths of the soul.

If he evokes the image of "anointing" with reference to this matter, it is an attempt to characterize the nature of this experience.

Fruit in us of the action and presence of the Spirit who makes the soul capable of knowing and tasting God through these "spiritual senses," this experience is nothing but a prolongation of faith and the Word. It is not a new reality, but the full expansion of these. It renders faith more living, sheds light upon the mystery of the divine Word, and increases the certitude we already possess by indelibly imprinting it in the soul.

The soul's relationship with God becomes an "histoire" written by God Himself.

As it intensifies and becomes more frequent and loving, this experience comes to the point of being a prelude in the soul of that blessed state in which knowledge and experience become one. "Then we shall know as we are known" (1 Cor. 13, 12), St. Paul cries out, and his meaning is that our present experience of God will intermingle with the very life of God Himself. And St. John writes: "Now this is eternal life, that they may know thee, just Father, and him whom thou hast sent, Jesus Christ" (17, 3).

Criterions for the "experience" of God

How are we to qualify this experience of God brought us by the Holy Spirit? When Paul declares: "The Spirit himself gives testimony to our spirit that we are the sons of God" (Rom. 8, 16), he seems to do away with all intermediaries. This is also the meaning of the Johannine expression which designates the Spirit. He says: "But we have an anointing from the Holy One" i.e., Christ, and this anointing "dwells in you and you have no need that anyone teach you" (1 Jn. 2, 20; cf. Is. 11, 2; 61, 1; 1 Jn. 2, 27).

The Spirit communicates an intimate knowledge and taste of God to the soul which are unmistakable. His anointing is "true and is no lie" and permeates the soul in such a manner that the latter "knows that God dwells in her" (1 Jn. 3, 24). "And in this we know that we abide in him and he in us, because he has given us of his Spirit" (1 Jn. 4, 13).

John bears witness then to an experience of God which may be termed "quasi-immediate" and he does this with the greatest certainty. And one of the proofs that he is really dealing with an experience of this kind is the care he exercises in stating that definite criterions must be present to vouch for its authenticity.

In fact, if this experience were "immediate," all proof of its authenticity would be rendered useless since there would be no possibility of illusion or error. But if the soul experiences God in the innermost depths of its being in a manner that is "quasi-immediate," it is absolutely necessary to join to this experience objective signs which cannot err and which place the soul outside the danger of "illuminism."[1]

1. On this point, as on so many others, John's recommendations are similar to Paul's. The latter states: "Do not extinguish the Spirit ... But test all things" (1 Thess. 5, 19-21). John: "Beloved, do not believe every spirit, but test the spirits to see whether they are of God; because many false prophets have gone forth into the world. By this is the spirit of God known: every spirit that confesses that Jesus Christ has come in the flesh, is of God" (1 Jn. 4, 1,2). Cf. also: Mouroux, L'experience chretienne, pp. 166-191.

Thus we find especially in the first Epistle (that work which condenses John's long pastoral and apostolic experience) the "criterions" which help us in making a definite distinction between an authentic life "in the spirit" and its many counterfeits.

The *first criterion* demands that we be among the number of those who do not deny but acknowledge their sins. "If we say that we have no sin, we deceive ourselves and the truth is not in us" (1 Jn. 1, 8), and we even "make God a liar and his word is not in us" (1 Jn. 1, 10).

Recognizing our sins need not prevent "our hearts from being at rest" for even if "our heart blames us, God is greater than our heart and knows all things" (1 Jn. 3, 20). Before Him our human frailty like our good will is evident and His mercy is infinite.

"This act of absolute abandonment which contains humility, confidence, and hope within itself, is the principle of our peace and the sign that we are in the truth" (Mouroux, op. cit).

The *second criterion* consists in "observing the commandments." "And by this we can be sure we know him, if we keep his commandments" (1 Jn. 2, 3-5).

Among the commandments the most characteristic of the presence of the Spirit of God in us is undoubtedly love of neighbor. Because this must be proved by exterior manifestations, it constitutes a criterion easily verified, to which John returns repeatedly (1 Jn. 3, 11-17; 4, 11-20; 5, 1). The love we practice towards our neighbor is an imitation of Christ's conduct towards us (1 Jn. 2, 6-12), as it is patterned upon the love with which God has loved us. "Beloved, if God has so loved us, we ought also to love one another" (1 Jn. 4, 11).

The one who loves his brother is in "the light" (1 Jn. 2, 10), in the "truth" (1 Jn. 3, 19); "he has passed from death to life" (1 Jn. 3, 14), and he is "born of God" (1 Jn. 3, 9-15). Finally, this love takes its origin in the very movement which makes us love God. It bears witness perfectly to God's presence in us and the Spirit's activity.

The *third criterion* is not to love the world but God (1 Jn. 2, 15). This is an interior and exterior attitude which presupposes an essential choice, constantly maintained and renewed, and it bears testimony of the victorious action of the Spirit of God in the soul.

The Christian's faith is the clearest mark of this "victory over the world" (1 Jn. 5, 4) and of this living presence of the Spirit, for the one who overcomes the world is the one who is born of God.

Finally, a *last criterion* consists in confessing Christ and in guarding oneself against antichrists, which must undoubtedly be understood as a belonging and a fidelity to the Church and her magisterium.

Humility and confidence in God, fidelity to His commandments, and especially that of fraternal charity, fidelity and submission to the Church: such are the criterions without which there cannot be an authentic experience of God in the Spirit.

Gifts of the Holy Spirit

Having strongly insisted upon the possibility of an experience of God as well as the necessary conditions for its authenticity, John attempts to make us understand its intimate nature through the word "anointing" already encountered and always applied by him to the Spirit. Undoubtedly he hopes to make us "feel" spiritually the Spirit's action in our soul, and he transmits his own personal experience through this word which has real biblical savor.

Anointing which is placed among the symbols of the Spirit is strength and gentleness simultaneously. It places in the soul, along with the perfume of the divine Presence, gifts inseparable from that Presence, viz., Wisdom, Understanding, Knowledge, Counsel, Fortitude, Piety, and Fear of the Lord. These gifts are understood in the passage of the Epistle where John says to the Christians: "And as for you, let the *anointing* which you have received from him, dwell in you, and you have no need that anyone teach you. But as his anointing teaches you concerning all things, and is true and is no lie, even as it has taught you, abide in him" (1 Jn. 2, 27); and we can also understand in this passage the intimacy established between God and the soul in which the "anointing" of the Spirit "abides." Better than any other expression, this one shows that we are dealing here with a slow and deep "osmosis" at the termination of which those words of Christ are fully realized: "He who is born of the Spirit is spirit" (3, 4).

The transformation effected by the Spirit is a veritable birth (3, 5-8). Bowing beneath the Spirit's breath and allowing herself to be penetrated by it, the soul passes more and more under His influence. A new light until then unknown lights up everything from within.

It is a new light because it is essentially the light of the Spirit; but, in direct proportion to the soul's being born of the Spirit and becoming "spirit" herself, this newness gradually ceases to remain impenetrable to her. Born to this new life which dwells in her, the soul actually lives from its continual and everlasting influence. Better adapted each day to the life of the Spirit within her, and to the life "in the spirit," she becomes capable of knowing God in an intimate way and of uniting herself to Him. Although obscure, this knowledge and union are more enlightening and intimate to her than any other. It is of a real "communion" that we must speak here.

At the same time the Spirit fills the soul with His presence and strength and gives her the power to nourish herself on the mystery of God as spirit. She is sustained by a hidden manna, and this food, to which she feels herself becoming more and more accustomed and which she longs for more and more, is a constant source of life.

She can now set out upon the way on which the Spirit would have her advance. It is a way which is "in the world" where she is called upon to dwell and which she must pass through without becoming its prisoner through attachments. And it is exactly the Spirit's presence that heightens the desire of not becoming attached. He makes her more capable of using temporal realities to advantage, of making them bear fruit for "eternity."

Interior Guest of the Soul

"If you love me, keep my commandments. And I will ask the Father and he will give you another Advocate to dwell with you forever, the Spirit of truth whom the world cannot receive because it neither sees nor knows him. But you shall know him, because he will dwell with you, and be in you" (14, 15-17). "And as for you, let the anointing which you have received from him, dwell in you" (1 Jn. 2, 27).

The soul in whom the Spirit "abides" knows that if she remains faithful, her desire of never being separated from God will be fulfilled. The Spirit gives her the assurance of this interiorly. "And in this we know that he abides in us, by the Spirit whom he has given us" (1 Jn. 3, 24). To abide does not simply mean to escape changes, to go out from the relative to enter into the absolute, but it also means to allow the divine exchanges to realize themselves more frequently, intimately, and fruitfully.

On the plane of human affairs, time is a necessary factor in order for any work to acquire quality, depth, and stability; and the very word "dwelling," which was used to designate the home of families that desired to perpetuate themselves, gives us an idea of these things. Time is likewise necessary for the Spirit to build his dwelling in us and live there with an intimate and fruitful presence. However, if the Spirit dwells in us, it is also in order that we might better accomplish our exodus and passage towards God.

Our life is a life of pilgrims who must advance each day, and the Spirit is the gentle breeze filling the sails which the soul must ever keep in readiness. Through Him the soul allows herself to be led and through Him she advances along the road to God.

"Stay with us" (Lk. 24, 29) the disciples of Emmaus begged when Christ seemed to wish to continue His journey and leave them. God has made man a pilgrim, but He desires that a presence dwell in him and accompany him everywhere, never ceasing to guide him in his long and painful pilgrimage, enlightening with divine rays the lights he gathers from his experience. This presence of the Spirit man has with him; it is strength and counsel on the way; it is the Way. Then all is changed for he is not alone since Someone is there, an interior Guest dwells within, converses lovingly with him, and this "divine Guest" brings him love along with life.

The Holy Spirit is this interior Guest. If the soul is faithful in allowing Him to dwell within her and places herself always under His guidance, then He will guide her, teach her all Truth, i.e., He will have her fulfill her pilgrimage and, while advancing towards the goal set by God, she will taste in the depths of her own heart, the Divine Heart.

CHAPTER 21

THE HOLY SPIRIT AND THE CHURCH

"Christ's privileged witness": such is the glorious title conferred on John and his Gospel gains much from it. And still this same Gospel was conceived and drawn up by the apostle in terms of a time when faith would be faith in the Church, or faith in Jesus Christ living in the Church.

John joins to his glance as "seer" enlightened by the Spirit an exceptional longevity which permitted him to be present at the organization and development of the Church during a period of almost three-quarters of a century. His writings will be destined then not for the witnesses of Christ's life, but for those generations that were to see the beginnings of the age of the Church.

That is why, important as is the place accorded to Christ in the Gospel, since all centers in Him, John nevertheless conceived his writings in such a way that Christ's words and actions are not confined to themselves, but are considered in their extension and their temporal and eternal import.

For this reason, the fourth Gospel, though deeply Christological, is nonetheless ecclesial. Or rather, if this gospel is so ecclesial, it is simply because it is totally Christological, considering in Christ not only the Head but also the body or members in whom He was to grow each day and to be formed gradually. In a word, this Gospel takes in the whole Christ.

A study of the first Epistle strengthens this conviction that John had his eye on the future. The time in which he is writing is no longer the time of Christ but that of the Church, and it is to form them and habituate them to living in this time according to a definite form of the Christian life that John busied himself in favor of his correspondents, his "little children" (1 Jn. 2, 1,12,14,18; 5, 21).

What goes to make up the uniqueness of the fourth Gospel is that it is a writing drawn up when the Church is already established, and it is drawn up by an ocular witness of Christ. It has these two essential dimensions, not separated or simply juxtaposed, but linked one to the other, in a vital continuity one with the other.

If the Church does not live totally from Christ, if she is not the living Christ who continues His work, she is nothing. "Without me you can do nothing" (15, 5). But, inversely, if she claims to transmit only a memorial of the Savior instead of the living reality, i.e., perpetually renewed, which it is her mission to communicate: "Do this in memory of me" (Lk. 22, 19), then she is nothing but a conservatory or a museum.

Now the Church must necessarily be vibrant with the life of Christ, and though she is human in her members, yet she must possess and transmit this divine life. That is why John likens her to a person, the Spouse, in his Apocalypse, in order to make her principle of life and fecundity better understood, while her power is completely dependent upon her Bridegroom, Christ.

If, on this latter point, the Apocalypse brings lights not contained in the Gospel except under an inceptive form, the ensemble of the remarks we have just made are verifiable in the Gospel; and this in such a way that every Christian can discover there, as in a pure mirror, both the Savior's face and the traits His Spouse must reflect if she is to bring Him forth in souls.

The Spirit working in the Church

It is not under her historic form, but rather her spiritual form that John would have us assist at the birth of the Church. She is in no way (at least in the Gospel faithful to essential data) an organization whose perfection would explain her diffusion; she is Pentecost continuing. Just as the Spirit presides over those days spent in the Cenacle until the day on which He descends upon the apostles, filling them with His fire, and sends them out for the conquest of the world, so also in the fourth Gospel the Spirit appears as the soul of the Church, just as Christ had promised in His Father's name.

"And while eating with them, he charged them not to depart from Jerusalem, but to wait for the promise of the Father, 'of which you have heard,' said he, 'by my mouth; for John indeed baptized with water, but you shall be baptized with the Holy Spirit not many days hence'" (Ac. 1, 4-5).

John does not speak of Pentecost in his Gospel, but simply points out that after the Resurrection the Master appeared to His disciples, the doors being closed, and said to them: " 'As the Father has sent me, I also send you.' When he said this, he breathed upon them, and said to them, 'Receive the Holy Spirit . . .' " (20, 21-23).

In the Apocalypse John is considering the Church in a different atmosphere. He now sees it with the eyes of a pastor and a father. He clearly states her deviations, abuses, and defections. He attempts to apply the proper remedy. He is working to maintain purity of doctrine and firmness of faith. And in the Epistle he gives his children counsel based upon his pastoral experience.

In the Gospel John is content with stressing the divine presence which goes to make up the Church and is the Church. It makes her the Incarnation continued. Since this Spirit is the Spirit of Christ, where the Spirit is there also is Christ, and where Christ is there also is the Church. "He who hears you hears me" (Lk. 10, 16).

Shall we say that in limiting himself to this spiritual aspect of the Church, John has eliminated or under-estimated the human, material, temporal, and visible part of the Church? Would his Church be a "church in the spirit" as opposed to a visible Church? When making such a claim one sets out upon a way as false as that which interprets the words: ". . . the flesh profits nothing" (6, 63), or: "God is spirit, and they who worship him, must worship him in spirit and truth" (4, 23) as excluding the reality and necessity of Christ's flesh in the Eucharist, or the necessity of fidelity to the commandments in Christ's true disciples.

The plenitude of the Spirit in the Church is similar to the plenitude of the Spirit in Christ. "He whom God has sent speaks the words of God, for not by measure does God give the Spirit" (3, 34). The plenitude of the Spirit is, so to speak, linked to the reality and plenitude of the Incarnation. It is because the Word is made flesh that the fullness of the Spirit must come upon this flesh, in order that everything that is visible through it and all that it accomplishes may be purely "spiritual" in its significance and power. Thus it is with the Eucharist, Christ's flesh, which draws its power from the fact that it conveys the Spirit in plenitude. And so it is likewise with the Church.

If the Church stands in such need of the Spirit, it is precisely because she herself is flesh, and in her as in the Eucharist, the flesh profits nothing if the Spirit did not give it life. That is why John, deeply convinced of this supernatural truth, judged that in recalling the Spirit's presence and action in the Church, he has set down the essentials and all the rest flows from this.

Church of the Spirit and the visible Church

The fourth Gospel gives us proof that John does not underestimate the necessary incorporation of the Church in the temporal order. First, this is proved by the importance accorded to testimony. The Church is founded upon testimony. Scripture is one of the forms of Tradition, and is itself a privileged testimony. Christ was the first witness of His Father. "I speak what I have seen with the Father" (8, 38). After Him, those whom He chose "bore witness" (1, 7), viz., first, John the Baptist; then the disciples, the evangelists, and among these latter, John the beloved disciple who enjoyed a privileged rank.

The Gospel is the sum total of these testimonies put down in writing and which remain alive through the strength and power of the Testimony which dwells in them and which they transmit to us. This divine Testimony, so manifold and so bound up with the facts, remains nonetheless eminently spiritual. It acts through the power and activity of the Spirit who is manifest in it. Neither the government, nor the organization, nor the power, nor the expansion of the Church would have any meaning or value, if, more deeply and essentially, the testimony and the grace of the Incarnate Word and the testimony and the action of the Spirit were not manifest in the Church.

It is not simply because He "was made flesh" (1, 14) that Christ was Savior; it was because having been made flesh, "he received the Spirit without measure" (3, 34), and because through His death He transmitted the Spirit to those who would bear testimony to Him throughout the world until the end of time (19, 30).

In the same way, it is not solely through the presence or the power of His "body" that the Spouse pursues the saving mission confided to her by her Bridegroom; but through the life of the Spirit present and acting in her. In her, as in Christ, the Spirit uses flesh and temporal realities to pass on His message and communicate Himself to men. "It is the Spirit that gives life; the flesh profits nothing" (6, 63).

If Christ pronounced these words with reference to a sacrament which borrows the eucharistic species from the earth, so that the wheat of our fields and the wine of our grapes serve as support to the presence of His body and bood, it is in order to remind us that the power of this sacrament is entirely spiritual. And nevertheless the flesh remains necessary. "Unless you eat my flesh you shall not have life in you" (6, 53). The same may be said of the Church. In her it is the Spirit who gives life: if she were not incarnate, she would not be! Like her Master and Bridegroom, she needs a body: ". . . and the two shall become one flesh. This is a great mystery, I mean in reference to Christ and to the Church" (Ephes. 5, 32).

Hence, in spite of the fact that the fourth Gospel is the most spiritual Gospel, it remains true that John has been careful to show the Church founded by Christ under an "incarnate" appearance, with all that this demands, and primarily, the necessity of a hierarchy and an organization. Though Christ prays to his Father to "keep" those confided to Him in the Truth, Love, and Unity: "Holy Father, keep in thy name those whom thou hast given me, that they may be one even as we are" (17, 11), and though He communicated to them His Spirit before leaving them (21, 21), He likewise prepared them to go into the world to struggle and suffer persecution just as He himself had been in the world, struggled and suffered there.

"If the world hates you, know that it has hated me before you. . . . If they have persecuted me, they will persecute you also; but if they have kept my word, they will keep yours also" (15, 18-20).

Christ has sent them that they go forth and bear fruit (15, 16). "Amen, I say to you, he who believes in me, the works that I do he also shall do, and greater than these shall he do. . . . No servant is greater than his master" (14, 12; 15, 20).

He asks the Father not that they be taken from the world, but that they be kept from evil (17, 15). If He Himself "is no longer in the world, . . . these are in the world" (17, 15). And "In the world you will have affliction, but take courage, I have overcome the world" (16, 33).

He has endowed His Church with a principle of hierarchic organization and the fourth Gospel bears testimony of this, but in the usual Johannine manner, viz., without emphasizing a reality that may be seen in the context. The words to Simon-Peter already gives proof of a primacy: "Peter, lovest thou me more than these? . . . Feed my lambs . . . Feed my sheep" (21, 15-17).

The respect John pays to the future head of the Church on so many occasions, or rather to the one whom he felt must one day hold the first place, is another proof of this.[1] This attitude is evident especially in the Resurrection episode at the tomb, where he does not enter first but gives preference to Peter and allows him to enter.

We find other indications in the "Acts," e.g., in the list of the apostles where there is order of pre-eminence (1, 13). Peter is mentioned first here and John, in spite of his youth, is mentioned immediately afterwards. It is in this same order, John placing himself under Peter's authority, that

1. John could not have failed to understand, as his companions did, the words of Christ to Peter in answer to his profession of faith at Caesarea: "Thou art Peter and upon this rock I will build my church . . . I will give you the keys to the kingdom of heaven" (Mt. 16, 18-19).

the two apostles reappear in the second and third chapters of the Acts. It is worthy of note that John is silent when with Peter and it is always Peter who speaks up as head (Ac. 2, 37; 3, 3,11; 4, 13,19).

The reading of the Johannine Epistles as well as the Apocalypse only confirms this certainty already evident in the Gospel. The Church is an incarnate reality. The Church is in the world. It is a "body," and this body must be made up in such a way as to make it materially and spiritually viable if it is to live and develop. In other words, it must have organization, union, and authority which will guarantee its expansion, cohesion, and unity in one Spirit (Ac. 1, 14). John, head of the churches in Asia and Patriarch of Ephesus, when assuming and exercising his power, is doing nothing but making very explicit what his Gospel shows us of the Church in its nascent state but already really established.

Christ's words reported by John: "As the Father has sent me, I also send you ... Receive the Holy Spirit ..." (20, 21) simply repeat what He had already said at the Supper (17, 18). But this time when placing them directly under the vivifying influence and breath of the Spirit, Christ shows by these words His will to continue His work through the Church in a spiritual manner, but by using the same means as He had used. These means were: His coming into the world, appearing and acting as a man, setting to work the processes suitable for making Truth known in word and action. This is what the last pages of the Johannine Gospel contain.

"Receive the Holy Spirit"

A certain number of elements are gathered together and incorporated into his account which trace out the physiognomy of the Church such as Christ willed it and instituted it.

The notion of "one sent" makes up the first trait of this Church. It is sufficient to recall the insistence with which Christ laid claim to this title of the one "sent by the Father" to understand that the apostles too were to bear in mind that they were sent and must remain interiorly dependent on Him who sent them. They must act according to His orders and keep themselves dependent upon and under the inspiration of the Spirit whom they received when Christ made them His representatives. "'As the Father has sent me, I also send you.' And breathing upon them he said, 'Receive the Holy Spirit'" (20, 21-22).

We have here a true Pentecost, for here are found communicated to the apostles two characteristics to which Christ laid claim and which made of Him the "envoy" and the one who possesses the Spirit in plenitude, as St. John wrote in his reflections on the Baptist's declarations. "For he whom God has sent speaks the words of God, for not by measure does God give the Spirit" (3, 34).

However, there is more here than a delegation of powers, there is a participation. Also the comparison between Christ and His apostles follows through. Just as the "Father" who loves the Son "and has given all things into his hands" (3, 35), so Christ has done with regard to those whom He has set up as heads and pastors of His Church. He communicates His spiritual powers to them. When prescribing the preaching of the "gospel," He confides to them the protection of the Truth. When entrusting to them the care of assuring the life and communication of the sacraments, He places Himself in their hands and gives them in some way power over the Life of grace in souls.

"The Father has given all things into his hands" and "As the Father raises the dead and gives them life, even so the Son also gives life to whom he will" (5, 21). "For as the Father has life in himself, even so he has given the Son to have life in himself" (5, 26).

In His turn Christ gives all power to His apostles, but being spiritual these powers are linked to the sending of the Holy Spirit. "Receive the Holy Spirit; whose sins you shall forgive they are forgiven; whose sins you shall retain, they are retained" (20, 23).

Christ's declaration made at the commencement of the Supper is fulfilled: "He who receives you receives me" (13, 20). He promises to remain closely associated with those whom He sends no matter what their weakness or limitations, as appears in His choice of Peter as head of the Church. This solidarity and continuity work on the supernatural plane, and that is why Christ can thus engage Himself, not only in recognizing the apostles as His own, but also in ratifying through time the decisions they will make under the guidance of the Spirit. It is likewise in virtue of this same principle that "whatever you bind on earth shall be bound also in heaven" (Mt. 18, 18).

"Feed my lambs ... Feed my sheep"

Another trait of the Church may be drawn from the scene on the banks of the sea of Tiberias. The account shows us the apostles resuming their accustomed trade, following Peter's example. "Simon Peter said to them, 'I am going fishing.' They said to him, 'We also are going with thee.' And they went out and got into a boat. And that night they caught nothing" (21, 3). But with Christ's arrival on the scene everything changes.

"But when day was breaking, Jesus stood on the beach; yet the disciples did not know that it was Jesus. Then Jesus said to them, 'Young men, have you any fish?' They answered him, 'No.' He said to them, 'Cast your net to the right of the boat and you will find them.' They cast therefore, and now they were unable to draw it up for the great number of fishes. The disciple whom Jesus loved said therefore to Peter, 'It is the Lord.' Simon Peter therefore, hearing that it was the Lord, girt his tunic about him, for he was stripped, and threw himself into the sea. But the other disciples came with the boat . . . dragging the net full of fishes" (21, 4-8).

This is a vivid account of a scene actually lived in which not a detail has been missed, even to the number of fishes caught, and that remark is worthy of a fisherman filled with admiration: "And though there were so many, the net was not torn" (21, 11).

Who would not see that each detail has a spiritual significance? If the apostles resumed their former work, it was because Christ did not intend that they shelter themselves in a state of passivity. If prayer is necessary to draw down the Holy Spirit and to remain in contact with Him, to prayer must be added action and apostolic labor; we must "launch out into the deep" in order to become fishers of men like Christ (Lk. 5, 4; Mt. 4, 19; Mk. 1, 17).

However, reduced to its own resources this work remains ineffective. "Without me you can do nothing" (15, 5). "That night they took nothing" (21, 3). Only the presence of Christ could transform their work into something miraculously fruitful.

All through the account Peter retains his role as head. It is to him that John says, "It is the Lord," and he casts himself into the water in order to come more quickly to Jesus, and it is Peter still who "went aboard and hauled the net onto the land full of large fishes, one hundred and fifty-three in number" (21, 11) which, despite its weight, did not break: symbol of the Church destined to grow without losing its unity. And it is to him, finally, that Christ speaks, confiding the direction of His Church to him, and confirming him very definitely in what He had already allowed to be understood at Caesarea Philippi.

"Feed my lambs . . . Feed my sheep" (21, 15,16). The pre-eminence to which Peter is called is not one of honor, but it is essentially one of service. The expression employed by Christ leaves the field free for the most varied initiative, while succinctly pointing out the orientation of His thought.

When inviting Peter to become a "good shepherd," to take care of the sheep that will be left to him and lead them into rich pastures, Jesus does not content Himself with what He had already said to His apostles as reported in Chapter 10 by St. John. He wants Peter to understand that such a role entails care, attention, decision, authority, kindness, everything that is expected of a shepherd solicitous for the good of his flock and obliged to lead them daily into pastures which give life in abundance. And while the allusion to "lambs" emphasizes the solicitude and goodness which the shepherd must exercise towards the "weakest of the flock" (Is. 40, 11), the reference to "sheep" underscores the pastoral obligations with regard to the flock as a whole and its "common good."

These powers and this authority imparted to Peter and his successors are not discretionary. The sheep are simply confided to him, they don't belong to him. "Feed *my* sheep," said Christ. And these sheep are always the property of the unique Shepherd who has received them from the Father. "Those whom thou hast given me I have guarded . . ." (17, 12). And this is what the apostle is expected to do and all those henceforth entrusted with a pastoral office.

Set side by side, these various traits bring out the figure of the Church and show the spirit that should underlie its life and development. Directly dependent upon Christ, it derives from Him powers that are essentially spiritual. For it to enter time and reach out to men, these powers of the Church demand that a certain liberty of movement, of judgment be left to the apostles. This freedom is limited, however, in two ways: the apostles are always to consider themselves only Christ's lieutenants, and decisions are always closely associated with the common good of the flock.

As for the qualities of government necessary for such a function, the apostles are invited not only to be instructed by the Good Shepherd (10, 14), and by the passage of Ezechiel which Christ has evidently come to fulfill and which prophetically announces Him: "I will myself seek and will visit them. As the shepherd visits his flock, in the day when he shall be in the midst of his sheep, and will deliver them out of all the places where they have been scattered" (Ez. c. 34, passim).

Such is the line of conduct given to pastors. And if Peter was still unaware of the spirit of his mission, the Master's threefold question enlightened him. "Simon, son of John, dost thou love me more than these? . . ." (21, 15-17). Love for the Master permits the apostles to exercise the power conferred upon them, and the lambs to submit in the proper spirit. "He will lead them with bonds of love" (Os. 11, 4).

This love must take on the form of sacrifice, even to giving up of one's life for the flock (10, 15). "The disciple is not above the Master" (15, 20). ". . . And where I am there also shall my servant be" (12, 26). "Amen, amen, I say to thee, when thou wast young thou didst gird thyself and walk where thou wouldst. But when thou art old thou wilt stretch forth thy hands, and another will gird thee, and lead thee where thou wouldst not" (21, 18).

We see how John has been careful to trace out with firm and pliant stroke the traits of this power confided to the heads of the Church. We should not be surprised that the portrait drawn by the evangelist is that of a mother and teacher. Is it not the "children of God" that have been confided to her?

"If I wish him to remain until I come, what is it to thee?"

The fourth Gospel, about to come to a close, gives us a final episode marked with a mysterious character. Christ's words to Peter are full of mystery. He has just announced to Peter that his life will be crowned with martyrdom, and He adds: "Follow me." Coming from one "risen from the dead" and who no longer belongs to the earth, these words necessarily take on the meaning of fidelity in spirit. However, Peter, who has just heard this order, complies with it physically: "Turning round, he saw following them the disciple whom Jesus loved, the one who, at the supper, had leaned back upon his breast and said, 'Lord, who is it that will betray thee?' " Then addressing Christ Peter asks, "And what of this man?" And Jesus answers, "If I wish him to remain until I come, what is it to thee? Do thou follow me" (21, 20-22).

The meaning of these words is not only mysterious for us, but it was mysterious also for John's contemporaries. In fact, "This saying therefore went abroad among the brethren that that disciple was not to die. But Jesus had not said of him, 'He is not to die'; but rather, 'If I wish him to remain until I come, what is it to thee?"

Was He making a comparison between the two vocations of these men? The active and missionary vocation of Peter as opposed to John's contemplative vocation? As tempting as such an interpretation may be, it seems hardly possible to adopt it. The word "remain" does not have the meaning here that it does in the discourse after the Supper. Besides, the interpretation given by those living at the time shows that they applied it not to the form of life Christ would have him lead, but rather to its duration.

Undoubtedly the conviction of an impending Parousia held by the first Christian generations joined to the apostle's exceptional longevity could have given the idea of his being in the world when the Son of Man would come on the clouds of heaven. However, the text of Chapter 21 (whether written by John or a disciple) shows that there was no intention of allowing such a belief to be held. "But Jesus had not said . . ." The meaning of these words remains covered with a veil which John and his disciples did not wish to remove.

It is possible to draw some light from the fact that not only does John receive again the title of the "disciple whom Jesus loved," but that the most proper attitude to persuade us of this fact is recalled here: "he who leaned back upon his breast and said . . ." It appears as though John were desirous that such an image be preserved of him through the centuries.

Furthemore, it is no doubt intentional that we likewise come upon the word dear to John: "demeurer" (21, 22). We have already stated that it does not have its spiritual meaning here. But if it is used twice in this final chapter, is it not because of its value as testimony and because, better than any other word, it makes up the apostle's signature? It sets a seal upon what singled out his vocation from that first encounter with Christ. "Come and see. They saw where he was staying, and they stayed with him that day." From start to finish, John is the "one that stays."[2]

How finally would we not note how much of a contrast there is with the expression used by Christ regarding John and the command given to Peter? "If I wish him to remain until I come, what is that to thee? Do thou follow me."

Through this discreet and veiled sign, perhaps John wished to evoke his ardent longing and expectation of Christ and the assurance of His return. In the conclusion to the Apocalypse John presents the Church and the faithful soul successively. "And the Spirit and the bride say, 'Come'!" "And let him who hears say, 'Come'!" To this faithful soul Christ brings the words of consolation, "It is true, I come quickly," and this promise renews the soul's ardor, "Yes, come, Lord Jesus!" (Ap. 22, 17-22).

It matters little then whether the expression "demeurer" refers to the longevity of the apostle or characterizes his vocation. What the Johannine Gospel wants to do on the verge of its close is to place both the faithful soul and the entire Church in an attitude of vigilant love, awaiting and preparing for the return of the Bridegroom.

---

2. Demeurer has the general meaning of: to live, remain, stay, abide.

Many other signs also Jesus worked in the
sight of his disciples, which are not written
in this book. But these are written that
you may believe that Jesus is the Christ
the Son of God, and that believing you
may have life in his name (Jn. 20, 30,31).